Property and Trust Law in Greece

Property and Trust Law in Greece

Yianna Karibali-Tsiptsiou

This book was originally published as a monograph in the International Encyclopaedia of Laws/Property and Trust Law.

General Editor: Roger Blanpain
Associate General Editor: Michele Colucci
Volume Editors: Alain Verbeke, Vincent Sagaert

Wolters Kluwer
Law & Business

Published by:
Kluwer Law International
PO Box 316
2400 AH Alphen aan den Rijn
The Netherlands
Website: www.kluwerlaw.com

Sold and distributed in North, Central and South America by:
Aspen Publishers, Inc.
7201 McKinney Circle
Frederick, MD 21704
United States of America
Email: customer.service@aspenpublishers.com

Sold and distributed in all other countries by:
Turpin Distribution Services Ltd.
Stratton Business Park
Pegasus Drive, Biggleswade
Bedfordshire SG18 8TQ
United Kingdom
Email: kluwerlaw@turpin-distribution.com

Printed on acid-free paper.

ISBN 978-90-411-4708-0

This title is available on www.kluwerlawonline.com

Printed and Bound by CPI Group (UK) Ltd, Croydon, CR0 4YY.

To my beloved son Dimitris

The Author

Dr Yianna Karibali-Tsiptsiou is Professor of Civil Law at the Law School of the Faculty of Law, Economic and Political Sciences at the Aristotle University of Thessaloniki. From 2006 to 2010 she served as Dean of the above-mentioned Faculty and since 2010 she has been President of the Legal Committee of the same University.

She studied at the Aristotle University of Thessaloniki, where she obtained her Law Degree, her Master's Degree in Private Law and her Doctor's Degree. She has written books, papers and articles in the general area of Civil Law and the Law of Antiquities. Her books include: *The Complete Personal Servitude of Habitation* (1985; in Greek); *The Approval of Juridical Acts* (1990; in Greek); *Nullity due to Simulation* (1st edn 1999; 2nd edn 2004; in Greek); *Monuments and their Detention* (2004; in Greek); *Legal Status of Monuments (Collectors, Antique Dealers, Merchants of Recent Monuments)* (2009; in Greek); *Property and Trust Law in Hellas* (1st edn 2003; in English).

She currently teaches Civil Law (mainly Property Law, Law of Inheritance and Law of Juridical Acts) at graduate and postgraduate levels.

The Author

Table of Contents

Table of Contents

List of Abbreviations

A. Abbreviations of Periodical Titles

AID	Archeio(n) Idiotikou Dikaiou (Archive of Private Law)
AchNom	Achaiki Nomologia (Court Rulings of Achaia)
ArchN	Archeio(n) Nomologias (Archive of Court Rulings)
Arm	Harmenopoulos
ChrIdD	Chronika Idiotikou Dikaiou (Annals of Private Law)
D	Diki
EEmbD	Epitheorisi(s) Emborikou Dikaiou (Review of Commercial Law)
EfAD	Efarmoges Astikou Dikaiou (Applications of Civil Law)
EpiskEmbD	Episkopisi Emborikou Dikaiou (Survey of Commercial Law)
EEN	Ephimeris Hellinon Nomikon (Newspaper of Greek Jurists)
HellD	Helliniki Dikaiosyni (Hellenic Justice)
NoB	Nomiko(n) Vima (Law Tribune)

B. Other Abbreviations

AP	Areios Pagos (Greek Supreme Court in civil and criminal matters)
Art.(s)	Article(s)
BC	Bankruptcy Code
BGB	German Civil Code
CAL	Code of Aviation Law
CC	Civil Code
CCProc	Code of Civil Procedure
CPrMarL	Code of Private Maritime Law
Ed.(s)	Edition, editor(s)
E.L.	Emergency Law
ErmAK	Erminia Astikou Kodikos (Interpretation of the Civil Code)
GenPrinc	General Principles of Civil Law
IntrLCC	Introductory Law of the Civil Code
IntrLCCproc	Introductory Law of the Code of Civil Procedure

List of Abbreviations

Komm	Kommentar
L.	Law
L.D.	Law Decree
MünchKomm	Münchener Kommentar
NOMOS	NOMOS Legal Database (http://lawdb.intrasoftnet.com)
PC	Penal Code
P.D.	Presidential Decree
PrL	Property Law
RCADI	Recueuil de cours de l'Académie de Droit International
R. Hell. D.I.	Revue Hellénique de Droit International
SachR	Sachenrecht
SchuldR	Schuldrecht
Sub-para.	Edaphio (sub-paragraph)

Preface to the Second Edition

The lapse of nine years since the 1st edition of the present book was published has made it necessary to bring out a 2nd edition. Within the framework of this 2nd edition consideration has been given to the recent special legislation concerning Greek Property Law, as well as recent Greek court rulings and the recent Greek and foreign bibliography. However, the opinions which were expressed in the 1st edition, the general structure of the book and the citation method used in it remain unchanged.

I would like to thank warmly the editors of the International Encyclopaedia of Law series for the present 2nd edition of my book.

I would also like to express my warm thanks to the lecturer Dr Timoleon Kosmides for the assistance he afforded me in gathering recent court rulings and updating the bibliography used in the 1st edition.

Thessaloniki, August 2012

Yianna Karibali-Tsiptsiou
Professor of Civil Law
Aristotle University of Thessaloniki/Greece

Preface to the First Edition

This monograph forms an integral part of the series on 'Property and Trust Law' in the International Encyclopaedia of Law. However, as the institution of 'trust' does not exist in Greece, the present monograph provides an exposition of Greek Property Law.

In writing this monograph efforts were made to follow the detailed outline elaborated, for reasons of uniformity, by the editors of the series. However, due to the peculiarities of Greek Property Law, it did not prove possible to adhere strictly to this outline. Thus, the monograph includes three Parts (I, II and VI) which were not in the outline, while the content of the General Introduction and other Parts which are proposed in the outline have undergone certain alterations in order to suit the structure of Greek Property Law. Moreover, as the outline mentions institutions and concepts of Anglo-Saxon Law which are unknown in Greece it was deemed necessary to provide a brief presentation of these and correlate them with corresponding institutions and concepts in Greek Property Law, wherever this was feasible.

Owing to the fact that this is the first time that a monograph of this length on Greek Property Law has appeared in English, coupled with the fact that fundamental differences exist between Greek and Anglo-Saxon Property Law, translating the concepts of Greek Property Law into English terms posed considerable problems. Therefore, Latin terms are sometimes used when the English translation does not appear adequate.

In the notes in the text of the present monograph, references have been made to the books and articles listed in the bibliography only where original opinions or controversial issues are presented in the text. Both in the bibliography and in the textual notes Greek titles appear in English translation, while at the end of each reference the indication 'in Greek' appears. The works written in languages other than Greek are always referred to by their original titles. The guidelines laid down by the editors of the encyclopaedia relating to the method of citation in the textual notes are followed only when the relevant book or article is cited for the first time. The same applies in the case of titles with the indication 'in Greek', i.e., a Greek title translated into English. Books or articles which have already been cited are referred to by the name of their author, title (which is frequently shortened or abbreviated) and relevant paragraph, page or marginal number, or all of these combined.

Preface to the First Edition

I would like to express my warm thanks to the editors of the International Encyclopaedia of Law series for entrusting me with the writing of this monograph.

January 2003

Yianna Karibali-Tsiptsiou
Associate Professor of Civil Law
Aristotle University of Thessaloniki

General Introduction

Chapter 1. The General Background of the Country

§1. Geography

1. Greece lies at the south-eastern extremity of Europe and constitutes the most southerly country of the Balkan peninsula. It covers an area of 131,957 km^2 and has a current population of about 11,000,000 inhabitants.

Greece is divided geographically into the Peloponnese, Central Greece, Thessaly, Epirus, Macedonia, Thrace and the Islands of the Ionian and Aegean Seas, of which Crete is the largest.

§2. Cultural Situation

2. The modern Greek State was founded after the Greek Revolution of 1821, while before the Greek people had lived under Ottoman occupation for almost four centuries.

Culturally, in the last period of the Byzantine State before Constantinople fell to the Turks in 1453, but especially after independence in the modern period, two worlds were present in Greece: on the one hand, its ancient tradition and, in connection with it, western values and the need for rationalism and modernization; on the other, Eastern romanticism, religious traditions and devotion to Byzantium.[1] Modern Greece preserved the values of both the former and the latter strands of cultural heritage. Furthermore, however, the Greek people came to realize that the country had to be brought into line with developments in the rest of Europe. Thus, in 1979 Greece acceded to the European Community (European Union after the Maastricht Treaty of 1992)[2] while, from 1 January 2002, its national currency (drachma) was replaced by the euro.

The Greek population has great ethnic (Greek) and religious (Christian Orthodox) homogeneity. The official spoken language in the country is Greek. However, the knowledge of foreign languages is very common among the Greek people.

---

1. M. Stathopoulos, *Contract Law in Hellas* (The Hague/Athens: Kluwer/Sakkoulas, 1995), No. 2.
2. The treaty of accession was signed on 28 May 1979 and ratified on 29 Jun. 1979 (L. 945/1979). Greece became a member of the European Communities on 1 Jan. 1981. The main transition period expired on 31 Dec. 1985, while the remaining transition period expired on 31 Dec. 1987.

§3. Political System

3. The Greek Revolution of 1821 marks the beginning of a new era in the political history of Greece. This era is characterized by constant and major upheavals,[3] as may be seen in the following historical outline.

The Constitutions of Epidaurus (1822) and Astros (1823) were followed by the Constitution of Troizena (1827), which vested all executive functions in Ioannis Kapodistrias, the first Governor of modern Greece. The assassination of Ioannis Kapodistrias resulted in an absolute monarchy (1833–1844), while a successful revolution in 1843 compelled King Otto, the first King of Greece, to grant the constitution of 1844. This constitution made Greece a constitutional monarchy. The revolution of 1862 overthrew Otto and a new democratic constitution was enacted in 1864 with George I as the King of the Greeks. The constitution of 1864 was revised in 1911. During the following First World War, the revised constitution was suspended a number of times and was finally replaced in 1925/1927 by a constitution which abolished the monarchy. However, the monarchy was restored in 1935 and the constitution of 1911 was reintroduced to be quickly rendered inoperative during the dictatorship of Ioannis Metaxas (1936–1941). A constitutional reversion followed the Second World War and the civil war which came after. It resulted in the adoption of the constitution of 1952 which reintroduced a new version of the constitution of 1911 and again a regime of crowned democracy. A *coup d'état* in 1967 resulted in the establishment of a seven-year military dictatorship which abolished the constitution of 1952. In 1974 the dictatorship collapsed and democratic institutions were quickly restored. The referendum of December 1974 abolished the monarchy, while in June 1975 an elected parliament voted in a new constitution, according to which Greece is a 'presidential parliamentary democracy'.[4] The constitution of 1975 was revised in 1986 and again in 2001 and in 2008. After the constitutional revision of 1986,[5] the broad powers granted to the President of the Republic by the constitution of 1975 were virtually transferred to the government and, in particular, to the Prime Minister. On the other hand, through the revision of 2001, which became effective on 17 April 2001, 79 articles of the constitution of 1975 were amended, updated or enriched with new provisions. Even after this broad

3. See P. Zepos, 'The Greek Legal System', *R. Hell. D.I.* 14 (1961): 1 et seq.; P. Zepos & M. Tourtoglou, 'Griechenland', in *Handbuch der Quellen und Literatur der neuren europäischen Privatrechtsgeschichte*, vol. III/5, ed. H. Coing, Max Planck Institut (München: Beck, 1988), 473 et seq. (483 et seq.); P. Yessiou-Faltsi, *Civil Procedure in Hellas* (Athens/The Hague: Sakkoulas/Kluwer, 1995), No. 2; Ath. Yiannopoulos, 'Historical Development', in *Introduction to Greek Law*, 3rd edn, ed. K. Kerameus & Ph. Kozyris (AH Alphen aan den Rijn/Athens: Kluwer/Sakkoulas, 2008), 8–11. However, for a more detailed treatment of this point see St. Koutsoubinas, *Les peuple dans la constitution hellénique de 1975* (Nancy, Presses Universitaires, 1989), 21 et seq.; Ph. Spyropoulos, *Constitutional Law in Hellas* (The Hague/Athens: Kluwer/Sakkoulas, 1995), No. 1 et seq.
4. See P. Dagtoglou, 'Constitutional and Administrative Law', in *Introduction to Greek Law*, 3rd edn, ed. K. Kerameus & Ph. Kozyris (AH Alphen aan den Rijn/Athens, Kluwer/Sakkoulas, 2008), 23 et seq. and, for a more detailed treatment, D. Tsatsos, *Constitutional Law*, vol. I, 4th edn (Athens/Komotini: Sakkoulas, 1994), 304 et seq. [in Greek].
5. On the relevant revision see D. Tsatsos, *Constitutional Law I*, 324 et seq.; Ph. Spyropoulos, *Constitutional Law in Hellas*, Nos 34 et seq., 136 et seq.

revision, however, the constitution of 1975 did not undergo any substantial institutional amendment[6] as the revision of 2008 was very limited and focused on some institutionally secondary points.

4. According to the constitution currently in force, Greece is a 'presidential parliamentary democracy', 'popular sovereignty is the foundation of the regime' and 'all powers are derived from the People and exist in favour of them and the Nation' (Article 1). 'Respect and protection of the value of human beings as the primary obligation of the State' (Article 2 paragraph 1), 'equality of all Greek people before the law' and 'equal rights and obligations of all Greek men and women' are guaranteed (Article 4 paragraphs 1, 2). The constitution provides for the protection of human beings, as individuals and as members of society, and raises Greece to the status of a 'welfare State' (Articles 5 et seq.). More specifically, among other things, it safeguards the free development of the personality, personal liberty, the right to access to justice, the right to enjoy protection of one's genetic identity, the right to be informed and participate equally in the information society, the right to be protected from the collection and processing of personal data and the right of privacy. Furthermore, it takes special care of freedom of assembly and association, freedom of expression (in particular that of the press), individual property, trade union freedom, employment, family, marriage, motherhood and childhood and also weak, disabled and homeless people.[7]

The constitution (Articles 26 et seq.) divides State authority into the three traditional powers (functions): legislative, executive and judicial. Legislative power is exercised by Parliament and the President of the Republic; executive power by the President of the Republic and the government; and judicial power by the courts. The Parliament, nowadays, consists of 300 members elected for a maximum term of four years by direct, universal and secret ballot. Every citizen over the age of 18 is entitled to vote. The government must enjoy the confidence of Parliament. Finally, the President of the Republic is elected by the Parliament, for a five-year term, by a special majority and procedure.

The structure of the State is based on the aforementioned separation of powers and the rule of law over both Parliament and the administration through judicial review (Article 93 paragraphs 4, 95) and an independent judiciary (Articles 87 et seq.).

5. The major political parties, which over the last thirty-seven years have alternated in power in Greece, are the conservative liberal New Democracy Party (ND) and the centrist social democratic Panhellenic Socialist Movement (PASOK). Actually (August 2012), the Cabinet is formed by a coalition of the above two parties and of a smaller one, the pro-european Demokratic Left (DIMAR). The major party of the opposition is the left wing SYRIZA. Also represented in the parliament are the Greek Communist party, an other right wing party and a pure nationalistic party.

---

6. See preface of An. Manitakis to the 'Constitution of Greece. 1975/1986/2001' (Athens-Thessaloniki: Sakkoulas, 2002), p. v et seq. [in Greek].
7. On all these points see K. Chrysogonos, *Individual and Social Rights*, 3rd edn (Athens: Nomiki Bibliothiki, 2006), 119 et seq. [in Greek].

Chapter 2. The Legal Background of the Country

§1. The Position of the Greek Legal System in the Legal Families

6. The sources of Greek civil law down to the time of the Revolution of 1821 were Roman law,[8] as it had developed in Byzantium, and customary law, which had taken shape in several different places. However, certain legal relations, such as real relations associated with immovables, were regulated by Turkish law, while, from the beginning of the nineteenth century, French law used to be applied to some extent in commercial relations, especially on the islands.[9] With regard to the Byzantine-Roman law, it should be noted that it was initially codified in Latin in the *Corpus Juris Civilis* of the Emperor Justinian (in the sixth century); later (in the ninth century), it was systematically presented by the Emperor Leo the Wise in the collection called *Basilika*, which was to a large extent a translation into Greek of the legislation of Justinian; finally (in the fourteenth century), it was summarized, again in Greek, in a private collection called *Hexabiblos* by the Thessaloniki judge Constantine Harmenopoulos. *Hexabiblos* was based, at least indirectly, on the *Basilika*.

7. Byzantine-Roman law and customary law remained the actual sources of private law even after the revolution of 1821 and the establishment of the independent Greek State. At the same time, the first major Greek codes were drafted by Professor Ludwig von Maurer in his capacity as member of the Regency Council of King Otto. These codes, which were based on both French and German models and were published in the German language, are: the Code of Civil Procedure (1834), which was replaced only in 1968; the Code for the Organization of Courts and of Notaries (1834), which was replaced in 1988; and the Penal Code (1833) and the Code of Penal Procedure (1834), which remained in force until 1951. On the other hand, in 1928, by an ordinance of Ioannis Kapodistrias, the French Napoleonic Code of Commerce of 1807 was adopted by the Greek State to regulate commercial relations. Since then, though, this code (parts of which had been translated into Greek) has undergone many amendments so that actually only a few articles of its first book remain in force.[10]

As for the civil law, in particular, the legislative act which finally resolved the issue of which system should apply was the decree of 23 February 1835. The latter

---

8. It should, however, be borne in mind that Roman law was considerably influenced by fundamental ideals of the ancient Greek (i.e., Athenian) legal system and especially the Greek political philosophers. Indeed, a number of abstract legal notions, such as the concept of 'equity' (*aequitas*) or 'good faith' (bona fides), were introduced into Roman law through the doctrines of ancient Greek philosophy. However, Greek law made an impressive impact on Roman law after 30 B.C., when, due to the transformation of Roman law by Hellenistic influences, the Graeco-Roman phase of the historical evolution of Roman law began (see P. Yessiou-Faltsi, *Civil Procedure in Hellas*, No. 7 and, for a detailed discussion, N. Pantazopoulos, *Roman Law in a Dialectic Coherence to Greek Law*, vol. I (Thessaloniki: Sakkoulas, 1974), 20–21, 162 et seq., 176 et seq. [in Greek]; G. Nakos, *History of Greek and Roman Law* (Thessaloniki: University Studio Press, 1991), 49 et seq. [in Greek]).
9. See M. Stathopoulos, *Contract Law in Hellas*, No. 4.
10. N. Deloukas & E. Perakis, 'Commercial Law', in *Introduction to Greek Law*, 3rd edn, ed. K. Kerameus & Ph. Kozyris (AH Alphen aan den Rijn/Athens: Kluwer/Sakkoulas, 2008), 217.

declared that 'the civil laws of the Byzantine emperors contained in the *Hexabiblos* of Harmenopoulos shall remain in force until the promulgation of the civil code whose drafting we have already ordered' and that 'the customs, sanctioned by long and uninterrupted use or by judicial decisions, shall have the force of law wherever they prevail'. The decree of 1835 was broadly interpreted as referring, through the *Hexabiblos* of Harmenopoulos and the *Basilika*, to the *Corpus Juris Civilis*. Thus, a link was reestablished between modern Greek law and the legislation of Justinian. This legislation, though, constituted the source of civil law in Germany, where it had been studied and applied in such a way as to lead to the creation of the famous German science of the law of the *Pandects*. Adherents of the doctrine of the law of *Pandects* in Greece became the first professors at the Law School of the University of Athens, which had been set up in 1837. These jurists (Paulus Kalligas, Petros Paparrigopoulos and Vasilios Ekonomides), having knowledge of the law of *Pandects*, had contributed decisively to its introduction into Greece.

In this way a link began to be formed between Greek civil law and the teachings of German nineteenth century Pandectists. Since then, Greek civil law has developed under the strong influence of pandectist legal science. However, special civil laws have been influenced by other legal systems (such as the French and Austrian),[11] while in the law of inheritance and especially in family law the impact of Byzantine laws and Greek customs has been dominant. Furthermore, the generation of legislation of local nature in the area of private law was abundant in the second and third decades of the twentieth century. Many of these laws were of a social character or concerned with employees' rights.[12] At the same time, preparatory work on the drafting of a Civil Code was going ahead. This Code was finally drawn up in the 1930s and came into force on 23 February 1946. The relevant Code also extended its application to the areas previously dominated by local Civil Codes, that is, to the Ionian islands, Crete and Samos, where the Ionian Civil Code of 1841 (of French origin), the Civil Code of Crete of 1904 (of German origin) and the Civil Code of Samos of 1899 (of French and Italian origin) were, respectively, in force.

The Greek Civil Code is based, on the one hand, on Byzantine-Roman law, as it had been developed under the impact of pandectist legal science, and on the other, on the civil laws of modern Greece. Furthermore, it has been influenced first and foremost by the German Civil Code (BGB) and to a somewhat lesser extent by the two Swiss Codes (the Civil Code and the Code of Obligations), by the French Civil Code and by the Austrian Civil Code. Following the model of the BGB, the Greek Civil Code is divided into five books. The first is devoted to the General Principles of Civil Law (Articles 1–286 CC), while the other four cover the Law of Obligations (Articles 287–946 CC), Property Law (Articles 947–1345 CC), Family Law (Articles 1346–1709 CC) and the Law of Inheritance (Articles 1710–2035 CC).

The Greek Civil Code underwent two major reforms, while by Law 1250/1982 civil marriage was introduced as an alternative to the religious type. The aforementioned major reforms occurred as a consequence of laws 1329/1983 and 2447/1996. The first revised all the provisions of the Code involving unequal treatment of the

11. On this issue in the area of property law see *infra* para. 18.
12. See M. Stathopoulos, *Contract Law in Hellas*, No. 5.

sexes,[13] while both the first and the second transformed mainly, though not exclusively, a significant number of Family law provisions. On the other hand, changes, especially in the area of Family Law, have also occurred as a consequence of the entry into force of Law 3089/2002 and Law 3305/2005 concerning medically assisted human reproduction.

8. If, in bringing the present section to a close, we wanted to classify the modern Greek legal system as a whole within a certain legal family, we could say that it belongs to the Romano-Germanic family of law, although in certain branches of law, and especially in commercial and public law, it displays a strong French influence. However, in view of the fact that modern Greek law has undergone the impact of several legal systems, adopting them however to the Greek legal tradition and the realities of life in modern Greece, it seems correct to accept that it constitutes a 'selective' or 'mixed' legal system[14] which nonetheless has its own original form.[15] Furthermore, it should be borne in mind that the accession of Greece to the European Community (already the European Union) in 1979 marked a new period for Greek law. Indeed, since then, the Greek legal order has been connected with that of the European Union, in the sense that one substantially penetrates the other and not in the sense that they exist in parallel.[16]

§2. Relations between the Sources of Law and their Hierarchical Structure

9. The sources of law are distinguished into primary and secondary types, depending on whether they are self-contained (in the sense that rules of law derive directly from them) or not. As emerges from Article 1 CC, together with Article 28 paragraph 1 sub-paragraph a of the Constitution, the primary sources of (internal Greek) law are: legislation, customs and 'the general accepted rules of international law'. In addition, as a result of Greece's accession to the European Community, those rules of Community law which are directly applicable in the Member States and, consequently, in Greece constitute a primary source of (internal Greek) law. On the other hand, the secondary sources of law are: international treaties, which become part of the Greek legal system only after ratification (Article 28 paragraph 1 sub-paragraph a of the Constitution), and also collective labour agreements, arbitral awards, business practices, morality and objective good faith.

---

13. In the light of the explicit provision of the Constitution of 1975 which proclaimed that 'all Greek men and women have equal rights and obligations'.
14. See G. Michaelides-Nouaros, 'Les systèmes juridiques des peuples Européens', *R. Hell. D.I.* 10 (1957): 40 et seq. (67, 106, 110 et seq.); Ph. Franceskakis, D. Evrigenis & S. Symeonides, *Comparative Law* (Thessaloniki: Sakkoulas, 1978), 257–258, 264 et seq. [in Greek].
15. P. Yessiou-Faltsi, *Civil Procedure in Hellas*, No. 9.
16. See D. Papasteriou, *General Principles of Civil Law*, 2nd edn (Athens-Thessaloniki: Sakkoulas, 2009), para. 2 X, XI No. 27 et seq., 41 et seq. [in Greek] and, for a detailed discussion, P. Ladas, *General Principles of Civil Law*, vol. I (Athens-Thessaloniki: Sakkoulas, 2007), para. 3 VI No. 42, 72 [in Greek]; P. Ladas, *From the Civil Code to the European Law. National consciousness and European spirit* (Thessaloniki: Sakkoulas, 1993), passim [in Greek].

10. Although the Civil Code places customs on the same level as legislation by naming it a source of law, the superiority of legislation in relation to customs is obvious.[17] This de facto superiority is quantitative, as customs today are of extremely limited extent, and also qualitative, because of the clarity, precision and certainty of legislation in comparison with customs.[18]

With regard to legislation, that is, the statutes enacted by the State, the following should be borne in mind:

(a) The statutes are either substantive or formal, depending on whether they contain a legal rule or not. Thus, for example, the budget, although it appears in the form of a statute, does not contain legal rules and, therefore, is a formal statute. Such a formal statute, though, may not constitute a source of law.
(b) The legal rules exist in the form of a hierarchy, at the top of which stand the provisions of the Constitution. Due to this hierarchy, a rule of a higher rank may not be suspended, transformed or abolished by a rule of lesser rank. On the other hand, on account of the said hierarchy, a rule of a lesser rank must be in harmony with rules of higher rank. Consequently, ordinary legislation must be harmonized with the Constitution, while a law contrary to the Constitution is invalid and the courts are required not to apply it (Article 93 paragraph 3 of the Constitution). More specifically,[19] the monitoring of the constitutionality of laws is carried out by all the courts, but only in terms of the specific case in front of them. The relevant control is suppressive, in contrast to the preventive checking of the constitutionality of legislation which is carried out by Parliament. The courts check, ex officio or in subsequence to an objection, the substantive unconstitutionality of legislation, that is, the possible conflict of the content of a law with an explicit constitutional provision or a generally accepted main principle of the Constitution. Finally, it should be noted that the courts do not have the power to repeal a law which they judge to be unconstitutional; they are simply entitled and obliged not to apply it in the case which they are hearing. Only one court can repeal a law (with general applicability and beyond the case being heard): the Special Supreme Court (Article 100 of the Constitution). However, this court has the relevant power only when contradictory decisions as to the constitutionality of a law have been issued by the Supreme Courts of the three jurisdictions which exist in Greece (the Council of State, i.e., the supreme

17. On the disputed issue of whether the custom can abolish statute law see K. Simantiras, *General Principles of Civil Law*, 4th edn (Athens/Komotini: Sakkoulas, 1988), para. 10 Nos 100–103, 96–98 [in Greek], where the relevant overall discussion is presented. See also Ap. Georgiades, *General Principles of Civil Law*, 3rd edn (Athens/Komotini: A. Sakkoulas, 2002), para. 3 II 3 No. 5, 29–30 [in Greek]; Ph. Doris, *Introduction to the Civil Law*, vol. I (Athens/Komotini: A. Sakkoulas, 1991), 82–85 [in Greek]; P. Filios, *General Principles of Civil Law*, 3rd edn (Athens/Komotini: A. Sakkoulas, 2009), para. 36 D II, 116 [in Greek]; Y. Karibali-Tsiptsiou, 'Sources of Positive Law', *Harmenopoulos/Scientific Year-Book* 1 (1980): 233 [in Greek] (who maintains that the custom cannot abolish statute law).
18. M. Stathopoulos, *Contract Law in Hellas*, No. 7.
19. See, in particular, D. Papasteriou, *GenPrinc*, para. 9 No. 3, 111; M. Stathopoulos, *Contract Law in Hellas*, No. 8. See also An. Manitakis, *Greek Constitutional Law*, vol. I (Athens-Thessaloniki: Sakkoulas, 2004), 287 [in Greek].

administrative court, the Court of Cassation of Areios Pagos and the Court of Audit[20]).

11. As has already been stated, the primacy of legislation, as a source of law, is a characteristic of the Greek legal system. Judicial rulings, that is, the decisions of the courts, are not considered to be a source of law.[21] As the saying goes, 'the judge is subject to the law and he does not make law'.

However, the constructive influence of a judge, as a shaper or developer of the law, is indisputable.[22] Indeed, judges are regarded as 'creators' of the law in several ways: by interpreting unclear provisions, by supplementing or correcting them through the interpretative process and also by giving concrete form to general clauses and abstract notions contained in these provisions, so that they can be applied to the case being heard. A judicial decision, though, is binding only in the specific case under judicial review. Its binding nature (res judicata) does not imply that it creates a rule for the future. The judicial precedent perhaps influences but does not bind the next judge who has to give a decision in a similar case, precisely because it is not a legal rule. In any event, notwithstanding the non-binding character of judicial precedent, the actual influence of court rulings, particularly of those emanating from Supreme Courts, and, even more so, the influence of the consistent practice of these courts is considerable. But this influence should not be confused with the legal force of a rule of law. However, in the case where the consistent practice of courts creates a sense of general binding (*opinio juris*) in the citizens, a rule of customary law is generated. In this case, though, the reason for the legal force of the relevant rule and, furthermore, the source of production of law is not the court decision but the custom.[23]

12. Doctrine also does not constitute a source of law in the formal sense. However, its influence on the formation and interpretation of written law is of great importance. In fact, it creates the ideas that influence the legislator and supports the judge in interpreting the legal rules and in formulating his or her opinion.[24]

---

20. These Supreme Courts maintain, in every other respect, each in its own jurisdiction, the unity of interpretation and implementation of law in Greece.
21. Unlike what happens in the Anglo-American system, where case law to a certain extent serves as an actual source of law.
22. On this issue see A. Ligeropoulos, *Case law As a Factor in the Formation of Private Law* (Thessaloniki, 1932), passim [in Greek]; G. Michaelides-Nouaros, 'L' oeuvre créatrice de la jurisprudence grecque en cas de silence de la loi', *R. Hell. D.I.* 4 (1951): 163 et seq.; N. Papantoniou, *General Principles of Civil Law*, 3rd edn (Athens: Sakkoulas, 1983), 45 et seq. [in Greek]; Yessiou-Faltsi, *Civil Procedure in Hellas*, No. 10; D. Papasteriou, *GenPrinc*, para. 3 No. 5 et seq., 54 et seq.; P. Ladas, *GenPrinc I*, para. 9 III No. 20 et seq., 170 et seq.; Ap. Georgiades, *GenPrinc*, para. 2 IV No. 26 et seq., 26–27; M. Stathopoulos, *Contract Law in Hellas*, No. 7; Ph. Doris, *Introduction to the Civil Law I*, 67 et seq.; P. Filios, *GenPrinc*, para. 34 B, 109–110; A. Grammatikaki-Alexiou, 'Sources and Materials', in *Introduction to Greek Law*, 3rd edn, ed. K. Kerameus & Ph. Kozyris (AH Alphen aan den Rijn/Athens: Kluwer/Sakkoulas, 2008), 15; Y. Karibali-Tsiptsiou, 'Sources of Private Law', 237.
23. M. Stathopoulos, *Contract Law in Hellas*, No. 7.
24. P. Yessiou-Faltsi, *Civil Procedure in Hellas*, No. 10; A. Grammatikaki-Alexiou, 'Sources and Materials', 15; Y. Karibali-Tsiptsiou, 'Sources of private law', 237–238.

Chapter 3. Introduction to the Law of Property

§1. Definitions and Classification

I. The Concept and Content of Property Law

13. According to Greek law, people exercise authority over objects through real rights (i.e., ownership, servitudes, pledges and mortgages), possession and detention. The determination of these means of exercising authority, the definition of their concept, content and legal nature and the regulation of their acquisition, exercise, loss and protection constitute the subject-matter of property law. Real rights, possession and detention establish relationships between persons and things and, at the same time, relationships between persons with regard to a certain thing. These relationships, due to their importance, come under the control of law and constitute legal relations and more specifically real relations. Consequently, property law may be defined[25] as the set of rules of private law which regulates real relations.[26]

On the basis of the distinction made by the Greek legal system between private and public law,[27] civil law, and therefore property law, come under the former. Furthermore, in the light of the division of civil law into law dealing with persons and law concerning pecuniary relations, property law falls within the sphere of the latter.

14. In terms of content, property law concerns dominance over things and other objects (e.g., rights),[28] though not dominance over all economic goods. Thus, for example, property (*universitas bonorum*) as a unity,[29] rights of intellectual property and invention do not fall within the scope of property law.

II. The Concept of Ownership (The Characteristic of Unity)

15. The concept of ownership in Greek law is examined in detail in the third part of this monograph.[30] Here we intend only to point out that three categories of ownership are distinguished in Greece: 'full', 'limited' and 'revocable'. Full ownership is that which is not encumbered with a limited real right, that is, ownership which has not been stripped of the powers contained in a servitude (real or personal, which

25. See D. Papasteriou, *Property Law*, vol. 1 (Athens-Thessaloniki: Sakkoulas, 2008), para. 1I B Nos 6–7, 4 [in Greek]; Chr. Kousoulas, *Property* Law (Athens-Thessaloniki: Sakkoulas, 2004), para. 1, 1 [in Greek].
26. On the concept of 'real relation' see also *infra* para. 46.
27. In spite of the overlapping of these two broad branches of law, which renders the distinction between them relative, the main criterion for this distinction remains the extent to which in a legal relation one of the parties is a public authority (or an agent thereof) acting in this capacity or not. In the first case we speak of public and in the second of private law relations.
28. On the distinction between an object and a thing see *infra* para. 57.
29. The provisions of property law are applicable to each of the things included in the property (see *infra* para. 61).
30. See *infra* paras 160–162.

includes usufruct, habitation and limited personal servitudes), a pledge or a mortgage. By contrast, limited ownership is that which is encumbered with one of the above-mentioned real rights. In particular, ownership which is encumbered with usufruct and has been stripped of the powers to make use of and collect the fruits of the thing (Article 1142 CC) is called 'naked' ownership. In this case, naked ownership exists on the same level together with a self-existent real right of usufruct, which may not be regarded as a right of separate or concurrent ownership.[31] Finally, revocable ownership is that which is dependent on a suspensive or resolutory condition or term.

Apart from these categories, no other distinction of ownership exists in Greece. The distinction between 'legal' and 'equitable' ownership is unknown to Greek law. In Greece, a person is either an owner or not. He or she cannot be an owner for management purposes (legal owner) without also being an owner for beneficial purposes (equitable owner). In this sense, the unity of ownership is a fundamental principle of Greek law.[32] Two or more persons cannot be owners of an asset except as co-owners. In this case, each co-owner is the absolute owner of his or her individual share of the whole.[33]

The 'fragmentation' of the concept of ownership and the distinction between legal and equitable ownership apply in Anglo-Saxon law[34] and are due to the existence and parallel enforcement, in the relevant legal system, of two different sets of legal rules: those of the 'common law' and 'equity'. Common law is the set of legal rules created through the jurisprudence of the Royal Courts of England in the twelfth and thirteenth centuries. Equity is the set of legal rules which was developed after the thirteenth century, through the jurisprudence of the Court of Chancery, to correct some of the harsh injustices of the rigid and inflexible common law.[35] The concepts of legal and equitable ownership owe their creation to common law and equity, respectively.[36]

III. Ownership and Possession

16. Possession,[37] in contradistinction to ownership, is not a real right. However, like ownership, possession also offers its holder universal power over a thing.

31. See also *infra* para. 40 (under f).
32. On the same issue in the area of Belgian law see J.H. Herbots, 'Belgium', under 'Contracts' in *International Encyclopedia of Laws* (The Hague: Kluwer, 1998), No. 88.
33. See *infra* para. 208.
34. An analogous 'fragmentation' of ownership can be found in classical Roman law, where, in parallel with the ownership recognized by *jus civile* (*proprietas ex jure quiritum*), the ownership in praetorian law (*proprietas ex jure praetorio* or *proprietas in bonis esse*) had been created through the jurisprudence of the praetor, who applied the rules of *aequitas* (see G. Petropoulos, *History and Institutions of Roman Law*, 2nd edn (Athens, 1963), 203–204, 623 et seq. [in Greek]).
35. On the dual structure of Anglo-Saxon law see F.H. Lawson & B. Rudden, *The Law of Property*, 2nd edn (Oxford: Clarendon Press, 1982/reprinted 1991), 53–54; J.G. Riddall, *Land Law*, 6th edn (London/Edinburgh/Dublin: Butterworths, 1997), 76; R. Sexton, *Land Law*, 2nd edn (Great Britain: Blackstone Press Limited, 1997), 39, 42.
36. See also *infra* para. 38.
37. On the institution of possession see, in detail, *infra* paras 104 et seq.

Nevertheless, whereas ownership offers legal, direct, absolute and universal power over a thing, possession offers physical authority over the thing with the mind of an owner. Furthermore, while ownership exists only if it has been validly acquired in one of the ways provided for by the law,[38] possession exists as soon as the physical power over the thing has been acquired, regardless of whether this acquisition is approved of or not by the law. Thus, the thief of a movable thing or the encroacher of another's land is a possessor but not an owner.

Usually ownership and possession coexist in the same person. However, sometimes one person is the owner and another is the possessor of the same thing. Thus, the thief of a movable thing is possessor and not owner of the thing, while the person from whom the movable has been stolen has ownership, though not possession of it.[39]

IV. Classification of Property Law: Law of Immovable and Law of Movable Property

17. Owing to the fact that Greek property law treats the real rights pertaining to immovable things in a different way from those pertaining to movables, in respect of their acquisition, abolition or protection, it could be divided into the 'law of immovable property' and the 'law of movable property'.[40] This division is adopted in the present monograph. More specifically, in this monograph the term 'immovable property' denotes the real rights which may have as their object an immovable thing. On the other hand, the term 'movable property' is used to denote the real rights relating to movable things and incorporeal objects.[41] Although Greek law does not treat the real rights on all types of incorporeal objects in the same way as it treats the real rights on movable things, the creation of a third division of property law, that of the 'law of incorporeal property', is in our opinion superfluous and, from a certain point of view, contrary to the law. Indeed, the interpretative rule of Article 949 CC, referring to the case where by law or a juridical act[42] a distinction is made between the immovable assets of a person, as a whole, and his or her movable assets, states that '... any and all claims shall be included in the movables'. Hence, by interpreting the word 'claims' in a broad sense, we may include in its scope, and consequently in the category of movable property, all types of real rights which may have as their object incorporeal objects.

Furthermore, it should be borne in mind that most foreign legal systems divide property (and rights in the area of property) into two types: 'immovable' and 'movable property'. Immovable property denotes all property rights relating to immovables, while movable property includes all other property rights. However, English law (and other legal systems derived from English law) distinguishes between 'real' and 'personal property'. According to this law, all property rights relating to land,

38. See also *infra* para. 48 and n. 123.
39. See also *infra* para. 104.
40. See also D. Papasteriou, *PrL I*, para. 11 I A No. 1, 186.
41. On the real rights which may be acquired on incorporeal objects see *infra* paras 50 (under c), 256, 260 et seq., 411, 443–444, 490 et seq.
42. From this point on the terms 'juridical act(s)' and 'legal transaction(s)' will be used alternatively.

except leases, belong to real property, while rights in all other types of property and leases belong to personal property.[43]

§2. Historical Origins of Property Law

18. Before the Greek Civil Code was introduced, pandectist legal science had also permeated property law. However, a great part of the latter was regulated by modern laws which had been drawn up by following the models of other legal systems. Examples of such laws are: the law concerning pledges of 1836 (of French origin), the law relating to mortgages of 1836 (of Bavarian and French origin), the law concerning distinction of lands of 1837 (of Austrian and French origin), the law relating to transcription of ownership and other real rights on immovables of 1856 (of French origin), Law 1339/1918 concerning discovery of lost property (of German and Swiss origin) and Law 3741/1929 relating to the ownership of storeys (of Belgian origin).

19. The property law of the Greek Civil Code derives from Byzantine-Roman law, as interpreted by pandectist legal science. This law has been doubly influenced by pandectist legal science: on the one hand, through the property law which was in force in Greece at that time, to the extent that the latter coincided with the law of pandects; on the other, through the BGB which was also influenced by the pandectist legal science and which constituted the main[44] model for the drafting of the Greek Civil Code. However, through the BGB, elements of ancient German law were also introduced into the Greek Civil Code. This is due to the fact that the property law of the BGB is the result of a mixture of Roman and ancient German law. Thus, of Roman origin are: the distinction between ownership and possession and between ownership and limited real rights, the individualistic character of ownership and the distinction between promissory and dispositive juridical acts. On the other hand, of German origin are: the distinction between immovable and movable property, the principles of publicity and specificity and the possibility of ownership being acquired from a person who is not the owner by an acquirer acting in good faith.[45]

§3. Sources of Property Law

20. The basic provisions of property law are contained in the third book of the Greek Civil Code (consisting of Articles 947–1345), while rules of property law are scattered throughout the other books of this code as well. Thus, such rules also occur in the General Principles (Articles 27, 175, 239), Law of Obligations (Articles 604, 626, 695, 838), Family Law (Articles 1394–1395, 1398) and in the Law of

43. See F.H. Lawson & B. Rudden, *PrL*, 19; J.G. Riddall, *Land Law*, 50–51; R. Sexton, *Land Law*, 20.
44. The influence of the French and the Swiss Civil Codes is also noticeable.
45. On all these points see Ap. Georgiades, *Property Law*, vol. I, 2nd edn (Athens-Thessaloniki: Sakkoulas, 2010), para. 1 IV 1, 4, 5 Nos 18, 23 et seq., 8, 10–11 [in Greek].

Inheritance (Articles 1872, 1874 et seq., 1906, 1908, 1918, 1996, 2003 et seq.). On the other hand, provisions of property law are also found in other codes, such as the Code of Civil Procedure (CCProc), the Bankruptcy Code (BC), the Code of Private Maritime Law (CPrMarL) and the Code of Aviation Law (CAL).

21. In addition, various special laws are of great importance to property law. This is due to the fact that the property law of the Civil Code contains only a part of the so-called private substantive property law, that is, only a part of the provisions referring to movable or immovable things and to the powers exercised over them by people. Thus, special laws regulate: (a) certain institutions belonging to private substantive property law (e.g., the institutions of horizontal and vertical ownership); (b) the so-called public property law, which contains rules pertaining to things belonging to the State or public entities, and (c) the so-called procedural property law and, for example, issues relating to the transcription of transactions associated with immovables in the transcription registers.

Of the aforementioned special laws, some regulate institutions belonging entirely to property law,[46] whereas others, without regulating institutions of property law, simply contain provisions of property law.[47] On the other hand, by virtue of explicit provisions of the Introductory Law of the Civil Code, those of the above laws which were in force before the Civil Code was introduced preserve their legal validity.

22. Finally, mention should be made of public law as a source of property law. Indeed, the significance of property law to the social and economic life of the country on the one hand, and the individualistic character of ownership on the other, make it necessary for the State to take measures to restrict this characteristic and promote the public interest. In this respect, various rules of public law are promulgated. These rules, by imposing on the owner of a thing serious obligations, lead to major changes in the area of property law. Owing to this influence of public law, property law, without moving from its original starting place, i.e., private law, nowadays has important sources in the field of public law as well.[48]

§4. Ideological Trends and Developments in Property Law

23. The property law of the Greek Civil Code, deriving as it does from Byzantine-Roman law and influenced by the German and, to a lesser extent, other

46. See, for example, Law 3741/1929 and L.D. 1024/1971 concerning, respectively, the ownership of storeys and the divided ownership of buildings erected on a single building plot, as well as Laws 2882/2001 and 2985/2002 relating to compulsory expropriations and also Law 2844/2000 concerning contracts on movables or claims subject to publicity and other security contracts.
47. See, for example, L.D. 17 Jul./13 Aug. 1923 concerning special provisions relating to companies limited by shares, the General Building Regulation (Law 1577/1985 as amended by Law 1772/1988 and already by Law 2831/2000), Laws 2308/1995 and 2664/1998, as currently in force, concerning the constitution and function of land registers in Greece, Law 2971/2001 relating to seashores and beaches and Law 3028/2002 concerning protection of archaeological objects and the cultural heritage in general.
48. On these points see Ap. Georgiades, *PrL*, para. 1V 4 Nos 35–37, 14; D. Papasteriou, *PrL I*, para. 1IV No. 28, 13–14; Chr. Kousoulas, *PrL*, para. 4 I, 16.

foreign civil codes which were in force at the beginning of the twentieth century, to a large extent reflects the ideas of the nineteenth century relating to civil and economic liberalism. However, the property law of the Civil Code projects ownership as a right subject to restrictions.[49] These restrictions, though, pertain to the exercise of ownership and not to the right of ownership itself. Consequently, ownership, within the scope of the Greek Civil Code, preserves its individualistic character aiming first and foremost at the satisfaction of the personal needs of its holder.

24. During the course of time, ownership felt the impact of modern social, economic, political and cultural developments. The object of ownership, particularly land, began to interest, in addition to the individual, society as a whole. Thus, ownership gradually lost its individualistic character and its social function began to be promoted.

However, as the Greek legislator rarely interferes in the third book of the Civil Code, the property law laid out therein does not accurately reflect the above-mentioned developments. It should be borne in mind, though, that through restrictions imposed on the right of ownership by provisions of public law,[50] the social function of ownership is strongly promoted in Greece.

25. Since the Greek Civil Code was introduced, modifications in the area of property law have been brought about, on the one hand, in the chapter concerning mortgages, by the Code of Civil Procedure, its Introductory Law and special laws and, on the other, in certain provisions which have to conform to Laws 1329/1983 and 2447/1996.[51] Furthermore, among the recent developments occurring in the field of property law are Laws 2308/1995 and 2664/1998, as currently in force, concerning the constitution and function of land registers in Greece[52] and Law 2844/2000 relating to contracts on movables or claims subject to publicity and other security contracts.[53]

§5. Fundamental Principles of Property Law

I. The Principle of *Numerus Clausus* of Real Rights

26. One of the major principles governing Greek property law is the principle of *numerus clausus* of real rights. This is understood to mean, on the one hand, that real rights are only those enumerated by statute and thus limited in number and, on the other, that the content of real rights is determined by statute in a binding manner.

The principle of *numerus clausus* is based on Article 973 CC which recognizes as real rights ownership, servitudes (distinguished into real [or predial] and personal types, further distinguished into complete [i.e., usufruct and habitation] and limited

49. See Art. 1000 CC *infra* para. 164.
50. See *infra* para. 168.
51. On the reformation of the Greek Civil Code in subsequence to these laws see *supra* para. 7.
52. See *infra* para. 31.
53. See *infra* paras 412 (under c), 471 et seq., 485, 489, 491, 495–497, 500–503, 504, 505 (under a).

personal servitudes), pledges and mortgages. The same principle also emerges from those provisions of the Civil Code which determine the content of the above real rights in a binding way. However, it may be observed that the law gives to the private will a certain freedom in shaping the content of real and limited personal servitudes. As in these cases, though, the private will may act only within the constraints imposed by the Civil Code,[54] the above freedom must not be interpreted as constituting an exception to the principle of *numerus clausus*.[55] In addition, it should be noted that Article 973 CC does not preclude the legal creation of other real rights than those it declares. Such rights are actually provided for in special laws.[56] Consequently, the exact meaning of the principle of *numerus clausus* is that individuals of their own volition can neither constitute other real rights apart from those provided for by statute (Civil Code or special laws) nor change the content of such rights from that specified by the statute in question.

The principle of *numerus clausus*, which is neither self-evident[57] nor known by all foreign legal systems,[58] serves to safeguard the security of transactions. Indeed, the immediate (direct) power of the holder of a real right over a thing and the absolute character of the real right[59] justify the need of the third parties to know the types and the exact content of the real rights, so that certainty with regard to the real relations can be achieved. On the other hand, the said principle prevents ownership from being segmented into pieces. This segmentation would actually occur if the law recognized that the private will may freely create limited real rights[60] without a predetermined content.

27. The principle of *numerus clausus* is dominant in the area of property law, though not in the field of the law of obligations. In the latter, the principle of private autonomy and, more specifically, the principle of freedom of contracts (Article 361 CC) is dominant. As freedom of contract may be defined, on the one hand, the freedom of individuals to attempt or not attempt declarations of will, to execute or not execute legal transactions, to conclude or not conclude contracts and to choose their contracting parties and, on the other, the ability of the contracting parties to create

---

54. See also *infra* paras 232, 252.
55. Thus, Ap. Georgiades, *PrL*, para. 2 II3 No. 14, 25; Y. Karibali-Tsiptsiou, 'Fundamental Principles Governing Greek Property Law', *Cyprus Law Review* 11 Nos 43–44 (July-December), 1993, 6410–6411 [in Greek]. For the opposite view see S. Banakas, in *Civil Code*, Vol. VI: *Property Law*, ed. Ap. Georgiades & M. Stathopoulos (Athens: Sakkoulas, 1985), Arts 1119–1120 No. 1 [in Greek]; I. Spyridakis & M. Spyridakis, *Property Law*, vol. A (Athens/Komotini: Sakkoulas, 2001), No. 19.5., 77–78 [in Greek].
56. See *infra* para. 51.
57. The usefulness of this principle is disputed. See A. Yiannopoulos, *Louisiana Civil Law Treatise*, Vol. 2: *Property*, 3rd edn (St. Paul, Minn.: West Publishing Co., 1991), para. 237, 469; and, on a critical approach, Ph. Hech, *Grundriß des Sachenrechts* (Tübingen: Scientic Malen, 1960), para. 23 No. 10, 91; I. Spyridakis & M. Spyridakis, *PrL*, vol. A, No. 19.3.3., 75; Y. Karibali-Tsiptsiou, 'Fundamental principles etc.', 6412.
58. See M. Wolf & L. Raiser, *Sachenrecht*, 10th edn (Tübingen, 1957), para. 2 n. 5, 9.
59. On which see *infra* para. 48.
60. Servitudes, pledges and mortgages constitute the so-called limited real rights (on the distinction between ownership and limited real rights see *infra* para. 50 [under a]).

an unlimited number of contractual personal[61] relations, and therefore of personal rights, freely defining their content.

The principle of private autonomy is known in the area of property law as well. In this area, though, it denotes the freedom to constitute, transfer, alter or abolish real rights, within the constraints imposed by the principle of *numerus clausus*, and also the freedom to choose of the person in favour of whom the real right will be constituted.[62]

II. The Principle of Publicity

A. *Content and Justification*

28. The principle of publicity, combined with the principle of *numerus clausus* of real rights and the principle of specificity, aim at the production of indisputable real relations and, thus, at the securing of transactions. Indeed, the protection of third parties presupposes, first of all, that they know the real rights of a certain legal order and their content (principle of *numerus clausus*) and, in addition, that they are able to ascertain – at the time they intend to execute a transaction – the legal status of a certain object (principle of specificity) with regard to the real relations associated with it (principle of publicity).

The demand for publicity, in its simplest form, means that the law must ensure that the real relations in a particular case become clear to third parties (demand for 'formal publicity'). However, the satisfaction of the demand for formal publicity does not in itself succeed in achieving the ultimate goal, which is the protection of third parties. The achievement of this ultimate aim presupposes, furthermore, that the law safeguards the third parties who trust the external elements which determine the real relations (demand for 'substantive publicity').

B. *Formal and Substantive Publicity in the Area of Movables*

29. The demand for formal publicity is served in the area of movables through the acquisition and abandonment of possession.[63] In fact, the acquisition of ownership or other real rights on a movable thing presupposes delivery of its possession (see Articles 1034, 1067, 1075, 1143 [in combination with 1034], 1211 CC), while the abolition of a real right on a movable requires abandonment of its possession (see *Articles* 1076, 1243 point 2 CC). However, it should be stressed that through the acquisition and abandonment of possession the demand for formal publicity is not completely satisfied, especially, for the following reason: notwithstanding the

61. From this point on the terms 'personal' (or 'in personam') and 'obligational' will be used interchangeably (see also *infra* paras 53, 54).
62. See D. Papasteriou, *PrL I*, para. 2 II No.11 32–33. See also J. Baur & R. Stürner, *Sachenrecht*, 18th edn (München: Beck, 2009), para. 1 II b No. 7, 3.
63. However, in the area of fictitious pledges, formal publicity is achieved through registration in public registers (see *infra* paras 471, 473, 476).

fact that the possessor's physical power over the thing gives third parties the impression that the possessor is also the owner of the thing in question, in several cases the holder of the physical power over a thing is neither possessor nor owner.

Insofar as substantive publicity is connected, to a certain extent, with formal publicity, the incomplete satisfaction of the latter has a negative impact on the satisfaction of the former as well. However, it should be borne in mind that, in the field of movables, the demand for substantive publicity is satisfied, to a great extent, through the institution of acquisition of ownership from a person who is not the owner by an acquirer acting in good faith (Articles 1036 CC et seq.).

C. *Formal and Substantive Publicity in the Area of Immovables*

1. System of Transcription and Mortgage Registers

30. Of the two basic systems of publicizing the real relations associated with immovables, namely the system of transcription registers or personal system and the land registry system or objective system, the Greek Civil Code has adopted the former, which is combined with a system of mortgage registers.[64] Only the islands of Rhodes and Cos and the town of Porto-Lagos on the island of Leros have preserved (Article 8 Law 510/1947), even after the introduction of the Civil Code, the land registry system which had been introduced into the Dodecanese by Decree 132/1929 of the Italian governor at that time.

Within the framework of the system of transcription and mortgage registers, alphabetical indexes are kept of the persons who have executed real transactions associated with immovables.[65] Consequently, a person, e.g., a purchaser, who desires to be informed about the legal status of a certain immovable, from the point of view of the real relations attaching to it,[66] takes as his or her starting point a certain person, e.g., the seller, searches for his or her name in the alphabetical index and from there he or she is led to the real transactions which are connected with the immovable in question and have been constituted by the seller in question. However, in this way, he or she may be informed about the real changes to a certain immovable only to the extent that these changes are connected with the person with whom his or her research began. On the other hand, real changes which are connected with another, unknown person – who may be the real owner of the immovable – cannot become known to him or her. As can be clearly seen, these public registers do not fully inform the people who consult them. Thus, the opinion which holds that, in the field of immovables, the principle of formal publicity is inadequate is to a certain extent correct.

---

64. The whole system is completed by the keeping of seizure (attachment) and vindication registers.
65. With regard to the acts which must be transcribed in the transcription registers of the district in which the immovable is located see Arts 1192, 1193 and 1208 CC. See also Arts 1194–1197 CC (which pertain to the way in which the transcription is effected and the content of the transcription) and Arts 1198–1199 and 1202–1204 CC (which refer to the results connected with the transcription).
66. According to Art. 1200 CC, transcription registers are public and accessible to anyone wishing to consult them, while according to Art. 1201 CC, the registrar who keeps the transcription registers is under obligation to issue to all applicants copies, attestations or summaries of the contents thereof.

Whereas, in the area of the transcription and mortgage registers system, the demand for formal publicity is served to a certain degree, the demand for substantive publicity, as a rule, is not satisfied at all. Indeed, insofar as real transactions are registered without their legality being checked, the relevant registrations are not presumed to be precise. Consequently, the registers are not publicly reliable sources and so the person of good faith who trusts them is not protected.

2. Land Registry System

31. The disadvantages of the transcription and mortgage registers system do not, as a rule, exist in the land registry system. Indeed, because this system is land-centred and not person-centred, the registrations are effected on a land basis and not on a personal basis. Therefore, the land registers offer the enquirer a complete picture of the real relations associated with the immovable under investigation and, in this way, the principle of formal publicity is fully satisfied. Furthermore, in the land registry system the principle of substantive publicity is also served. In fact, as in this system the legality of the registered acts is checked by the competent officer before their registration, the content of the land registers is presumed to be precise. Consequently, these registers are regarded as publicly reliable sources and, for this reason, the person in good faith who trusts them may be protected.

The advantages of the land registry system compared with the transcription and mortgage registers system finally led the Greek legislator to enact Law 2308/1995 and Law 2664/1998 which form the basic legislation concerning the constitution and function of land registers in Greece. The first of these laws (Law 2308/1995, as currently in force) refers to the procedure to be followed up until the initial entries in the land registers, while the second (Law 2664/1998, as currently in force) regulates the construction, maintenance and updating of the land registers.[67] Thus, within the framework of the said laws, the land registry system has gradually been introduced into Greece.

Here, it is worth noting that, according to Law 2664/1998 (National Land Register and other provisions), the National Land Register is a system organized on the basis of land-ownership containing legal, technical and other additional information concerning all immovables in the dominion (Article 1 paragraph 1 sub-paragraph a) and is governed by certain principles. These principles are declared in Article 2 and are as follows: the principle of organizing relevant information on a land-ownership basis; the principle of checking the legality of titles and other necessary documents;[68] the principle of temporal priority; the principle of providing (formal) publicity of the land registers; the principle of securing public faith in order to protect

67. On these laws see, in detail, Chr. Kousoulas, *The Law Relating to the Land Register* (Athens-Thessaloniki: Sakkoulas, 2001), passim [in Greek]; P. Matthaiou, *The National Land Register* (Athens: A. Sakkoulas, 2000), passim [in Greek]; L. Kitsaras, *The Initial Entries in the Land Register* (Athens: P. Sakkoulas, 2001), passim [in Greek].

68. On this principle see, in particular, D. Papasteriou, 'The Principle of Legality within the Scope of the National Land Register', *HellD* 40 (1999): 1469 et seq. [in Greek].

the person of good faith who trusts the entries in the land registers;[69] and the principle of providing an open land register.[70]

III. The Principle of Specificity

32. The principle of specificity is understood to mean, on the one hand, that a real right may be constituted only on an individually determined thing and, on the other, that a real legal transaction is effective only if it refers to an individually determined thing. The consequences of this principle are clearly seen in the legal treatment of aggregates of things and rights, property and enterprise.[71]

IV. The Principle of Unity of Economic Purpose

33. The principle of unity of economic purpose pertains to composite objects[72] and expresses the aspiration of the law that the physical unity and, through the latter, the unity of the economic purpose of the composite objects should be preserved. This principle is mainly expressed in the provisions of the Civil Code which refer to the legal treatment of component parts and accessories, the acquisition of ownership by union, connection, amalgamation or merger and the acquisition of products or other components of an object after their separation.[73]

V. The Principle of Economic Utilization

34. The principle of economic utilization means that the law, for reasons relating to the social economy, is well disposed towards diligent people who take care of, exploit and utilize to good effect economic goods. This principle justifies many

69. The efficacy of this principle (on which see, in particular, Y. Karibali-Tsiptsiou, 'Presumption of Accuracy of the Registrations in the Land Registers and Public Faith', *HellD* 40, 1480 et seq. [in Greek]) is based on two facts: (a) the fact that the initial entries, which have become definitive in the way provided for by law, produce a non-rebuttable presumption that the persons who appear in them as beneficiaries really are beneficiaries (Art. 7 paras 1–4 L. 2664/1998); (b) the fact that the entries following the initial registrations produce a relevant rebuttable presumption that may be overturned as a result of a legal action and a concomitant irrevocable judgment (Art. 13 para. 1 L. 2664/1998). However, before the above legal action is inscribed in the land register, a third party may validly acquire a right from the person who appears in the land register as a beneficiary or from his or her heirs, provided that he or she acted in good faith and did not base his or her acquisition on a *donandi causa* (Art. 13 para. 3 sub-para. b L. 2664/1998). On these points see D. Papasteriou, *PrL 1*, para. 2 VIII E No. 33, 43–44.
70. Insofar as the land register also records '... other additional information concerning all immovables in the dominion', it offers information which may lead to important conclusions which are useful for the exercise of legislative policy and for the formulation of environmental, economic and social policies.
71. See *infra* paras 59–62.
72. On the distinction of objects into single and composite objects see *infra* para. 65.
73. On these items see, respectively, *infra* paras 82, 87, 331–334, 336.

of the original modes of acquisition of ownership, such as acquisition by *usucaption*, the elaboration or transformation of material owned by another, concession and occupancy of movables without an owner.[74]

VI. The Principle of Protection of Good Faith

35. The term 'good faith' signifies, on the one hand, the criterion on the basis of which a certain type of human behaviour is evaluated in transactions ('objective' or 'transactional good faith') and, on the other, the internal status of an individual to which the law attaches legal consequences which are useful to that individual (subjective good faith). This internal status may be either incorrect knowledge of an event or ignorance of it, provided both are justifiable.

In the area of property law, both the above-mentioned concepts of good faith are found. However, when speaking about protection of good faith in the context of property law, we mean the protection of subjective good faith. The main expressions of the principle of protection of subjective good faith, in the field of property law, are as follows: the acquisition of ownership by ordinary *usucaption* (Articles 1041 et seq. CC), the acquisition of ownership of a movable good from a person who is not the owner and the concomitant extinction of the limited real rights which probably encumber the thing (Articles 1036 et seq., 1040 CC), the acquisition of fruits by a possessor of good faith (Article 1066 CC), the acquisition of ownership in the case of the partial erection of a building on neighbouring land (Article 1010 CC) and the publician action (Article 1112 CC).[75]

74. On these issues see, respectively, *infra* paras 280 et seq., 329, 335, 296–299, 337.
75. On all these cases see, respectively, *infra* paras 281 et seq., 329, 315 et seq., 327, 336 (under b), 184–186, 397–399.

Chapter 4. Fiduciary Mechanisms in the Greek Legal System

§1. The Greek Legal System and the Institution of Trusts

I. Non-existence of the Institution of Trusts in Greece

36. Trusts are non-existent in Greece.[76] However, even countries which do not include the institution of trusts in their domestic law are prepared to recognize foreign trusts as a matter of private international law when matters involving such trusts arise in their jurisdictions. This is the aim of the Hague Trust Convention (of 1 July 1985) on the law applicable to trusts and their recognition.[77] It should be noted, though, that Greece has not yet ratified the relevant Convention.

Furthermore, it should be stressed that the Regulation 44/2001 (Brussels I Regulation) on international jurisdiction, recognition and enforcement of judgments in civil and commercial matters, which has been in force in Greece from 1 March 2002, includes provisions relating to trusts.[78] Of these, Article 5 point 6 in particular is worth mentioning. According to the latter, a person domiciled in a Member State may, in another Member State, be sued 'in his capacity as settlor, trustee or beneficiary of a trust created by the operation of a statute, or by a written instrument, or created orally and evidenced in writing, in the Courts of the State Member in which the trust is domiciled'. It should be borne in mind that a provision corresponding to the one above was also contained in Article 5 point 6 of the Brussels Convention (of 1968), which (Convention) has already been substituted by the Brussels I Regulation after having been effective in Greece since 1989.[79] On the other hand, according to Article 1 paragraph 2 h of the Regulation 593/2008 (Rome I Regulation) on the law applicable to contractual obligations 'the constitution of trusts and the relationship between settlors, trustees and beneficiaries' is excluded from the scope of this Regulation. Moreover, the Regulation 864/2007 (Rome II Regulation) on the law applicable to non-contractual obligations does not apply to 'non-contractual obligations arising out of the relations between the settlors, trustees and beneficiaries of a trust created voluntarily' (Article 1 paragraph 2 e).

As can be clearly seen, Greek courts will have to carry out a process of classification of the subject-matter of the disputes brought before them, in order to determine whether they involve a trust, for purposes of their jurisdiction.[80] Therefore, a succinct reference to the institution of trusts should be useful.

76. The only provisions of Greek law which refer to trusts are Art. 17 para. 5 of L.D. 118/1973 relating to tax issues and P.D. 96/1993, which permits Greek people to invest capitals in Unit Trusts established in a Member State of the European Community.

77. See J.H. Herbots, 'Belgium/Contracts', No. 94.

78. See Art. 5 point 6, Art. 23 paras 4, 5 and Art. 60 para. 3.

79. The Brussels Convention also contained provisions corresponding to Art. 17 paras 4, 5 and Art. 60 para. 3 of the Brussels I Regulation (see, respectively, Art. 5 para. 6, Art. 17 paras 3, 4 and Art. 53 para. 2).

80. See also J.H. Herbots, 'Belgium/Contracts', No. 94.

II. General Overview of Trusts

37. The institution of the 'trust', a developed form of the medieval institution of 'use'[81] and a special and completely elaborated form of the Roman *fiducia cum amico*,[82] constitutes equity's[83] biggest contribution to the English legal tradition and probably the most impressive expression of the fiduciary idea worldwide.[84]

Due to the variety of functions served by a trust, a complete definition of the latter is difficult to provide. Indeed, trusts aim especially at the long-term regulation and neutral administration of family properties, the management of property which has been devoted to public, charitable or non-charitable, purposes, the management of capital belonging to associations of individuals or groups of investors, and also at the securing of claims.[85] However, for the meaning of the term of 'trust',[86] we can refer to Article 2 of the Hague Trust Convention which stipulates the following:

> For the purpose of this Convention, the term 'trust' refers to the legal relationships created – *inter vivos* or on death – by a person, the settlor, when assets have been placed under the control of a trustee for the benefit of a beneficiary or for a specified purpose.
>
> A trust has the following characteristics:
>
> (a) the assets constitute a separate fund and are not part of the trustee's own estate;
> (b) title to the trust assets stands in the name of the trustee or in the name of another person on behalf of the trustee;
> (c) the trustee has the power and the duty, in respect of which he is accountable, to manage, employ or dispose of the assets in accordance with the terms of the trust and the special duties imposed upon him by law.

81. The institution of 'use' took the form of a transfer of immovables by one person (feoffor) to another person of confidence (feoffee to uses) who was obliged to keep and manage them for the benefit of one or more other persons (*cestuis que use*). On the concept of 'use', the circumstances which imposed it and the evolution of 'use' into the modern trust see, in particular, Gr. Moffat, G. Bean & J. Dewar, *Trusts Law. Text and Materials*, 2nd edn (London/Dublin/Edinburgh: Butterworths, 1994), 24 et seq.; Chr. Deliyianni-Dimitrakou, *Trust and Fiducia* (Thessaloniki: Sakkoulas, 1998), 71 et seq. [in Greek] with a further wealth of references.
82. Ap. Georgiades, *GenPrinc*, para. 29 XIII 8 No. 89, 366–367. On the Roman *fiducia cum amico* see *infra* para. 45 and n. 121.
83. On common law and equity see *supra* para. 15.
84. See P. Kornilakis, *The Fiduciary Assignment of Claims* (Thessaloniki: Sakkoulas, 1978), 30–31 [in Greek]; P. Kornilakis, 'The Birth and Evolution of the Institution of Trusts in Anglo-Saxon law', *Arm* 31 (1977): 243–244 [in Greek].
85. See P. Kornilakis, 'The Birth and Evolution of the Institution of Trusts in Anglo-Saxon law', 246 and for a detailed discussion Chr. Deliyianni-Dimitrakou, *Trust and Fiducia*, 195 et seq.
86. On this meaning see also A. Yiannopoulos, *Property*, para. 236, 463; K. Gray, *Elements of Land Law*, 2nd edn (London/Dublin/Edinburgh: Butterworths, 1993), 34–35; Gr. Moffat, G. Bean & J. Dewar, *Trusts Law*, 3–4; J.G. Riddall, *Land Law*, 75–76; P. Kornilakis, *The Fiduciary Assignment of Claims*, 31; J.G. Riddall, 'The Birth and Evolution of the Institution of Trusts in Anglo-Saxon law', 244–245; I. Voulgaris, 'Issues Relating in the Fiduciary Transfer of Ownership under the Anglo-Saxon laws (Trust) According to Private International Law', EEN 36 (1969): 798 [in Greek].

The reservation by the settlor of certain rights and powers, and the fact that the trustee may himself or herself have rights as a beneficiary, are not necessarily inconsistent with the existence of a trust.

38. Furthermore, with regard to trusts, the following points should be borne in mind:

A trust normally involves three parties (or groups of parties): the settlor, the trustee and the beneficiary (*cestuis que trust*).

A settlor creates the trust by a non-formal, unilateral act *inter vivos* or *mortis causa* (express trust – implied trust). However, a trust may also be created by virtue of the law (statutory trust) or a judicial decision founded on the rules of equity (imputed trust, either of the resulting or constructive variety).[87] Once a valid trust has been created, it can be enforced only by the beneficiaries and not the settlor. However, even after the creation of the trust, the settlor reserves certain powers, such as, for example, the power to revoke the trust, to remove the trustees and replace them with others or to delete certain beneficiaries.

A trustee is an individual or company in whom the trust property[88] is vested. This property, which is held and managed by the trustee and on which the latter has 'legal ownership' (or 'legal estate') – recognized and protected by the common law[89] – constitutes an independent fund available only for the beneficiaries or the charitable or other permitted purpose.[90] The personal creditors of the trustee have no recourse against the trust assets and the latter cannot be used as part of the trustee's own property whether at death or divorce or bankruptcy.[91] In the case where several trustees exist, they hold the trust property as joint tenants, in the sense that on the death of one of them the property passes automatically to the surviving trustee(s).[92]

The beneficiary or beneficiaries are entitled to the income from the trust property.[93] The arrangement between the settlor and the trustees under the trust instrument confers extensive enforceable rights on the beneficiary, although he or she neither provides a consideration[94] for this arrangement nor is a party to the latter. The beneficiary's major right is his or her 'right to follow the trust property'.

87. On the creation of trusts see, in particular, Gr. Moffat, G. Bean & J. Dewar, *Trusts Law*, 91 et seq.; Chr. Deliyianni-Dimitrakou, *Trust and Fiducia*, 99 et seq.
88. All sorts of things, movables or immovables and corporeals or incorporeals, may be held in trust; but the things most frequently held so are lands, stocks and bonds (A. Yiannopoulos, *Property*, para. 236, 463).
89. See also *supra* para. 15.
90. However, the trust instrument will expressly give the trustees, as an incident of their holding and managing the trust fund, the power to pay themselves out of the fund for their services and expenses (A. Yiannopoulos, *Property*, para. 236, 464; J.H. Herbots, 'Belgium/Contracts', No. 98).
91. See Art. 11 paras 2 and 3 (a, b and c) of the Hague Trust Convention.
92. See J.H. Herbots, 'Belgium/Contracts', No. 95; Chr. Deliyianni-Dimitrakou, *Trust and Fiducia*, 109–110. On the relationship between 'joint tenancy' and 'tenancy in common' see *infra* para. 159 (under g).
93. Even unborn or unascertained persons may come to have rights under trust for their benefit (J.H. Herbots, 'Belgium/Contracts', No. 98).
94. In England, for contracts to have a binding force, a consideration is required; on this point see M. Stathopoulos, *Contract Law*, Nos 26, 72–73; S. Symeonides, 'The General Principles of Civil Law', in *Introduction to Greek Law*, 3rd edn, ed. K. Kerameus, Ph. Kozyris (AH Alphen aan den Rijn/Athens: Kluwer/Sakkoulas, 2008), 92–93.

Because of this right, he or she is entitled to vindicate the trust property in the case where the latter, whether in its original form or transmuted into some new form, wrongfully enters the possession of a third party who is not a purchaser of it without notice of the trust, that is, he or she is not a purchaser acting in good faith.[95] The extensive powers of the beneficiary, which are similar to those deriving from a real right, constitute a creation of equity. The same powers justify the recognition of a right of 'ownership' on the trust property in favour of the beneficiary. This 'ownership', a creation of equity, is known as 'equitable ownership'[96] (or 'equitable interest') and exists on the trust property in parallel with the legal ownership of the trustee.[97]

III. Needs Which Have Led to the Development of Trusts in the Anglo-Saxon Countries and Legal Possibilities through Which the Relevant Needs Are Met in Greece

39. The development of trusts in the Anglo-Saxon countries is due to the fact that it serves, in these countries, needs which cannot be met by other institutions or legal possibilities, which, in contrast, are effective in continental legal orders. If we attempted to summarize the most important factors in the development of trusts in the Anglo-Saxon countries, we ought to put forward the following:[98]

(a) the narrow framework of privity[99] in Anglo-Saxon law and the non-recognition of contracts for the benefit of third parties not participating in the contract block;
(b) the requirement of a consideration as a condition for the validity of a contract, a requirement which renders gratuitous acts difficult;[100]
(c) the non-existence of the institution of usufruct, which allows the coexistence of ownership and usufruct on the same object; and finally;
(d) the non-recognition of 'foundations', in the sense of legal entities under civil law which have as their basis a property dedicated to serve a specific purpose.

40. The aforementioned factors which have led to the development of trusts in the Anglo-Saxon countries do not exist in Greece. Actually, the needs which are

95. See also Art. 11 para. 3 (d) of the Hague Trust Convention.
96. See also *supra* para. 15.
97. It is debatable whether the beneficiary's right with regard to the trust property is a real or personal right or a peculiar form of right which may not be classified either as real or personal (on this point see A. Yiannopoulos, *Property*, para. 236, 465; P. Kornilakis, 'The Birth and Evolution of the Institution of Trusts in Anglo-Saxon Law', 245; Chr. Deliyianni-Dimitrakou, *Trust and Fiducia*, 116 et seq.).
98. See M. Stathopoulos, *Contract Law in Hellas*, No. 43.
99. In English terminology, what corresponds to the principle of relativity is the 'doctrine of privity' (M. Stathopoulos, *Contract Law in Hellas*, No. 185).
100. On this issue see M. Stathopoulos, *Contract Law in Hellas*, Nos 72–73.

served by trusts in these countries are met in Greece, mainly, by the following legal possibilities (or a combination of them):[101]

(a) By the conclusion of nominate, innominate or mixed contracts which may have as their object the management of the property of another and which have in Greece binding force without any need for the existence of a consideration.
(b) By contracts for the benefit of a third party (Articles 410 CC et seq.). This third party[102] 'may demand the performance directly from the promissor if it appears that such was the intention of the contracting parties or if such conclusion results from the nature and purpose of the contract' (Article 411 CC).
(c) By the institution of representation,[103] that is, the institution through which a person (representative) has the power to carry out juridical acts with third parties in the interest of another person (the party represented – the principal). Representation is distinguished into voluntary and legal (or statutory) types, depending on whether the power of the representative is created by the person represented or *ex lege*. Thus, for example, the representation of a minor by his or her parents (Articles 1510, 1516 CC) or a tutor (Articles 1589 CC et seq.), as well as the representation of a person under privative judicial assistance by a judicial assistant (Article 1676 CC) are legal types of representation. Furthermore, whereas legal representation is always direct, voluntary representation is distinguished into direct (Articles 211 CC et seq.) and indirect types. Direct representation means that the representative is entitled to carry out juridical acts with third parties not only in the interest but also in the name of the person represented, who alone (and not the representative) becomes subject to the consequences of the relevant legal transaction.[104] On the other hand, in the area of indirect voluntary representation, which is an incomplete form of representation, the representative carries out juridical acts with third parties in the interest of the person represented, though not in the name of the latter but in his or her own name.[105] The function of direct voluntary representation presupposes the

---

101. See M. Stathopoulos, *Contract Law in Hellas*, No. 44. See also A. Yiannopoulos, 'Property', in *Introduction to Greek Law*, 3rd edn, ed. K. Kerameus & Ph. Kozyris (AH Alphen aan den Rijn/ Athens: Kluwer/Sakkoulas, 2008), 159–160; P. Kornilakis, 'The Birth and Evolution of the Institution of Trusts in Anglo-Saxon Law', 245 and for a detailed discussion Chr. Deliyianni-Dimitrakou, *Trust and Fiducia*, 193 et seq.
102. In the case where, at the time of the conclusion of the relevant contract, the third party does not as yet exist, it may emerge from the interpretation of the contract that the parties have concluded it on the suspensive condition that this third party should exist, e.g., should be born or should acquire a legal personality (M. Stathopoulos, *Contract Law in Hellas*, No. 195).
103. On this institution see, among others, D. Klavanidou, in *Law of Juridical Acts*, ed. D. Papasteriou & D. Klavanidou (Athens-Thessaloniki: Sakkoulas, 2008), paras 65 et seq., No. 1 et seq., 465 et seq. [in Greek]; M. Karasis, *Textbook of General Principles of Civil Law. Law of Juridical Acts* (Thessaloniki: Sakkoulas, 1996), 153 et seq. [in Greek]; P. Ladas, *General Principles of Civil Law*, Vol. II (Athens-Thessaloniki: Sakkoulas, 2009), para. 50 No. 1 et seq., 721 et seq. [in Greek]; Ap. Georgiades, *GenPrinc*, para. 46 No. 1 et seq., 585 et seq., M. Stathopoulos, *Contract Law in Hellas*, Nos 191, 324, 329 et seq.; P. Filios, *GenPrinc*, paras 208 et seq., 530 et seq. [in Greek]; S. Symeonides, 'The General Principles of Civil Law', 95–97.
104. See D. Klavanidou, in *JuridActs*, ed. D. Papasteriou & D. Klavanidou, para. 65 I B No. 4, 466–467.
105. See D. Klavanidou, in *JuridActs*, ed. D. Papasteriou & D. Klavanidou, para. 65 I B No. 3, 466.

existence of a power of attorney (Article 216 CC). The latter, although it takes the form of a non-causal (abstract) unilateral juridical act, usually has as *causa* a contract of mandate or a contract for partnership or work.

(d) By the institutions of consent and approval (Articles 236–239 CC),[106] which signify the approbation of a juridical act, before (consent) or after (approval) its constitution, by a third person who is not a party of the relevant act. This third person is either called to protect the interest of the person who carries out the juridical act (and who, for example, is receiving concurrent judicial assistance [Article 1676 CC]) or is the principal whose legal interest is affected by the relevant juridical act (which, for example, has been carried out by a person not invested with a power of attorney [Articles 229, 233 CC] or constitutes a disposal of property by someone not entitled to do so [Article 239 CC]).

(e) By the fiduciary transfer of ownership or another right. This transfer, which will be discussed in detail in later units,[107] aims either at the security of the acquirer for a claim on his or her part against the transferor (*fiducia cum creditore*) or at the management without restrictions by the former of the items of property transferred to him or her by the latter (*fiducia cum amico*).

(f) By the possibility of the ownership of a thing being encumbered with limited real rights and especially with the complete personal servitude of usufruct, which, as already mentioned, offers its holder the power to make use of and collect the fruits of a thing belonging to another (Article 1142 CC). In these cases, the powers contained in the relevant real right are deducted from ownership and form another right. This right is a self-existent real right which exists in parallel with the restricted ownership and may not be regarded as a right of separate or concurrent ownership.[108] On the other hand, upon the disappearance of the above right, ownership regains its original completeness.

(g) By certain institutions of the law of inheritance which aim to determine the fortune of one's property after one's death. The main examples of such institutions are:

  (i) The substitution of an heir (Article 1809 CC et seq.) or a legatee (Article 2008 CC), which takes place if the testator indicated a substitute heir or legatee in the event that the original heir or legatee forfeited his or her rights either before or after devolution.[109]

  (ii) The *fideicommissum* (Articles 1923 CC et seq.), family *fideicommissum* (Articles 1929–1930 CC), *substitutio fideicommissaria* (Article 2009 CC) and family legacy (Article 2010 CC), which are examined in the next section.[110]

  (iii) The institution of forced heirship (Articles 1825 CC et seq.), which aims to protect the closest relatives of the decedent and, more specifically, his or her descendants, parents and surviving spouse. The latter, known as 'forced heirs', are always – even in spite of the contrary will of the testator

106. See, in particular, Y. Karibali-Tsiptsiou, *The Approval of Juridical Acts* (Thessaloniki: Sakkoulas, 1990), passim [in Greek].

107. See *infra* paras 45, 504 et seq.

108. See also *supra* para. 15.

109. See also Art. 1791 CC concerning the substitution of an heir by virtue of the law.

110. See *infra* paras 41–43.

(disinheritance in its broad sense; Article 1713 CC) – entitled to a certain percentage of the estate and they have all the rights and duties of other heirs. However, if there are descendants, the parents are excluded, while the testator may exclude a forced heir from his or her forced heirship if a reason for disinheritance in its narrow sense exists (Articles 1839 et seq. CC).

(iv) The institution of the executor of a will (Articles 2017 CC et seq.), whose task is the faithful execution of the dispositions contained in a will. The executor has the right to take actions allowed by the testator or necessary for the execution of the testamentary dispositions. He or she is also entitled, under the same conditions, to manage the estate in whole or in part.

(v) The judicial liquidation of succession (Articles 1913 CC et seq.), which may be requested from the court by the creditors of an estate. Upon the publication of the decision ordering liquidation, the rights and obligations pertaining to the estate are separated *ipso jure* from the personal assets of the heir and constitute a separate group available for the satisfaction of the creditors of the estate. This group comes under the administration of a liquidator appointed by the aforementioned court decision.

(vi) The institution of vacant succession (Articles 1865 CC et seq.). Vacant succession exists when the heir is unknown or it is not certain if he or she has accepted the succession. In this case, the court appoints a curator to the succession who represents the heir and manages the estate.

(h) By the use of special institutions provided for by the law for special needs, such as, for example, the institution of liquidation of a legal entity (Articles 72 CC et seq.) or a partnership (Article 777 CC et seq.) and the institution of compulsory administration (Articles 1034 CCProc et seq.).

(i) By the recognition of the institution of 'foundations' (Articles 108 CC et seq.). According to Article 108 CC 'if by means of a deed of constitution a property has been designated to serve a certain purpose the foundation shall acquire substance by means of a decree approving its constitution'.

(j) By the recognition of bodies which aim to manage collective investments in movable values.[111]

§2. The Greek Legal System and the Institution of *Fideicommissum*

41. As has already been mentioned,[112] through the Roman institution of *fideicommissum*, which is also regulated by the Greek Civil Code,[113] needs are met in Greece which in Anglo-Saxon countries are served by the institution of trusts. As

111. See L. 3283/2004 which has integrated into Greek legislation EC Directive 2001/107, EC Directive 2001/108, EC Directive 2000/64 and regulates the mechanisms through which collective investments in movable values are managed.

112. See *supra* para. 40 (under g).

113. On the evolution of *fideicommissum* from its creation up until that time see, in particular, K. Bourandas, *Fideicommissum*, vols I, II (Thessaloniki: Sakkoulas, 1993), passim [in Greek].

has already been stated, *fideicommissum*, without being the equivalent of a trust in civil law jurisdictions, is closely related to the latter.[114]

The concept of *fideicommissum* appears in Article 1923 CC. According to this legal rule, the testator[115] may impose on an heir the obligation to surrender, after the occurrence of a certain event[116] or after a certain moment in time, the estate acquired by him or her, or a portion thereof, to another (*fideicommissarius*), while such obligation may not be imposed on a *fideicommissarius*. The *fideicommissarius*, who may even be a natural person not yet conceived or a legal entity not yet constituted at the time of the decedent's death (Article 1924 CC), is a future heir who acquires the decedent's estate indirectly, that is, through the heir burdened with the *fideicommissum*.

Until the devolution of the estate on the *fideicommissarius*, the instituted heir, though a temporary owner of the property, has both management and beneficial enjoyment of the latter, while, upon conditions laid down by the law, he or she is also permitted to dispose of objects belonging to the estate (Articles 1937, 1939 CC). However, upon the devolution of the estate on the *fideicommissarius*, the instituted heir ceases to have the capacity of heir and is bound to surrender the estate to the *fideicommissarius* (Article 1941 CC). The latter then acquires the estate automatically, like any other heir.[117] This means that if the original heir burdened with the *fideicommissum* refuses to restore the estate to the *fideicommissarius*, the latter may initiate against the former, not a simple personal (obligational) action, but an action claiming a portion of the inheritance (Articles 1871 CC et seq.), namely an action which is available only to heirs.

42. The Greek Civil Code also regulates the so-called family *fideicommissum*. The latter exists in the case where the testator has instituted an heir and stipulated that the estate, or a portion thereof, must be preserved within his or her family or the family of the instituted heir. In such a case, Articles 1929 and 1930 CC specify the person belonging to the testator's or the original heir's family who will be called upon to inherit the estate, in the capacity of *fideicommissarius*, after the death of the original heir.

43. A distinction should be drawn between the institution of *fideicommissum* and the institution of *substitutio fideicommisssaria* (specific *fideiocommissum* or *fideicommisaria* legacy). The latter applies to legacies[118] and denotes the disposition of the testator according to which an asset given to a legatee passes after a certain time or event to another person. The relevant disposition is null unless it is for the public benefit or in favour of those close relatives of the testator which are stipulated by Article 2009 CC.

114. On this point see Waters, 'The Institution of the Trust in Civil and Common Law', RCADI 252 (1995): 117 (136 et seq., 150 et seq.); A. Yiannopoulos, *Property*, para. 236, 465; A. Yiannopoulos, 'Property', in *Introduction to Greek Law*, ed. K. Kerameus & Ph. Kozyris, 160.
115. The *fideicommissum* is constituted by testament and in the cases of Arts 1924–1929 CC by virtue of the law.
116. For example, after the *fideicommissarius* has come of age.
117. See *infra* para. 278.
118. On which see *infra* para. 279 (under b).

Furthermore, mention should be made of the family legacy which exists in the case where, according to the will expressed by the testator, the assets given to a legatee must be preserved in perpetuity within the family of the testator. In such a case, Article 2010 CC determines which of the testator's close relatives will be called upon to inherit the estate, in the capacity of *fideicommissarii* legatees, after the death of the original legatee.

§3. The Greek Legal System and Fiduciary Juridical Acts

44. Greek legal doctrine and judicial rulings have recognized the pandectist theory relating to fiduciary juridical acts (*Treuhandgeschäfte*), a theory which was developed under the impact of the Roman instructions concerning the institution of *fiducia.* However, the Greek Civil Code does not include any provision relating to fiduciary juridical acts, while Greek legal doctrine and mainly court rulings approach the latter with reservations.[119] In any event, it should be borne in mind that Articles 190–194 CPrMarL regulate the fiduciary transfer of ownership of ships, whereas the fiduciary transfer of ownership of movables and the fiduciary assignment of business claims or other rights with a view to securing a claim has already been recognized in law, respectively, by Article 10 paragraph 1b and Articles 11–15 of Law 2844/2000.

45. Fiduciary juridical acts, in the Greek legal order, will be discussed in the last part (Part VIII) of this monograph. Here, we will merely define their concept and general attributes and the possible forms in which they may appear.[120]

A fiduciary juridical act is a legal transaction through which somebody transfers a right to another person who undertakes to use it for a particular purpose and then to transfer it back to its original holder. In the context of a fiduciary juridical act an external and an internal relationship is created between the transferor and the acquirer. The former is a dispositive juridical act through which the relevant right is transferred. This act, which leads to the transfer of more powers than those which are necessary for the accomplishment of the purpose intended by the contracting parties, is serious and not simulated (in the sense of Article 138 CC). Consequently, it is valid and renders the acquirer holder of the right transferred. On the other hand, the internal relationship is a promissory juridical act from which arises the acquirer's obligation to use the right for a particular purpose and then to transfer it back to its original holder.

A fiduciary juridical act may appear in one of the following forms:

(a) It is possible for the ownership of a movable or immovable thing to be transferred (fiduciary transfer of ownership) with a view either to securing a claim

119. See *infra* paras 508, 515.
120. On these points see K. Simantiras, *GenPrinc*, para. 33 X, 435 et seq.; N. Papantoniou, *GenPrinc*, para. 54 d, 272 et seq.; D. Klavanidou, in *JuridActs*, ed. D. Papasteriou & D. Klavanidou, para. 19, No. 1 et seq., 74 et seq.; M. Karasis, *GenPrinc*, 53–54, 55; Ap. Georgiades, *GenPrinc*, para. 29 XIII, No. 73 et seq., 359 et seq.; P. Ladas, *GenPrinc II*, para. 32 XII, No. 92 et seq., 72 et seq.

by the acquirer against the alienator (securing transfer [*Sicherungsübereignung*]) or the management of the thing by the acquirer (*Verwaltungstreuhand*).[121] In the first case, the acquirer is bound to transfer the ownership back to the alienator after the settlement of the debt. In the second case, the acquirer is also obliged to retransfer the ownership of the thing and, if the latter has been alienated, the value.

(b) Furthermore, it is possible for a claim to be assigned (fiduciary assignment of a claim) with a view either to securing a claim on the part of the assignee against the assignor (securing assignment [*Sicherungsabtretung*]) or the management and, more specifically, the collection of the claim by the assignee in his or her own name but in the interest of the assignor (*Inkassozession*). In these cases, the assignee is, respectively, bound either to reassign the claim to the assignor after the settlement of the debt or to restore the proceeds of the collection to the latter.

121. These forms of fiduciary legal transactions correspond to the Roman *fiducia cum creditore* and *fiducia cum amico*, respectively.

Part I. Basic Concepts of Property Law

Chapter 1. Real Rights

§1. Real Relations and Real Rights

46. A real relation is a relationship between a person and a thing and at the same time a relationship between persons with regard to a certain thing from which issue real rights and/or possession or detention on the one hand and obligations or commitments based on the law on the other. As can be clearly seen, the concept of real relation is broader than the concept of real right. Indeed, real rights arise from real relations and are either identified (temporarily or definitively) with the latter or are one of the elements that make up a real relation and coexist with one or more other real rights, with possession or with one or more real or personal (obligational) claims.

§2. The Concept and Distinctive Characteristics of Real Rights

47. The Greek Civil Code, in its Article 973, defines a real right (or right in rem) as a right securing over a thing a direct (immediate) power that can be invoked against all persons. In addition, it should be borne in mind that a real right arises from a certain real relation and constitutes, according to the most correct opinion, a relationship between a person and a thing. Consequently, a real right may be defined as a relationship between a person and a thing which is characterized by the elements of directness and absolute effect.[122]

48. Taking the above definition as a starting point and taking into account the Civil Code's provisions referring to the various forms of real right, we come to the conclusion that the elements of the concept of real right are as follows:

122. With regard to disputed issues: (a) if the real right is a relationship between a person and a thing or a relationship between persons and (b) if the real right's main characteristic is directness or absolute effect see Ap. Georgiades, *PrL*, para. 3 I No. 2 et seq., 38–41; D. Papasteriou, *PrL I*, para. 3 III A 3, Nos 16 et seq., 54–56.

(a) power over a (movable or immovable) thing. However, it should be borne in mind that there are real rights, such as usufruct, pledges and mortgages, which contain power that refers to rights as well;
(b) legal power, namely power the acquisition of which presupposes that the conditions provided for by the law come into effect;[123]
(c) direct (immediate) power, in the sense that the object of the real right is directly subject to the sovereign will of the beneficiary and that the will of a third party does not intervene between the holder of the real right and the thing;
(d) absolute power, that is, the power of the holder to oppose any third party who breaches his or her authority over the thing;[124]
(e) universal or partial power, depending on whether the power over the thing exhausts all its utility (as happens in the case of ownership) or only a part of it (as happens in the case of limited real rights, i.e., of servitudes, pledges and mortgages).

49. On account of their direct (immediate) and absolute character, real rights are also characterized by the following distinctive characteristics: (a) power to pursue the thing regardless of whose hands that thing is in, that is, power of the holder to protect his or her right against any offence caused by a third party. This power characterizes those real rights that confer on their holders physical power over the thing, namely all real rights except for that of mortgage; (b) power to follow, which characterizes only limited real rights. This power entails that, where ownership encumbered with a limited real right (e.g., usufruct) is transmitted to a third party, the limited real right follows the ownership and the new owner acquires the right of ownership encumbered with the relevant real right; (c) rule of separation or preference. According to this rule, in the case where a thing is delivered by its owner to a third party (e.g., a depositary) who becomes overburdened with debts, the owner in question is entitled to separate the thing from the property of the debtor even when the remaining property of the latter is insufficient to satisfy his or her creditors (rule of separation). According to the same rule, the holder of a real right has a priority, i.e., he or she is preferred if there is a conflict (e.g., with creditors) concerning the object of his or her right (rule of preference); (d) rule of temporal priority which comes into effect when more than one limited real right coexist over the same thing and which means that the right which has temporary precedence is preferred.

§3. Classification of Real Rights

50. The Greek Civil Code, in its Article 973, recognizes as real rights ownership, servitudes (which are divided into real [or predial] and personal, which include usufruct, habitation and limited personal servitudes), pledges and mortgages. These

123. Legal power, as an element of the concept of real right, is distinguished from physical power, as an element of the concept of possession (see *infra* para. 104).
124. The power of the holder of the real right which is generated by the breach of this right and aims to restore of the direct (immediate) power of the beneficiary over the thing is called 'real claim'.

real rights, on the basis of their content, object and subject, may be classified into the following groups:

(a) Ownership and limited real rights. In contradistinction with ownership, which confers universal power over the thing, all other real rights, known as 'limited real rights', confer limited power. Indeed, while the owner has, as a rule, a unique, general and abstract power to perform any activity over the thing (see *Article* 1000 CC), the holder of a limited real right has a limited power the content of which varies in accordance with the kind of right. Thus, for example, a usufructuary has the power to make use of and collect the fruits of a thing belonging to another (Article 1142 CC), whereas the holder of a habitation is entitled to use as a habitation the building of another or an apartment therein (Article 1183 CC).
(b) Rights of substance and rights of value. The specific content of the rights of substance consists in the power of their holders to derive certain utilities directly from the substance of the thing, although not the power to alienate the thing. Such rights are servitudes. On the other hand, the specific content of the rights of value consists in the power of their holders not to use but to alienate the thing, under certain conditions, in order to gain satisfaction from its value. Such rights are pledges and mortgages, i.e., the so-called rights of real security.
(c) Rights on immovables, movables or rights. Starting with ownership, it should be noted that such rights may be constituted on an immovable or a movable thing. Continuing with servitudes, it should be noted that, whereas usufruct may have an immovable or movable thing or a right as its object, real servitudes, habitation and limited personal servitudes may be constituted only on immovable things. Finally, as concerns the rights of real security, it should be stressed that a mortgage may be obtained on immovables as well as on the usufruct thereof, while a pledge may have as its object a movable thing or a right.
(d) Rights the holder of which is each individual owner of a certain immovable thing and rights the holder of which holds the right independently of his or her relationship towards a thing. All real rights, except for real servitudes, belong to the second group.

51. Apart from the above real rights, recognized by the Civil Code, there are other real rights which have been introduced into the Greek legal system by special legislation. Such rights are: (a) the ownership of a mine, namely the – as distinguished from the ownership of the ground – real right which confers on its holder (State or natural person) the power to search for, extract and exploit minerals; (b) the State's ownership of therapeutic sources, which is independent of the ownership of the land where the source is located; (c) the State's right of preference in the case where an immovable which is useful for society as a whole (e.g., a private forest) is sold; (d) the right of *superficies* which was in force in Greece before the Civil Code was introduced and which has been reintroduced to Greece by the relatively recent L. 3986/2011 (Articles 18–26). According to the latter law (Articles 18 and 25), *superficies* is the real right which confers on its holder, natural person or legal entity, against payment of an exchange, the power to erect a building on a piece of public land belonging to another and to exercise over the building the powers afforded by ownership.

52. Finally, mention should be made of the law which was in force in Greece before the Civil Code was introduced and which recognized, in addition to the real rights enumerated in Article 973 CC, the following real rights as well: (a) *emphyteusis*, that is, the real right which is constituted on an immovable belonging to another and confers on its holder a power almost identical to that of the owner against payment of an annual rent; (b) as has already been mentioned, *superficies*, which, at that time, was defined as the real right which, against payment of an annual rent and public dues, confers on its holder the power to have a building on the land of another and to draw profit from this building as owner; (c) the right of separate ownership on a plantation, a tree or a building located on the land of another.

The above rights were abolished by the Civil Code. Nevertheless, pursuant to Articles 58–59 IntrLCC, those of the previous rights which were already constituted at the time the Civil Code was introduced are preserved and are governed by the provisions of the previous law.

§4. The Distinction between Real and Personal (Obligational) Rights

53. Real rights, as rights that confer legal, direct (immediate) and absolute, universal or partial power over a thing (or right), differ from personal (in personam or obligational) rights, that is, rights which are generated by an obligation.[125] An obligation is a relationship whereby a person (debtor) is bound, towards another person (creditor), to fulfil a performance, i.e., an act, an omission or a forbearance (Article 287 CC). The obligation creates a personal bond between debtor and creditor, from which arises, on the one hand, a personal right (or claim) of the creditor to require from the debtor a performance and, on the other hand, an obligation on the part of the debtor towards the creditor to fulfil the relevant performance.

As can be clearly seen, the power of the holder of a personal right differs from the power of the holder of a real right. Indeed, while a real right confers power over a thing (or a right), the object of a personal right is a performance. Also, in contradistinction with the direct power of the holder of a real right over the thing, a personal right, even when the subject of the performance is a thing, confers power over the will of the specified debtor and only indirectly over the thing. In addition, personal rights, unlike real ones, are not absolute but relative rights, that is, rights which may be invoked not against all persons but only against the specified debtor.[126] Furthermore, it should be stressed that the power to pursue and the power

125. For a critical approach to the relevant distinction see Ath. Yiannopoulos, *Property*, para. 237, 467–468.

126. However, sometimes, by virtue of special provisions of the law (Arts 479, 599 paras 2, 614, 819, 1953 CC), personal rights may be invoked not only against the initial debtor, but against third parties too. Thus, for example, in the case of a sub-lease or assignment of the leased thing to a third party, the lessor can, upon the expiration of the lease, claim the leased thing also from the sub-lessee or from the person to whom the use was assigned (Art. 599 para. 2 CC). In these cases, the personal right does not become absolute, but, as is rightly accepted, the obligation alters in regard

to follow, as well as the rule of separation or preference and the rule of temporal priority, characterize only real rights and are absent from personal ones. Finally, it should be added that, whereas real rights are limited in number (the principle of *numerus clausus*[127]), the private will can, in principle, create an unlimited number of personal rights, freely defining their content (the principle of contractual freedom; Article 361 CC).

§5. The Distinction between Real and Personal (Obligational) Juridical Acts

54. A real (or in rem) juridical act is one in which a real right is constituted, transferred, encumbered or abolished *inter vivos* (Article 1192 point 1 CC).[128] The main characteristic of a real juridical act is its direct (immediate) effect on the legal status of the object (thing or right). Thus, for example, by the real contract of Article 1034 CC the ownership of a movable thing is transferred from its owner to a third party, while the real contract aiming at the constitution of a pledge (Article 1211 CC) entails the encumbrance of the ownership with a right of pledge in favour of a third party. As a rule, real juridical acts are bilateral (contracts). However, there are also unilateral real juridical acts, such as a declaration of renunciation of usufruct (Article 1169 CC).

Apart from real juridical acts, there is the personal (in personam or obligational) type of juridical act. A personal juridical act and, as a rule, a personal contract is one in which a personal (obligational) right is produced, transferred, altered or abolished.[129]

55. The distinction between real and personal juridical acts is not identical to the distinction between dispositive and promissory juridical acts. Dispositive juridical acts are those that have as a direct juridical consequence the disposal of a right, that is, the transfer, encumbrance, abolition or alteration of this right.[130] On the other hand, in promissory juridical acts, only an obligation is generated.[131] Real juridical acts are always dispositive acts, while personal juridical acts, depending on whether they aim at the constitution or at the transfer and abolition of a personal right, are, respectively, promissory juridical acts or dispositive juridical acts.

Of great importance in property law are the personal-promissory types of juridical acts, chiefly contracts, that aim at the constitution or transfer of a real right. Examples of such transactions are contracts of sale, exchange or donation. These contracts do not have as a direct juridical consequence the constitution or transfer

---

to its subject (thus, Ap. Georgiades, *PrL*, para. 4 II 3 No. 12, 53). Compare, however, K. Larenz & M. Wolf, *Allgemeiner Teil des Bürgerlichen Rechts*, 8th edn (München: Beck, 1997), para. 15 III 5b No. 62, 301, who maintain that in such a case *man spricht von einer Verdinglichung obligatorischer Rechte*.

127. On which see *supra* paras 26–27.
128. See D. Klavanidou, in *JuridActs*, ed. D. Papasteriou & D. Klavanidou, para. 10 II No. 5, 47.
129. See D. Klavanidou, in *JuridActs*, ed. D. Papasteriou & D. Klavanidou, para. 10 I No. 2, 46.
130. See D. Klavanidou, in *JuridActs*, ed. D. Papasteriou & D. Klavanidou, para. 11 II A No. 6, 50.
131. Compare D. Klavanidou, in *JuridActs*, ed. D. Papasteriou & D. Klavanidou, para. 11 I No. 2, 49.

of a real right. They only aim at the creation of an obligation, i.e., of a liability on the part of one or both of the contracting parties and of a corresponding claim on the part of the other party. Thus, for example, in the conclusion of a contract for sale of an immovable or a movable thing, only an obligation on the vendor to transfer the ownership of the object and to deliver it to the purchaser is generated (Article 513 CC). For the transfer to occur, another juridical act, the real dispositive contract of Article 1033 or 1034 CC, respectively, is required. Before this act, the purchaser has only a personal right towards the vendor and not a real right of ownership over the thing. This distinction between the personal-promissory type of contract and the dispositive-real (in the case of our example) type of contract has been described as 'the backbone of the whole of private law'. However, the same distinction does not preclude the possibility of both types of contract being concluded simultaneously, as is frequently the case in practice.

56. Also of great importance in property law is the distinction drawn between causal and non-causal types of juridical acts. This is because the Civil Code characterizes real contracts aiming at the transfer of the ownership of an immovable as causal (Article 1033 CC), in contradistinction with real contracts whereby a movable is transferred (Article 1034 CC), which are considered to be non-causal.

A real contract is characterized as causal or non-causal depending on whether the realization of its legal consequences presupposes or not the existence of a valid just cause. On the other hand, the just cause of a real contract is not its direct juridical aim, i.e., the transfer of property itself, but its indirect juridical aim, which justifies the said transfer, i.e., the aforementioned personal-promissory contract (e.g., the contract of sale)[132] by which the obligation to transfer is undertaken.

132. See *supra* para. 55.

Chapter 2. Things

§1. The Concept of a Thing

57. Article 947 paragraph 1 CC, pertaining to the concept of things, stipulates that things in the legal sense are only corporeal objects. This definition, though, which refers only to the characteristic of corporeality, is incomplete. Thus, taking into consideration all the Civil Code's provisions relating to things and to real rights, we may complete the above definition by defining a thing in the legal sense as an individual (self-existent) corporeal object of impersonal nature that is susceptible of human appropriation. From this definition it can be clearly seen that the Civil Code distinguishes between an object and a thing. Indeed, the concept of an object is broader than the concept of a thing as it includes not only all sorts of corporeal objects but incorporeal objects (e.g., rights or claims) as well.

58. The above definition permits the conclusion that a thing in the legal sense constitutes an object in the following senses: (a) a corporeal object, i.e., an object that has a material, regardless of whether it is solid, fluid or gaseous in form, foundation. However, natural forces or energies and, particularly, electrical current and heat, although incorporeal objects, are, by means of a legal fiction, classified as things insofar as they are concentrated within a limited space and are therefore susceptible of human appropriation (Article 947 paragraph 2 CC). Thus, in Greece producers of energy enjoy full proprietary protection; (b) an object of impersonal nature. Consequently, living human beings (as subjects and not objects of legal relations), the (natural or artificial[133]) members or parts of the living human body[134] and the human corpse[135] are not things in the legal sense; (c) an individual (self-existent) object, namely an object having, in accordance with the notions prevailing in trade,[136] a well-defined existence in space. Thus, for example, lands acquire individuality when boundaries are fixed; fluid and gaseous substances acquire individuality (self-existence) and become things in the legal sense as soon as they are placed in containers; fruits of trees prior to separation are parts of trees rather than indi-

133. Artificial members of the human body (e.g., artificial teeth or legs), although lifeless objects, are not things in the legal sense insofar as they are found in durable connection with the body.
134. However, under certain conditions, parts of the human body, such as blood, hair or internal organs, may become things upon their separation from the living human body. However, L. 3984/2011 'concerning the transplantation of human tissues and organs' determines the conditions under which a 'donor' (alive or dead) may offer an organ or organs from his or her body. Furthermore, mention should be made of L. 3089/2002 and L. 3305/2005 concerning 'medically assisted human reproduction', in view of the debates that have taken place before and after the enactment of these laws with regard to the possibility of bringing human genetic material under the concept of a thing.
135. The human corpse, in that it is directly connected with the personality of the man deceased, is not a thing in the legal sense. However, taking into consideration that, as time goes by, the above-mentioned bond is broken, it is accepted that a skeleton or an embalmed corpse may be an object of transactions so long as this is not contrary to public policy and morality.
136. According to the notions prevailing in trade, the individuality (self-existence) of a thing depends on its economic value. Thus, for example, a grain of wheat, although an individual thing in the natural sense, is not an individual thing according to the notions prevailing in trade and, therefore, not a thing in the legal sense. A thing in the legal sense is a mound of wheat as, in accordance with the notions prevailing in trade, it is an individual object.

vidual objects and, therefore, not things in the legal sense; (d) an object susceptible of human appropriation. Objects insusceptible of human appropriation are chiefly those which are 'common to all', i.e., the atmospheric air and the open sea.[137]

§2. Groups of Objects

I. Aggregate of Things (*Universitas Facti*)

59. An aggregate of things is the ideal sum of several, similar or dissimilar, individual things (in the legal sense), which, on account of the unity of their economic purpose, are regarded in trade as an economic unity. Thus, for example, a collection of paintings, postage stamps or coins, a herd of animals, a bookcase, the equipment of a restaurant or a clinic as well as the furnishings of a house constitute aggregates of things.

An aggregate of things is not a thing in the legal sense, but an incorporeal object. Therefore, an aggregate, as a unity, is not susceptible of possession and real rights and may not be transferred or vindicated. On the contrary, each of the things which constitute it is susceptible of possession and real rights, while the transfer or vindication of the aggregate presupposes the transfer or vindication of each of the above things. Nevertheless, an aggregate of things, as a unity, on account of its incorporeal character, may become the object of an obligation.

II. Aggregate of Rights or of Assets (*Universitas Juris*)

60. An aggregate of rights is a sum of things and/or rights which is separated from the rest of one's property, by virtue of the law, and is subject to a special legal status. Thus, for example, the assets of a person in bankruptcy and the assets of a legal entity which has been dissolved (which are devolved to the State; Article 77 CC) constitute aggregates of rights.

As can be clearly seen, an aggregate of rights differs from an aggregate of things in respect of its composition (as it is composed of things and/or rights) and the source of its creation (which is the law and not the notions prevailing in trade). In addition, in contrast to an aggregate of things, the administration of an aggregate of rights does not always belong to the holder of the relevant rights but may be entrusted, by the law, to a third party, e.g., to a trustee in bankruptcy. Furthermore, an aggregate of rights, like an aggregate of things, is not a thing in the legal sense but an incorporeal object and, therefore, receives a legal treatment similar to that of an aggregate of things.

III. Property (*Universitas Bonorum*)

61. Property in the broad sense is the sum of one's legal relations and actual situations which are capable of being evaluated in financial terms. Consequently,

137. These objects, although not things in the legal sense, are characterized by the law (Art. 966 CC) as 'things out of commerce'.

property in its broad sense includes rights, liabilities and actual situations (such as, for example, clientage or good fame) which can be evaluated in financial terms. On the other hand, property in the narrow sense is the sum of one's rights that are capable of financial evaluation.

Property, in both of the above senses, is a sum of incorporeal objects[138] and constitutes an economic unity. As a unity, property may become the object of an obligation, is susceptible of compulsory execution and, upon the demise of its holder, may be transmitted to the heirs. From the point of view of property law, however, it is not a separate and unique object and, therefore, is not susceptible, as a unity, of real rights or possession. Consequently, the provisions of property law (pertaining, for example, to the transfer or vindication of a thing) are applicable to each of the things included in the property and not to the latter as a unity.

IV. Enterprises

62. An enterprise is the sum of things, rights and actual situations or relations which constitute an organized economic unity around their holder and pursue a profit-making purpose (e.g., industrial, handicraft or commercial enterprise).

An enterprise differs from an aggregate of rights and from property (*universitas bonorum*) not only in respect of its composition but also because it constitutes an organized economic unity around its holder and pursues a profit-making purpose. However, the legal treatment of an enterprise is similar to that of an aggregate of rights and to that of property. Thus, as a unity, an enterprise may become the object of an obligation, though not the object of real rights or possession. Concomitantly, insofar as it also includes things, the provisions of property law are applicable to each one of these things.

§3. Classification of Things

I. Movables and Immovables

63. The concepts of immovable and movable things are defined by Article 948 CC. According to this article, immovables consist of the ground and its component parts, while movables consist of anything which is not an immovable. The term 'ground' in this article signifies a part of the ground which has the features of a thing in the legal sense and, above all, the characteristic of individuality.[139] On the other hand, a component part of the ground, in the above sense, is a movable or immovable thing which is in steady and permanent corporeal (natural or artificial) connection with the ground and constitutes, together with the latter, one thing.[140]

---

138. Even when it includes things, since an element of the property is the right on the thing (see D. Papasteriou, *PrL I*, para. 10 III D No. 41, 181 [in Greek]).
139. On this point see *supra* para. 58 under c.
140. For further details on the component parts see *infra* paras 79 et seq.

Article 948 CC is completed by the interpretative rule of Article 949 CC. According to this last article, in the case where by law or a juridical act (e.g., a testament) a distinction has been made between the immovable assets of a person, as a whole, and his or her movable assets, the usufruct of an immovable, as well as any real servitude encumbering an immovable shall be included in the immovables, while any and all claims shall be included in the movables. This rule does not mention anything about habitation, limited personal servitudes, pledges or mortgages. However, it is obvious that habitation and limited personal servitudes, which may be constituted only on immovables, are included in the immovables. On the other hand, on the basis that pledges and mortgages secure claims, it is generally accepted that both of them are included in the movables.

64. Immovable things are divided into two categories: urban (*praedia urbana*) and agrarian (*praedia rustica*), depending on whether, according to the notions prevailing in trade, they are destined, respectively, to be built (regardless of whether they are already built or not) or to be used for cultivation and the collection of fruits.

As regards movable things, it should be mentioned that some of them are characterized by peculiarities. Thus, cars, ships and aeroplanes, money, negotiable instruments and merchandise, although movables, are governed, to various extents, by special rules different from those governing movables in general.[141]

II. Single and Composite Things

65. Single things are material objects, such as stones, pieces of metal or wood, which, according to popular rather than scientific notions, appear to be one thing. Composite things, on the other hand, consist of several single things that have lost their individuality and are regarded as one thing. Thus, for example, a building, a car, a ship or an aeroplane are composite things.

III. Principals and Accessories

66. A principal is a thing served by another thing or a thing on which another thing depends. An accessory[142] is a thing which is destined, by the private will or the notions prevailing in trade, to serve the economic purpose of a principal thing. Thus, for example, a house is a principal thing and the keys of its doors are accessories.

141. On this point see, among others, Ap. Georgiades, *PrL*, para. 10 I 4 No. 13 et seq., 111–114; D. Papasteriou, *PrL I*, para. 11 I E No. 13 et seq., 192–195. See also *infra* para. 308 n. 543 and para. 411 n. 726.

142. For further details on accessories see *infra* paras 85–87.

IV. Fungibles and Non-fungibles

67. According to Article 950 CC, fungible things are movables which in trade are ordinarily determined by number, measure or weight (e.g., material, oil, money or wheat). In contradistinction to Article 950 CC, it emerges that non-fungible things are immovables, as well as movables which in trade are not ordinarily determined by number, measure or weight (e.g., paintings or furniture).

The division of things into fungible and non-fungible types is not identifiable with the division of obligations into generic (or 'in kind') and specific types. However, as a rule, generic obligations relate to fungible things, while specific obligations pertain to non-fungible things. Nevertheless, as the classification of obligations as generic or specific depends on subjective criteria (i.e., the private will), it is possible for a fungible thing to become the object of a specific obligation and for a non-fungible thing to become the object of a generic obligation.

V. Consumables and Non-consumables

68. As emerges from Articles 951–952 CC, consumable things are movables the use of which according to their very purpose consists in their being either consumed or alienated. To the first group belong things the use of which according to their very purpose consists in the immediate and complete destruction of the whole thing or of a part of it. Examples of such things are food, drinks and fuel, though not clothes, as their deterioration and ultimate destruction is the result of prolonged use rather than their destined purpose. The second group includes, in particular, coins and bank notes, matured interest or dividend coupons that have become due, as well as movables which, without being consumables by nature, form part of a commercial establishment or an aggregate of things and are destined to be alienated individually (Article 952 sub-paragraph b CC).

In contradistinction to the concept of consumable things, non-consumable things may be defined as immovables, as well as those movables the use of which according to their very purpose does not consist in their being consumed or alienated. Examples of such things are the books in a bookcase (and not in a bookstore), the clothes of a certain person and the furniture of a certain house.

VI. Things Divisible and Indivisible

69. A divisible thing, in the legal sense, is a (movable or immovable) thing that can be physically divided into several self-existent parts of the same kind without any substantial decrease in its value. Thus, for example, cloths, liquids, metals, grain, money and unimproved tracts of lands (on condition that divisions of the latter do not entail the constitution of non-complete building grounds) are divisible things. On the other hand, an indivisible thing, in the legal sense, is a (movable or immovable) thing that in subsequence to its physical division either does not preserve its value (e.g., precious stones, mirror) or is destroyed (e.g., animals, paintings).

It should, however, be stressed that all things, regardless of whether they are divisible or indivisible, are susceptible of division in ideal shares. Thus, for example, co-ownership may exist not only on a divisible thing (e.g., 500 kg of grain), but on an indivisible thing (e.g., a painting) as well. The first case, however, involves distribution of the common thing itself, while, in the second case, the distribution is accomplished by sale of the common thing in a public auction and distribution of the proceeds of the auction between the co-owners.[143]

VII. Things in Commerce and Out of Commerce

A. General Remarks

70. Things which are out of commerce are those which, according to the law, are either insusceptible, or susceptible upon certain restrictions, of real relations. All other things are in commerce.

A distinction must be drawn between things which are out of commerce and things of forbidden commerce. The latter are things in respect of which the law prohibits or submits to restrictions certain types of commerce. Thus, for example, the sale of guns, explosive materials, drugs and archaeological treasures is prohibited.

Article 966 CC declares that 'things out of commerce are those common to all, those subject to common use and those dedicated to serve public, municipal, communal or religious purposes'.

B. Things Common to All

71. As is generally accepted, the atmospheric air and the open sea are common to all, insofar as they are found in a free state.[144] Otherwise, that is, when they are concentrated within a delimited space, they are susceptible of human appropriation.

Things which are common to all do not belong to anybody. However, the airspace and the part of the sea that occupies an area of six nautical miles from the coastline of a State are subject to the dominion of that State. However, the relevant sovereign rights of the State are not property rights but rights of public law.

It should also be stressed that things which are common to all may be used by everyone. This power arises from the right attaching to one's own personality. Consequently, when the relevant use is prohibited the provisions pertaining to the protection of personality apply (i.e., Articles 57, 59 and 914 CC).

C. Things of Common Use

72. Things of common use are those which may be used freely and in accordance with their designated purpose by any person. These things, unlike those

---

143. On the concept of co-ownership and its dissolution through distribution see *infra* paras 208 and 214–215.

144. See also, however, the remark made *supra* para. 58 n. 137.

which are common to all, are enumerated by the law. Indeed, Article 967 CC declares that 'things of common use are, in particular, freely and constantly running water,[145] roads, public squares, the seashore,[146] harbours and roadsteads, the banks of navigable rivers,[147] large lakes[148] and their shores'. As can be clearly seen ('... in particular ... '), the previous list is indicative. Concomitantly, other things may also become of common use by virtue of the law, an administrative act or the private will of their owners.[149]

73. 'Common use' means enjoyment by all to the benefit of the public interest. The content and the extent of common use varies and depends, for example, on the kind, the designated purpose or the sufficiency of the thing which is subject to common use. However, common use does not mean speculative exploitation of the thing.

The power to use a thing of common use arises from the right attaching to one's own personality. Therefore, when this power is infringed by material acts, it is protected as the right attaching to one's own personality (Articles 57, 59, 914 CC). The above power is not transferable, is not extinguished by renunciation, disuse or prescription and lasts as long as the thing retains its identity as a thing of common use.

74. Things of common use, as a rule, are used equally by all the rightful claimants. However, this rule may be broken. This is because the law recognizes the possibility of particular rights being acquired on the thing subject to common use. Indeed, Article 970 CC declares that 'in the matter of things of common use particular private rights[150] may be acquired by a concession of the public authority[151] in conformity with the conditions laid down in the law provided that common use shall thereby be served or shall not be impeded'.

The rule of equal use may be broken, as well, in the event of conflict between several claimants of common use. This conflict is regulated by the relevant administrative authority and also by Article 969 CC. This article, regulating conflicts over

145. Which forms navigable or unnavigable rivers or rivulets.
146. Namely, the part of the land that borders on the sea and is washed by the highest but usual reach of the waves (Art. 1 para. 1 L. 2971/2001).
147. As well as their beds. Consequently, the banks and beds of unnavigable rivers are not of common use and belong to the adjacent landowners. However, since running water is of common use, remote landowners are entitled to its use and may have access to it by means of ditches or pipe lines (see Arts 1029, 1031 CC).
148. That is, lakes formed by freely and constantly running water, regardless of their extent.
149. As an acquisition, and thus the abolition of the qualification of a thing as a thing of common use, is accomplished by virtue of the law or the private will.
150. Examples of such rights are the right to establish a kiosk on a pavement or a public square, the right to establish a refreshment room in a park, the right to place the tables and the chairs of a restaurant or a pastry-shop on a pavement or on a public square, etc. It is debatable whether the relevant rights are real, personal or sui generis rights governed by the rules of administrative law (on this point see Ap. Georgiades, *PrL*, para. 13 III 5 No. 27, 156). However, from the point of view of property law, the holder of the above rights has the detention of the thing and is protected as the possessor (Art. 997 CC).
151. The act of concession is a unilateral administrative act or an administrative contract and not a simple administrative licence (e.g., licence to sell merchandise on the street) which has a temporary character and is freely revocable.

the common use of water, gives priority, in order of preference: (a) to the use which is more important for the public interest; (b) to the use that promotes the social economy to a greater extent; (c) to the use which goes back the furthest in time; (d) to the use for the benefit of an enterprise connected with a certain locality and (e) to the use for the benefit of the riparian.

75. The classification of a certain thing as a thing of common use does not mean that it does not belong to anybody or that it is insusceptible of the right of ownership. In fact, as emerges from Article 968 CC, things subject to common use belong to municipalities or communities, to private persons when this is authorized by statute or, in the final analysis, to the State. This ownership, even when limited on account of the common use, is governed by the provisions relating to ownership in general insofar as the relevant provisions are compatible with the common use. Thus, for example, the provisions pertaining to the protection of ownership, to the acquisition of fruits by the owner (Article 1064 CC) or to the acquisition of a hoard (Article 1093 CC) are all applicable, though not the provisions relating to *usucaption*, as things out of commerce – which include things of common use – are insusceptible of *usucaption* (Article 1054 CC).

D. Things Dedicated to Serve Public, Municipal, Communal or Religious Purposes

76. The last category of things out of commerce includes all sorts of things dedicated to a public purpose.[152] These things either belong to the public property[153] of the State[154] or municipalities and communities[155] or serve religious purposes.[156] These things differ from things dedicated to common use in that the public purpose served by them is not of common use. However, like things dedicated to common use, things dedicated to a public purpose are susceptible of ownership.

E. Loss of Qualification as a Thing out of Commerce

77. Pursuant to Article 971 CC, 'things out of commerce shall lose this qualification the moment they lose their intended function as things of common use or cease to serve public, municipal, communal or religious purposes'. As emerges from

152. These things, together with the things of common use that belong to the State, constitute the so-called public things.
153. Things belonging to the private property of the State (or of the municipalities and communities) are not things out of commerce in the sense of Art. 966 CC.
154. For example, State-owned buildings housing government offices and educational and health institutions.
155. For example, municipal or community buildings housing municipal or community offices and institutions as well as certain movables dedicated to serve similar purposes, e.g., dustcarts.
156. For example, religious institutions and cemeteries as well as consecrated vessels and sacred vestments, images and books after their sanctification.

this article, of the things out of commerce only those of common use and those dedicated to serve public, municipal, communal and religious purposes – though not those common to all – may lose their qualification as things out of commerce.

The loss of the above qualification means that the thing becomes a thing in commerce and that all limitations of ownership on it are lifted. Change of ownership does not occur (except in the cases of Articles 1071 and 1072 CC).

§4. Component Parts and Accessories

I. General Remarks

78. Composite things are of great importance to the economy of a State. Hence, the law endeavours, on the one hand, to ensure that their physical unity is preserved and, on the other, to decree real relations on them which are simple and profitable for the economy.

One of the ways in which the law aspires to attain these purposes is the distinction it draws between component parts and accessories and the mandatory rule that the (essential) component part 'may not become a distinct object of ownership or other real right' (Article 953 CC). On the other hand, with regard to accessories – which, first, do not constitute elements of a composite thing, as they are not firmly and permanently connected with the principal thing, and second, together with the principal thing constitute an economic unity – there exists the interpretative rule that 'a real juridical act dealing with the principal thing in case of doubt shall also include the accessory' (Article 958 CC).

II. Component Parts

A. Concept

79. Interpreting Articles 953, 954 and 955 CC in combination with each other, we may define a component part as a movable or immovable thing which is not self-existent, but is found in steady and permanent corporeal connection (natural or artificial) with another movable or immovable, and together with the latter constitutes one thing.[157]

B. Essential and Inessential Component Parts

80. Article 953 CC permits the conclusion that component parts are distinguished into those which are insusceptible (essential, inseparable, not self-existent) and those which are susceptible (inessential, separable, self-existent) of a distinct real right. Commonly quoted examples of inessential component parts are a ring in

157. A component part of an immovable may be a movable or an immovable thing, while a component part of a movable may only be a movable thing.

relation to its precious stone and a frame in relation to a photograph. However, the distinction between essential and inessential component parts has been censured. This is because of the argument that the triple distinction between essential and inessential component parts and accessories is practically useless as inessential component parts do not differ from accessories in respect of their nature and their legal treatment.

C. Essential Component Parts in Particular

1. Classification

81. From the combination of Articles 953 and 954 CC it may be concluded that the category of essential component parts includes those defined as such according to the general criterion of Article 953 CC and those determined by the law, i.e., by Article 954 CC. More specifically:

Component parts, according to the general criterion of Article 953 CC, are things which cannot be separated from the thing of which they form part without deterioration or alteration of their own substance or intended purpose or those of the thing of which they form part. Examples of such things are the wheels of a car, the main and subsidiary engines of a ship and the accessories of a clock. In any event, in case of doubt, the notions prevailing in trade ultimately determine the classification of a thing as a component part in accordance with the general criterion.

On the other hand, component parts by virtue of the law (i.e., Article 954 CC), regardless of whether the conditions provided for by Article 953 CC occur, consist of: (1) things firmly attached to the ground, especially buildings;[158] (2) the produce of an immovable as long as it is connected with the soil;[159] (3) underground waters and springs and (4) seeds upon their being sowed and plants upon their being planted (Article 954 paragraph 1 CC). Furthermore, the component parts of a building are the movables used for its erection or incorporated in it[160] (Article 954 paragraph 2 CC).

2. Legal Treatment

82. In accordance with the mandatory rule of Article 953 CC, an (essential) component part 'may not become a distinct object of ownership or other real right';[161]

158. Exceptions to this rule are introduced by Art. 955 CC (see *infra* paras 83–84), Art. 1002 CC in combination with L. 3741/1929 and L. 1024/1971 (see *infra* paras 216 et seq.) as well as by Art. 1010 CC (see *infra* para. 184).
159. For example, plants, trees and their fruits, stones, sand, minerals and metals.
160. For example, construction materials, stairs, windows, window-shutters, window-panes, doors, electric, telephonic and hydraulic installations, washstands and bathtubs, elevators and central heating installations.
161. Consequently, it may become a distinct object of possession (see *infra* para. 108).

in other words, it follows the legal fate of the composite thing.[162] This rule has certain consequences, the most important of which are the following:

(a) as long as the component part is connected with the composite thing, it is insusceptible of separate ownership or any other real right, while the ownership or other real rights which exist on the composite thing extend to the component part as well;
(b) any real juridical act[163] relating to the composite thing also includes the component part, even when this is added after the relevant act has been made;
(c) real rights that existed on the component part before its connection to the composite thing are permanently extinguished;
(d) retention of ownership or any other real right on the component part before its connection to the composite thing is invalid;
(e) any real right existing on the component part, as part of the composite thing, remains unchangeable even after the separation of the component part from the composite thing;[164]
(f) separate vindication of a component part is not permissible;
(g) distribution of the component thing separately from the composite thing is impossible;
(h) the attachment of an immovable extends to the component parts as well; finally;
(i) the compulsory expropriation of an immovable includes *ipso jure* the component parts as well.

D. Component Parts in Appearance

83. The classification of a thing as a component part presupposes, on the one hand, its stable and, on the other, its permanent corporeal connection with the composite thing. Hence, the absence of such stability or permanence from such a connection renders the above classification inapplicable.

Article 955 CC is a rule which makes clear that the temporary purpose of an – even stable – connection means that the relevant thing may not be classified as a component part. Indeed, Article 955 CC, pertaining to things that in accordance with Article 954 paragraph 1 point 1 and paragraph 2 CC should be characterized as component parts – that is, to things that appear to be component parts – excludes the relevant characterization if the connection of the component part with the composite thing has a temporary purpose.

---

162. Exceptions to this rule are introduced chiefly by Art. 1023 CC (see *infra* para. 198) and Art. 1002 CC in combination with L. 3741/1929 and L. 1024/1971, as well as by Arts 953 para. 5 and 968 CCProc (concerning attachment and sale by public auction of fruits even before their separation from the trees).
163. Though not any personal one.
164. An exception is provided for by Art. 1283 CC, which declares that 'where a movable which forms a component part or an accessory of a mortgaged immovable has been separated from the immovable and transferred to a third party, the mortgagee shall not be entitled to claim the movable back from the third party'.

More specifically, in accordance with the above article, the following may not be deemed component parts:

(a) things that have only been attached to the ground for a temporary purpose (Article 955 paragraph 1 sub-paragraph a CC);[165]
(b) buildings or constructions in general which have been erected on an immovable belonging to another by a person owning a real right thereon and in the exercise of such right (Article 955 paragraph 1 sub-paragraph b CC);[166]
(c) movable things which are only attached to a building for a temporary purpose (Article 955 paragraph 2 CC).[167]

84. The things enumerated in Article 955 CC, known as component parts in appearance, are movable things and are governed by the provisions relating to movables. This is because immovables are considered to be the ground and its component parts (Article 948 CC), whereas the things enumerated in Article 955 CC may not be characterized as component parts.

III. Accessories

A. Concept

85. The concept of accessories arises from Articles 956 and 957 paragraph 1 CC. From these articles it may be concluded that an accessory is a movable thing which, without being a component part of a principal thing, has been destined to serve permanently the economic purpose of the latter and has already been placed in a spatial relationship in regard to the principal thing corresponding to the above purpose. This applies provided that the relevant movable is regarded as an accessory in accordance with the notions prevailing in trade.

In view of the above definition, it should be noted that an accessory is:

(a) a movable thing;
(b) a self-existent movable, unlike a component part;
(c) a movable connected with another principal (movable or immovable) thing, that is, with a thing which performs the main function;

165. For example, huts erected for crews engaged in construction projects, kiosks of a commercial exhibition organized for a single occasion only.
166. Buildings or other constructions erected by the holder of a personal right, e.g., by the lessee, may not be deemed component parts because they fall by analogy into the sphere of application of Art. 955 para. 1 sub-para. b CC (according to one opinion: see Ap. Georgiades, *PrL*, para. 11 II 4 No. 31, 131) or into the area of application of Art. 955 para. 1 sub-para. a CC (according to a second opinion: see D. Papasteriou, *PrL I*, para. 12 II D Nos 47, 48, 245–246).
167. For example, an awning attached to the balcony or a water-heater attached to the bathroom of an apartment by the lessee.

(d) a movable destined[168] to serve permanently the economic purpose of the principal thing;
(e) a movable that has already been placed in a spatial relationship to the principal thing[169] corresponding to the economic purpose of the latter;
(f) a movable that possesses the previous attributes and, in addition, is deemed an accessory in trade.

Consequently, the following may be mentioned as examples of accessories: keys in relation to a house, an anchor in relation to a ship, a spare tyre in relation to a car, furniture in relation to a house and a barrel in relation to wine, though not telephonic apparatus, as this may not be deemed an accessory in accordance with the notions prevailing in trade.

86. Besides the things which qualify as accessories according to Articles 956 and 957 CC, Articles 959 and 960 CC explicitly characterize certain movables as accessories. These are movables destined to serve the economic purpose either of a building constructed for the purpose of serving permanently an industrial enterprise[170] (Article 959 CC)[171] or of an agrarian immovable (Article 960 CC).[172] To be specific, Articles 959 and 960 CC, on the assumption that the above movables permanently serve the economic purpose of the principal thing, declare that the said movables may be deemed accessories, providing however that the other conditions of Articles 956 and 957 are also fulfilled.

B. *Legal Treatment*

87. The interpretative rule of Article 958 CC – pursuant to which 'a real juridical act dealing with the principal thing in case of doubt shall also include the accessory' – permits the conclusion that the private will may make an accessory the object of distinct ownership or another real right. Consequently, an accessory may be transferred, pledged, abandoned, occupied, attached or vindicated separately from the principal thing.

---

168. Either by those who have permanent rights on the principal thing (i.e., the owner and the possessor of good faith, though not, as a rule, the lessee or the usufructuary) or directly by the law (Arts 959–960 CC).
169. A spatial relationship does not necessarily mean bodily contact as well. Thus, for example, the ships or the railway wagons used to carry raw materials or prepared products may be accessories of a factory. On the other hand, according to Art. 957 para. 2 CC, a temporary separation of the accessory from the principal thing does not disqualify it as an accessory. Thus, for example, keys remain accessories of a house even when they are not in the lock but in another place (e.g., a pocket or desk).
170. Or, as is accepted, a handicraft or a commercial enterprise.
171. According to Art. 959 CC, such movables are: machines, utensils and tools.
172. According to Art. 960 CC, such movables are: utensils, tools, cattle, agricultural products that are necessary for the further cultivation of the land until the new harvest and also the fertilizers existing on and originating from the said land.

However, the above Article 958 CC, taking into account the fact that the principal thing and the accessory – in spite of their physical individuality – form an economic unity, declares that 'in case of doubt', that is, in a case where a contrary stipulation has not arisen, the real juridical act dealing with the principal thing should also include the accessory.[173] This applies without there being any need to preserve the conditions necessary for the transfer of the accessory.[174]

Moving in a similar direction to Article 958 CC, the interpretative rule of Article 370 CC, pertaining to personal (obligational) contracts dealing with the principal thing, declares that the relevant contracts in case of doubt should also include the accessory.

§5. Fruits, Benefits and Charges

I. Fruits

88. The concept of fruits is declared in Article 961 CC which distinguishes, on the one hand, between the fruits of a thing and the fruits of a right and, on the other hand, between natural and civil fruits.[175]

The natural fruits of a thing are the (organic) products thereof,[176] as well as everything that is extracted therefrom in conformity with its destined use,[177] whereas the civil fruits of a thing are the proceeds which a thing yields by virtue of a legal relation.[178]

---

173. The rule of Art. 958 CC is broadened by Art. 1282 CC ('a mortgage shall extend to the whole of the mortgaged immovable as well as to the component parts and accessories thereof'). See, however, and Art. 1283 CC *supra* para. 82 n. 164.
174. Thus, for example, the sale and transfer of ownership of a farm, pursuant to Art. 1033 CC, also entails the transfer of ownership of the water-pump without the delivery of its possession also being necessary (see Art. 1034 CC). However, when the alienator is the owner of the principal thing, though not of the accessory as well, the acquisition of ownership on the accessory by the acquirer of good faith (pursuant to Art. 1036 CC) presupposes the delivery of possession of the accessory as well (thus, G. Balis, *General Principles of Civil Law*, 8th edn (Athens: Sakkoulas, 1961), para. 196, 516 [in Greek]; D. Papasteriou, *PrL I*, para. 12 III D 1 No. 83, 261; Ph. Dimakou, in *Civil Code*, Vol. V: *Property Law*, ed. Ap. Georgiades & M. Stathopoulos (Athens: Sakkoulas, 1985), Art. 958 No. 6 [in Greek]). Compare Ap. Georgiades, *PrL*, para. 11 III 2 No. 50, 137–138.
175. E. Kounougeri-Manoledaki, *The Law of Fruits* (Thessaloniki: Sakkoulas, 1979), 43–44 [in Greek]) suggests the distinction of fruits into natural fruits or the fruits of a thing and civil fruits.
176. Namely, anything that, in accordance with the laws of nature, is produced periodically and organically by the fruit-producing thing without the latter being destroyed or suffering any deterioration. Examples of such things are eggs, milk, the fruits of plants or trees and the timber therefrom.
177. Namely, anything that is produced by the fruit-producing thing in accordance with the laws of nature and the destined use of the thing, such as meat and leather from animals, ore from a mining operation, a mineral from a mine, stones from a quarry and electric, nuclear or other forms of energy produced by certain installations. These products, unlike organic ones, are not produced periodically, while their receipt entails the destruction or deterioration of the fruit-producing thing.
178. For example, the rent paid by the lessee to the owner-lessor.

The fruits of right are the revenues which a right yields according to its destined use (natural fruits)[179] or by virtue of a legal relation (civil fruits).[180]

II. Benefits

89. According to Article 962 CC, benefits are not only the fruits of a thing or a right but also any advantage which the use of the thing[181] or the right[182] procures.

III. Charges

90. Article 965 CC refers to the apportionment of the charges which encumber a thing, without defining them. However, charges, in the sense of Article 965 CC, are not the limited real rights that encumber the ownership of a thing but the various liabilities that are connected with the thing and follow it. Examples of such liabilities are public, municipal or communal taxes, the obligation to grant right of way (Articles 1012–1016 CC)[183] or the obligation to insure a thing.

---

179. That is, the natural fruits derived from a thing (see *supra* nn. 176 and 177) not by their owner but by the holder of a limited real right (e.g., the usufructuary) or of a personal right (e.g., the lessee) by virtue of his right.
180. For example, the interest encashed by the creditor of a claim or the rent paid by the lessee to the usufructuary-lessor (compare *supra* n. 178).
181. For example, the advantage of the owner of an apartment who uses it as his or her habitation.
182. For example, the advantage of the usufructuary of a flat who uses it as an office or the advantage of the shareholder of a company limited by shares deriving from the exercise of his or her right to participate and vote in the general meetings of the shareholders.
183. See *infra* paras 187 et seq.

Part II. Detention and Possession

Chapter 1. Detention

§1. Introductory Remarks

91. An element of the concept of real right is the 'direct power', though not 'physical power', over a thing. Consequently, a real right exists even when a thing is not dominated physically by the holder of the real right but by someone else, e.g., a lessee or a thief.

92. The Civil Code, through its provisions relating to possession, recognizes and protects the physical power over a thing regardless of whether it is based on a real right or not.[184] This choice of the law is not accidental. It aims, on the one hand, to support peaceful cohabitation and public policy and, on the other, to prolong the economic exploitation of a thing, which, as a rule, is carried out by the person who has the physical authority over the thing.

93. The simplest type of physical power over a thing is detention. This concerns the physical authority which is exercised with the mind of a detentor, that is, with the intention of acting as detentor. Detention is one of the utilities offered by a real right to its holder; it constitutes one of the elements of the concept of possession; and, finally, it is of great importance as a form of relationship between a person and a thing which (relationship) is not based on a real right or on possession. Consequently, a detentor may be the holder of a real right, the possessor and any other person in whom the elements of the concept of detention may occur. Thus, for example, a lessee, a depositary or somebody who borrows an item for use are detentors in that they exercise physical power over a thing, though it is recognized that the ownership belongs to the lessor, depositor or person who lends an item for use by another.

§2. Concept and Legal Nature of Detention

94. Article 974 CC defines detention as physical power over a thing. However, this imperfect definition may be completed by adding that detention is a legal and,

184. However, in cases where the physical power is not based on a real right, while the holder of physical power over a thing is temporarily vindicated if his or her power is violated, he or she faces outright defeat if sued by the holder of a real right on the thing.

more specifically, a real relation, in which a person has the power physically to dominate a thing, and to do it voluntarily, in accordance with the notions prevailing in trade and within the limits determined by the law.

The above definition, on the one hand, determines the legal nature of detention, as it characterizes the latter as a real relation, while, on the other, it permits the conclusion that the elements of the concept of detention are as follows:

(a) legal relation of a person towards a thing;
(b) physical (or material or actual) authority over the thing;
(c) desire for physical authority over the thing;
(d) determination of this authority in accordance with the notions prevailing in trade;
(e) exercise of the same authority within the limits determined by the law.[185]

As can be clearly seen, the terms 'detention' and 'physical power or authority' are not synonymous. Indeed, the concept of 'detention' is broader and includes 'physical power' as one of its constituent elements. Consequently, where physical power over a thing is ascertained, the existence of detention is not an undoubted fact, while the ascertainment of detention entails the existence of physical power as well.[186]

§3. Types of Detention

I. Protected and Non-protected Detention

95. Detention is divided into two types: protected and non-protected, depending on whether the law protects it or not. Thus, according to the law (Article 997 CC in combination with Article 974 CC), protected detention, almost like possession,[187] is detention which has been acquired either by virtue of a contract with the possessor[188] or by virtue of the law,[189] provided that the detentor has the intention of exercising physical power over the thing in the name of the possessor and not in his or her own name or in the name of a third person. Contrariwise, any form of detention which does not include the above elements (e.g., the physical power of a lessee which is exercised on the leased thing, after the expiration of the lease, without the consent of the lessor) is non-protected.[190]

185. On all these points see D. Papasteriou, *PrL I*, para. 14 VI, IX No. 18 et seq., 70, 283 et seq., 303–304 [in Greek].
186. See D. Papasteriou, *PrL I*, para. 14 VI No. 25, 287.
187. For further details on the protection of detention see *infra* paras 155–156.
188. For example, a contract for the hire of a thing or a contract of deposit, loan for use or transport.
189. Examples of detentors by virtue of the law, are voluntary agents, the parents or tutor of a minor, testamentary executors, liquidators of succession, trustees in bankruptcy and the holders of a private right on a thing of common use.
190. Non-protected detention must be distinguished from the accidental or temporary physical authority over a thing belonging to another which is exercised, for example, by the passer-by who takes a

II. Graduated Detention

96. Graduated detention[191] exists when the detentor, e.g., a lessee A, grants the physical power over the thing to another person, e.g., to a sub-lessee B. In this case, A and B preserve the status of detentor. However, A becomes an indirect and B a direct detentor. Concomitantly, the detention of A is indirect, while the detention of B is direct.

III. Universal, Partial and Quasi Detention

97. Universal detention (or simply detention) is the universal physical authority over a thing, i.e., the physical power pertaining to all the utilities (or benefits) of the thing. Such physical authority is exercised by the possessor and, naturally, by the owner.

Partial detention is partial physical authority over the thing, i.e., the physical power relating to one or more, though not all, the utilities of the thing. Such physical authority is exercised, on the one hand, by the person who has acquired the partial physical power over the thing from the possessor in his or her capacity as lessee or depositary or through some other similar relationship (Article 997 CC) and, on the other hand, by the holder of a limited real right of servitude or pledge, by the quasi possessor (even when he or she is not holder of one of the rights just mentioned) and, finally, by the person who has acquired partial physical power over the thing from the quasi possessor in his or her capacity as lessee, depositary or through some other similar relationship (Article 997 CC). In our opinion, the partial physical authority exercised by the persons in the last three cases represents an example of so-called quasi detention. This is because, in the last case, the relevant physical power is offered by the quasi possessor, while the physical authority that is exercised by the persons in the other two cases is a constituent of their quasi possession.[192]

IV. Detention of a Thing and Detention of Part of a Thing

98. In contradistinction to the detention of a thing, namely the physical power that occupies the whole of the thing, detention of part of a thing[193] is the physical

rest on a park bench (see D. Papasteriou, *PrL I*, para. 14 VI No. 22, fn. 30, 286 in combination with para. 14 VII, Nos 51–52, 295–296. Compare, however, Ap. Georgiades, *PrL*, para. 14 III 1 No. 13, 167).

191. On this subject see Ap. Georgiades, *PrL*, para. 14 III 1 No. 14, 167; Chr. Kousoulas, *Possession and Hereditary Succession* (Thessaloniki: Philotas, 1996), 108–113 [in Greek]; D. Papasteriou, *PrL I*, para. 14 VII No. 53 et seq., 296–298.

192. See also *infra* para. 107. However, see also D. Papasteriou, *PrL I*, para. 14 VII Nos 57 et seq., 298–299 in combination with para. 17 IV Nos 37 et seq., 333–335.

193. The recognition of this type of detention is justified by Art. 993 CC concerning the possession of part of a thing (see D. Papasteriou, *PrL I*, para. 14 VII No. 60 et seq., 300–301; Chr. Kousoulas, *PrL*, para. 27 II 1, 164–165).

power that relates to a part of the thing. This part must be externally distinguished and the separate authority over it must be conceivable and materially possible. An example of such a part is a room of a flat.

V. Detention, Co-detention and Common Detention

99. Detention, in the sense of universal physical power over a thing, cannot be exercised on one and the same thing by several persons separately. Nevertheless, it is possible for several persons to exercise detention in undivided ideal shares[194] on the same thing. This type of detention is called 'co-detention'.

In addition, Article 9 Law 2844/2000, pertaining to the institution of a pledge under common detention, recognizes the common type of detention. To be specific, according to this article, it is possible for a pledge to be constituted even when the thing pledged is not delivered to the creditor, but is placed under the common detention of the creditor and the pledger in such a way that neither of them may undertake it without the cooperation of the other.[195]

§4. Acquisition, Preservation, Exercise and Loss of Detention

I. Acquisition of Detention

100. Detention is acquired originally or derivatively. Detention is acquired originally when it is obtained either without the preceding detentor's free will or regardless of whether a previous detentor exists. Thus, the acquisition of physical power over a lost thing or over a thing without an owner entails original acquisition of detention insofar as the acquirer has the intention of acting as detentor. On the other hand, we speak of derivative acquisition when the physical power of the (new) detentor over the thing is acquired with the preceding detentor's consent and is based on the physical power of the latter. Derivative acquisition presupposes: (a) an agreement between the old and the new detentor to the effect that, for just cause,[196] detention is transferred and (b) delivery of the physical power over the thing from the old to the new detentor. However, derivative acquisition takes place not only in the aforementioned case of particular succession in detention but also in the case of universal succession (Article 983 CC).

II. Preservation of Detention

101. Acquired detention is preserved until a good reason for its termination arises. However, during the period between the acquisition and the loss of detention,

194. In regard to the concept of the undivided ideal share see *infra* para. 208.
195. See also *infra* para. 481.
196. For example, delivery of the thing so that the obligation arising from a contract for the hire of a thing may be fulfilled. However, the contract to the effect that detention is transferred is non-causal (see D. Papasteriou, *PrL I*, para. 15 I No. 11, 308).

the elements of its concept must occur, although it is not necessary for the same elements to remain constantly effective.

III. Exercise of Detention

102. The exercise of detention is the performance of various actions on the thing through which (actions) physical control is realized over the thing and the actor manifests the intention of acting as detentor. Detention may be exercised personally by the detentor,[197] e.g., a lessee, or through another, e.g., a sub-lessee, in the name of the detentor. However, the person who has commenced detention in the name of another, as long as he or she remains in detention, is presumed to be exercising detention in the name of the other.[198]

IV. Loss of Detention

103. Loss of detention may be due to general grounds (e.g., destruction of the thing) or to specific grounds (e.g., expiration of the term of the contract for the hire of a thing). Furthermore, in view of the fact that detention may be exercised personally or through another, the following should also be stressed.

Detention which is exercised personally is lost[199] as soon as, for any reason, either physical contact with the thing has definitely ceased or the exercise of physical power over the thing has become definitely and permanently impossible.

On the other hand, detention which is exercised through another may be lost for reasons relating either to the detentor himself or herself (e.g., a lessee) or to the person who exercises the detention in the name of the detentor (e.g., a sub-lessee). Thus, detention may be lost as soon as the (original) detentor or the subsequent detentor has lost the physical power over the thing. However, detention is not lost in the case where, although the subsequent detentor has abandoned the thing, the (original) detentor may exercise physical power over it in such a way as to prevent the opposite situation from arising.[200]

---

197. Personal exercise of detention also occurs in the case where the detentor uses a detention-aid (or detention-helper). On the analogy of Art. 986 CC (dealing with the possession-aid; see *infra* para. 129), a detention-aid may be defined as a person who exercises physical power over a thing on behalf of the detentor so long as he or she is dependent upon the detentor in a domestic sense or as a hired servant and is bound to follow the detentor's instructions regarding the thing. An example of such a person is a driver hired by the lessee of a car.
198. See also Art. 980 CC, dealing with possession, *infra* para. 128.
199. See also Art. 981 CC, dealing with the loss of possession, *infra* para. 132.
200. On all these points see D. Papasteriou, *PrL I*, para. 16 III Nos 11–12, 316.

Chapter 2. Possession

§1. Concept, Functions and Legal Nature of Possession

I. Concept of Possession

104. Physical power over a thing, not necessarily connected with a real right, is enjoyed not only by the detentor but also by the possessor.

Taking into consideration Article 974 CC, which deals with the concept of possession, and also the provisions governing possession, all in all, possession may be defined as the legal relation and, more specifically, the real relation in which a person exercises physical power over a thing with the mind of an owner.[201] This definition, which is not the only one that has been expressed in respect of possession,[202] declares, like most of the other definitions, that the concept of possession consists of two elements: the physical power over a thing (objective or material element: *corpus*) and the intention of acting as owner (subjective or spiritual element: *animus*).

The physical power has already been mentioned as an element of the concept of detention. However, the physical power of the possessor differs from that of the detentor in that it is exercised not with the mind of a detentor but with the mind of an owner.

'Mind of an owner' means the desire to have authority over a thing in a manner befitting an owner, i.e., with the intention of acting as owner. The mind of an owner must be distinguished, on the one hand, from the conviction of being the owner and, on the other, from the mind of a detentor. Indeed, the conviction of being the owner is something more than the intention of acting as owner and is not a prerequisite for the existence of possession. Thus, the thief of a movable who knows that he or she is not the owner and, concomitantly, does not have the conviction of being the owner, is the possessor insofar as he or she has the intention of acting as owner. On the other hand, the mind of a detentor is something less than the mind of an owner. In fact, while the mind of an owner denotes an intention to possess permanent, universal (unlimited) and exclusive authority over a thing, the mind of a detentor denotes an intention to possess temporary and limited, in regard to manner and extent, physical authority over a thing.

---

201. See D. Papasteriou, *PrL I*, para. 17 II No. 7, 322.

202. For a critical presentation of these definitions see Chr. Kousoulas, *Possession*, etc., 65 et seq. and, especially, 123, where the author defines possession as 'the relationship of a person towards a thing and, simultaneously, the relationship of a person towards other persons, in regard to the thing, which relationship is characterized by the inclusion of the thing in the sphere of dominance of the assets of a certain person as the holder of a real right, but regardless of whether a relevant real right exists.'

II. Functions of Possession

105. The law invests possession with a number of functions as a result of which possession plays a major role in the area of private law. The most important of these functions are the following:

(a) The way it helps to maintain the material relationships of persons towards things. This is because possession is protected regardless of whether its holder is at the same time the holder of a real right or not.
(b) The way it helps to realize the principle of (formal) publicity, in the field of movables, as from the acquisition or loss of possession arises publicity of the real relations pertaining to movables.[203] Indeed, the acquisition of ownership, usufruct and pledges on movables, by contract, presupposes the transfer of possession (Articles 1034, 1143, 1211 CC); the acquisition of ownership on things without an owner presupposes occupation of possession (Article 1075 CC); and the renunciation of ownership presupposes abandonment of possession (Article 1076 CC). In addition, there is a presumption of ownership in favour of the possessor of a movable (Articles 1110–1111 CC), while the law connects with possession the possibility of real rights being acquired on movables by a person who is not the owner (Articles 1036 et seq., 1143, 1215 CC).
(c) Finally, a note should be made of the way in which possession contributes to the acquisition of real rights through *usucaption* (Articles 1041 et seq. CC).

III. Legal Nature of Possession

106. Various opinions have been expressed on the legal nature of possession.[204] To be precise, these range from the opinions which characterize possession as an actual situation with which the law connects legal effects to those which regard possession as a right. Among the latter, there is disagreement regarding what kind of right possession is.

However, taking into account the provisions governing possession as a whole, it seems correct to accept the opinion which holds that possession is a legal relation and, specifically, a real relation.[205]

§2. Types of Possession

I. Quasi Possession

107. Taking into account Article 975 CC in combination with the rules dealing with possession, the latter may be defined as the legal relation and, more specifically, as the real relation[206] in which a person exercises partial physical power over

203. See also *supra* para. 29.
204. On these see Chr. Kousoulas, *Possession*, etc., 127 et seq.
205. Thus, Chr. Kousoulas, *Possession*, etc., 132 et seq.; D. Papasteriou, *PrL I*, para. 17 VI No. 75, 347.
206. D. Papasteriou, *PrL I*, para. 17 IV No. 36, 333.

a thing with the mind of the holder of a pledge or a certain servitude. Consequently, the elements of the concept of quasi possession are: partial physical power over a thing[207] (objective or material element: *corpus*) and the mind of the holder of a pledge or a certain servitude, namely the intention of acting as holder of a pledge or a certain servitude (subjective or spiritual element: *animus*).

In comparing the concept of possession with that of quasi possession, we come to the following conclusion: Article 974 CC, which defines possession as physical authority over a thing that is exercised with the mind of an owner, means the universal physical authority which embraces all the utilities of the thing. Concomitantly, possession corresponds with the right of ownership, regardless of whether it coexists with the latter or not.[208] On the other hand, quasi possession entails partial physical authority over a thing, that is, authority which extends to some of the utilities of the thing and, more specifically, to those which form the content of a pledge or a certain servitude.[209] Consequently, quasi possession corresponds with the rights of a pledge or servitude, regardless of whether it coexists with one of them or not.[210]

II. Possession of Part of a Thing

108. Possession of part of a thing (which is recognized by Article 993 CC) is the real relation[211] in which a person exercises on a distinct part of a thing either universal physical power with the mind of an owner or partial physical power with the mind of the holder of a pledge or a certain servitude (quasi possession of part of a thing). However, the part of the thing must be externally distinct and the authority over it must be conceivable and materially possible. Examples of such a part are the drawer of a wardrobe and the room of a flat.

Insofar as, pursuant to Article 953 CC, a distinct object of possession may become an (essential) component part,[212] the latter constitutes part of a thing susceptible of possession or quasi possession. However, as Article 953 CC excludes the possibility of any (essential) component part becoming a distinct object of ownership or other real right, the above possession or quasi possession may not lead to

207. With regard to the issue of when this partial physical power denotes quasi detention, see *supra* para. 97.
208. Thus, the possessor is not only A, the owner of farm X, who exercises physical power over it, but also B, who arbitrarily detains farm Z (belonging to C) and enjoys all its utilities with the mind of an owner.
209. On account of the partial character of the physical authority over the thing, it is possible for two or more persons to have separate quasi possession on the same thing. Thus, it is not impossible for the following to be constituted on the same immovable: a usufruct in favour of A, a real servitude of way in favour of B and a real servitude regarding the cutting of wood in favour of C.
210. Thus, A, the owner and possessor of the immovable X, who passes through the neighbouring immovable Z (belonging to B) with the mind of a holder of a real servitude of way, has quasi possession on Z not only when he or she is the rightful beneficiary of the relevant servitude but also in the case where the constitution of the above servitude is null and void or non-existent.
211. D. Papasteriou, *PrL I*, para. 17 IV No. 46, 336.
212. See *supra* para. 82 n. 161.

the acquisition of ownership or a certain servitude, on the component part, through *usucaption*.[213]

III. Co-possession

109. Possession, in the sense of universal physical power over a thing which is exercised with the mind of an owner, may not be exercised on one and the same thing by several persons separately.[214] Nevertheless, it is possible for several persons to enjoy possession in undivided ideal shares[215] of the same thing (Article 994 CC). This type of possession is called 'co-possession'.

To be precise, co-possession is the legal relation and, more specifically, the real relation in which two or more persons exercise, in common, physical power with the mind of a co-owner on one and the same thing.[216] Consequently, the elements of the concept of co-possession are: first, the physical power[217] which is exercised on the same thing by several persons in common, i.e., in undivided ideal shares (objective or material element: *corpus*) and, second, the mind of a co-owner, that is, the intention of each co-possessor to act as a co-owner (subjective or spiritual element: *animus*).

In the context of co-possession, on the one hand there are external relationships (between co-possessors and third parties), which are governed by the provisions dealing with possession, and, on the other, internal relationships (between co-possessors), which are governed by the provisions concerning undivided joint rights[218] (Article 785 et seq. CC).

IV. Possession by Means of a Fiction

110. Sometimes the law recognizes the existence of possession although the elements of its concept do not occur. Thus, the heirs of a possessor[219] are deemed possessors regardless of whether they have acquired physical power over the thing or whether they know or not that devolution by succession has occurred. Also, the State is deemed possessor of lands without an owner and of State lands, in general, even when it has not undertaken, on these lands, any action denoting exercise of possession.

These cases are examples of the so-called possession by means of a fiction which is associated with certain legal consequences similar to those with which

---

213. Compare, however, *infra* para. 344.
214. Compare *supra* para. 107 n. 209.
215. In regard to the concept of the undivided ideal share see *infra* para. 208.
216. D. Papasteriou, *PrL I*, para. 17 IV No. 53, 339.
217. In the case where the physical power is not universal but partial quasi co-possession exists, whereas if the physical power of co-possessors refers to a part of a thing co-possession of part of a thing exists.
218. See, however, *infra* para. 154.
219. On the transfer of possession to the heirs of a possessor (Art. 983 CC) see *infra* paras 124–125.

possession, in the sense of Article 974 CC, is associated. Thus, for example, it is protected like the possession of Article 974 CC.

§3. Further Categories of Possession

I. Possession of Bad and Good Faith

111. Possession of bad faith exists when the possessor is aware or ignorant, due to gross negligence, of the fact that he or she is not entitled to possession. On the other hand, possession of good faith exists when the possessor is ignorant, without being guilty of gross negligence, of the fact that he or she is not entitled to possession.

II. Defective and Non-Defective Possession

112. Defective possession is that which has been acquired as a consequence of the eviction of the possessor in an illegal manner and without his or her consent (Article 984 CC). Contrariwise, non-defective possession is that which has not been acquired as a consequence of the eviction of the possessor in an illegal manner and without his or her consent.

The effects of defective possession are relative in the sense that defective possession exists only in regard to the dispossessed possessor and not to third parties. On the other hand, the relevant defect of possession also weighs against the heirs and the particular successors of the possessor, although, in the last case, this is so only if the particular successor (and generally each successive possessor) is aware, at the time of acquisition, of the defect in the possession of his or her predecessor (Article 984 paragraph 2 CC) and is consequently a possessor of bad faith. However, in the case where a series of possessors of bad faith is interrupted by a possessor of good faith, the following possessor acquires non-defective possession regardless of whether he or she is aware of the defect of the initial acquisition.

§4. Acquisition of Possession

I. Original Acquisition of Possession (Concept and Legal Nature)

113. Original acquisition is that which occurs either without the previous possessor's free will or regardless of whether a previous possessor exists. Thus, for example, the possession of stolen or lost things and of things without an owner is acquired originally. Original acquisition of possession is realized by occupation of the thing and presupposes a concurrence of the constitutive elements of possession in the person of the acquirer.

114. The legal nature of the original acquisition of possession is debatable. In fact, while according to one opinion the relevant acquisition constitutes a real fact,[220] according to a second opinion the same acquisition is a unilateral juridical act.[221]

II. Derivative Acquisition of Possession

A. *Concept and Legal Nature*

115. The derivative acquisition of possession is that in which the latter is transferred voluntarily by the previous to the new possessor. To be precise, the derivative acquisition of possession presupposes:

(a) possession by the person who transfers it at the time of the transfer;
(b) an (explicit or implicit) declaration of will addressed by the previous possessor to the new one to the effect that he or she transfers his or her possession to the latter with regard to both of the elements of its concept;
(c) an (explicit or implicit) declaration of will on the part of the new possessor to the former to the effect that he or she accepts the acquisition of possession with regard to both of its constitutive elements.[222]

The derivative acquisition of possession encompasses both particular and universal succession in possession. However, only particular succession in possession is being examined here, while universal succession will be discussed later on.[223]

116. As emerges from the above observations, the acquisition of possession by the new possessor is inconceivable without a previous agreement between the former and the new possessor to the effect that possession is transferred. Consequently, it seems correct to adopt the opinion which holds that the derivative acquisition of possession presupposes the drawing-up of a contract between the former and the new possessor.[224] However, it is also argued that derivative acquisition of possession is not transactional[225] and that, in the case of acquisition through

220. See chiefly K. Vavouskos, *Property Law*, 6th edn (Thessaloniki: Sakkoulas, 1986), No. 67, 76 [in Greek]; Ap. Georgiades, *PrL*, para. 17 III No. 9, 197 as well as Magistrates' Court of Patmos 4/1997, 53 Arm, 1999, 361 (363). See also I. Spyridakis & M. Spyridakis, *PrL*, Vol. A, No. 72.3, 230.
221. See mainly G. Balis, *Property Law* 4th edn (Athens: Sakkoulas, 1961), para. 3, 12–13 [in Greek]; Chr. Thibaios, *Law of Possession*, vol. II (Athens, 1953), 27 [in Greek]; D. Papasteriou, *PrL I*, para. 18 II No. 10, 354.
222. On these subjects see D. Papasteriou, *PrL I*, para. 18 III Nos 13 et seq., 355–356.
223. See *infra* paras 124–125.
224. See chiefly G. Balis, *PrL*, para. 4, 16; Chr. Thibaios, *Law of Possession*, vol. II, 132; D. Papasteriou, *PrL I*, para. 18 III Nos 16 et seq., 356–357; I. Spyridakis & M. Spyridakis, *PrL*, vol. A, No. 73.3.4., 234, as well as Plenary Session of AP 1593/1979, 28 NoB, 1980, 1120; AP 218/2008, 50 HellD, 2009, 1059 (1060); AP 1082/2000, 42 HellD, 2001, 429; AP 1368/1996, 38 HellD, 1997, 1127 (1128); AP 695/1994, 37 HellD, 1996, 155 (156); AP 1605/1992, 34 HellD, 1994, 430; AP 603/1992, 35 HellD, 1994, 81; AP 809/1989, 38 NoB, 1990, 1434; AP 1605/1987, 29 HellD, 1988, 1371 (1372).
225. Thus, K. Vavouskos, *PrL*, No. 69, 77–78.

(material) delivery (Article 976 sub-paragraph a CC),[226] the material delivery constitutes a material act.[227]

B. Cases of Derivative Acquisition of Possession

1. (Material) Delivery of a Thing

117. According to Article 976 sub-paragraph a CC, 'in the case of a thing that is in the possession of another, possession shall be acquired through delivery effected voluntarily by the current possessor'. From this article it emerges that the acquisition of possession through material delivery of the thing presupposes, first, a declaration of will on the part of the current possessor that he or she is estranged from the physical authority over the thing and that he or she transfers this authority, together with the mind of an owner, to the acquirer and, second, a corresponding declaration of acceptance by the acquirer.

As can be clearly seen, the material delivery of the thing indicates a coincidence of declarations of will on the part of the current possessor and the acquirer and, consequently, the drawing-up of a contract. This contract is real (in that possession constitutes a real relation), non-formal, even when it refers to immovables,[228] and non-causal.[229]

2. *Longa* and *Brevi Manu* Delivery

118. According to Article 976 sub-paragraph b CC, 'an agreement between the former possessor and the new one shall be sufficient for the acquisition of possession where the new possessor is in a position to exercise power over the thing'. On this article are based the *longa* and *brevi manu* forms of delivery. From the same article it emerges that, insofar as the acquirer has the ability to exercise (*longa*

---

226. See *infra* para. 117.

227. See mainly Ap. Georgiades, *PrL*, para. 18 V1 No. 40 p.213; P. Filios, Chr. Filios, *Property Law*, 3rd edn (Athens/Komotini: Sakkoulas, 2009), para. 34 B I 100–101 [in Greek], as well as Magistrates' Court of Patmos 4/1997, 53 Arm, 1999, 361 (363). See also J. Baur & R. Stürner, *SachR*, para. 7 B II 2b No. 17, 71; H. Prütting, *Sachenrecht*, 34th edn (München: Beck, 2010), para. 7 I 1 No. 55, 23; H. Westermann, et al., *Sachenrecht*, 7th edn (Heidelberg: Müller, 1998), para. 13 II 2, 94.

228. See, in particular, D. Papasteriou, *PrL I*, para. 18 III No. 19, 357. See also Plenary Session of AP 1593/1979, 28 NoB, 1980, 1120; AP 218/2008, 50 HellD, 2009, 1059 (1060); AP 1082/2000, 42 HellD, 2001, 429; AP 220/2000, 41 HellD, 2000, 762; AP 1368/1996, 38 HellD, 1997, 1127 (1128); AP 695/1994, 37 HellD, 1996, 155 (156); AP 1605/1992, 35 HellD, 1994, 430; AP 603/1992, 35 HellD, 1994, 81; AP 809/1989, 38 NoB, 1990, 1434; Court of Appeal of Athens 4889/1999, 41 HellD, 2000, 861; Court of Appeal of Patras 479/1996, 13 AchNom, 1997, 124.

229. See, in particular, G. Balis, *PrL*, para. 4, 16; D. Papasteriou, *PrL I*, para. 18 III No. 26, 359. See also Plenary Session of AP 1593/1979; AP 1368/1996; AP 695/1994; AP 1605/1992; AP 603/1992; AP 809/1989; Court of Appeal of Larissa 845/2003, 45 HellD, 2004, 914 (917); Court of Appeal of Athens 4164/2001, 42 HellD, 2001, 1371; Court of Appeal of Athens 4889/1999 *supra*, Court of Appeal of Patras 479/1996 *supra*.

manu delivery)[230] or does in fact exercise physical power over the thing (*brevi manu* delivery),[231] he or she is considered to possess only the material element of possession (*corpus*) and that the acquisition of possession by him or her presupposes only the transfer of the spiritual element (*animus*). This transfer is realized by virtue of an agreement between the former and the new possessor.

3. Constitution of Possession and Anticipatory Constitution of Possession (*Constitutum Possessorium* and *Constitutum Possessorium Anticipatum*)

119. *Constitutum possessorium* is referred to in Article 977 sub-paragraph a CC, which declares that 'delivery to an acquirer shall also be effective where it has been agreed between him and the former possessor that the latter shall remain on the strength of a certain legal relation in detention of the thing'. From this article it emerges that the acquisition of possession by *constitutum possessorium* presupposes an agreement (contract) between the former possessor and the acquirer which includes two specific stipulations: (a) the stipulation that possession is transferred from the former possessor to the acquirer by transmission only of the mind of an owner; (b) the stipulation that the former possessor will remain in detention of the thing on the strength of a certain legal (personal or real) relation, for example, as lessee (detentor) or usufructuary (quasi possessor and, consequently, quasi detentor).

120. While *constitutum possessorium* presupposes that the person who executes the transfer is possessor, in *constitutum possessorium anticipatum*, there is a transfer of possession (according to the terms which apply in the case of *constitutum possessorium*) which has not yet been acquired by the person who executes the transfer. Thus, acquisition of possession by *constitutum possessorium anticipatum* occurs in the following case: B buys a flat from A and, before the possession of this flat is transferred to him or her, he or she sells the same flat to C and agrees with the latter that, as soon as he or she (B) acquires the possession, he or she will transfer it to him or her (C) although he or she himself or herself (B) remains in detention of the thing as lessee.

4. Delegation of Possession

121. Acquisition of possession by delegation (Article 977 sub-paragraph a CC) occurs when the possessor is not also the detentor, because the thing is detained, on the strength of a certain legal relation, by a third party. In this case, the transfer of possession presupposes an agreement between the former possessor and the acquirer which includes, on the one hand, the stipulation that possession is transferred by

---

230. For example, because he or she has taken delivery of the only key to the storehouse where the agricultural products which are going to be transferred to him or her are kept.
231. On the strength of a legal relation, e.g., a contract of hire or a loan for use with the former possessor.

transmission only of the mind of an owner and, on the other, the stipulation that the said third party will continue to detain the thing on the strength of the above legal (personal or real) relation, for example, as lessee (detentor) or usufructuary (quasi possessor and, concomitantly, quasi detentor). However, 'in such a case the possession shall in regard to the third party be transferred to the acquirer the moment the transfer is brought to the knowledge of the third party by the former possessor' (Article 977 sub-paragraph b CC). This notification, which is a quasi juridical act, is not an essential precondition for the transfer of possession to the acquirer but a condition for effecting the relevant transfer to the third party. Consequently, before the notification of the third party, in relation to the latter, the person who transfers remains possessor.

5. Transmission of Warehouse Warrant or Bill of Lading

122. According to Article 978 CC, 'in the matter of goods and generally of movable things deposited in a warehouse or taken over by a transporter, if a warehouse warrant or bill of lading has been issued, the transfer of possession is effected by the transmission of the warehouse warrant or the bill of lading'.

Taking into consideration the fact that, on the one hand, the warehouse-keeper or the transporter becomes detentor in accordance with the will of the depositor or the consignor and, on the other, that the warehouse warrant or the bill of lading incorporates the depositor's or the consignor's possession of the things deposited or taken over by the transporter, it is obvious that Article 978 CC introduces a case of acquisition of possession by delegation.

III. Special Ways of Acquiring Possession

A. Acquisition of Possession through a Representative

123. In view, first, of the fact that Articles 211–235 CC, concerning representation and power of attorney, refer to declarations of will and juridical acts and, second, of the dispute over the issue of whether acquisition of possession is effected by juridical or material act,[232] the usefulness of Article 979 CC, concerning acquisition of possession through a representative, is obvious. Indeed, on account of Article 979 CC, there is no doubt that possession can be acquired (originally or derivatively) not only personally but through a representative as well 'when the latter acquires physical power over the thing for the purpose of rendering possessor thereof the person represented'. On the other hand, it is self-evident that representation is possible not only for the acquirer, as Article 979 CC declares, but also for the person who executes the transfer. This possibility is based on Article 211 CC or Article 979 CC, which in this case is applied by analogy.

232. See *supra* paras 114, 116.

Furthermore, it should be stressed that Article 979 CC, which declares that possession can be acquired through a representative, justifies the application of Articles 211–235 CC and, consequently, permits direct, voluntary or legal, representation. Nevertheless, Article 979 CC does not exclude the possibility of possession being acquired by an indirect representative as well.

B. Acquisition of Possession by Hereditary Succession

124. According to Article 983 CC, 'possession is transmitted to the heirs of a possessor'. Consequently, provided that the deceased was possessor (quasi possessor, possessor of part of a thing, co-possessor or detentor) at the time of his or her death, his or her possession[233] (or detention) is transmitted automatically, by the operation of the law alone, to his or her intestate, testamentary or forced heirs.[234] This transmission is effected even before the heir acquires the constitutive elements of possession[235] and regardless of whether the latter is ignorant of the death of the possessor, his or her status as heir or the existence of the things belonging to the succession. In addition, possession is transmitted to the heirs even if it is based on a right – such as habitation (Article 1185 CC), non-inherited usufruct (Article 1167 CC) or a limited personal servitude (Article 1190 CC) – which expires upon the demise of its holder.[236] Finally, the transfer of possession on immovables may be effected without the need to make a declaration of acceptance of the succession in a public document and relevant transcription.[237]

125. Heirs receive exactly the same possession (or detention) that was enjoyed by the deceased. In the case where the deceased's possession was defective, the possession transmitted to the heir is also defective (Article 984 paragraph 2 subparagraph b CC). On the other hand, in the case where the deceased possessor had suffered a violation of his or her possession while he or she was alive, upon his or

233. And, more precisely, the legal relation of possession (thus, Chr. Thibaios, *Law of Possession*, Vol. II, 100; Chr. Kousoulas, *Possession*, etc., 171–172; D. Papasteriou, *PrL I*, para. 20 IV No. 19, 386, where other views are also mentioned).
234. On the subject of hereditary succession see *infra* para. 278.
235. This explains the prevailing opinion which holds that the heir's possession is possession by means of a fiction (see, in particular, G. Balis, *Law of Inheritance*, 5th edn (Athens: Sakkoulas, 1965), para. 4, 10 [in Greek], as well as AP 875/2001, 1 ChrIdD, 2001, 609; AP 679/1994, 37 HellD, 1996, 65 (66); AP 1004/1983, 32 NoB, 1984, 650; Court of Appeal of Patras 479/1996, 13 AchN, 1997, 124; Court of Appeal of Athens 942/1995, 37 HellD, 1996, 367; Court of Appeal of Patras 69/1995, 12 AchN, 1996, 202; Court of Appeal of Thessaloniki 6385/1991, 34 HellD, 1993, 1646; Court of Appeal of Thessaloniki 1801/1992, 46 Arm, 1992, 799; Magistrates' Court of Florina 33/1999, 48 NoB, 2000, 310). See also, however, other views in Chr. Kousoulas, *Possession*, etc., 147 et seq., 153 et seq. and D. Papasteriou, *PrL I*, para. 20 IV No. 18, 385 (who maintain, though, that this type of possession is authentic).
236. However, in such a case, the heir must restore the thing to the owner (Y. Karibali-Tsiptsiou, *The Complete Personal Servitude of Habitation* (Thessaloniki: Sakkoulas, 1986), 75 [in Greek]).
237. See AP 43/2008, 50 HellD, 2009, 760 (761); AP 165/2004, 45 HellD, 2004, 816; AP 1004/1983, 32 NoB, 1984, 650; Court of Appeal of Patras 900/1997, 14 AchN, 1998, 289. Compare *infra* para. 278 and n. 492.

her death, his or her claims against the offender, insofar as they have not been prescribed, are transmitted to the heirs. Furthermore, the heir is protected like any other possessor (or detentor) even in the case where he or she has not yet acquired physical power over the thing.

C. Acquisition of Possession by the State

126. The acquisition of ownership on an immovable thing by the State also automatically entails the acquisition of possession, without it being necessary for the State to acquire physical power over the immovable.[238] However, in the case where the State has not acquired ownership, it acquires possession, as would any other person.

§5. Preservation, Exercise and Loss of Possession

I. Preservation of Possession

127. Acquired possession is preserved until a ground justifying its loss occurs. During the period between acquisition and loss, the elements of the concept of possession are considered to exist. During the same period, possession is preserved without it being necessary either for the elements of its concept to coexist – either at a particular moment in time or constantly – or for the same elements to remain constantly effective. More specifically, the physical authority which was perceived at the time of the acquisition of possession is believed to be retained insofar as it may be manifested at any moment. On the other hand, the mind of an owner which existed at the time of the acquisition of possession is preserved without there being any need for its renewal.

II. Exercise of Possession

128. Exercise of possession is understood to mean any action through which physical authority is gained over a thing and the mind of an owner is evinced.[239] Examples of such actions are the fixing of boundaries, the fencing, measuring or cultivation of an immovable, as well as the hire of a movable or an immovable thing and the keeping, conservation or consumption of a movable thing.

Possession can be exercised personally or through another. However, the person who has began to detain a thing in the name of another, as long as he or she

238. Articles 2 para. 1, 3 para. 1 E.L. 1539/1938, whose legal validity was preserved by Art. 53 IntrLCC. The relevant provisions apply by analogy in the area of municipalities and communal authorities (Art. 1 L.D. 31/2.12.1968).

239. It is self-evident that there are also actions through which quasi possession, possession of part of a thing and co-possession are exercised.

preserves the detention, is presumed to detain the thing in the name of the other (Article 980).

129. Possession is exercised personally either in the case where the possessor is also detentor or in the case where, in spite of the existence of a representative, certain actions are undertaken by the possessor and detentor. Furthermore, personal exercise of possession also occurs in the case where the possessor and detentor uses a possession-aid (or possession-helper).

A possession-aid is neither a possessor nor a detentor. He or she is a person who exercises power over a thing on behalf of the possessor providing that he or she is dependent upon the possessor in a domestic sense or as a hired servant and is bound to follow the possessor's instructions regarding the thing (Article 986 CC).[240] Examples of such persons are the spouse, children, parents, brothers and sisters of the possessor, as well as receivers of his or her hospitality, workmen and employees.

130. Possession is exercised through another in the case where, by reason of a personal (obligational) contract, e.g., a contract of hire, loan for use or deposit, the detention of the thing has been granted by the possessor to a third party and also in the case of graduated detention.[241] Thus, for example, the possession of the owner-lessor is exercised by the lessee (indirect detentor) or the sub-lessee (direct detentor). Furthermore, possession is exercised through another in the case where a pledge or usufruct has been constituted on the thing. Indeed, the usufructuary and the pledgee exercise over the thing the possession of the owner, while, at the same time, as holders of the relevant limited real rights, they also have quasi possession (and therefore quasi detention) over the thing.

III. Loss of Possession

131. Loss of possession, in the sense of invalidation of the elements of its concept, is referred to in Articles 981–982 CC. Taking these articles into account, the following should be stressed in regard to the loss of possession which is exercised personally or through another:

132. Possession which is exercised personally is lost as soon as the physical power over the thing has definitely ceased or a contrary intention of the possessor has been expressed (Article 981 CC).

To be precise, loss of physical authority is effected as soon as, for any reason, either corporeal contact with the thing has definitely ceased or the exercise of physical power over the thing has become definitely and permanently impossible. Examples of actions that may lead to the definitive loss of physical authority over the thing are the abandonment of the thing by its possessor, the destruction of the

240. A possession-aid must be distinguished from a detention-aid (see *supra* para. 102).
241. On this point see *supra* para. 96.

thing, the removal of the movable thing to an unknown or inaccessible place or the arbitrary occupation of the movable or immovable thing by a third person.[242]

On the other hand, loss of possession on account of loss of the mind of an owner occurs when the possessor has declared clearly, explicitly or implicitly, his or her definite, serious and true intention not to act in a manner befitting an owner. In this case abandonment of possession occurs.[243]

133. Possession which is exercised through another is lost in the case where the (represented) possessor has declared his or her intention not to possess the thing for himself or herself and has brought this intention to the knowledge of the (representative) detentor or quasi detentor, e.g., the borrower of an item for use, lessee or usufructuary.[244]

However, possession which is exercised through another may also be lost for reasons involving the (representative) detentor or quasi detentor. Indeed, loss of possession entails either the loss of physical authority over the thing by the detentor or the declaration of the latter that he or she intends to possess the thing not on behalf of the (represented) possessor but for himself or herself or a third party. This last case constitutes the so-called usurpation of possession. To be precise, in the area of movables, usurpation leads to loss of possession as soon as the detentor has expressed, by actions, a change of intention: for example, as soon as the borrower of an item for use has written his or her name on a borrowed book and has put it in his or her bookcase or as soon as a lessee, appearing as owner, has transferred a movable to a third party of good faith. On the other hand, in the field of immovables, usurpation does not entail loss of possession before the possessor has taken cognizance of the matter (Article 982 CC). To be precise, the possessor who has been informed about the usurpation loses the *animus* of possession if he or she takes no action and the *corpus* if his or her judicial or extra-judicial attempt to reacquire possession fails. However, the same possessor does not lose his or her possession if his or her judicial or extra-judicial attempt to reacquire possession is successful.

---

242. It seems correct to accept the opinion which, taking into consideration Art. 982 CC (see *infra* para. 133), holds that the arbitrary occupation of an immovable thing may not lead to loss of possession before the possessor has taken cognizance of the matter (thus, G. Balis, *PrL*, para. 11, 36; K. Vavouskos, *PrL*, No. 79, 85; Ap. Georgiades, *PrL*, para. 20 II No. 6, 231; D. Papasteriou, *PrL I*, para. 22 III No. 10, 403–404). For the opposing point of view see Chr. Thibaios, *Law of Possession*, Vol. II, 254–255; AP 1897/1999, 41 HellD, 2000, 1646–1647; AP 1199/1982, 50 EEN, 1983, 544; AP 1001/1981, 49 EEN, 1982, 676; Court of Appeal of Patras 990/2001, NOMOS = AchNom 2002, 54.

243. Within the framework of the opinion which characterizes original and derivative acquisition of possession as transactional, it is accepted that abandonment of possession constitutes a (unilateral, non-addressed and non-formal) juridical act (thus, G. Balis, *PrL*, para. 11, 38; Chr. Thibaios, *Law of Possession*, vol. II, p. 271; D. Papasteriou, *PrL I*, para. 22 III No. 16, 406). The opposing view, however, has also been expressed (see Ap. Georgiades, *PrL*, para. 20 III No. 9, 232; P. Filios, Chr. Filios, *PrL*, para. 35 B, 104, as well as J. Baur & R. Stürner, *SachR*, para. 7 B II 3a No. 26, 72 et seq.; H. Prütting, *SachR*, para. 7 II No. 60, 24).

244. See *supra* para. 130.

Chapter 3. Protection of Possession and Detention

§1. Protection of Possession

I. General Remarks and Classification

134. Protection of possession is rendered necessary when the latter is violated[245] either by disturbance or by eviction of the possessor in an illegal manner and without his or her will (Article 984 paragraph 1 CC).

An eviction is any act that entails a complete or partial loss of possession. It constitutes a total violation of possession as it leads to complete deprivation of physical power over the whole thing or a part of it.[246] A disturbance, on the other hand, is any hindrance of the exercise of physical power over the thing which falls short of dispossession. It constitutes a partial violation of possession insofar as the possessor is deprived of some utilities of the thing on account of an act[247] or omission[248] of the offender.[249]

An eviction or disturbance constitutes a violation of possession when it is illegal, that is, not authorized by law. The illegality is judged objectively without taking into account the fault or bad faith of the offender. However, the opinion has been expressed, by drawing an analogy with Article 915 paragraph 1 CC, that when the offender is unable to 'bear responsibility for violation of possession', no violation occurs.[250]

Finally, it should be stressed that an illegal eviction or disturbance constitutes a violation insofar as it is not in accord with the will of the possessor.

135. In a case of violation, possession is protected, on the one hand, by self-help and, on the other, by judicial means. Protection by judicial means takes the form of two possessory actions: the eviction action and the disturbance action.

However, in urgent situations or in order to avert an imminent danger, rights to possession (or detention) may be determined, independently of any possessory

245. Insofar as the effects of defective possession are relative (see *supra* para. 112), the defective possessor also enjoys protection (see, however, *infra* para. 142).
246. For example, stealing a painting, the arbitrary occupation of an immovable or the partial erection of a building on a neighbouring immovable.
247. For example, passing through a field belonging to another or hindering a possessor from drawing water from his or her well.
248. For example, non-construction of the roof of a building, in spite of a relevant obligation (Art. 1026 CC), and concomitant direction of rain water towards the property of a neighbour.
249. A simple dispute of possession does not constitute a disturbance (see chiefly AP 1038/1996, 38 HellD, 1997, 1837; Court of Appeal of Athens 848/2009, 51 HellD, 2010, 821 (822); Court of Appeal of Patras 202/2001, NOMOS = AchNom 2002, 29; Magistrates' Court of Amvrissos 7/1998, 43 Arm, 1999, 1539). However, if, on account of a serious threat, the possessor is hindered from doing something, the relevant threat may be considered to be a disturbance.
250. D. Papasteriou, *PrL I*, para. 23 II No. 9, 417.

action, in a proceeding for provisional remedies initiated by a petition to the Magistrates' Court (Articles 682 paragraph 1 sub-paragraph a, 733–734 CCProc).[251] In the summary proceedings of provisional remedies the court may award possession to either litigant on the basis of a cursory examination of the merits of each case. However, this disposition has no res judicata effect in a subsequent possessory trial.[252]

Possession is further protected by actions for declaratory judgment (Article 70 CCProc), unjust enrichment (Articles 904 et seq. CC) and damages in accordance with the provisions governing unlawful acts (Articles 987 sub-paragraph b, 989 sub-paragraph b, 914 or 919 CC).

In addition, mention should be made of: (a) Article 995 CC, according to which if a movable thing has escaped from the possessor's power and reached the immovable of another, the possessor of the immovable is bound to allow a search for and the recovery of the movable against payment of compensation for any damage caused by the search;[253] (b) Article 936 paragraph 1 sub-paragraph b CCProc, which deals with the right of the possessor of the seized thing to request a stay of execution.

Finally, it should be noted that the possession of the State is protected judicially like that of any other person as well as by special provisions aiming at its more effective and rapid protection.

136. Of the aforementioned methods of protecting possession, protection by self-help and protection by eviction and disturbance actions will be examined in detail in the following sections.

II. Protection by Self-help

137. Article 985 CC, pertaining to the protection of possession by self-help, offers the possessor, on the one hand, a right of defence (Article 985 paragraph 1 CC) and, on the other, a right to private justice or recovery (Article 985 paragraphs 2–3 CC).[254]

---

251. As soon as the petition for provisional remedies has been brought and until the relevant judgment has been rendered, it is at the discretion of the judge to issue, even ex officio, a provisional order, usually by a simple note on the application itself (Art. 691 para. 2 CCProc).
252. If the provisional remedy has been ordered before the possessory action is brought, the court may determine a term, not less than thirty days, within which the relevant action must be commenced (Art. 693 CCProc).
253. However, the relevant claim is made on the condition that the possessor of the immovable has not acquired the possession of the movable, as, in this case, a violation of possession has taken place, thus permitting the possessor of the movable to commence an eviction action.
254. Rights in general are protected by private justice and defence in accordance with the provisions of Arts 282–284 CC. However, this general protection (which applies in the area of possession as well), on account of the restrictions which accompany it, would be insufficient and, therefore, ineffective for the possessor. Indeed, according to Art. 282 CC, private justice is only permitted when the authorities cannot provide assistance in time and by reason of this delay the realization of the claim runs the risk of being frustrated or of becoming substantially more difficult. Furthermore, according to Art. 284 CC, defence is only permitted with a view to averting an actual and unjust

To be precise, the possessor has the right to repel by reasonable force any disturbance of, or threatened expulsion from, possession of a movable or an immovable thing (right of defence), regardless of whether the disturbance or the expulsion is due to a human action or a fortuitous event and regardless of whether the offender acted fraudulently, in error or in good faith.

Furthermore, in a case of illegal dispossession, the possessor has the right to recover possession by reasonable force (right to private justice or recovery). In this regard, a distinction is drawn between movables and immovables. Thus, the possession of movables may be recovered when the usurper is caught or pursued in the act, that is, at the time of dispossession or immediately after it, while the possession of immovables may be recovered by expulsion of the usurper immediately following dispossession, that is, within the time required in that particular case. However, in the case where the possessor is absent or ignorant of the illegal dispossession, the starting point for immediate recovery is the time when the relevant dispossession is brought to the knowledge of the possessor.

138. The violated possessor has rights to defence and private justice not only in regard to the offender but also the latter's successors in respect of whom the defect of possession is relied upon[255] (Article 985 paragraph 4 CC).

On the other hand, self-help may be exercised by any possessor, even a defective one, by the universal and particular successors of the possessor insofar as the conditions of Article 985 CC are fulfilled, by a possession-aid (Article 986 CC), by a (voluntary or legal) representative of the possessor and, according to the most correct opinion, by a detentor.[256]

III. Protection by Judicial Means

A. *Eviction Action*

139. An eviction action is a legal action through which a person who has been dispossessed, illegally and without his or her consent, demands recovery of

assault. However, the protection of possession by private justice must not 'exceed the measure required to avert the risk' (Art. 283 CC), whereas the defence of the possessor must be of a kind which is 'rendered necessary' by the situation (Art. 284 CC).

255. See Art. 984 para. 2 CC *supra* para. 112.

256. This opinion, which provides an extensive interpretation of the term 'possessor' in Art. 985 CC, holds that the possibility of self-help being exercised by the detentor (e.g., by a lessee), first, entails indirect protection of the possession itself and, second, is justified in view of the regulation of Art. 986 CC which offers protection by self-help even to the possession-aid, namely to a person who does not have separate power over the thing (see Ap. Georgiades, *PrL*, para. 22 I 5 Nos 12–13, 251–252 and para. 26 I 3 No. 12, 308; D. Papasteriou, *PrL I*, para. 24 II Nos 21–22, 436–437 and para. 28 II Nos 14–15, 510–511, as well as Court of Appeal of Thessaloniki 2832/1999, 55 Arm, 2001, 648 [649]). However, the prevailing opinion, adhering to the text of Arts 985 and 997 CC (see *infra* paras 155–156), deprives the detentor of protection by self-help (see chiefly G. Balis, *PrL*, paras 27, 48, 48, 79; Chr. Thibaios, *Law of Possession*, Vol. III (Athens, 1957), 331, 338 [in Greek]; K. Vavouskos, *PrL*, Nos 95, 109, 97, 110; A. Tousis, *Property Law*, 4th edn (Athens: Sakkoulas, 1988), para. 36, 166 [in Greek]; K. Papadopoulos, *Actions of Property Law* (Athens, 1989), 47 [in Greek]; P. Filios & Chr. Filios, *PrL*, para. 48 B, 125).

possession from the person who has wrongfully dispossessed him or her (Article 987 sub-paragraph a CC).

The plaintiff[257] may be the person who had possession at the time of dispossession, his or her heirs or his or her particular successors, insofar as the relevant action has been assigned to them. The plaintiff may also be a possessor evicted as the result of a judgment of provisional remedies. This is because this judgment has no res judicata effect in a subsequent possessory trial.[258] When possession is exercised by a detentor, e.g., a lessee, the relevant action may be brought against a third party by either the possessor or the detentor (Article 997 CC).[259] However, an eviction action may not be brought by a possession-aid as he or she enjoys only protection by self-help (Article 986 CC).

The defendant is any natural person or legal entity[260] who has dispossessed the plaintiff, illegally and without his or her consent, and also his or her successors in respect of whom the defect of possession is relied upon.[261] These persons may be sued only if they are still in possession at the time of the commencement of the action. Otherwise, the plaintiff may sue them only for damages in accordance with the provisions governing unlawful acts (Articles 987 sub-paragraph b, 914, 919 CC). If, after commencement of the action, the defendant transfers possession to a third party, the proceedings are continued against the initial litigant, whereas the judgment is executed against the person who has taken over possession, except if the latter has acquired, during the trial, both possession and ownership in accordance with the provisions concerning transfer from a person who is not the owner (Articles 225, 325, 919 CCProc).

The type of relief requested in eviction actions is the recovery of possession of the thing. However, the above action may be accompanied by an action for damages (Article 987 sub-paragraph b CC) in accordance with the provisions concerning unlawful acts (Articles 914, 919 CC), by a revendicatory action (Article 1094 CC)[262] when the possessor is also the owner,[263] by an action for declaratory judgment (Article 70 CCProc) or by an action for unjust enrichment (Articles 904 et seq. CC). However, the same action may not be accompanied either by a disturbance action which conflicts with the first (Article 218 paragraph 1 point a CCProc)[264] or by an action for recovery of a leased thing on the expiry of the lease because this action is judged in a different type of proceeding.

257. In the case of a minor plaintiff who is under tutelage the formalities of Art. 1621 CC must be observed.
258. See *supra* para. 135.
259. See *infra* paras 155–156.
260. Even the possession-aid who has begun to enjoy possession for himself or herself or the detentor who usurps the possession of the represented possessor (see *supra* para. 133).
261. See Art. 984 para. 2 CC *supra* para. 112.
262. On this action see *infra* paras 366, 369 et seq.
263. See, in particular, G. Diamandopoulos, *The Contradictory Behaviour of Litigants in Civil Trials* (Athens/Komotini: A. Sakkoulas, 1996), p. 339 [in Greek].
264. This combination of an eviction action and a disturbance action is conceivable only in the event of failure of the first action as a reserve option (Art. 219 CCProc) (see, in particular, G. Diamandopoulos, *The Contradictory Behaviour etc.*, 342–343).

B. Disturbance Action

140. A disturbance action (Article 989 sub-paragraph a CC) is conferred on a possessor who has not been evicted from possession but who is only being hindered, illegally and without his or her consent, in exercising physical power over the thing. By this action the possessor demands the cessation of the disturbance as well as its future prevention. Consequently, the commencement of the relevant action presupposes the existence of a disturbance, which either has a certain duration or includes the risk of repetition.

The plaintiff is the illegally disturbed possessor, provided that he or she was possessor at the time of the disturbance as well as at the time of commencement of the action. The plaintiff may also be the heir of the disturbed possessor provided that the disturbance is continuing at the time of death of the latter. On the other hand, in the case where the disturbed possessor dies after the disturbance action has been brought, the trial may be continued by his or her heirs. The particular successor of the disturbed possessor may commence the disturbance action provided that the disturbance continues after the succession. However, if the disturbance occurred during the time the ancestor was in possession, the particular successor may commence the relevant action so long as it has been assigned to him or her. Finally, an unlawfully disturbed detentor may bring this type of action against third persons but not against the possessor (Article 997 CC).

The defendant is any natural person or legal entity[265,266] who has caused the disturbance or his or her heirs or particular successors in the case where the latter have succeeded the disturber in the possession of a construction which was built on his or her land and which continues to disturb the possession of the plaintiff. In the case where disturbance is caused as a consequence of a mandate of another person, both the mandatory and the mandator may be sued. Finally, in the event of a disturbance caused by more than one person, the action may be brought against each of the disturbers or against all of them together.

The relief requested in a disturbance action is, on the one hand, the cessation of the disturbance and, on the other, its future prevention. However, the relevant action may be accompanied by an action for damages (Article 989 sub-paragraph b CC) in accordance with the provisions concerning unlawful acts (Articles 914, 919 CC), by a negatory action (Article 1108 CC)[267] when the possessor is also the owner[268] or by an action for declaratory judgment (Article 70 CCProc), though not by an eviction action.[269]

265. The State cannot be sued in the case of disturbances arising from acts which are undertaken in the course of carrying out administrative functions or exercising political power.
266. Even the possession-aid who does not follow the possessor's instructions or the detentor who exercises detention by infringing the personal (obligational) contract which connects him or her with the possessor.
267. On this action see *infra* paras 366, 393 et seq.
268. See, in particular, G. Diamandopoulos, *The Contradictory Behaviour etc.*, 340.
269. See also *supra* para. 139 n. 264.

C. The Defendant's Defence

141. The defendant in an eviction or disturbance action may deny the basis of the action. This denial may be simple or justified, depending on whether the defendant alleges, without[270] or with justification,[271] that the elements of the basis of the action are, wholly or partially, unfulfilled. In the case of denial, the plaintiff is obliged to prove the facts which support his or her action (Article 338 paragraph 1 CCProc).

142. The defendant is also entitled to file the so-called plea of defective possession. This plea, which entails the dismissal of the eviction or disturbance action as legally and substantially unfounded, is based on Articles 988 and 990 CC. According to the latter, an eviction or disturbance action is not admissible if the plaintiff acquired possession wrongfully with regard to the defendant or his or her ancestors during the year prior to his or her eviction or disturbance.[272] As can be clearly seen, Articles 988 and 990 CC presuppose dispossession or disturbance of the defendant by the plaintiff, which comes first, and dispossession of the plaintiff by the defendant, which follows. The same articles maintain that the plaintiff, who was the first to display wrongful behaviour, deserves to be protected less than the defendant. However, so long as the law offers the possibility of filing the relevant plea to any true possessor, the same plea may also be raised by the plaintiff against the defendant, by means of a counter-plea, in the case where the defendant, before being dispossessed by the plaintiff, had wrongfully dispossessed the plaintiff himself or herself. However, this only applies if, between the eviction on which the plea of the defendant is based and the eviction on which the counter-plea of the plaintiff is based, a period of not more than one year has elapsed.

143. Furthermore, the defendant, on account of a disturbance or eviction, may invoke, by means of a plea, a real or personal right granting to him or her power over the thing. However, this plea may be advanced only exceptionally and, to be precise, only in the case where the relevant right has been recognized by a final judgment in litigation between the defendant and the plaintiff (Article 991 CC).[273] This choice of the law results from the fact that possession is protected regardless of whether it is based on a right or not so that peaceful cohabitation, which is disturbed in the case of violation of possession, can be quickly restored. On the other hand, the possibility of the aforementioned plea being advanced only when the relevant right has been recognized by a final judgment averts the danger of delay which might arise if the said right had to be proved within the framework of a trial to settle the question of possession.

---

270. For example, the defendant may simply deny that the plaintiff was possessor at the time of eviction or disturbance or at the time of commencement of the action.
271. For example, the defendant may allege that he or she and not the plaintiff was possessor at the time of eviction or disturbance or at the time of commencement of the action.
272. This term is justified by Art. 992 CC concerning the time of prescription of the claims on eviction and disturbance (see *infra* para. 144).
273. The State, municipalities and communal authorities may raise the relevant plea regardless of whether this condition is fulfilled.

It should, however, be stressed that the above-mentioned plea must be distinguished from the invocation of a right enabling the defendant to justify denial of the basis of the action. Indeed, the allegation 'I dispossessed you because I am the usufructuary or the lessee of the thing' must be distinguished from the allegation 'I dispossessed you because the thing was legally delivered to me by virtue of my right of usufruct on it'. The first allegation constitutes a plea and as a rule is prohibited, while the second constitutes a justified denial of the basis of the action and is not included in the prohibition of Article 991 CC.

144. Considering the fact that the claims on eviction and disturbance are prescribed after a lapse of one year from the date of the eviction or the disturbance[274] (Article 992 CC),[275] it is obvious that the defendant may defend himself or herself by advancing the plea of prescription. It should, however, be borne in mind that the term of prescription may be suspended or interrupted on the grounds determined in Articles 255–270 CC.[276]

145. The defendant in an eviction action who has a claim against the plaintiff that is due to and connected with disbursements made on the thing is entitled, by filing the plea of retention specified in Articles 325–326 CC, to refuse the restitution

274. The time of prescription begins to run from the day which follows the day of eviction or disturbance (Art. 241 CC), regardless of whether the possessor was aware or ignorant of such facts. However, in the cases of usurpation and arbitrary occupation of possession of an immovable the time of prescription does not begin before the possessor has taken cognizance of such matters (see also *supra* para. 132 note 242 and para. 133). If the disturbance is permanent, because it derives from a construction, the term of prescription begins from the time when the construction was built. If the disturbance derives from periodically repeated acts, each act constitutes a separate disturbance and therefore a new time of prescription begins after each act.

275. This prescription concerns only possessory actions, though not also any accompanying claim for damages in accordance with the provisions governing unlawful acts, which claim is subject to five (or twenty) years' prescription (Art. 937 CC), or a claim for unjust enrichment, which is subject to twenty years' prescription (Arts 904, 249 CC).

276. It is debatable if the term of prescription is interrupted by the commencement of a petition for provisional remedies. According to one opinion, it is not interrupted. This opinion invokes Art. 261 CC, which declares that the term of prescription is interrupted by the commencement of a 'legal action' (see G. Balis, *PrL*, para. 22, 68; Chr. Thibaios, *Law of Possession*, Vol. III, 145, as well as AP 575/1989, 39 NoB, 1991, 54; Court of Appeal of Patras 990/2001, NOMOS = AchNom 2002, 54; Court of Appeal of Thessaloniki 2832/1999, 55 Arm, 2001, 648 (650); Three-member District Court of Larissa 72/2002, NOMOS = Dikografia 2002, 122; Three-member District Court of Thessaloniki 5344/1993, 55 Arm, 2001, 473; One-member District Court of Rhodos 30/2006, NOMOS; Magistrates' Court of Ilion 19/2001, 52 ArchN, 2001, 223). However, the opposite opinion puts forward the convincing argument that the commencement of a petition for provisional remedies makes it clear that the possessor did not remain inactive but attempted to solve the dispute albeit through the institution of provisional remedies (thus K. Vavouskos, *PrL*, No. 103 n. 3, 105–106; K. Beys, *The Proceedings before the One-Member District Court*, Vol. II (Athens: Klisiounis, 1969), 267 [in Greek]; Ap. Georgiades, *PrL*, para. 23 IV 4 No. 51, 273; D. Papasteriou, *PrL I*, para. 25 IV No. 68, 471, para. 26 VI No. 26, 494; G. Daskarolis, 'Interruption of Prescription by Petition of Provisional Remedies in Disputes Concerning Possession', 36 EEN, 1969, 603 et seq. [in Greek]; L. Pipsou, 'Issues Arising from Interruption of Prescription by the Commencement of Legal Action or the Undertaking of Other, Introductory to a Trial, Procedural Acts', Arm 46 (1992): 323 et seq. [in Greek] with a further wealth of references to both of the aforementioned opinions).

of the thing until he or she has been satisfied in respect of these disbursements.[277] However, advancing a plea of retention is excluded in the case where the defendant has acquired the possession or detention of the thing by an unlawful act involving fraud (Article 327 in combination with Article 450 paragraph 1 CC).

146. In addition, the defendant may advance the pleas of renunciation of the action, abuse of right and of impossibility of restitution of the thing.

147. Finally, the possibility must not be excluded that the defendant may demand legal protection by commencing a cross action. However, this cross action is admissible on the condition that, on the one hand, the same type of proceedings can be used for both the action and the cross action (Article 268 paragraph 3 CCProc) and, on the other hand, that the defendant does not invoke by his or her cross action a right granting to him or her power over the thing, except if such right has been recognized by a final judgment in litigation between him or her and the plaintiff (Article 991 CC).[278]

D. Procedural Issues

148. Eviction and disturbance actions are judged within ordinary proceedings.[279] The subject-matter competent court is the One-member District Court (Articles 16 point 13 CCProc), while the Magistrates' Court may also be competent in cases where the value of possession does not exceed the sum of money determined in Article 14 paragraph 1 CCProc.[280] The court with territorial jurisdiction, in the area of immovables, is the court of the district in which the immovable is situated (Article 29 CCProc), whereas, in the field of movables, it is the court of the district where the defendant has his or her domicile or residence (Articles 22, 23 paragraph 1 CCProc).

149. Eviction and disturbance actions are subject to payment of a judicial stamp-tax. Furthermore, possession actions pertaining to immovables, except for petitions for provisional remedies, must be registered within thirty days of the date of their disposition in the vindication registers of the district in which the immovable is situated or, within the framework of the Land Registry System, on the record sheet of the land register which is devoted to the relevant immovable (Article 12 paragraph

277. On the same issue in the area of revendicatory actions see *infra* para. 390.
278. Compare *supra* para. 143.
279. On the subject of adversary (ordinary and for provisional remedies), default and ex parte proceedings as well as particular proceedings see P. Yessiou-Faltsi, *Civil Procedure in Hellas*, Nos 232 et seq., 451 et seq.
280. N. Nikas, in *Interpretation of the CCProc*, Vol. I, ed. K. Kerameus, D. Kondilis & N. Nikas (Athens-Thessaloniki-Komotini: Sakkoulas, 2000), Arts 11 No. 1, 16 No. 1, 14 [in Greek]; D. Papasteriou, *PrL I*, para. 25 V No. 81, 475; L. Pipsou, *Procedural Issues of Real Actions* (Thessaloniki: Sakkoulas, 2000), 18–19 [in Greek]. See also Court of Appeal of Athens 1101/1996, 50 Arm, 1996, 1331.

1 point xii of L. 2664/1998), as otherwise they are dismissed as inadmissible (Article 220 CCProc).

150. On the subject of proof, it should be noted that the plaintiff must allege and prove: (a) in an eviction action, that he or she enjoyed possession at the time of eviction and that he or she was dispossessed illegally and without his or her consent by the defendant; and (b) in a disturbance action, that he or she was possessor at the time of disturbance as well as at the time of commencement of the action and that he or she was disturbed by certain actions of the defendant. On the other hand, the defendant must prove the factual events on which his or her pleas are based.

However, the litigant who invokes possession is bound to prove, using any means of proof including testimony (Article 339 in combination with Article 393 CCProc), not only the acquisition but also the existence of possession at the critical moment. This proof is made easier by the two (rebuttable) presumptions deriving from Articles 980 paragraph 2[281] and 1046 CC.[282]

151. The final judgment which accepts an eviction or disturbance action has a res judicata effect with regard to the possession of the plaintiff at the time of eviction or disturbance and the exercise of the action, though not to the possession of the plaintiff and his or her ancestors in a previous period, even when the relevant subject has been examined in the justification of the judgment. In addition, the above judgment does not have a res judicata effect in respect of the ownership of the plaintiff, even when the court has examined the relevant issue.

§2. Protection of Particular Types of Possession

I. Protection of Quasi Possession

152. According to Article 996 CC, an illegally disturbed or dispossessed quasi possessor is protected by the actions protecting possession, that is, by the eviction or disturbance actions. On the other hand, a quasi possessor is also entitled to choose judicial protection in the form of a petition for provisional remedies. Although not declared in Article 996 CC, the prevailing opinion correctly accepts that there is no reason to deprive a quasi possessor of protection by self-help as well.

II. Protection of Possession of Part of a Thing

153. As may be concluded from Article 993 CC, the possessor of part of a thing is protected by self-help, by an eviction or disturbance action and by a petition for provisional remedies.

---

281. According to Art. 980 para. 2 CC 'a person who has commenced detention in the name of another, so long as he remains in detention, is presumed to be detaining the thing in the name of the other.'
282. According to Art. 1046 CC 'a person who at the commencement and at the termination of a certain time period has had a thing in his possession is presumed to have possessed the thing during the intervening time as well.'

III. Protection of Co-possession

154. Article 994 CC, pertaining to the protection of co-possession, distinguishes between two categories of protection depending on whether the violation has been caused by a third party or a co-possessor. In the first case, it offers each co-possessor protection by self-help, an eviction or disturbance action and a petition for provisional remedies. In the second case, the same article, distinguishing between eviction and disturbance, offers the dispossessed co-possessor protection by self-help, an eviction action and a petition for provisional remedies. However, in the case of disturbance, that is, in a case of dispute concerning the limits within which each co-possessor may make use of the thing,[283] it excludes the application of the provisions referring to protection of possession[284] and prefers the relevant dispute to be solved on the basis of the internal relationship between the co-owners. This internal relationship may be derived from a contract made between the co-owners[285] or directly from the law.[286] In the second case, the method of management and use of the common thing will be determined in accordance with the provisions governing an undivided joint right (Articles 788–790 CC). This is because, due to the existence of co-possession, a personal relation of undivided joint right is constituted.

§3. Protection of a Detentor and Protection against a Detentor

I. Protection of a Detentor

155. The mandatory rule of Article 997 CC declares that, in the case of illegal disturbance of, or eviction from, possession or quasi possession, the person who has acquired detention or quasi detention from the possessor or quasi possessor[287] in the capacity of lessee or depositary or by reason of some other similar (personal) relation[288] may also[289] commence against third parties[290] actions protecting possession.[291]

283. For example, in the case where the co-possessor A, who believes that the common field must remain uncultivated for one year, hinders his or her co-possessor B from sowing the field.
284. However, this inhibition does not include either protection by self-help in accordance with the general provisions of Arts 282 and 284 CC or claims for damages in accordance with the provisions governing unlawful acts (Arts 914, 919 CC).
285. For example, A and B jointly bought a field and, at the same time, they determined the method of its joint exploitation.
286. For example, A and B became co-heirs and co-possessors of a field.
287. The law presupposes delivery of detention to the detentor or to his or her ancestor with the consent of the possessor (Ap. Georgiades, *PrL*, para. 26 I 2 No. 6, 307).
288. Not necessarily valid.
289. That is, in parallel with the possessor.
290. And not against the possessor or quasi possessor, in relation to whom he or she enjoys only the protection deriving from the relevant personal relation.
291. He or she may also commence a petition for provisional remedies, while, as is generally accepted, he or she also enjoys protection by self-help in accordance with the provisions of Art. 985 CC and certainly of Arts 282 and 284 CC (see also *supra* para. 138 and n. 256).

156. In the case of graduated detention – for example, in the case where a lessee A grants the physical power over the leased thing to a sub-lessee B[292] – it seems correct to adopt the opinion[293] which holds that both the direct (B) and the indirect detentor (A) enjoy the protection of Article 997 CC.[294] This opinion solves the conflicts of interests and serves the security of law and trades in a satisfying manner.

II. Protection against a Detentor

157. Article 998 CC determines the means of protection for a possessor who has been illegally disturbed or dispossessed by the person who acquired detention from him or her as a lessee or depositary or by reason of some other similar (personal) relation.[295] The same article declares that the above possessor is protected against the detentor[296] by the actions protecting possession,[297] that is, by the disturbance or eviction action and also by the petition of provisional remedies. In addition, the possessor may commence against the detentor claims deriving from the personal relation which exists between him or her and the latter.

292. See *supra* para. 96.
293. For a critical presentation of other opinions which have been held on the same issue see Ap. Georgiades, *PrL*, para. 26 III Nos 23–25, 313–315; I. Spyridakis, M. Spyridakis, *PrL*, Vol. A, No. 100.3.2, 356–358.
294. Thus, Ap. Georgiades, *PrL*, para. 26 III Nos 26–28, 315–316; D. Papasteriou, *PrL I*, para. 28 IV No. 23, 515; P. Kornilakis, *Concise Law of Obligations. Special Part* (Athens-Thessaloniki: Sakkoulas, 2000), para. 65 II 3, 213 [in Greek]; I. Spyridakis, *Action on a Disturbance of Possession* (Athens: A. Sakkoulas, 1997), 103–104 [in Greek]; I. Spyridakis, *Action on an Eviction from Possession* (Athens: A. Sakkoulas, 1997), 108–109 [in Greek]; I. Spyridakis & M. Spyridakis, *PrL*, Vol. A, No. 100.3.2, 357–358.
295. Disturbance occurs, for example, when the detentor exceeds the limits of the personal relation which connects him or her with the possessor. On the other hand, eviction occurs, for example, when a lessee usurps possession, denying the restitution of the leased thing at the termination of the contract of hire or claiming that he or she is the possessor.
296. The possessor is protected not only against the direct but also against the indirect detentor in the case of graduated detention (D. Papasteriou, *PrL I*, para. 28 IV No. 23, 515).
297. The above possessor is not offered protection by self-help in accordance with Art. 985 CC.

Part III. Immovable Property

Chapter 1. General Classification

158. The term 'immovable property' is used in the present monograph to denote real rights which may have as their object an immovable thing;[298] that is, ownership and, of the limited real rights,[299] servitudes and mortgages.[300] Of these rights, ownership and servitudes will be examined in this section. The mortgages will be discussed in a separate section (Part VII), together with pledges. This is because they both constitute real securities.

More specifically, the present section will discuss, from the point of view of their concept, content, nature and the rights and obligations of their holders: (a) ownership (Chapter 2), placing importance on the legal restrictions on the latter, especially those derived from the rules of the Civil Code which regulate the relations between the owners of neighbouring, urban or agrarian, immovables (neighbour law); (b) the specific types of ownership (Chapter 3), that is, co-ownership[301] and horizontal and vertical ownership.[302] However, among the specific types of ownership time-sharing will also be examined, although Greek law does not regard time-sharing as a form of ownership but as a form of hire of an immovable. This section will close with a fourth chapter, which will be devoted to servitudes.

159. However, before the aforementioned issues are discussed, the following points should be noted:

(a) In this monograph the term 'immovable property' is used instead of the term 'real property', which is used by English law to denote property rights relating to land.[303]

298. See also *supra* para. 17.
299. On the relationship between ownership and limited real rights see *supra* para. 50 (under a).
300. It should, however, be recalled: (a) that ownership and, of the servitudes, usufruct may also have a movable thing as an object; (b) that usufruct may be constituted on incorporeal objects as well (see *supra* para. 50 (under (c)), as well as *infra* paras 260 et seq.) and (c) that the usufruct of an immovable is also susceptible of mortgage (see *supra* para. 50 (under (c)), as well as *infra* paras 443–444). On the other hand, the interpretative rule of Art. 949 CC should also be borne in mind (see *supra* paras 17, 63).
301. Immovable and movable things are susceptible of co-ownership.
302. Only immovables are susceptible of horizontal and vertical ownership.
303. See also *supra* para. 17.

(b) The distinction between 'legal interests' and 'equitable interests' is unknown in Greece. This distinction applies in English law and is due to the parallel existence, in the relevant legal system, of the common law and equity.[304] More specifically, of the property rights relating to land, these which were recognized by the common law were (and still are) classified as 'legal estates' (e.g., fees simple or leases) or 'legal interests' (e.g., easements, profits or rent charges), whereas those which were recognized by equity became known as 'equitable interest'. For every kind of legal estate or legal interest in land which is recognized by the common law, an equivalent equitable interest may exist ('equity follows the law', that is, equity has copied the various types of property rights recognized by the common law). Thus, for example, as legal fees simple, easements and profits can exist, so too can equitable fees simple, easements and profits. However, there are certain types of equitable interests (restrictive covenants, licences by estoppel, constructive trusts and estate contracts) which have no legal equivalent.[305]

(c) According to Greek property law, limited real rights relating to immovables include, on the one hand, the various types of servitudes – that is, the real (or predial) and the personal servitudes, which include usufruct, habitation and limited personal servitudes – and, on the other, mortgages.[306]

The real[307] and the limited personal servitudes[308] of Greek property law may be compared, respectively, with the easements and the profits *à prendre* of English land law. Furthermore, the function of the restrictive covenants of English land law seems to be similar to that of the real servitudes of Greek property law. In order to justify this conclusion, a reference to the concept of easements, profits *à prendre* and restrictive covenants is necessary. Thus:

An easement is the right of one landowner to use or to restrict the use of another, neighbouring piece of land (servient tenement) for the benefit of his or her own land (dominant tenement). Examples of easements are the right of way or light, the right to extract water and the right to support buildings.[309]

A profit *à prendre* is the right to go onto somebody else's land (servient tenement) and to remove from that land something which exists there naturally. Thus, for example, the right to extract minerals such as gravel or chalk, the right to go hunting or shooting over somebody else's land, the right to fish in someone's lake/river/pond and the right of a farmer to graze sheep or other animals on land which does not belong to him or her constitute profits *à prende*. A profit

304. On which see *supra* para. 15.
305. On all these points see, in particular, R. Sexton, *Land Law*, 39–40, 42–43.
306. See, however, on the possible objects of usufruct and mortgages *supra* para. 158 n. 300.
307. On which see *infra* paras 231 et seq.
308. On which see *infra* paras 252–254.
309. On easements see J. Stevens & R.A. Pearce, *Land Law*, 3rd edn (London: Sweet&Maxwell, 2005), 397 et seq.; E.H. Burn, *Modern Law of Real Property*, 15th edn (London/Dublin/Edinburgh: Butterworths, 1994), 518, 519 et seq.; K. Gray, *Elements of Land Law*, 1044, 1059 et seq.; F.H. Lawson & B. Rudden, *PrL*, 129–130; J.G. Riddal, *Land Law*, 311 et seq.; R. Sexton, *Land Law*, 5, 294 et seq.

may exist *in gross*, i.e., as a totally separate right not attached to any dominant tenement.[310]

Finally, a restrictive covenant is a covenant restricting the use of land and, more specifically, a promise by one landowner to a neighbouring landowner or landowners that he or she will not do certain things upon his or her/their land. For example, a farmer promises a neighbouring farmer not to develop his or her own land but to keep it for agricultural purposes only; or a shop-owner promises a neighbouring house-owner that he or she will not sell takeaway food. In each of these two cases the land restricted is the servient tenement, while the land which benefits is the dominant tenement.[311]

(d) Greek property law does not recognize the right of 'use' as a self-contained real right. However, the right 'to make use … of a thing belonging to another … ' and the right 'to use as habitation the building of another or an apartment therein' are contained, according to Greek law, in the concepts of usufruct (Article 1142 CC) and habitation (Article 1183 CC), respectively. In addition, the right to make simple use of a servient tenement is classified as a limited personal servitude.[312]

(e) The real rights of *emphyteusis, superficies* and of separate ownership on a plantation, a tree or a building located on the land of another, which were in force in Greece before the Civil Code was introduced, were abolished by the Civil Code.[313] However, as regards the right of *superficies*, it should be noted, on the one hand, that it has already been reintroduced to Greece by the relatively recent L. 3986/2011 (Articles 18–26)[314] and, on the other, that the relevant institution is compared with the English institution of 'leasehold', as well as with the institutions of 'Erbbaurecht', 'Baurecht', 'superficie' and 'superficie' or 'bail à construction', which are in force in Germany, Switzerland, Italy and France, respectively.[315]

(f) The institutions of rent charges[316] and licences,[317] which apply in English law, are unknown in Greece.

---

310. On profits *à prendre* see E.H. Burn, *Real Property*, 519, 562 et seq.; K. Gray, *Elements of Land Law*, 1045 et seq., 1087 et seq.; F.H. Lawson & B. Rudden, *PrL*, 130; J.G. Riddal, *Land Law*, 351 et seq.; R. Sexton, *Land Law*, 6.
311. On restrictive covenants see E.H. Burn, *Real Property*, 609 et seq.; F.H. Lawson, B. Rudden, *PrL*, 130–132; J.G. Riddal, *Land Law*, 403–404; R. Sexton, *Land Law*, 5, 329 et seq.
312. See *infra* para. 252.
313. See also *supra* para. 52.
314. See *supra* para. 51.
315. See preamble to L. 3986/2011 under D. In particular, on leasehold interests in land see *infra* para. 257 (under (b).
316. A rent charge is the right which, independently of any lease or mortgage, gives the holder of it a right to a periodical sum of money secured on land (F.H. Lawson & B. Rudden, *PrL*, 98–100). For example, A, a builder of new houses on land which he or she owns, sells one of these houses to B for a certain amount of money and a perpetual, usually annual, sum of money. A, who is entitled to receive payment of this perpetual sum of money from the current owner of the house B (and his or her successors), owns a rent-charge (see R. Sexton, *Land Law*, 6–7).
317. A licence is defined as 'a permission given by the occupier of land to do some act which would otherwise be a trespass' or 'permission to enter upon land' (see E.H. Burn, *Real Property*, 529, 585 et seq.; K. Gray, *Elements of Land Law*, 890 et seq.; F.H. Lawson & B. Rudden, *PrL*, 219–220).

(g) Greek property law knows only one form of co-ownership, which is identifiable with the 'tenancy in common' of English law. The English form of co-ownership known as 'joint tenancy' is unknown in Greece.[318] Tenancy in common is usual (but not obligatory) where the co-owners are in a business relationship, while joint tenancy is the usual (but not obligatory) form of co-ownership where the co-owners are members of the same 'family'. The crucial distinguishing feature of joint tenancy is the right of survivorship. This means that, on the death of a joint tenant, his or her interest[319] does not pass under the law of succession, but rather passes to the surviving joint tenant(s). In contrast, when a tenant in common dies, there is no right of survivorship, but his or her share passes under the normal rules of succession. Furthermore, an essential feature of both joint tenancy and tenancy in common is 'unity of possession', in the sense that the co-owners have concurrent rights to enjoy the whole of the common thing (land). On the other hand, while for co-owners to be joint tenants 'unity of interest', 'unity of title' and 'unity of time' must be present,[320] the relevant features may be present in a tenancy in common, but are not necessary.

318. On tenancy in common and joint tenancy see E.H. Burn, *Real Property*, 214 et seq.; K. Gray, *Elements of Land Law*, 461 et seq.; F.H. Lawson & B. Rudden, *PrL*, 82–84; J.G. Riddal, *Land Law*, 155 et seq.; R. Sexton, *Land Law*, 160 et seq.

319. The joint tenants have 'interests' or 'rights', while the tenants in common own the property in 'undivided shares' (R. Sexton, *Land Law*, 162, 163).

320. Consequently, all the co-owners: (a) must have absolutely identical rights over the land in question (unity of interest), (b) must have acquired their interest from the same document or transaction (unity of title) and (c) their rights must have commenced at the same moment (unity of time) (R. Sexton, *Land Law*, 162).

Chapter 2. Ownership

§1. Concept of Ownership

160. The Greek Civil Code does not define the term ownership.[321] However, Article 973 CC (pertaining to the concept of a real right), combined with Article 1000 CC (referring to the content of ownership), permits the conclusion that ownership is the direct (immediate), absolute and universal power over a thing recognized by the law.[322] In other words, ownership is the broadest, in regard to content, real right and offers its holder any power over the thing owned, unless this power has been limited by provisions of law or by a juridical act.

Furthermore, in view of the fact that from ownership arise not only rights but also obligations, towards neighbours and the members of society in general,[323] ownership has also been defined as the legal relation from which derive the real right of ownership and, probably, obligations, charges or commitments.[324] It seems correct to adopt this definition since the qualification of ownership as a legal and, more specifically, real relation expresses precisely and completely the legal status of an owner.

161. Taking Articles 973 and 1000 CC as a starting point, we come to the conclusion that the elements of the concept of ownership are as follows: power over a thing, power recognized by the law, power direct (immediate) and absolute – as is the case with the other real rights – and also – unlike the other (limited) real rights – power universal. This means that, whereas the other real rights have a limited content and confer on their holders the right to dominate the thing for certain purposes, the owner has a uniform, general and abstract power to perform any activity over the thing.[325] Indeed, the owner, so long as he or she does not infringe the law or the rights of third parties, can occupy and use the thing, collect its fruits, change or destroy it and, in addition, transfer, encumber or renounce his or her ownership.

162. Owing to the universal character of ownership, it is inconceivable for the owner to have a limited real right, e.g., usufruct, on his or her own thing. Therefore, when the holder of a limited real right on a thing also acquires the ownership of the same thing, the relevant limited real right is extinguished because of confusion.[326] On the other hand, as a consequence of the extinction of the limited real right which encumbered the ownership, the content of the latter – which was restricted so long

321. D. Papasteriou, *Property Law*, vol. 2 (Athens-Thessaloniki: Sakkoulas, 2008), para. 29 II No. 6, 3.
322. D. Papasteriou, *PrL II*, para. 29 II No. 6, 4.
323. See *infra* paras 164 et seq.
324. I. Sontis, 'Strukturelle Betrachtungen zum Eigentumsbegriff', *Volume in Honour of K. Larenz* (München: Beck, 1973), 981 et seq.; Ap. Georgiades, 'Eigentumsbegriff und Eigentumsverhältnis', *Volume in Honour of I. Sontis* (München: Beck, 1977), 159 et seq.; Ap. Georgiades, *PrL*, para. 29 IV No. 32, 344; D. Papasteriou, *PrL II*, para. 29 II No. 7, 4 [in Greek]. See also H. Prütting, para. 27 IV Nos 322–323, 126–127.
325. See also *supra* para. 50 (under a).
326. See *infra* paras 357, 361, 364, 365, 441, 454, 466, 480.

as the above right existed – becomes universal again. This attribute of ownership is called 'elasticity'.

§2. Content of Ownership

163. According to Article 1000 CC, 'the owner of a thing, provided that he does not infringe the law or the rights of third parties, may dispose of it at will and exclude any action thereon by another'. From this Article it may be concluded that the owner's – at first unlimited and exclusive – power over the thing has a positive and a negative aspect.[327]

The positive aspect of ownership refers to the relationship between the owner and the thing and means that the owner has the power, on the one hand, to act on the thing in a physical way (e.g., to cultivate the land or to collect fruits) and, on the other, to dispose of his or her right through juridical acts (e.g., to transfer, encumber or renounce it). The first of the above powers is known as the 'power to dispose of the thing', whereas the second one is known as the 'power to dispose of the right'.[328]

The negative aspect of ownership refers to the owner's position in relation to third parties and means the owner's absolute power to prevent anyone's unauthorized interference with the thing he or she owns and, by extension, his or her absolute power to protect his or her ownership in the event of any attack upon it.[329]

164. From Article 1000 CC it may also be concluded that the owner's power over the thing is unlimited only initially and that the provisions of the law and the rights of third parties constitute the framework within which the above power may be exercised. The term 'law' is understood to cover any rule of private or public law that binds or limits the owner's power over the thing. On the other, the term 'rights of third parties' includes, mainly, limited real rights (servitudes, pledges and mortgages) and, second, personal rights. However, the latter count only when they give their holders the power to possess or detain the thing belonging to another and on the condition that the possession or detention is already exercised. However, in this last case, the possession or detention in fact limits the ownership and can be brought against the owner (see for example Articles 1095, 1108 paragraph 2 CC).[330]

165. Generally speaking, the restrictions imposed on ownership by the rights of third parties also belong to the group of restrictions introduced by the law, i.e., the group of so-called legal restrictions. This is because the law recognizes the possibility of their constitution and also because they restrict the owner's power

327. D. Papasteriou, *PrL II*, para. 30 IV No. 17, 21.
328. On this point see D. Papasteriou, *PrL II*, para. 30 IV Nos 18–22, 21–22; Ap. Georgiades, *PrL*, para. 28 I 1 No. 3, 328; P. Filios & Chr. Filios, *PrL*, para. 61 A, B, 142–143; I. Spyridakis & M. Spyridakis, *Property Law*, vol. B/1 (Athens/Komotini: A. Sakkoulas, 2001), No. 105.2., 381–382 [in Greek].
329. D. Papasteriou, *PrL II*, para. 30 IV Nos 23–24, 23.
330. Thus, G. Balis, *PrL*, para. 30, 86; Ap. Georgiades, *PrL*, para. 28 II 2 No. 16, 331–332. Compare P. Filios & Chr. Filios, *PrL*, para. 63 A,B, 146–147.

according to the law. Nevertheless, there are differences between legal restrictions and restrictions based on rights of third parties.

Indeed, with regard to legal restrictions, it should be stressed that there are restrictions from which derive rights in favour of third parties (e.g., Articles 1006, 1007, 1012, 1028 CC) and also restrictions (such as certain restrictions based on the General Building Regulation) from which no rights derive at all. In the latter case, transgression of the law has penal and administrative consequences and only when the conditions of an unlawful act are fulfilled does the prejudiced person have a claim for compensation. On the other hand, the rights which probably derive from legal restrictions are not real but personal and offer their holder a personal claim enabling him or her to demand from the owner an act (e.g., Article 1006 CC), an omission (e.g., Articles 1004, 1007 CC) or a forbearance (e.g., Articles 1003, 1018 CC).

Furthermore, according to the prevailing opinion, the restrictions imposed by limited real rights are 'restrictions' in the exact sense of the word, insofar as they encumber ownership and restrict its content with regard to a number of utilities. On the other hand, again according to the prevailing view, the restrictions imposed by law are elements which exist in the concept of ownership and aim at the 'determination' and not restriction of the content of the latter. However, with regard to legal restrictions, it is argued by some that they constitute 'restrictions' in the exact sense of the word, while others argue that they create 'restrictions' which do not restrict the owner's power over the thing but the possibility of this power being exercised.[331]

§3. Legal Restrictions on Ownership

I. General Remarks

166. Modern ideas about the social function of property involve the imposition of various restrictions on the positive or negative content of ownership. These restrictions are based on the law and aim at supporting the general interest of society.

167. If we wanted to classify the above legal restrictions, we could begin with those based on general provisions of the law. Such provisions are contained in Articles 281 (abuse of right), 282–283 (private justice), 284 (defence) and 285–286 CC (state of necessity) and refer to rights in general and not only to ownership.

168. A second group of legal restrictions are those which refer to ownership in particular. These 'specific' restrictions, as we may call them, arise from provisions in private as well as public law.

The most important of the specific restrictions which derive from rules of private law are those based on Articles 1001 and 1003–1031 CC. In regard to these restrictions, it should be noted that Articles 1003–1031 CC, which will be examined in

331. On all these points see, in particular, Ap. Georgiades, *PrL*, para. 28 II 1 No. 12, 330–331 and para. 29 III Nos 26 et seq., 343–344.

the next section, constitute the law governing relations between the owners of neighbouring, urban or agrarian, immovables (neighbour law). As to the restriction imposed by Article 1001 CC, it should be emphasized that, according to this article, although the ownership of an immovable, unless the law ordains otherwise, extends to the space above and below the ground, the owner may not prohibit an action undertaken at a particular height or depth if no interest is affected by the prohibition. The above interest – which may be pecuniary or not, present or future – should be judged objectively, taking into consideration the notions prevailing in trade, the local circumstances and the circumstances of the particular case.

However, the greatest number of specific legal restrictions of ownership arise from public law. This incursion of public law into the area of property law is motivated by the ideas of the managed economy and the State interventionist policy and aims at supporting social policy, public interest and the safety of the State. Restrictions of this type may be classified into the following groups:[332]

(a) restrictions for purposes connected with public order and the safety of the State (e.g., restrictions on building houses, cultivating the land or planting trees in so-called zones of defence);
(b) restrictions attached to public health (e.g., prohibition on the cultivation of hashish);
(c) restrictions relating to the street-plan, constitutional order and appearance of a town (e.g., restrictions arising from the General Building Regulation);
(d) restrictions for reasons of technical development (e.g., restrictions based on laws which bind the owner of an immovable either to permit electricity or telephone lines or cables to go through his or her land or to tolerate the construction of an underground tunnel under his or her land);
(e) restrictions referring to the protection of the landscape, archaeological sites or treasures and monuments in general (e.g., the obligation of the owner of an immovable to tolerate excavations by the State aimed at discovering antiquities);
(f) restrictions for reasons connected with the social economy and policy (e.g., forced prolongation of the hire of immovables, i.e., rent control);
(g) restrictions arising from rules aimed at the protection of the environment and especially the protection of forests or forest areas.

169. The last group of legal restrictions which should be mentioned includes the restrictions arising from rules which prohibit or limit the owner's power to dispose of his or her right. Such rules are contained, for example, in Article 1937 paragraph 2 CC (concerning the prohibition of the disposal of *fideicommissum*) or in Article 997 CCProc (concerning the inability of the debtor to dispose of the things seized).

332. The most important restriction on ownership, on the strength of the rules of public law, is compulsory expropriation. The latter, which must be distinguished from the legal restrictions on ownership (see, amongst others, Ap. Georgiades, *PrL*, para. 40 II Nos 7 et seq., 460 et seq.), is examined in the section of the present book which is devoted to the acquisition of ownership (see *infra* para. 297).

II. Neighbour Law

A. *Introduction to Neighbour Law*

1. Justification, Concept, Content and Nature of Neighbour Law

170. The establishment of neighbour law is justified by the nature of things. Indeed, the owners of neighbouring immovables, exercising their power over their own land, frequently come into conflict. For example, the owner of an immovable X, in establishing a lime-kiln on his or her land, disturbs the owner of the neighbouring immovable Z, who chokes because of the emitted dust. In this case the positive content of the ownership of X (power to dispose of the thing) comes into conflict with the negative content of the ownership of Z (power to exclude anyone's unauthorized interference in the thing). In the same case, if the law had not made provisions for the above conflict, restricting the positive content of the ownership of X and the negative content of the ownership of Z, the peaceful coexistence of the owners of X and Z, as well as the economic utilization of their immovables, could not be achieved.

171. Thus, neighbour law is the set of rules which impose restrictions on the ownership of neighbouring immovables (whether these immediately border each other or not) in such a way that quarrels between the neighbours can be avoided and a peaceful coexistence between them may be achieved. Neighbour law is embodied in Articles 1003–1032 CC (private neighbour law) and also in special laws, e.g., the General Building Regulation (public neighbour law).[333] However, in this book only the rules arising from the Civil Code will be examined.

172. After studying the above rules we come to the conclusion that the restrictions based on them relate to the negative or positive content of ownership insofar as these rules oblige the owners of neighbouring immovables not only to forbear interference in their land (e.g., Article 1003 CC) but also to refrain from acting (e.g., Article 1004 CC) or to take specific action on it (e.g., Article 1006 CC).

173. Finally, it should be stressed that neighbour law contains non-mandatory rules. Consequently, the restrictions based on these rules may be changed or abolished by agreements between the interested parties and, concomitantly, by the establishment of a real or limited personal servitude. This servitude will involve the owner's restriction or exclusion from the rights which belong to him or her by virtue of the neighbour law.

333. D. Papasteriou, *PrL II*, para. 32 II No. 4, 41.

2. Classification of the Restrictions Based on Neighbour Law and the Relationship between the Neighbours

174. The restrictions arising from neighbour law can be divided into direct and indirect ones.[334]

The direct ones derive directly from the law and establish between neighbours an obligation whereby they are mutually bound to forbear, act or refrain from acting. These restrictions are general and reciprocal. General, in the sense that they refer to all kinds of immovables (e.g., Article 1003 CC) or to all the immovables of a certain category (e.g., Article 1024 CC which refers to agrarian immovables), and reciprocal because, although they restrict the power of an owner, at the same time they support him or her to the extent that the neighbours are liable to the same restriction.

We speak of indirect restrictions when the law offers the owner of an immovable X the possibility to demand from the owner of a neighbouring immovable Z, that his or her immovable Z should be encumbered with a real right – and, as a rule, with a real servitude (called 'legal' or 'forced') – in favour of him or her (i.e., in favour of the applicant). In this case, the restriction arises directly from the above real right and indirectly from the law[335] which permits the constitution of the relevant real right. Restrictions of this kind refer only to the immovable encumbered and may therefore be characterized as specific and unilateral (and not mutual).

175. The rights and obligations which derive directly from neighbour law are personal. However, the relevant obligation is equivalent to *obligatio propter rem* or *obligatio ob rem* insofar as the creditor or debtor is the current owner of a certain immovable. Therefore, the legal action through which a claim derived from neighbour law is exercised is mixed (*actio* in rem *scripta*) and for this reason subject to transcription (Article 220 CCProc).[336]

B. Restrictions which are Peculiar to Neighbour Law

1. Emissions (Article 1003 CC)

176. According to Article 1003 CC:

> the owner of an immovable shall be bound to tolerate the emission of smoke, soot, exhalations, heat, noise, vibrations or other similar side effects originating from another immovable provided that such effects do not substantially

334. Thus, I. Sontis, *Compulsory Servitudes* (Athens/Komotini: A. Sakkoulas, 1981), 3 et seq. [in Greek]; Ap. Georgiades, *PrL*, para. 30 II Nos 9 et seq., 348–350; D. Papasteriou, *PrL II*, para. 32 III Nos 12–17, 44–46; I. Spyridakis & M. Spyridakis, *PrL*, vol. B/1, No. 116.2. 3., 432–444; Ph. Tsetsekos, *Neighbour law* (Athens: Sakkoulas, 2000), 16–17 [in Greek].

335. Articles 1012–1017 (on which see also *infra* para. 187 n. 351), 1028, 1029–1030, 1031 CC, as well as Art. 1010 CC.

336. Thus, Ap. Georgiades, *PrL*, para. 30 II 3 No. 16, 350–351.

> prejudice the use of the owner's immovable or result from a use which is usual to the immovables of the region in which the offending immovable is situated.[337]

The above rule restricts the negative content of the ownership of the prejudiced immovable, binding its owner – as well as the holder of a limited real right or the possession or detention over it – to tolerate various emissions originating from a neighbouring immovable, regardless of whether it is used by its owner or by a third party. Interpreting Article 1003 CC – where the emissions enumerated are indicative – we come to the conclusion that it refers to material interventions resulting from imponderable factors, such as (besides those mentioned in the previous article) dust, glaring light, magnetic or electrical energy, music or a bad smell and not, for example, stones, water, garbage, rats or bees. Emissions in the sense of Article 1003 CC are only those which issue from the offending immovable and not those caused by an activity (e.g., the planting of trees) which takes place in the offending immovable and offends the prejudiced one reflectively (e.g., by blocking its view). However, it seems correct to accept the opinion which holds that Article 1003 CC also includes the so-called ideal emissions, e.g., those resulting from a brothel, a hospital or a school situated on the neighbouring immovable.[338]

177. Article 1003 CC binds the owner to tolerate the aforementioned emissions on one of two possible conditions.[339] First, on the condition that the emissions do not substantially prejudice the use of his or her own immovable or, second, on the condition that the emission results from a use which is current in regard to the immovables of the region in which the offending immovable is situated. Moreover this applies regardless of whether the offending or the prejudiced immovable is established first. However, it should be added, on the one hand, that the essence of the offence caused must be judged objectively by taking into consideration the designated purpose of the prejudiced immovable (e.g., as a house, factory or clinic)

337. Articles 1003–1005 CC in combination with Arts 989 and 1108 CC are used, among others (e.g., Arts 966 et seq. CC in combination with Art. 57 CC, Arts 914 et seq. CC and Art. 281 CC), to deal with problems relating to environmental protection. On environmental protection see, among others, I. Karakostas, *Environment and Law*, 2nd edn (Athens/Komotini: Sakkoulas, 2006), passim [in Greek]; D. Klavanidou, 'Preventative Mechanisms of Environmental Protection in the System of Civil Law', *EpiskEmbD* 5, No. B (April-June), 1999, 370 et seq. [in Greek]; D. Papasteriou, *PrL II*, para. 32 IV No. 31 et seq., 53–54; compare H.P. Westermann, *BGB-Sachenrecht*, 11th edn (Heidelberg: Müller, 2005), para. 3 I No. 62, 33.

338. Thus, Ap. Georgiades, *PrL*, para. 31 I No. 8, 362; I. Spyridakis & M. Spyridakis, *PrL*, vol. B/1, No. 118.2.2., 440–442; Ph. Tsetsekos, *Neighbour Law*, 27–29; H. Prütting, *SachR*, para. 28 II 1c No. 330, 129–130. On the opposing view see, chiefly, G. Balis, *PrL*, para. 33 No. 1, 95–96; K. Vavouskos, *PrL*, No. 125, 124.

339. In the event that the relevant conditions do not arise, the owner may be protected by a negatory action (Art. 1008 CC), an action of disturbance (Art. 989 CC) or by provisional remedies, whereas a claim for compensation pursuant to the provisions governing unlawful acts (Arts 914, 919 CC) may not be excluded. However, it has been accepted that, in the case of emissions issuing from immovables serving public purposes (e.g., schools or airports), the owner is bound to tolerate them even when the above conditions do not arise (Ap. Georgiades, *PrL*, para. 31 II No. 16, 365; I. Spyridakis & M. Spyridakis, *PrL*, vol. B/1, No. 118.4.1, 447–448).

and, on the other hand, that the 'use which is current' in certain regions must be determined in the light of the notions prevailing in trade.[340]

2. Repulsion of Threatening Effects (Articles 1004–1007 CC)

a. Harmful Installations

178. According to Article 1004 CC, the owner of an immovable has the right, acting preventively, to prohibit the construction or maintenance of installations of permanent character (e.g., tanks, cesspits, stables or pigsties) on a neighbouring immovable if it can be foreseen with certainty – and not probability – that their existence or use will entail illegal side effects[341] on the owner's immovable.

179. An exception to the preventive action of Article 1004 CC is introduced by Article 1005 CC. The latter provides for repressive action if, in the case contemplated in Article 1004, the installation is attempted following the issue of an authorization as required by law or with due observance of special conditions laid down in the law. Indeed, the issue of the authorization or the observance of the above conditions guarantees that the harmful side effects will not take place. Therefore, when the conditions of Article 1005 CC are fulfilled, a removal of the installation may only be demanded after the harmful side effects resulting from the installation have actually materialized in regard to the immovable in question.

b. Danger of Collapse of Buildings and Digging Close to the Foundations of a Neighbour's Immovable

180. According to Article 1006 CC, if there is a danger that a building or other work might wholly or partially collapse, thus threatening to cause harm to a neighbouring immovable, the owner (or possessor or usufructuary) of such an immovable has the right to demand from the person who would in conformity with the provisions governing unlawful acts be liable for damages[342] to take the steps required to prevent the danger.

181. According to Article 1007 CC, 'an immovable may not be dug up to such a depth as to deprive the soil of the neighbouring immovable of the required

---

340. According to the grammatical expression of Art. 1003 CC, if the prejudicial emissions are current in the region of the offending immovable, the neighbour is bound to tolerate them even when, because of them, the use of his or her immovable becomes excessively difficult or impossible. However, this solution sometimes seems unkind (e.g., when a florist is forced to change his or her profession because of the emissions from a neighbouring factory which make it impossible for him or her to engage in floriculture in his or her immovable). Therefore, the opinion has been expressed that the owner's obligation to tolerate the current emissions ceases when the previous emissions could be avoided or reduced by taking the required measures (Ap. Georgiades, *PrL*, para. 31 II No. 15, 364–365; see also I. Spyridakis & M. Spyridakis, *PrL*, vol. B/1, No. 118 3.2, 444–447 and along the same lines para. 906 satz 2 BGB).

341. The illegality of the effects will be judged according to Art. 1003 (D. Papasteriou, *PrL II*, para. 33 II No. 30, 69; Ap. Georgiades, *PrL*, para. 32 II No. 6, 371).

342. See Art. 925 CC.

support, except if precautions have been taken to secure an appropriate consolidation of the soil in some other way'. This means that it is permitted to dig to such a depth that no danger to the neighbouring immovable can be caused or to a great depth, when appropriate measures have been taken to shore up the ground supporting the neigbouring immovable.

3. Acquisition of Component Parts and Fruits of Neighbouring Immovables (Articles 1008–1009 CC)

182. Article 1008 CC declares that 'the owner of an immovable may cut off and keep for himself roots that intrude into his property from trees grown on the neighbouring immovable' and that 'the same rule shall apply in regard to branches of trees grown on the neighbouring immovable which extend over his property, provided he has given reasonable notice to the possessor of the neighbouring immovable of his intention to cut off such branches'. However, according to the same article, 'such right shall not be granted if the roots or the branches do not prevent the use of the immovable'.

183. According to Article 1009 CC, 'fruits falling on the neighbouring immovable from a tree shall be considered fruits of the immovable on which they fall'. This article introduces a legal fiction according to which the above fruits belong, in order of priority, to the possessor of good faith, to the holder of a limited real right or to the owner[343] of the immovable on which they fall, and not of the immovable on which the trees are situated. However, the fruits belong to the person who has one of the above rights on the immovable on which the trees are situated either when the immovable on which they fall 'is destined for common use' (Article 1009) or when the falling has been caused by an action of the person who, pursuant to Article 1009 CC, has the right to appropriate them. Furthermore, the cause of the falling is irrelevant.

4. Buildings Erected Partially on a Neighbouring Immovable (Articles 1010–1011 CC)

184. Sometimes the owner of an immovable, in erecting a building on his or her property, acting in good faith, extends it onto neighbouring land. In this case, the application of the Roman rule *superficies solo cedit* would mean that the owner of the occupied land becomes the owner of the part of the building erected on his or her land. In the same case, the owner of the occupied land could demand the demolition of the building erected on his or her land. However, such solutions would be contrary not only to the interests of the person who had erected the building, but also to the interests of the national economy. This is because they would result in a decrease in the financial value of the building and the work carried out. On the other

343. See Arts 1064–1066 CC *infra* para. 336.

hand, the above solutions could encourage extortion and huge financial demands for the purpose of transferring the occupied land.

Therefore, Article 1010 CC, introducing an exception to the above Roman rule, defines the conditions under which the court may adjudicate the ownership of the occupied land in favour of the owner of the erected building.[344]

185. According to Article 1010 CC, the court may, in its reasonable appreciation of the situation, award[345] the ownership of the occupied land to the owner of the building erected[346] on the following conditions:

(a) the building erected is a new and self-contained[347] building (e.g., house, shop, storehouse or factory) and not another type of work (e.g., separating wall or shed);
(b) the building is erected by the owner (or co-owner) of an immovable (and not by the holder of another real right on the immovable or by its lessee);
(c) only part and not the whole of the building extends onto the neighbouring land;
(d) there is good faith on the part of the person who erects the building, in the sense that he or she acts in the belief that he or she is erecting the building within the limits of his or her own land (subjective good faith);
(e) there is no timely (i.e., before a large part of the building has been completed) protest by the owner of the occupied land (or by the holder of another real right on it);[348]

344. Article 1010 CC introduces an original mode of acquisition of ownership related to those of Arts 1057–1060 CC. Therefore, the position of Art. 1010 CC in the Civil Code should be after Art. 1057 CC and not amongst the provisions of neighbour law (I. Sontis, 'Contribution to the Interpretation of Art. 1010 CC', *NoB* 2 (1954): 1029; Ap. Georgiades, *PrL*, para. 34 I No. 3, 386; I. Spyridakis & M. Spyridakis, *PrL*, vol. B/1, No. 135.1, 520). However, the inclusion of Art. 1010 CC in neighbour law is due to the influence of the German Civil Code (Ap. Georgiades, *PrL*, para. 34 I No. 3, 386). However, it should be made clear that the corresponding paras 912–916 BGB, unlike Art. 1010 CC, do not declare adjudication of ownership but obligation on the part of the owner of the occupied land to tolerate the erected building against payment of an annuity.

345. Subsequent to a constitutive action or a cross action or a plea (against the revendicatory action or the eviction action of the owner of the occupied immovable) (Ap. Georgiades, *PrL*, para. 34 V No. 31, 394). The relevant judicial decision is constitutive and, therefore, subject to transcription.

346. In the event that the court refuses to make the relevant adjudication, according to a first opinion, co-ownership is constituted on the erected building (K. Vavouskos, *PrL*, No. 134, 134), whereas, according to a second opinion, the owner of the occupied land becomes the owner of the part of the building sited on his or her land (Ap. Georgiades, *PrL*, para. 34 II No. 16, n. 25, 390).

347. A repair, rearrangement or extension (except if it constitutes a self-contained building) does not constitute an 'erection' in the sense of Art. 1010 CC.

348. As the raising of a protest presupposes knowledge of the extension, the opinion has been expressed that Art. 1010 CC should not be applicable if the absence of a timely protest is due to ignorance of the extension (see, chiefly, G. Balis, *PrL*, para. 39 No. 5, 111–112; K. Vavouskos, *PrL*, No. 133, 133–134 and n. 5; Three-member District Court of Athens, 357/1971, 22 ArchN, 1971, 664 [665]). However, the opposite view has also been expressed (see I. Sontis, 'Contribution etc.', 1027 et seq.; Ap. Georgiades, *PrL*, para. 34 II No. 16, 390; P. Filios & Chr. Filios, *PrL*, para. 73 B, 160; I. Spyridakis & M. Spyridakis, *PrL*, vol. B/1, No. 135.2.5, 524; Ph. Tsetsekos, *Neighbour Law*, 57–58 and, from the scope of German Law, H. Roth, in *Staudinger Komm zum BGB, Buch 3: Sachenrecht*, 13th edn (Berlin: Sellier-de Gruyter, 2002), para. 912 No. 30; F.J. Säcker, in *MünchKomm*, Vol. 6: *Sachenrecht*, 5th edn (München: Beck, 2009), para. 912 No. 26).

(f) the value of the occupied land at the time of the occupation is paid, together with any other compensation for the prejudice arising, chiefly, from a possible reduction in the value of the remaining plot.

186. The provision of Article 1010 CC is applicable by analogy in the case where the extension of the building on the neighbouring land and the judicial adjudication have harmed third parties who enjoy real rights (e.g., servitudes[349] or a mortgage[350]) on the neighbouring land (Article 1011 CC).

5. Obligation to Grant Right of Way (Articles 1012–1017 CC)

187. Articles 1012–1017 CC[351] refer in particular to agrarian immovables which are deprived of the necessary passage towards a road ('blind' immovables) and offer their owners the possibility of demanding a right of way[352] from their neighbours. This applies under the following conditions arising from Articles 1012 and 1014 CC:

(a) the immovable is deprived, in objective terms, of the necessary passage towards a public (see Article 1014) and, therefore, of common use road (or square). However, deprivation also occurs when the existing passage serves the immovable insufficiently or sufficiently but not during all the seasons of the year. On the other hand, deprivation does not exist when the owner of the immovable already has a personal claim to demand a right of way from somewhere else or when the owner himself or herself owns another immovable through which a passage can be laid out;
(b) the passage is demanded from the neighbours. This means that the immovable on which the passage is to be laid out must not be of common use;
(c) the deprivation is not caused by a wilful act or omission on the part of the owner of the 'blind' immovable. Nevertheless, Article 1015 CC introduces an exception, declaring that 'if by reason of the alienation of part of an immovable the communication with the public road of the alienated or the remaining part of the immovable has been cut off, the owner of the part through which the communication was up until that time secured shall be bound to grant a right of way'. According to the same article, 'the alienation of one among several

349. In this case, the application of Art. 1010 CC by analogy means that the holder of the servitude is entitled to claim for compensation because of the total or partial extinction of his or her right.
350. In this case, the application of Art. 1010 by analogy means that the mortgage should be limited on the remainder of the plot (see Art. 1322 CC), while, in regard to the occupied part of the land, it should be converted into a claim for compensation (see Art. 1288 CC).
351. On which see K. Koutourisis, *The Compulsory Granting of Passage* (Athens: Sakkoulas, 1986), passim [in Greek]; D. Papasteriou, *PrL II*, para. 38 Nos 1 et seq., 105 et seq.
352. It is disputed whether the granting of way constitutes a legal restriction on the ownership of the immovable on which the passage is granted or a real servitude for the benefit of the 'blind' immovable. On the other hand, according to a third, convincing opinion, the obligation of the neighbour to grant a right of way to the owner of the 'blind' immovable constitutes a restriction on his or her ownership. However, once passage is granted, a right of way, which has the nature and function of the homonymous real servitude, exists (on all these points see, amongst others, Ap. Georgiades [who adopts the third opinion], *PrL*, para. 35 I Nos 2–3, 398–399 and nn. 2–4).

immovables belonging to the same owner shall be classed as a partial alienation of an immovable';

(d) proper compensation is paid.

188. Those who are entitled to demand a right of way are persons who have ownership, co-ownership, usufruct or habitation of the 'blind' immovable as well as those who have acquired the possession of the same immovable under the conditions allowing an ordinary *usucaption*. On the other hand, those who are obliged to grant the right of way are only the owner or the co-owners of the immovable situated between the 'blind' one and the road.[353] In the case where passage is demanded from more than one neighbour, the owner of the 'blind' immovable can choose against whom he or she will bring the relevant legal action or he or she can sue all the neighbours demanding the way one by one.[354]

189. The granting of the right of way may be effected by an agreement between the person entitled to demand the right of way and the person obliged to grant it. This agreement must be incorporated in a notarial deed and is subject to transcription. If the parties do not come to an agreement, then the person entitled may apply to the court, which (taking into account the objective circumstances and not the personal perception of the plaintiff) will determine the direction of the passage and the extent of the right of way thereon as well as the amount of compensation payable (Article 1013 CC).[355]

190. According to Article 1016 CC, 'a person who is hindered or disturbed in his use of the passage shall be protected in accordance with the provisions protecting real servitudes which are applicable by analogy'.[356]

191. Finally, according to Article 1017 CC:

> if by the opening-up of a new passage or for some other reason the need for the previously constituted passage no longer exists, the owner of the immovable on which such passage was granted shall have the right to demand the abolition thereof against reimbursement of the compensation he had received.[357]

353. And not the holder of a limited real right on it. Nevertheless, this holder must be sued with the owner or co-owners (see, amongst others, Ap. Georgiades, *PrL*, para. 35 III 2 No. 22, 405–406).

354. Ap. Georgiades, *PrL*, para. 35 III 2 No. 23, 406.

355. It is disputed whether the judgment is declaratory and therefore not subject to transcription or constitutive of a real servitude and for this reason subject to transcription. On this dispute see, amongst others, Ap. Georgiades, *PrL*, para. 35 III Nos 37 et seq., 410–413, who supports the second opinion with convincing arguments (in No. 38, 330).

356. On the above article, in particular, is based the view which holds that the right of way does not constitute a real servitude (see *supra* para. 187 n. 352).

357. And more correctly, against reimbursement of the compensation which had possibly been received for the future.

6. Tolerance of Repairs (Article 1018 CC)

192. According to Article 1018 CC:

> if, on account of repairs to or restoration of a building, the entry and circulation in the neighbouring immovable of working personnel or the temporary storage therein of installations or building materials becomes necessary, the owner of the neighbouring immovable shall be bound, provided that the use thereof is not substantially hindered, to tolerate such nuisances against payment of compensation or the provision of security against possible prejudice.

7. Relations in Respect of Borders (Articles 1019–1023 CC)

a. Landmarks between Bordering Immovables and Determination of Borders

193. Article 1019 CC, which refers to adjoining (agrarian or urban) immovables with fixed borders, declares that, in the case where no landmarks between the immovables exist, the owner (co-owner or co-owners) of each of them has the right to demand from the owner (or co-owners) of the neighbouring property the joint construction, and at joint expense, of fixed landmarks or the restoration of displaced or decayed ones.

194. Whereas Article 1019 CC refers to bordering immovables with fixed borders, Article 1020 CC presupposes adjoining (agrarian or urban) immovables with confused borders and entrusts their demarcation to the court. In this case the court must try, first of all, to ascertain the exact borderline. However, if it does not succeed in doing this, the demarcation has to be executed in accordance with the existing state of possession. Finally, if possession cannot be ascertained either, the disputed area is allotted in equal parts to each of the immovables concerned.

195. In the case mentioned in Article 1020, the borders can be determined by an agreement[358] between the neighbours and only if they cannot come to an agreement is the owner (co-owner or co-owners)[359] of each immovable entitled to bring an

358. This agreement does not have to be incorporated in a notarial deed when the parties aim, simply, at putting an end to the existing uncertainty. However, even if one of the parties believes that he or she is transferring a part of his or her land, then the agreement has to be incorporated in a notarial deed and rendered subject to transcription (D. Papasteriou, *PrL II*, para. 40 III No. 19, 135; Ap. Georgiades, *PrL*, para. 37 II, n. 11, 424).

359. As well as the holder of any limited real right which is affected by the confusion (K. Vavouskos, *PrL*, No. 142, 142; see also I. Spyridakis & M. Spyridakis, *PrL*, vol. B/1, No. 125.2.1, 474) or only the holder of usufruct (G. Balis, *PrL*, para. 42 No. 1, 119–120; Ap. Georgiades, *PrL*, para. 37 II 1, n. 14, 424; H. Westermann et al., *SachR*, para. 65 III 2, 352). On the opposing view see P. Filios & Chr. Filios, *PrL*, para. 79 A I, 170; H. Roth, in *Staudinger Komm zum BGB, Buch 3: SachR*, para. 920 No. 8; F.H. Säcker, in *MünchKomm*, vol. 6: *SachR*, para. 920 No. 2.

action[360] against the owner (or co-owners) of the bordering immovable, demanding the determination of the borders.[361]

b. Rights on the Separation of Items

196. According to Article 1021 CC, if two adjoining immovables are separated by a path or other strip of land or by a fence or wall or a ditch or some other structure (e.g., a firebreak protecting a forest) lying on the borderline between the immovables and serving both of them, it is deemed (rebuttable presumption) not that the owners of the immovables are co-owners of such separating items,[362] but that they are entitled to the common use of them provided that an exclusive use by one of them does not arise from external marks or local usage.

197. Article 1022 CC, which refers to the case contemplated in the aforementioned Article 1021 CC, explains that 'if the use of the structure is common to both neighbours, each shall have the right to make use thereof according to its designated purpose without hindering use by the other' and that 'maintenance expenses shall be borne in equal shares'. According to the same article, so long as one of the neighbours has an interest in preserving the structure 'the latter may not be removed or altered without his consent'. Finally, according to the same rule, 'in all other matters their relations shall be governed by the provisions relating to an undivided joint right'.

198. The last article in this group is Article 1023 CC, which refers to a tree (or brush-wood) that has grown on the border and stipulates that it should be common to both neighbours, in the sense that they will be compulsory co-owners. The same article provides for the right of each neighbour to demand the felling of the tree if it does not serve as a landmark.

8. Relations in Respect of Water Flow (Articles 1024–1031 CC)

199. According to Article 1024 CC, the owner of a low-level agrarian[363] immovable is bound – and not entitled – to receive water (e.g., of rain or melted

360. It seems correct to accept that the relevant action is mixed and must be transcribed (Art. 220 CCProc) (*thus*, K. Vavouskos, *PrL*, No. 142, 142; Ap. Georgiades, *PrL*, para. 37 II No. 16, 425–426; I. Spyridakis & M. Spyridakis, *PrL*, vol. B/1, No. 125.2.5, 474–475).

361. According to the prevailing (and correct) opinion, the relevant judicial decision is declaratory if the borders are determined through ascertainment of their old position or in accordance with the existing state of possession and constitutive (and subject to transcription) in the event of allocation (adjudication) of the disputed area in equal parts to each litigant (*thus*, G. Balis, *PrL*, para. 43 No. 4, 120–121; K. Vavouskos, *PrL*, No. 142, 142; Ap. Georgiades, *PrL*, para. 37 II No. 19, 427; I. Spiridakis & M. Spyridakis, *PrL*, vol. B/1, No. 125.3.4, 476). *Compare*, P. Filios & Chr. Filios, *PrL*, para. 79 B 3, 171.

362. Each neighbour is the exclusive owner of the part of the separating item which belongs to his or her property. However, if the separating item lies totally on one of the bordering immovables, it is self-evident that the owner of this land is the exclusive owner and user.

363. According to AP 623/2001, 50 NoB, 2002, 691, due to the identical nature of the legal ground, Art. 1024 CC also applies, by analogy, in the area of urban immovables which are located in districts without an organized system of sewers.

snow and not of waters flowing freely which are of common use [Article 967 CC]) flowing naturally and without the aid of an artificial construction from a neighbouring agrarian immovable situated on a higher level, while the owners of both the low-level and the higher-level immovables are prohibited from setting up a structure which impedes or alters the natural flow of water. On the other hand, the owner of the higher-level immovable is bound to tolerate the repair or restoration of structures existing on his or her immovable for the purpose of checking the flow of the water, provided that this is done without prejudicing him or her. The cost of such repair or restoration should be borne by those benefiting thereby and in proportion to the advantages they respectively derive (Article 1025 CC).

200. Article 1026 CC declares that the owner of any kind of building is bound to construct the roof so as to prevent rain water running towards the neighbouring (agrarian or urban) immovable.

201. Article 1027 CC refers to the water springing from a source which, as a component part of the immovable in which the source is situated (Article 954 paragraph 1 point 3), belongs to the owner of this immovable. The same article stipulates that the owner of the immovable may not, by using the above water or by excavating a well in his or her property, cut off or substantially reduce the quantity of water already used by the inhabitants of a village for their needs and not for other purposes, such as, for example, the operation of a factory.

202. Article 1028 CC restricts the right of the owner of an immovable in which a well or a source is situated to have exclusive use of the water from it. To be precise, it declares that the above owner is bound, without being deprived himself or herself, to provide, against compensation, the owner of the neighbouring property with the water which is indispensable for his or her domestic needs, provided that he or she (the neighbour) can only obtain water from elsewhere at a disproportionate cost.

203. Articles 1029–1030 CC offer the owner of an agrarian or urban immovable the right to demand – against payment of compensation – the conveyance of water originating from a source or well or river through the agrarian immovable of another. This applies on condition:

(a) that the above owner has a right (arising from a servitude, a personal [obligational] contract or directly from the law, e.g., when the water is of common use) to such water;
(b) that the conveyance is effected in the most suitable and less cumbersome manner for the immovable encumbered; and
(c) that the beneficiary takes care to build the structures that are necessary to prevent the owners of adjoining immovables from being hindered in the exercise of their rights.

204. Finally, according to Article 1031 CC, the owner of an urban or an agrarian immovable is under obligation, taking his or her own interest also into consideration, to allow – against proper compensation – the passage across the immovable of water or gas pipes or electrical cables either in the air or underground for the service of other immovables. The installation has to be executed in the most suitable and least cumbersome manner for the immovable encumbered. On the other hand, the owner of such an immovable has the right to demand the displacement of the installation to another position in the immovable at the expense of the beneficiary of the right of passage.

C. Final Remarks on Neighbour Law

205. From neighbour law arise (real) obligations,[364] which encumber the owners of immovables, and corresponding claims in favour of the owners of the neighbouring immovables. On the other hand, negatory actions (Article 1108 CC)[365] and actions following a disturbance (Article 989 CC)[366] play a decisive role in setting disputes between neighbours.

206. The subject-matter competent court for resolving the disputes arising from Articles 1003–1009, 1018–1020 and 1023–1031 CC is, in accordance with Article 15 point 3 CCProc, the Magistrates' Court. However, the previous article does not mention anything about the disputes arising from Articles 1010–1011, 1012–1017 and 1021–1022 CC. Nevertheless, from the diverse opinions which have been expressed on this point, it seems correct to adopt the one which, invoking Article 14 CCProc, holds that the value of the object of the dispute is decisive in determining the subject-matter competent court.[367]

As regards the territorial competence, the court responsible for the adjudication of cases relating to neighbour law should be the court of the region in which the relevant immovables are situated. On the other hand, the procedure which should be followed is that of ordinary proceedings and, in pressing cases, the summary proceedings of provisional remedies.

207. Completing this section on neighbour law, we must emphasize that most of the claims arising from the above law lose their value if their holder cannot exercise them indefinitely. Therefore, Article 1032 CC declares that the claims arising from Articles 1004–1007, 1012, 1015, 1018, 1019, 1020, 1023 paragraph 2, 1029 and 1031 are not subject to prescription. As to the claims not mentioned by Article 1032, it should be noted that they are prescribed after twenty years (Article 249 CC).

---

364. See also *supra* para. 175.
365. On which see *infra* paras 366, 393–396.
366. On which see *supra* paras 135, 140.
367. See, chiefly, K. Kerameus, *Civil Procedural Law. General Part* (Athens-Thessaloniki, Sakkoulas, 1986), 30 [in Greek]; K. Vavouskos, *PrL*, No. 157, 155; Ap. Georgiades, *PrL*, para. 39 III 1 No. 12, 453 (where the relevant overall discussion is presented); One-member District Court of Athens 8363/1984, 26 HellD, 1985, 319.

Chapter 3. Specific Types of Ownership

§1. Co-ownership

I. Concept and Nature

208. Co-ownership[368] is the ownership of an immovable or a movable thing which belongs to several persons (co-owners) in undivided ideal shares (Article 1113 CC). This means that in the case where A, B and C are co-owners of an immovable X, the ownership of each of them with regard to X extends not on a divided and visible part of it but on all the constituent elements of the immovable up to the percentage (e.g., one-third undivided) of his or her ideal share.

209. The ideal share of co-ownership is of the same nature as ownership. Therefore, as regards, for example, the transmission, encumbrance, protection or renunciation of the ideal share, the provisions governing ownership are to be applied, unless the special rules governing co-ownership (i.e., Articles 1113–1116 CC) make alternative provisions. However, the relationships between the co-owners are to be regulated by the provisions governing an undivided joint right (Article 1113 CC). This is because between the co-owners there exists an undivided joint right, established directly by the law.

II. Rights and Obligations between the Co-owners

210. As already mentioned above, Articles 1113–1117 CC and the provisions governing an undivided joint right (Articles 785–805 CC) regulate the relationships between co-owners. From these rules it may be concluded that each co-owner has the following rights:

(a) the right to use the common thing, provided that such use does not prevent its parallel use by the other co-owners (Article 787 CC);
(b) the right, even without the consent of the others, to take measures required to preserve the thing if it is in imminent peril (Article 788 paragraph 2 CC);
(c) the right to have a proportional share in the benefits of the common thing (Article 786 CC);
(d) the right to dispose of one's own share without the consent of the others, whereas the disposal of the whole of the common thing requires the joint consent of all the co-owners (Article 793 CC), and finally;
(e) the right to demand, at any time,[369] dissolution of the co-ownership, provided that such right has not been excluded by a legal transaction,[370] by the

368. On the two active forms of co-ownership which apply in English law, that is, tenancy in common and joint tenancy, see *supra* para. 159 (under g).
369. The (personal) claim for the dissolution of co-ownership is not subject to prescription (Art. 805 CC).
370. The relevant transaction may only exclude the dissolution of co-ownership for a period of up to ten years (Art. 795 para. 2 CC). However, the dissolution may be requested, on a serious ground, even

assignment to the common thing of a permanent purpose (Article 795 CC) or by the law.[371]

211. From the aforementioned rules it may also be concluded that each co-owner has the following obligations: (a) the obligation to participate, in proportion to his or her share, in the expenses incurred in connection with the maintenance, management and use of the common thing (Article 794 CC) and (b) in the event of imminent peril not only the right but also the obligation to take measures required for the preservation of the thing.[372]

III. Administration of the Common Thing

212. The administration of the common thing – that is, its management and its preservation, as well as the undertaking of actions aimed at changing its economic or legal status – belongs jointly to all the co-owners (Article 788 paragraph 1 subparagraph a). On the other hand, the proper method of administration is determined either by the common consent of all the co-owners (Article 788 CC combined with Article 790 CC) or by a majority (calculated by reference to the size of the shares) decision of the co-owners (Article 789 CC) or, where the administration cannot be regulated by one of the above methods, by a (declaratory) court decision (Article 790 CC). However, it should be stressed that the decisions on some important subjects must be of common consent only. Thus, according to Article 792 CC, a substantial alteration of, or a disproportionately expensive addition to the common thing, as well as any reduction in the co-owner's proportional share in the benefits deriving from the common thing, may not be decided by the majority nor pursued by a legal action.

213. The decision of the co-owners, as well as that of the court which determines the means of administration of the common thing, binds the particular successors in title of the co-owners (Article 791 CC) and their universal successors, too. However, where the common thing is an immovable, the binding of the particular successors in title is effective only if the relevant decision of the co-owners has been incorporated in a notarial deed and transcribed and the relevant court decision has been transcribed (Article 1115 CC).

before the agreed time, whereas an agreement limiting beforehand such right becomes null and void (Art. 797 CC). In addition, it should be noted that the agreement prohibiting a co-owner from dissolving the co-ownership for a fixed period of time binds his or her particular successors in title (Art. 796 CC), as well as his or her universal successors and the court. However, when the common thing is an immovable, the binding of the particular successors in title is effective if the relevant agreement has been incorporated in a notarial deed and transcribed (Art. 1115 CC).

371. In the case of compulsory co-ownership (on which see *infra* paras 216, 223).

372. P. Filios, in *ErmAK*, vol. III/B, issue 6/4 (Athens: Sakkoulas, 1974), Art. 788 No. 70 [in Greek]; Th. Skouras, in *Civil Code*, Vol. IV: *Law of Obligations. Special Part* ed. Ap. Georgiades & M. Stathopoulos (Athens: Sakkoulas, 1982), Art. 788 No. 36 [in Greek]; D. Papasteriou, *PrL II*, para. 66 V Nos 69–75, 574–576; Ap. Georgiades, *PrL*, para. 65 IV 2 No. 51, 817. For the opposite view see G. Balis, *PrL*, para. 110 No. 2, 260.

IV. Dissolution of Co-ownership

214. We speak of dissolution of co-ownership when the ownership ceases to belong to several persons jointly either because it has been transmitted to one person (late co-owner or not) or because the thing has been divided into several separate parts over each one of which an exclusive ownership has been established or, finally, because the common thing has disappeared (e.g., has been destroyed).

215. The Civil Code refers to the dissolution of co-ownership on the initiative of each co-owner by means of distribution of the thing co-owned (Article 798 CC). The distribution may be effected by either voluntary or judicial means, depending on whether the co-owners have agreed to it or not (Article 799 CC).

Voluntary distribution presupposes, on the one hand, an agreement (personal contract) between all the co-owners, whereby the obligation for distribution is undertaken, and, on the other, a real contract of distribution, by which the distribution of the thing and, consequently, the dissolution of co-ownership is effected. These contracts, in the area of immovables, must be incorporated in a notarial deed and transcribed.

Judicial distribution, which may be demanded by each of the co-owners[373] in the case where a voluntary distribution has not been achieved, is effected in accordance with the provisions of Articles 478–494 CCProc (Article 799 CC). It can be accomplished by physical division of the object itself, by public auction or partly by physical division and partly by public auction. To be precise, the court orders[374] a distribution by physical division when the common thing or things may, without reduction of their value, be distributed in portions of the same kind proportionate to the shares of the co-owners (Articles 800 CC and 480 CCProc). If distribution by physical division is impossible or unprofitable (as happens when the common thing is a car, a painting or an apartment), the court orders the sale of the common thing or things by public auction and the distribution of the proceeds of the auction among the co-owners in proportion to their shares (Articles 801 CC and 484 CCProc). Finally, if distribution by physical division is only partly possible (e.g., in the case where A and B jointly inherit an agrarian immovable which can be divided into two portions and an apartment), the court may decide in favour of a distribution partly by physical division and partly by public auction (Article 485 CCProc).

373. The relevant legal action must be brought against all the other co-owners, whereas to the relevant trial must be invited the holders of mortgages, pledges or usufruct as well as the persons who have imposed a seizure on the share of a certain co-owner (Art. 491 CCProc). See in detail L. Pipsou, *Judicial Distribution* (Athens-Thessaloniki: Sakkoulas, 2006), 54 et seq. [in Greek].

374. According to the prevailing view, the relevant court decision is constitutive (see, amongst others, M. Karasis, in *Civil Code*, Vol. V: *PrL*, ed. Ap. Georgiades & M. Stathopoulos Art. 1113 No. 92 and for a more detailed discussion on this point see L. Pipsou, *Judicial Distribution*, 188 et seq.).

§2. Horizontal Ownership

I. Concept, Justification and Legislative Status

216. The concept of horizontal ownership (or horizontal co-ownership or ownership of a storey) derives from Articles 1002 and 1117 CC. The first of these, which introduces a deviation from the principle that the component parts of a thing (such as a building in relation to the ground; Article 954 paragraph 1 point 1 CC) follow the legal fate of the composite thing (Article 953 CC), recognizes the possibility that a storey of a building or an apartment on a storey may come under separate ownership.[375] On the other hand, Article 1117 CC declares that the owner of a storey or an apartment therein is *ipso jure* an indivisible co-owner of a proportionate share[376] in the parts of the whole immovable that are also destined for the common use of the other co-owners. Such parts are, in particular, the building plot, the foundations, the supporting walls, the roof and the courtyard. From the above articles it may be concluded that horizontal ownership is a specific type of ownership over an immovable which is composed of two elements: the exclusive ownership of a storey or an apartment therein and the compulsory co-ownership of the common parts of the immovable.

217. The institution of horizontal ownership is a product of the urgent housing needs that have been created by the population increases in urban areas, the inability of towns to extend beyond their borders, the difficulties that exist in the communications between suburbs and city centres and the appearance of problems (regarding, for example, water supply, lighting or means of communication) in cases where the extension of a town becomes attainable. Thus, the institution of horizontal ownership, which means the extension of towns in a vertical direction, can be justified by the need to serve the housing needs of those who are unable to erect a building on their own plot not far from the centre of the town and the need to avoid the excessive horizontal spread of towns.

218. Horizontal ownership is regulated by the provisions of Articles 1002 and 1117 CC and Law 3741/1929 (concerning the ownership of storeys). However, some subjects are also regulated by L.D. 1024/1971 (concerning divided ownership on buildings erected on a single building plot) and by Law 1562/1985 (concerning the erection of co-owned immovables, etc.), whereas the provisions governing co-ownership and undivided joint rights also apply.

375. Whereas in accordance with the relevant principle, the ownership of the storey or the apartment should belong to the owner or to all the co-owners of the ground.

376. This share is usually defined in the juridical act by which the horizontal ownership is constituted. Otherwise, the same share is defined in accordance with the value of the storey or the apartment as a proportion of the value of the whole immovable.

II. Relationships between Co-owners

219. The relationships between co-owners are to be regulated, in order of priority by: (a) the mandatory rules of the legislation mentioned above (e.g., Article 1117 CC, 2 paragraphs 3, 10, 13 Law 3741/1929); (b) the private will of the co-owners (Article 4 Law 3741/1929); c) the non-mandatory rules of the aforementioned legislation (e.g., Article 5 Law 3741/1929); d) secondarily, and on condition that they might be reconciled with the special rules of horizontal ownership, the general rules governing co-ownership, ownership, an undivided joint right, co-possession, etc.

220. The most important organs of a union of co-owners are their general assembly and their manager. The latter is their mandatory and their representative in or out of court on subjects relating to the co-ownership.

221. As regards the rights and obligations of the co-owners, the following should be noted:

Providing that the regulation governing horizontal ownership[377] or a specific agreement between the co-owners does not state otherwise, each co-owner, as concerns his or her apartment, has an exclusive owner's rights (Article 1000 CC), provided that the exercise of these rights does not prejudice use of the property by the other co-owners or reduce their security or the security of the building (Article 3 paragraph 1 Law 3741/1929). On the other hand, as regards the parts of the building destined for common use, each co-owner is entitled to use, repair and renovate them so long as the rights of the other co-owners are not prejudiced and the designated use of the above parts is not changed (Articles 5 sub-paragraph a and 3 paragraph 2 Law 3741/1929). However, the right to extend the building either in the space above it, by adding a new storey, or below the ground, by digging a cellar, belongs to all the co-owners of the ground (Article 8 paragraph 1 Law 3741/1929).[378]

In regard to the obligations of the co-owners,[379] it should be stressed that each of them is bound to pay a share, in proportion to the value of the storey or the apartment that he or she owns, of the maintenance expenses for the areas of common use (Article 5 sub-paragraph b Law 3741/1929). In addition, in the case where a partial destruction of the building occurs, which costs less than three-fourth of the total value of the building, each co-owner is bound – unless there is a contrary agreement

377. This takes the form of a charter for the building and determines, among other things, the parts of the building destined for common use, the undivided ideal share of each co-owner in these parts and the conditions of their administration, a probable prohibition on the practice of specific professions or on the keeping of animals in the apartments of the building, the subject of central heating, etc.

378. Nevertheless, it is possible for the above right to be granted to a certain person, whether he or she is co-owner of the building plot or not. However, while in the first case it is not necessary to grant the beneficiary an additional percentage of co-ownership over the building plot, in the second case, a corresponding percentage of co-ownership thereon must be granted.

379. Compare also *supra* para. 211.

– to participate in the erection of the common parts in proportion to his or her rights over them (Article 9 paragraph 2 Law 3741/1929).

222. Any disputes arising from horizontal ownership between the co-owners of the building or between them and the manager are judged, regardless of the value of the object of the dispute, by the One-member District Court which is situated in the area of the immovable (Article 17 point 2 CCProc).

§3. Vertical Ownership

223. Vertical ownership (or co-ownership) presupposes the erection of more than one self-contained and independent building on a single building plot and can be defined as a mixture of exclusive ownership over one of the above buildings or a part of it (storey or apartment) and of compulsory co-ownership, as a proportional share, over the building plot and the other common parts.

There are two types of vertical ownership: simple and composite. We speak of simple vertical ownership when each of the above buildings, without being divided horizontally into storeys or apartments, constitutes a separate property belonging to one or more (in undivided ideal shares) of the co-owners of the building plot. On the other hand, in the case of composite vertical ownership, which presupposes the horizontal division of each of the above buildings into storeys or apartments, the object which is separately owned is not one of the buildings, but a storey or an apartment of one of them. Thus, in the context of composite vertical ownership, which is a mixture of horizontal and vertical ownership, there exists an undivided joint right between the co-owners of one building in regard to this building together with a similar right between the co-owners of the separate buildings in regard to the common building plot.

224. The institution of vertical ownership was put into practice as soon as it became obvious that the institution of horizontal ownership (in which the erection of only one building is permitted on a site which is fit for building on) was unable either to cover the pressing housing needs of people moving to urban centres[380] or to support the development of the country in respect of town-planning.[381] Nevertheless, the validity of the relevant institution was disputed,[382] until it was recognized by L.D. 1024/1971. This law recognizes vertical ownership 'in the sense of Article 1 Law 3741/1929 and Articles 1002 and 1117 CC' which refer to horizontal

380. Contrariwise, under the regime of vertical ownership, for example, two or more persons – each of whom cannot afford to buy a self-contained building plot – can buy the building plot in common and erect on it self-contained buildings, preserving the co-ownership over the plot.

381. The above development presupposes, for example, the possibility of erecting a group of self-contained buildings on a single building plot, on which gardens, courtyards, parking places or sports facilities, which are destined for the common use of all the residents of the buildings, may also be constructed.

382. See, for example, the Plenary Sessions of AP 107/1971, 19 NoB, 1971, 598 and 332/1970, 18 NoB, 1970, 830 as well as AP 388/1965, 14 NoB, 1966, 244.

ownership. Consequently, in the area of vertical ownership the provisions governing horizontal ownership are applicable *mutatis mutandis*.

§4. Time-Sharing

225. Time-sharing is an institution which offers the right to use as residence an immovable (building) or a part of it (apartment) for a specific period of time on an annual basis and for a specific number of years (or forever, as well). This right, known as 'time-share', is acquired upon payment of an agreed price which is paid once only. However, in addition, the beneficiary (time-sharer) is bound to pay an agreed annual sum for the maintenance of the immovable and for the provision of related services (cleaning, security, etc.).

Time-shares can have the nature of ownership and, more specifically, of horizontal ownership,[383] in the sense that for a specific period of time a time-sharer has separate ownership of a specific room or apartment in an immovable (tourist lodging) and a proportional co-ownership of the common parts of the immovable. However, time-shares may also have the nature of a personal right arising, for example, from a hotel accommodation contract or from a contract for the hire of a thing or of a fruit-bearing object.[384] Finally, it is also possible for the time-sharers to be shareholders of a company to which the immovable (tourist lodging) belongs.[385]

226. The appearance of the institution of time-sharing[386] is justified by the need to ensure that a standing tourist lodging is continually occupied by holiday-makers over a long period of time without considerable financial investment and at stable prices. On the other hand, the relevant institution becomes attractive because of the possibility of exchanging time-shares. Thus, for example, the holders of the right to take one week's vacation in Greece and Spain, respectively, may exchange their rights.

The above reasons, which have led to the institution of time-sharing becoming well established in the international tourist market, together with the concomitant need for Greece to remain competitive in the area of tourism, have resulted in the institution being introduced into our country as well. This was brought about by Law 1652/1986 (concerning contracts for time-sharing hire and the regulation of related subjects). On the other hand, by the Ministerial Decision Z1-130/21.2.2011 the Greek legislation was adapted to Community law (EC Directive 2008/122).

227. Greek law regards time-sharing not as a form of ownership but as a form of hire of an immovable. This means that it recognizes the time-share as a personal

383. In Portugal, for example, time-sharing has been recognized as a new real right similar to the right arising from horizontal ownership.
384. As happens in the countries with common law systems.
385. As happens in France, where the so-called *société civil d' attribution* exists.
386. The idea of time-sharing was born in Switzerland and France in the 1960s and spread to North America, South Africa, Japan, Australia, South America and, finally, the rest of Europe (especially, Spain, Portugal and Great Britain), in the 1980s.

right arising from a contract for the hire of a thing. Therefore, the provisions governing the latter form of contract (Articles 574 et seq. CC) are applicable in the area of time-sharing for the regulation of matters which are not covered by Law 1652/1986 and Ministerial Decision Z1-130/21.2.2011.

Of the matters that are regulated by the above legislation the following should be noted:[387]

(a) in a contract for time-sharing hire the vendor-lessor, on the one hand, is obliged to secure for the purchaser-lessee the use of the tourist lodging every year during the valid term of the contract (i.e., for three to sixty years) and to provide related services to him or her for a period of time determined by the contract, whereas the purchaser-lessee, on the other, is bound to pay the agreed rent;
(b) the establishment of a time-sharing hire presupposes the incorporation of the relevant contract in a notarial deed which must be transcribed;
(c) inseparable part of the said contract is a document which contains information relating to the status of the object of time-sharing;
(d) the purchaser-lessee is entitled to rescind or terminate by notice the above contact for certain grounds specified by law;
(e) the time-sharing hire is to be continued in the event of a universal or particular succession in title on the part of the vendor-lessor or the purchaser-lessee, whereas the latter also has the right to sub-lease or to assign to third persons the use of the tourist lodging for one or more seasons;
(f) mortgages, prenotices of mortgages[388] and seizures – which encumber the object of a time-sharing hire with a view to securing the satisfaction of claims held by the State or a public entity, a municipality, a communal authority, a social security organization, a bank or other lending body – are abolished in the case where a Greek or a foreign bank provides a letter of guaranty which completely covers the claim.

387. For a detailed treatment see, in particular, Chr. Themeli, *The Contract of Time-sharing Hire* (Thessaloniki, 2002), passim [in Greek].

388. On prenotice of mortgage see *infra* paras 411, 445 et seq.

Chapter 4. Servitudes

§1. Concept, Types and Governing Principles

228. A servitude is a limited real right on a thing belonging to another person which offers its holder the power to derive certain advantages from the substance of the thing. However, in view of the fact that from all types of servitudes arise not only rights but also obligations of their holders, it seems correct to accept that servitudes establish real relations from which derive the relevant real right, as well as obligations, charges or commitments.[389]

229. Depending on the way in which their holders are defined, servitudes are divided into two types: real (or predial) and personal. The first type involves the provision of a constant service by a certain immovable (the so-called servient tenement) to another immovable (known as the 'dominant tenement') and also to the current owner of the latter. On the other hand, personal servitudes – which are divided into complete (usufruct and habitation) and limited types, depending on the extent of the power granted to their holders – are established on a (servient) tenement for the benefit of a certain person regardless of his or her relationship to a dominant tenement.

230. Servitudes are governed by the following general principles:

(a) They may be established only on a thing in the legal sense. Exceptionally, usufruct may be constituted on a right as well.
(b) They can be established only on immovables. Exceptionally, usufruct may be constituted on movables as well.
(c) They may be established only on a thing belonging to another person (*nemini res sua servit*). This is because of the universal character of ownership, which renders the constitution of a servitude on a thing belonging to oneself meaningless and which also implies the extinction of a servitude because of confusion in the case where its holder acquires the ownership of the thing encumbered.[390] Nevertheless, Article 1114 CC, introducing an exception to the above rule, permits the establishment of a real servitude on a co-owned immovable for the benefit of the current owner of another immovable even if the latter is the co-owner of the servient tenement. The same article also permits the constitution of a real servitude on an immovable for the benefit of the current owners of a co-owned immovable even if one of these co-owners is the owner of the servient tenement.
(d) They must be directly or indirectly useful to their holders (*servitus utilis esse debet*).

---

389. See also D. Papasteriou, *Property Law,* vol. 3 (Athens – Thessaloniki: Sakkoulas, 2008), para. 70 No. 13, 5, para. 71 No. 6, 17, para. 76 No. 7, 108.
390. See also *supra* para. 162 as well as *infra* para. 416. Compare, though, Arts 1904–1905, 1914 and 1948 CC.

(e) The owner of the servient tenement is bound either to abstain from certain acts which he or she would have been entitled to perform by his or her right of ownership or to tolerate some use of his or her immovable by the holder of the relevant servitude.[391] On the other hand, a servitude cannot imply that the above owner has an obligation to perform positive actions (*servitus in faciendo consistere nequit*).[392]
(f) The constitution of a servitude on another servitude is impossible. This is because, as a rule, servitudes are established on things and not on rights and also because the above constitution would mean the alienation of the servitude, in whole or in part. However, the alienation of personal servitudes is contrary to their content and nature, whereas the alienation of real servitudes is impossible without the simultaneous alienation of the dominant tenement.

§2. Real (or Predial) Servitudes

I. Concept and Content

231. A real servitude is a limited real right which is acquired on an immovable in favour of the current owner of another immovable, who thus secures an advantage (Article 1118 CC).

To be precise, a real servitude is characterized by the following attributes:

(a) it is acquired on only one servient tenement and it secures an advantage for only one dominant tenement, while the constitution of a single real servitude on and in favour of more than one tenement is impossible;
(b) it is constituted on the whole servient tenement[393] and not on an ideal share of it and it secures an advantage not for an ideal share but for the whole dominant tenement. This means that real servitudes are undivided rights;
(c) it is constituted in favour of the current owner of the dominant tenement and, in this sense, it is a right which accompanies the ownership of the dominant tenement;[394]
(d) it must offer some kind of advantage to the dominant tenement. Therefore, the dominant and the servient tenements must be spatially related in such a way as to make it possible for the latter to grant the advantage to the former.

232. As to the content of a real servitude, it should be noted that this is determined by the private will, which may, however, act within the constraints imposed by law and, in particular, the provisions of Articles 1118, 1119 and 1124 CC. To be precise, according to Article 1119 CC, the benefit of the current owner of the dominant tenement must derive not from a positive action by the owner of the servient

---

391. See, for example, Art. 1119 CC.
392. An exception to this rule is introduced by Arts 1126, 1127 CC (see *infra* para. 235).
393. However, the exercise of a real servitude may be localized, after an agreement, on a specific part of the servient tenement.
394. This means that the transfer or the encumbrance (e.g., with usufruct) of the dominant tenement concerns *ipso jure* the real servitude as well.

tenement but from the fact that the latter tolerates some use of his or her immovable by the owner of the dominant one or abstains from certain actions which he or she would have been entitled to perform by his or her right of ownership. On the other hand, according to Article 1124 CC, the right of servitude may only exist insofar as is required to satisfy a need of the dominant tenement, while, in case of doubt, any new needs of the dominant tenement do not entail an extra encumbrance for the owner of the servient one.

II. Types of Real Servitudes

233. As has been mentioned, the law does not provide an exhaustive definition of the content or types of real servitudes. Indeed, Article 1120 CC lists some examples of real servitudes, whereas the private will may create, within the framework established by the law, other real servitudes with a different content as well.[395]

To be precise, according to Article 1120 CC, the main forms of real servitudes are as follows: the right of way, the right to convey or drain or draw water or water cattle belonging to a dominant tenement, the right to graze or cut wood, the right to let water from the roof of a dominant tenement flow over a servient one, the right of a roof to jut out or project over a servient tenement, the right to support a construction against a neighbouring building, the servitude of a sewer, of prohibiting construction, the right to prevent a servient tenement from blocking the light or the view of a dominant one. Mention may also be made of the right to dig sand or to quarry stones from a servient tenement, the right to maintain a hut on a servient tenement, etc.

234. Real servitudes can be divided into the following types:

(a) Positive servitudes or servitudes resulting in an obligation to show tolerance (*servitutes in patiendo*) and negative servitudes or servitudes aimed at an omission (*servitutes in non faciendo*). Positive real servitudes provide the owner of the dominant tenement with the power to act on the servient one and, at the same time, they oblige the owner of the latter to tolerate the above actions. To this group belong all the servitudes enumerated in Article 1120 CC, except for the last three. The latter are negative real servitudes in the sense that they oblige the owner of a servient tenement to abstain from certain actions which he or she would have been entitled to perform by his or her right of ownership.

395. It should, however, be noted that the possibility of real servitudes being formed is restricted by the General Building Regulation, which essentially abolishes the so-called urban real servitudes. Thus, according to Art. 25, since the General Building Regulation has come into force, it is prohibited to constitute a servitude which restricts the possibility of erecting or extending buildings or installations which are permissible under the rules currently in force pertaining to town-planning. As an exception, it is possible to constitute a right of way if this way is the only route of the dominant tenement to an area destined for common use. According to the same rule, all servitudes, except for the servitude relating to the uniform framework of a building and the servitude of way, which were constituted before the promulgation of the above Regulation, are abolished, against payment of proportional compensation, if their exercise is incompatible with construction works undertaken legally on the servient tenement.

(b) Continuous servitudes, which are exercised continuously, and intermittent servitudes, which are exercised periodically. Continuous servitudes include all the negative servitudes and those positive ones which provide the owner of a dominant tenement with the power to maintain a construction on a servient tenement. All the other real servitudes are intermittent.
(c) Visible and invisible servitudes, depending on whether they are physically visible. Thus, an example of a visible servitude is the protrusion of a construction onto a servient tenement, whereas an example of an invisible one is the servitude of a sewer.
(d) Servitudes of neighbour law, through which the non-mandatory rules of neighbour law are modified.[396]
(e) Servitudes imposing prohibitions or restrictions on financial or professional competition. An example of these is that which prohibits the establishment on a servient tenement of an enterprise that might enter into competition with another enterprise which is already in operation or may operate in the future on the dominant tenement.[397]

III. Exercise of Real Servitudes

235. A right of servitude can include any act by the beneficiary which is necessary for its exercise (Article 1125 sub-paragraph a CC). Thus, for example, in the case of a right of way, not only the owner of the dominant tenement is entitled to pass through the servient one but also the persons who cohabit with him or her, his or her lessee, his or her visitors, his or her domestic staff, etc. However, the beneficiary is bound to exercise his or her right with utmost regard to the interests of the owner of the servient tenement (Article 1125 sub-paragraph b). Otherwise, he or she is liable for compensation in order to repair the harm caused by his or her breach of the above obligation, whereas the owner of the servient tenement is protected by the negatory action (Article 1108 CC). Furthermore, the owner of the servient tenement has the right to demand, against prepayment of the amounts required, a change in the way the servitude has been exercised or in the place where the servitude has been exercised hitherto. This is possible provided that the financial purpose of the relevant servitude can be equally satisfied by the new method or place and that the method or place in which the servitude has hitherto been exercised was particularly onerous for the above owner (Article 1128 CC).[398] Finally, where a construction, e.g., a water course or an aqueduct, is maintained on a servient tenement with a view to securing exercise of a servitude, the beneficiary is bound to maintain it in an orderly state insofar as this is required by the interest of

396. See *supra* para. 173.
397. It has been correctly accepted that servitudes of this kind are valid only if they restrict the owner's power arising from the right of ownership and not when they restrict the owner of the servient tenement from exercising his or her legal freedom to carry out transactions or to engage in business (see Ap. Georgiades, *PrL*, para. 70 III 4 No. 37, 877–878 [in Greek]; D. Papasteriou, *PrL III*, para. 71IV No. 28, 28 [in Greek]).
398. Article 1128 CC as well as Art. 1125 sub-para. b constitute specific applications of Art. 281 concerning the abuse of right and, consequently, they are rules of public policy. Hence, the private will may not prevent their application (Art. 3 CC).

the owner of the servient tenement. However, where the construction also serves the interest of the owner of the servient tenement, the obligation of maintenance is, subject to any alternative agreement, to be borne by both owners in proportion to the interest of each (Article 1126 CC). On the other hand, where a servitude consists in the right of the beneficiary to maintain a construction on a construction of the servient tenement, e.g., in the right for a construction to protrude onto the servient tenement, the owner of the latter is, subject to any alternative agreement, bound to maintain his or her own construction to the extent that this is required by the interest of the beneficiary (Article 1127 CC).

236. The existence of a real servitude does not deprive the owner of the servient tenement of the right to make use of this immovable himself or herself in a similar (or a different) manner, unless it has been agreed differently[399] or the servient tenement is not sufficient to allow such use (Article 1129 CC). In addition, the owner of the servient tenement reserves the right to grant on his or her immovable other real servitudes of similar or different content.[400]

237. Because of its classification as an undivided right, according to Article 1130 CC, if the dominant tenement has been parcelled out, the servitude will continue to subsist for the benefit of each parcel, although its exercise may not become more onerous for the owner of the servient tenement. However, the servitude may no longer apply to the parcel for which it has lost its utility. On the other hand, because of the above characteristic, according to Article 1131 CC, where the servient tenement has been parcelled out, the servitude will continue to encumber each parcel. However, it will cease to apply to a parcel in respect of which by reason of the nature of the servitude or of an agreement the exercise thereof has ceased.

§3. Personal Servitudes

I. Usufruct on an (Immovable) Thing

A. Concept and Content

238. A personal servitude of usufruct consists in the real right of the usufructuary to make use and collect the fruits of a thing[401] belonging to another without essentially altering the substance of the thing (Article 1142 CC).

399. The relevant agreement must be incorporated in a notarial deed and transcribed.

400. If the servient tenement is not sufficient to serve all the servitudes, the relevant conflict is to be settled in accordance with the principle of temporal priority. If conflict occurs, despite the fact that the servient tenement is sufficient to serve all the servitudes, it is accepted that the provisions governing the undivided joint right should be applied by analogy (see Ap. Georgiades, *PrL*, para. 72 III No. 17, 898).

401. Usufruct may be constituted on immovable things (consumable and non-consumable) movable things, horizontal or vertical ownership, ownership of a mine as well as incorporeal objects. The present unit – in spite of its title, which has been chosen for systematic reasons – is devoted to the

Once the usufruct is constituted, the owner preserves only the power to dispose of his or her right,[402] whereas his or her ownership is stripped of the powers contained in the usufruct.[403] Therefore, the ownership encumbered with usufruct is called 'naked ownership'.

239. In order to define the content of usufruct the following points should be taken into account:

(a) A usufruct must be exercised in such a manner that the substance of the thing is preserved intact (Articles 1142, 1148 CC).
(b) The usufructuary has only the power to make use of the thing and to collect its fruits and not the power to dispose of it, i.e., to alienate it or to encumber it with a real right.
(c) The naked owner preserves only those powers which do not prohibit the exercise of the usufruct, e.g., the power to alienate the thing or to mortgage the naked ownership of the immovable encumbered with the usufruct.
(d) A usufruct extends to the component parts of the thing (Article 953 CC) and, in case of doubt, to its accessories that belong to the naked owner (Article 958 CC).
(e) A usufruct is a divisible right which may be constituted on an undivided ideal share of a thing (Article 1144 CC).
(f) Unless otherwise stipulated, usufructs are not transferable (Articles 1166, 1167 CC).
(g) The usufructuary may be a natural person or a legal entity.
(h) The constitution of a usufruct entails the establishment of a personal relation between the parties involved from which issue, on the one hand, rights and obligations in favour of and against the usufructuary and, on the other hand, corresponding obligations and rights against and in favour of the naked owner or the person who has granted the usufruct.[404]
(i) The principle of temporal priority regulates the relation between the usufruct and the other real rights which probably encumber the same thing, whereas the usufructuary enjoys the advantages which issue from the real servitudes which have been constituted for the service of the immovable encumbered with the usufruct.

---

usufruct of immovable and non-consumable movable things. The usufruct of consumable things and of incorporeal objects will be examined in Part IV.

402. See *supra* para. 163.

403. However, it is possible for an agreement to be reached whereby the owner may preserve some of the powers of the usufructuary which are removed from the usufruct. In this case, the usufruct is said to be 'limited'.

404. When the situation described in Art. 1161 sub-para. b occurs (see *infra* para. 245).

B. Rights and Obligations of the Usufructuary

1. Rights of the Usufructuary

240. The usufructuary has the right to make use of the encumbered thing and to collect its fruits[405] (Article 1142 CC). However, the exercise of this right presupposes the physical dominance of the usufructuary over the thing. Therefore, Article 1147 stipulates that the usufructuary has the right to possess the thing. This article does not conflict with Article 975 CC, according to which the usufructuary is quasi possessor of the thing encumbered. In fact, the usufructuary, on the basis of his or her real right, has quasi possession over the thing, while at the same time he or she exercises on the thing the possession of the naked owner, instead of him or her, as his or her representative.

241. Rights in favour of the usufructuary also issue from the personal relation[406] which exists between him or her and the naked owner. These rights are as follows:

(a) The right to demand confirmation of the condition of the thing through experts appointed by the court and paid by the usufructuary (Article 1145 sub-paragraph a CC).[407]
(b) Where the object of the usufruct is a group of things, the right to demand that the owner cooperates in compiling an inventory of the things (Article 1146 CC).[408]
(c) In the case where the usufructuary is faced with expenses which are not incumbent on him or her, the right to demand their payment, in accordance with the provisions governing the management of another's affairs, by the person who was the owner of the thing at the time the expenses were incurred (Article 1157 sub-paragraph a CC).
(d) The right to remove a construction made by him or her (the usufructuary) on the thing (Article 1157 sub-paragraph b CC).
(e) In the case where the usufruct encumbers a forest, a mine or a quarry, the right to demand from the owner a plan indicating the precise manner of exploitation of the forest, mine or quarry, the cost of which is to be borne by them both (Article 1149 CC).[409]

242. Finally, the usufructuary also possesses the rights deriving from the personal contract which constitutes the just cause of the real contract that led to the constitution of the usufruct.[410]

405. Taking into account that a hoard is not the fruit of a thing, Art. 1151 CC stipulates that the right of the usufructuary does not extend to the share belonging to the owner in a hoard discovered in the thing (on this point see *infra* para. 340).
406. See *supra* para. 239 (under h).
407. The same right belongs to the owner (Art. 1145 sub-para. b CC).
408. The same right belongs to the owner as well. However, the cost is to be borne by the party which made the request for the inventory (Art. 1146 sub-para. b CC).
409. The same right belongs to the owner as well (Art. 1149 CC).
410. See relevantly *supra* para. 56 and *infra* paras 274, 314 and 350.

2. Obligations of the Usufructuary

243. From the real right of usufruct issue not only rights but also the following obligations of the usufructuary:

(a) The obligation to preserve the substance of the thing intact (Article 1142 CC). This obligation is specified in further detail in Article 1148, pursuant to which the usufructuary, in exercising his or her right, is bound: to preserve the economic purpose of the thing in its current form (e.g., not to change a factory into a house); to make use of the thing with care and exploit it in an orderly manner (e.g., to cultivate the land even if the owner used to leave it uncultivated); and, finally, not to introduce substantial changes in the thing (e.g., not to erect a new storey on the building encumbered with usufruct).
(b) The obligation to take care, at his or her own expense, of the repair or restoration of the thing (e.g., to paint the building or to restore the roof) provided these form part of the normal maintenance of the thing (Article 1152 CC).[411]
(c) The obligation to notify the owner without any delay incurred by himself or herself of any deterioration in the thing or of the necessity of an emergency repair or a preventive measure that must be taken against a danger which had not been foreseen or in the case where a third person has usurped a right on the thing. If the owner neglects or refuses to take steps towards averting the deterioration or danger, the usufructuary is to take them at the owner's expense (Article 1153 CC).
(d) The obligation to return to the naked owner the fruits collected by him or her in a manner exceeding the bounds of an orderly exploitation (e.g., because of a predatory exploitation of the thing or a prohibited change of its substance) or as a result of extraordinary circumstances (Article 1150 CC).
(e) The obligation to insure the thing at his or her own expense and to the benefit of the owner[412] against the risk of fire or other dangers during the period of usufruct insofar as such insurance is required by the rules of an orderly exploitation. On the other hand, where the usufructuary has taken over an insured thing, he or she is bound to pay, on the same terms, the insurance premiums for the duration of the usufruct (Article 1154 CC).[413]
(f) The obligation towards the owner to pay during the period of usufruct the ordinary public charges relating to the thing, whereas, if there is a mortgage encumbering the thing at the constitution of the usufruct, he or she also bears an

411. However, the usufructuary is not responsible for any alteration or deterioration in the thing resulting from an orderly exercise of his or her right (Art. 1158 CC).
412. This constitutes a genuine contract for the benefit of a third person (Art. 411 CC).
413. The provision of Art. 1154 CC may be changed by a contrary agreement. However, where the usufructuary does not perform the obligation arising from Art. 1154 CC, the naked owner may insure the thing and demand compensation from the usufructuary, whereas, if the thing has been destroyed on account of a danger against which the usufructuary had an obligation to insure it, the usufructuary must restore to the naked owner the value of the thing at the time of its destruction (on these matters see Ap. Georgiades, *PrL*, para. 75 IV 2e Nos 56, 60, 936, 937;. Papasteriou, *PrL III*, para. 77 II No. 62 et seq., 177–178).

obligation towards the owner to pay during the period of the usufruct the interest on the debt or part thereof in proportion to any other mortgages securing the same debt (Article 1155 CC).

(g) Unless otherwise stipulated, the obligation to provide the owner with security where the exercise of usufruct is carried out in a manner that poses a serious threat to the rights of the owner. A donor who has reserved for himself or herself the right of usufruct is exempted from this obligation (Article 1159 CC). However, where the usufructuary does not or cannot provide the security as ordered or if he or she seriously harms the rights of the owner, the court may, at the owner's request, order the leasing of the thing or appoint a manager (who may also be the owner) entrusted with the exercise of usufruct on behalf of the usufructuary. The management ceases if and when security is finally provided or if the cause that justified the appointment of the manager ceases to exist (Article 1160 CC).

244. In particular, it should be noted that there is an obligation on the part of the usufructuary to restore the thing to the owner on the expiration of the period of usufruct (Article 1161 sub-paragraph a CC). Consequently, at the above time, the (naked) owner has, against the usufructuary (or his or her universal successors), not only the possibility of filing a revendicatory action (Article 1094 CC), but also a personal claim[414] aiming at the restitution of the thing.

Related to the subject under examination here is the provision of Article 1164 CC. This article regulates the fate of the lease of an immovable entered into by a usufructuary[415] in the case where the usufruct of the immovable comes to an end during the period of the lease. According to the same article, in this case, the provisions governing the alienation of a leased immovable during the period of lease apply by analogy, that is, Articles 614 et seq. CC, which permit the following conclusion: in the case where the lease is evidenced by deed bearing a certified date or, where the duration of the lease is longer than nine years, by a notarial deed that has been transcribed, provided that the lease contract does not include any contrary agreement, the (naked) owner assumes the rights and obligations flowing from the lease (Articles 614, 618 CC). Otherwise, he or she has the right to terminate the lease (Article 615 CC).

3. The Fiction of Article 1161 sub-paragraph b CC

245. Article 1161 sub-paragraph b CC, introducing a legal fiction, declares that in the relationship between the usufructuary and the owner of the thing the person who granted the usufruct is to be regarded as owner, in favour of the usufructuary, unless the usufructuary knows that the grantor is not the owner. This applies regardless of whether the above grantor ceased to be owner after the usufruct was constituted (e.g., because he or she transferred the thing encumbered to a third person)

---

414. The relevant claim belongs only to the person who was owner of the thing at the expiration of the period of usufruct (Ap. Georgiades, *PrL*, para. 75 IV 2 No. 73, 940; AP 90/1965, 13 NoB, 1965, 871 [872]).

415. On this possibility see *infra* para. 247.

or, in the area of movables, he or she was not owner even at the time the usufruct was constituted.[416]

The fiction of Article 1161 sub-paragraph b CC is always in favour of the usufructuary who is ignorant[417] of the fact that the grantor of the usufruct is not the owner of the thing. This means that the above usufructuary, even if the grantor of the usufruct is not the owner of the thing, may invoke the latter as owner and, concomitantly, claim that whatever was paid to him or her or was carried out with him or her was undertaken with the real owner and cannot be annulled. The same fiction never works against the usufructuary. Thus, the grantor of the usufruct may not demand that the obligations that the usufructuary bears towards the owner be fulfilled towards him or her if he or she does not prove his or her ownership of the encumbered thing.

4. The Special Prescription of Article 1165

246. According to Article 1165 CC, any claims put forward by an owner against a usufructuary as a result of alteration or deterioration of the thing owned, as well as any claims by the usufructuary for expenses or the removal of a construction are prescribed upon the expiry of a period of six months from the restitution of the thing (and not from the time at which the claim originated; Article 251 CC).

C. Transfer of Usufruct

247. The personal character of usufruct – the constitution of which expresses the good will and the confidence of the owner towards the usufructuary – is not consistent with the possibility of the above real right being an object of free transactions. Hence, Article 1166 sub-paragraph a CC declares that, unless otherwise stipulated, the usufruct is non-transferable.[418] As is obvious, this article contains a non-mandatory rule. Thus, at the constitution of the usufruct or later, the parties may stipulate that the usufruct may be transferable.[419] Furthermore, according to the same article, the exercise of the right of usufruct may be transferred to another for a period not exceeding the duration of the usufruct.[420] This means that, although the real right of usufruct is at first non-transferable, its exercise may be transferred by

---

416. On the possibility of usufruct being constituted on a movable not belonging to the alienator see *infra* para. 350 and n. 630.
417. It is generally accepted that ignorance due to gross negligence is not equated with knowledge (see Ap. Georgiades, *PrL*, para. 75 IV 3 No. 83, 943).
418. The transfer of usufruct, in spite of the relevant prohibition, is invalid. However, this invalid transfer may be interpreted as a valid transfer of the exercise of the right of usufruct.
419. On the issue of whether the usufruct may be stipulated as transferable with or without restrictions (e.g., with the restriction that the usufructuary, A, is entitled to transfer his or her right of usufruct to a third party, B, for a period of time which may not last longer than the length of time of the usufruct of A) see K. Roussos, in *Civil Code*, Vol. VI: *PrL*, ed. Ap. Georgiades & M. Stathopoulos Art. 1166 Nos 9 et seq.
420. See, however, Art. 1164 CC *supra* para. 244.

a personal contract (e.g., donation, sale, hire or loan of use) from the usufructuary (who remains the holder of the relevant real right) to another person.

248. Insofar as a usufruct is at first non-transferable, it cannot be encumbered with a real right as well. Exceptionally, it is possible for a mortgage to be acquired on the usufruct of an immovable (Article 1259 CC) even if the usufruct is non-transferable.[421]

Furthermore, on account of the initially non-transferable character of usufruct, it is disputed whether a usufruct may be an object of seizure. However, bearing in mind the fact that the usufruct may be the object of a mortgage and, concomitantly, the object of a compulsory alienation by the mortgagee, there is no reason why a compulsory alienation should not be made by the other creditors of the usufructuary as well. Therefore, it seems correct to adopt the opinion according to which a usufruct, regardless of whether it has been constituted as transferable or not, may be an object of seizure.[422]

II. Habitation

249. The personal servitude of habitation[423] consists in the real and exclusive right of the beneficiary to use as habitation the building of another or an apartment therein (Article 1183 CC).

From the above definition it may be concluded that the limited real right of habitation is an exclusive right in the sense that the beneficiary may use the building or the apartment[424] of another to the exclusion of its owner.[425] Because of this characteristic the relevant real right is classified as a complete personal servitude like usufruct.

Article 1183 CC, in combination with Article 1184 CC, permits the conclusion that the person entitled to habitation has the right to use the building or the apartment of another, together with his or her family and the domestic staff corresponding to his or her social position, only as a habitation and not as a work-place.[426] This concept of habitation justifies, on the one hand, the opinion that the above right is

421. See also *infra* para. 443.

422. Thus, Court of Appeal of Athens 8358/1991, 40 NoB, 1992, 287 (288); Court of Appeal of Athens 7567/1991, 34 HellD, 1993, 641; Court of Appeal of Piraeus 1175/1990, 33 HellD, 1992, 412; One-member District Court of Thessaloniki 13055/2008, 63 Arm, 2009, 412 (414); One-member District Court of Larissa 1380/1999, 21 D, 2000, 775; One-member District Court of Athens 20415/1997, 39 HellD, 1998, 953; One-member District Court of Chalkis 625/1997, 50 ArchN, 1999, 84. (On this issue see, amongst others, Ap. Georgiades, *PrL*, para. 76 II No. 6, 948, with further references to the above – also adopted by him – and to the contrary opinion.)

423. On this see, in particular, Y. Karibali-Tsiptsiou, *Habitation*, passim; D. Papasteriou, *PrL III*, para. 80 Nos 1 et seq., 223 et seq.

424. Regardless of whether it is an 'apartment' in the sense defined by L. 3741/1929 or L.D. 1024/1971, concerning horizontal and vertical ownership, respectively.

425. The real right of the beneficiary to co-inhabit a building or an apartment of another with the owner may not be characterized as habitation but as a limited personal servitude (see *infra* para. 252).

426. The real right of the beneficiary to use as a work-place the building or the apartment of another constitutes a limited personal servitude.

an undivided right which cannot be established on an ideal share[427] and, on the other hand, the view that the same right may be established only in favour of a natural person.

250. The establishment of habitation aims to serve the housing needs of a certain person and expresses the good will and the confidence of the owner of the building or the apartment towards the above person. Therefore, Article 1185 CC, introducing a mandatory rule, rightly stipulates that the right of habitation cannot be transferred and is extinguished by the demise of the beneficiary. Furthermore, as is generally accepted, the exercise of habitation is also non-transferable.

251. The similarity between habitation and usufruct, insofar as both of them are complete personal servitudes, justifies the provision of Article 1187 CC, according to which, 'in the case of a right of habitation in all other respects the general provisions governing usufruct of immovables shall be applicable by analogy insofar as they are compatible with the nature of the habitation'. Thus, habitation is established, extinguished and protected in the same way as the usufruct of immovables, with Articles 1145, 1147, 1148, 1151–1153, 1155, 1158, 1161, 1165 CC concerning usufruct being applicable by analogy in the area of habitation as well. However, unlike usufruct, in the field of habitation there is no claim for the provision of security and the beneficiary is not bound to secure the building (Article 1186 CC).

III. Limited Personal Servitudes

252. As emerges from Article 1188 CC, a limited personal servitude[428] is a real right which may be constituted on the immovable of another on behalf of a certain person and which affords him or her a certain, and concomitantly limited, authority or usefulness. Such a servitude may also be constituted on whatever forms the basis of a real servitude.

From the above definition it may be concluded[429] that limited personal servitudes, unlike usufruct and habitation, offer their beneficiaries not a complete but a limited authority or usefulness, e.g., the power to make a simple use of the servient tenement (e.g., to use it as a parking place), to make a simple collection of its fruits or to cohabit the encumbered immovable with its owner. However, a limited personal servitude may also have the same content as a real servitude, e.g., the right of

427. Indeed, the establishment of the right of more than one person, e.g., A, B and C, to inhabit an apartment up to an undivided share of one-third for each of them is likely to cause conflict between the rights of the beneficiaries. This is because the inhabitation of the apartment by one of them should exclude the others from the relevant use. However, the establishment of habitation in favour of more than one beneficiary is possible only in the sense that each of the beneficiaries inhabits the whole immovable.

428. For a detailed discussion on limited personal servitudes see I. Sontis, *Limited Personal Servitudes* (Athens: Sakkoulas, 1957), passim [in Greek]; see also D. Papasteriou, *PrL III*, para. 81 Nos 1 et seq., 231 et seq.

429. See, K. Vavouskos, *PrL*, No. 359, 359–360; Ap. Georgiades, *PrL*, para. 82 I 2 Nos 4–5, 992–993; A. Tousis, *PrL*, para. 202, 830–831; Y. Karibali-Tsiptsiou, *Habitation*, 99–102. Compare, however, I. Sontis, *Limited Personal Servitudes*, 185–191.

way, conveyance, drainage or drawing of water, on condition that the relevant servitude is constituted in favour of a certain natural person or legal entity,[430] regardless of his or her relationship to a dominant tenement, which, in the area of limited personal servitudes, does not exist. Therefore, Article 1189 CC, introducing an interpretative rule, stipulates that, in case of doubt, the extent of a limited personal servitude is to be determined by taking into account not the needs of a dominant tenement but the personal needs of the beneficiary.[431] However, the similarity of limited personal servitudes to real servitudes justifies the provision of Article 1191 CC, according to which, in the case of limited personal servitudes and on matters not specifically regulated by law, the provisions governing real servitudes shall be applicable insofar as these are also compatible with the nature of the personal servitudes.

253. Unless otherwise stipulated, a limited personal servitude is not transferable and is extinguished by the demise of the beneficiary or from the moment the legal entity that was the beneficiary disappears (Article 1190 CC). In the case where a limited personal servitude has been stipulated as transferable, its exercise may also be transferred. However, a transferable servitude may not necessarily be inherited and, *vice versa*, a servitude classified as being inherited upon its constitution is not always transferable. Finally, it should be added that, while the duration of a transferable servitude may not exceed the life-span of its initial beneficiary, the same does not occur when the servitude has been stipulated as transferable and inherited as well.[432]

254. A limited personal servitude may be constituted in favour of more than one person. In this case, it depends on the interpretation of the constitutive deed and, in particular, on the nature of the granted usefulness whether or not the relevant real right is undivided or common in ideal shares. Thus, if, for example, from the servitude arises the obligation not to restrict the light or the view of the dominant tenement, the relevant real right is to be undivided. On the other hand, in servitudes which offer the beneficiary the authority to derive products from the servient tenement, the relevant right may be common in ideal shares.[433]

430. See Art. 1190 CC *infra* para. 253.
431. As well as the needs of the members of his or her family and clients.
432. On all of these points see Ap. Georgiades, *PrL*, para. 82 II 4 No. 19, 998.
433. On all of these points see Ap. Georgiades, *PrL*, para. 82 II 2 No. 17, 997.

Part IV. Movable Property

Chapter 1. General Classification

255. The term 'movable property' is used in the present monograph to denote the real rights relating to movable things and incorporeal objects.[434] Examples of these real rights are: (a) ownership and, of its specific types, co-ownership, which may have as their object a movable or an immovable thing; (b) usufruct, which may be constituted on movable or immovable things and on incorporeal objects; (c) pledges, which may have as their object a movable thing or an incorporeal object. Finally, it should be borne in mind that the usufruct of an immovable may be the object of a mortgage.[435]

256. Of the aforementioned real rights, pledges will be examined in a separate part (Part VII) together with mortgages.[436] On the other hand, whatever was stated in the previous part (Part III) about ownership, co-ownership and usufruct on immovables characterizes relevant rights *mutatis mutandis* even when they pertain to movables.[437] Consequently, in the present section only topics which display peculiar characteristics will be discussed: namely, usufruct on consumable things or quasi usufruct (Chapter 2) and usufruct on incorporeal objects (Chapter 3), including usufruct on rights and claims, usufruct on property or enterprises, usufruct on corporate participation and usufruct on negotiable instruments.

257. However, before the aforementioned issues are discussed, the following points ought to be made clear:

(a) The term 'movable property' is used in this book instead of the term 'personal property' or 'chattels', which is used by English law to denote real rights in all types of property, except land, and leases.[438]
(b) The division of personal property (or chattels) into 'chattels personal', including real rights in all types of property except land, and 'chattels real', in the

434. See also *supra* para. 17.
435. See also *supra* para. 50 (under c).
436. See also *supra* para. 158.
437. Differences occur chiefly in the areas of acquisition and protection (see *infra* paras 271 et seq., 366 et seq.).
438. See also *supra* para. 17.

sense of leasehold interests in land, which is made in English law,[439] is unknown in Greece.[440]

(c) The distinction made by English law between 'choses in possession' and 'choses in action' does not apply in Greek law.[441] To be precise, according to English law, chattels personal are classified as 'choses in possession' or 'choses in action', according to whether they can be the objects of possession or only the objects of a legal action. The term 'choses in action' was first applied to debts. However, the term has been extended to all other intangible forms of property, such as patents and copyright. Therefore, as is generally accepted, the above distinction is better expressed as one between tangible and intangible things. Furthermore, it should be borne in mind that, according to English law: (i) tangible movables other than money are called 'goods'; (ii) money receives special treatment and is therefore distinguished from other movables; (iii) collective entities, such as the capital of a company or groups of investments managed by trustees are best called 'funds'.[442]

(d) The distinction between 'legal' and 'equitable' interests[443] does not exist in Greece, not even in the area of movables.

---

439. See E.H. Burn, *Real Property*, 36; F.H. Lawson & B. Rudden, *PrL*, 19; J.G. Riddal, *Land Law*, 51; R. Sexton, *Land Law*, 20–21 (as well as, 3, 202 et seq. concerning leases).

440. See, however, *supra* para. 159 (under e), where the institution of *superficies*, which has been reintroduced to the Greek legal system, is compared with the English institution of 'leasehold'.

441. On the concept of a thing, the types and legal treatment of groups of objects and the classification of things, according to Greek law, see *supra* paras 57 et seq.

442. On all these points see, in particular, F.H. Lawson & B. Rudden, *PrL*, 20 et seq.

443. On which see *supra* para. 159 (under b).

Chapter 2. Usufruct on Consumable Things (Quasi Usufruct)

258. Consumable things are not susceptible of usufruct in the sense of Article 1142 CC. Indeed, the right of the usufructuary to make use of and to collect the fruits of the encumbered thing while integrally preserving the substance of the thing is not reconcilable with the nature of consumable things, the use of which, according to their very purpose, consists in their consumption or alienation.[444] Thus, the term 'usufruct of consumable things' denotes a legal relation which is not identifiable with the usufruct of Article 1142 CC and which, therefore, is characterized as 'quasi usufruct'.

259. Quasi usufruct is regulated by Articles 1174–1175 CC. The first of these articles declares that, unless otherwise stipulated, where the object of usufruct is a consumable thing, the usufructuary becomes owner thereof, while, upon the expiry of the usufruct, he or she is obliged to restore, according to the choice of the person who granted the usufruct (and who has *ex lege* a relevant personal claim), either the value of the consumable as at the time of constitution of the usufruct or other things of the same quantity or quality. The second of the above articles states that, in the case of consumable things, the usufructuary, unless otherwise stipulated, is bound to provide security before their delivery, except if, on the one hand, the things take the form of money that has been deposited in a safe bank or other credit institution under reservation of the right of usufruct or, on the other hand, the usufructuary is the donor who has retained the usufruct for himself or herself.

However, in the area of quasi usufruct, some of the general provisions governing usufruct also apply by analogy. Examples of such provisions are Articles 1145 CC (concerning confirmation of the condition of the thing), 1146 CC (dealing with the inventory of a group of things), 1167 and 1169 CC (referring to extinction of usufruct by demise and declaration of renunciation by the usufructuary).[445] However, it ought to be noted that quasi usufruct is constituted by means of a juridical act *inter vivos* or *mortis causa* and not by *usucaption*.[446]

---

444. See *supra* para. 68.
445. Quasi usufruct is also extinguished by the fulfilment of the resolutory condition or the expiration of the resolutory term upon which it was constituted (Arts 202, 210 CC). On the other hand, the destruction of consumable things, the disuse and the impossibility of exercising usufruct (Art. 1170 CC) do not entail extinction of quasi usufruct in that they are not reconcilable with its nature. In addition, considering the fact that the usufructuary becomes owner of the consumable thing (Art. 1174 CC), it is correct to accept that Art. 1168 CC, concerning extinction of usufruct on account of merger (confusion) of the usufruct and of the right of ownership in the same person, does not apply in the area of quasi usufruct. However, the extinction of the relevant personal relation by merger (Art. 453 CC) is possible (on all these points see Ap. Georgiades, *PrL*, para. 76 VII 2 No. 36, 959–960).
446. See Ap. Georgiades, *PrL*, para. 76 VII 2 No. 35, 959.

Chapter 3. Usufruct on Incorporeal Objects

§1. Usufruct on Rights

260. The usufruct on (real or personal, absolute or relative) rights (Article 1178 CC) does not constitute a real right in the exact meaning of the term. This is because it does not have as its object a thing in the legal sense. Nevertheless, insofar as it offers to the beneficiary a direct (immediate) and absolute power over the encumbered right, it constitutes a right which possesses the characteristics of a real one.[447]

261. The usufruct of a right is constituted in the same manner as the transfer of the right (Article 1178 sub-paragraph b CC). However, non-fruitful[448] and non-transferable rights may not become the object of a usufruct (Article 1178 sub-paragraph c CC). Thus, the following, among others, are susceptible of usufruct: life annuity,[449] rights of intellectual property, rights deriving from participation in a partnership, rights in the area of so-called industrial property, pledges and mortgages with a secured claim and real servitudes with the dominant tenement. On the other hand, claims that cannot be assigned, habitation, limited personal servitudes, membership of an association, the claim of an employer against a worker for performance of work and claims for pecuniary reparation on account of moral prejudice are some examples of rights which are not susceptible of usufruct.

262. In the area of usufruct of rights the provisions governing the usufruct of things apply by analogy in all other respects so long as a different conclusion does not result from the law or the nature of the usufruct of the right (Article 1182 CC). Such provisions are contained, for example, in Articles 1166 (concerning the non-transferable character of usufruct) and 1167 et seq. CC (concerning the extinction of usufruct).

§2. Usufruct on Claims

263. Usufruct on claims, that is, on personal rights, is a type of usufruct of right. Therefore, in the area of the present type of usufruct whatever was stated in the previous paragraph about usufruct on rights also applies.[450] However, mention should

447. See Ap. Georgiades, *PrL*, para. 77 I 1 No. 1, 961–962 in combination with para. 78 I 4 No. 7, 86.
448. This characteristic is not provided for by law. It derives partly from the general principle according to which a servitude must be useful to its beneficiary (see *supra* para. 229 [under d]) and partly from the concept of usufruct as a right that offers to the holder the power to make use of and to collect the fruits of the encumbered thing or right (see Ap. Georgiades, *PrL*, para. 77 I 2 No. 2, 962).
449. According to Art. 1181 CC the usufructuary of a life annuity has the right to collect the periodic instalments that befit the right encumbered with the usufruct.
450. The usufruct on a claim is constituted in the same manner as the transfer of the claim (Art. 1178 sub-para. b CC), that is, by assignment (Art. 455 CC). However, the debtor's notification of the relevant constitution is also required for the usufructuary to be able, on the one hand, to exercise

be made of Articles 1179–1180 CC, which are devoted to usufruct of claims in particular. These articles makes it clear that the usufructuary of a claim has the right to enjoy its fruits (Article 1179 paragraph 1 CC), e.g., to enjoy the interest of a money claim. The same articles, distinguishing between claims which are pecuniary and those which are not, solve the problem of their collection as follows.

Where the claim is not pecuniary and has as its object the provision of another item of property, e.g., the transfer of ownership of a thing, the usufructuary is the only one who has the right to collect the claim (Article 1179 paragraph 2 sub-paragraph a CC). However, from the time of collection he or she becomes usufructuary of the thing (Article 1179 paragraph 2 sub-paragraph b CC), which, from now on, belongs to the creditor.[451]

Where the usufruct relates to a pecuniary claim, in conformity with the non-mandatory rule[452] of Article 1180 CC, both the creditor and the usufructuary have the right and the obligation to cooperate in order jointly to collect the principal of the debt. Instead of, or after, such a collection each of them is entitled to demand the safe deposit of the principal in an interest-bearing account under reservation of the right of the usufructuary, who is the one who determines the kind of deposit. However, from the collection of the claim onwards the ownership and the usufruct of the relevant amount of money belong, respectively, to the creditor and the usufructuary.

§3. Usufruct on Property or Enterprises

264. The possibility of usufruct being constituted on an existing[453] property is recognized by law and specifically by Articles 367 and 1156 CC. From Article 367 CC it emerges that a contract for the constitution of usufruct must be incorporated in a notarial deed.[454] On the other hand, Article 1156 CC permits the conclusion that the usufructuary is bound, on the one hand, to pay the interest which has accrued on the owner's debts at the time of the constitution of the usufruct and, on the other, to make periodic payments of alimony based on an obligation of the owner that had already arisen by the time the usufruct was constituted.

As regards the present type of usufruct, the following should be stressed: (a) that it is constituted on each of the objects which make up the property insofar as the latter, as a whole, does not constitute a thing in the legal sense;[455] (b) that, in the

---

his or her rights relating to the claim towards the debtor and, on the other, to defend his or her usufruct against third parties (see Art. 460 CC).

451. The method of collection varies according to the type of the encumbered claim. Thus, where the claim involves the transfer of ownership of an immovable, Art. 1033 CC applies (see *infra* paras 271 et seq.), while, where the object of the claim is the transfer of ownership of a movable, Art. 1034 CC applies (see *infra* paras 308 et seq.). However, in both cases, the usufructuary participates in the relevant real contracts in the name of the creditor who is the one who acquires the naked ownership of the thing.
452. Ap. Georgiades, *PrL*, para. 77 II 3 No. 22, 968.
453. And not future property (Art. 366 CC).
454. However, the constitution of usufruct on a property by testament is also possible and indeed usual in practice (see Ap. Georgiades, *PrL*, para. 78 I 2 No. 3, 970).
455. See *supra* para. 61.

area of usufruct on a property, Article 479 CC applies by analogy. This means that the creditors of the property, even after the constitution of the usufruct, are entitled to take in hand any object belonging to the property for the satisfaction of those of their claims which originated before the constitution of usufruct.[456]

265. An enterprise, like a property, cannot be the object of a real right as an economic unity.[457] Therefore, in this case, the relevant real right is constituted separately on each of the things or rights which make up the enterprise.[458]

In all other respects, in the area of usufruct on an enterprise,[459] the provisions governing the usufruct of a thing or a right (such as Articles 1148, 1152, 1157, 1158, 1163, 1174, 1179, 1180 CC) and the provision of Article 479 CC apply by analogy.[460]

§4. Usufruct on Corporate Participation

266. In the area of partnerships[461] without legal personality corporate participation is distinguished into corporate capacity and corporate share. The former refers to the administrative rights and the rights of the partner to receive a share of the profits of the company or the product of its liquidation, while corporate share denotes the per-percentage participation of the partner in the common property of the partnership.

Following the prevailing opinion, according to which corporate capacity (in the sense above) is transferable, it must be accepted that the latter is susceptible of usufruct as well and that the usufructuary has all the rights and obligations arising from the corporate capacity. On the other hand, as corporate shares are not transferable until the partnership's liquidation is terminated (Article 761 CC), it must be accepted that corporate shares are not susceptible of usufruct.

The distinction between corporate capacity and corporate share has no practical significance in the field of partnerships with legal personality, where the property of the company belongs to the body corporate of the company. Nevertheless, the relevant distinction is drawn in the above field, too, although, in this case, the term 'corporate share' is used to denote the right of the partner to receive a share of the profits of the company or the product of its liquidation. This means that in the said case the corporate share is based on a right which is detached from the rights which make up the corporate capacity. This right is susceptible of separate transfer and concomitantly susceptible of usufruct.

---

456. Ap. Georgiades, *PrL*, para. 78 I 3 No. 6, 971.
457. See *supra* para. 62.
458. It is accepted that the de facto relationships of an enterprise, e.g., its experience, clients, fame and organizational infrastructure in general, are susceptible of usufruct as well. This is because, as a whole, they make up a particular right (see Ap. Georgiades, *PrL*, para. 78 II 2 No. 11, 972–973).
459. For a detailed treatment of this point see K. Cristianakou-Fotiadi, *Usufruct on Enterprise* (Athens: Sakkoulas, 1994), passim [in Greek].
460. See Ap. Georgiades, *PrL*, para. 78 II 3 Nos 12 et seq., 973–974.
461. On the subject of usufruct on corporate participation in the area of partnerships see, amongst others, Ap. Georgiades, *PrL*, para. 79 II Nos 2 et seq., 976–978.

267. In the area of limited liability companies (E.P.E.)[462] corporate participation is susceptible of usufruct. This is because, according to law (Article 28 paragraph 1 Law 3190/1955), subject to any alternative provision in the articles of association, the corporate share (in the meaning of corporate participation) is transferable. The constitution of usufruct, in this case, presupposes a notarial deed (Article 28 paragraph 3 Law 3190/1955) and registration in the register of the partners (Article 25 L. 3190/1955).

§5. Usufruct on Negotiable Instruments

268. The Civil Code devotes specific articles, namely Articles 1176–1177 CC, solely to usufruct of title deeds in bearer form. From these articles emerge the following points:

(a) in the present case, the provisions governing usufruct of a thing apply insofar as they are compatible with the nature of title deeds in bearer form;[463]
(b) unless otherwise stipulated, the usufructuary is bound to provide security before the delivery of the title deeds, except if they have been deposited in a safe bank or other credit institution under reservation of the right of usufruct or if the usufructuary is a donor who has retained the usufruct for himself or herself;
(c) the usufructuary is entitled to possess, without providing security, the warrants for interest or dividends which remain attached to the title deeds;
(d) in the case of usufruct on shares of a company,[464] the usufructuary, unless otherwise stipulated, has the right to participate in the meetings of the shareholders of that company.

269. Registered title deeds are also susceptible of usufruct[465] providing that their transfer is not forbidden. The usufruct on them is treated like the usufruct of a right. This is because registered title deeds are characterized by absence of the element of complete incorporation, in the sense that the right which derives from the title deed surpasses the right which exists on the title deed.[466] Consequently, the usufruct on registered title deeds is constituted in the same manner as their transfer (Article 1178 sub-paragraph b CC), while the claims incorporated in the title deed are to be

---

462. On the subject of usufruct on corporate participation in the field of limited liability companies (E.P.E.) see, amongst others, Ap. Georgiades, *PrL*, para. 79 III Nos 10 et seq., 978.
463. Thus, for example, whereas Art. 1143 CC concerning the constitution of usufruct applies in this specific case, Art. 1170 CC does not apply and consequently the destruction or loss of the encumbered title deed does not entail the extinction of usufruct.
464. While the bearer shares are susceptible of usufruct in any case, the constitution of usufruct on registered shares may be liable to restrictions (see Ap. Georgiades, *PrL*, para. 80 IV No. 8, 981). However, as the usufruct of registered shares is substantially the usufruct of a right, in this area Arts 1178 et seq. CC applies (see also following para. 269).
465. On the subject of usufruct of registered title deeds see, amongst others, Ap. Georgiades, *PrL*, para. 80 II Nos 4–5, 980.
466. See, in particular, A. Kiandou-Pampouki, *Law of Negotiable Instruments*, 5th edn (Thessaloniki: Sakkoulas, 1997), para. 4 I, 16 [in Greek].

collected from the usufructuary in accordance with the provisions of Articles 1179 et seq. CC.

270. Finally, title deeds made payable in order (e.g., a bill) are also susceptible of usufruct.[467] The usufruct on these is constituted in the same manner as their transfer (Article 1178 sub-paragraph b CC), whereas the pecuniary claim incorporated in the title deed is to be collected from the creditor and the usufructuary jointly (Article 1180 CC). This method of collection is binding on the debtor only where the capacity of the bearer of the title deed as usufructuary derives from the title. However, the security of the interests of the creditor who granted the usufruct requires, in this specific case, Article 1176 CC (concerning the obligation of the usufructuary to provide security) to be applied by analogy.

467. On the subject of usufruct of title deeds made payable in order see, amongst others, Ap. Georgiades, *PrL*, para. 80 III Nos 6–7, 981.

Part V. Acquisition and Loss of Property Rights

Chapter 1. Acquisition and Loss of Ownership

§1. Acquisition and Loss of Ownership on Immovables

I. Acquisition by Contract

271. Article 1033 CC declares that 'for the transfer of the ownership of an immovable agreement between the owner and the acquirer is required to the effect that ownership is transmitted to the latter for a just cause'. The same article adds that 'the agreement shall be incorporated in a notarial deed and is subject to transcription'. From this article it may be concluded that the valid transfer of ownership of an immovable presupposes:[468]

(a) the ownership of the alienator;
(b) agreement to the effect that the ownership is transmitted;
(c) a just cause;
(d) a notarial deed; and
(e) transcription.

With regard to the above conditions, the following should also be noted.

468. In addition, the general conditions which are necessary for the valid constitution of any juridical act must also be fulfilled, such as the capacity to carry out legal transactions, the coincidence of will and declaration and will without defects. Furthermore, it should be borne in mind that restrictions to the transfer of ownership of immovables are introduced by special laws. Examples of such laws are: (a) the law which inhibits or restricts juridical acts related to immovables located in border regions of the State (Arts 24–32 L. 1892/1990 as it is in force today); (b) the legislation concerning town-planning (L. 947/1979 and L. 1337/1983) and (c) the legislation concerning forests (L. 998/1979 as modified by Art. 28 paras 14, 15, 18 L. 2644/1998).

A. *Ownership of the Alienator*

272. The Civil Code, on the basis of the principle *nemo plus juris ad alium transferre potest quam ipse haberet*, which governs every derivative acquisition,[469] declares that the alienator must be owner[470] of the transmitted immovable.[471] A general exception to this rule, similar to the one mentioned in Article 1036 CC which refers to movables,[472] is not recognized by the law. However, certain deviations from the same rule are recognized. Thus, Article 239 CC determines the conditions according to which the disposal of property by someone not entitled to do so may be valid. Articles 1963 CC and 822 CCProc declare the conditions according to which a juridical act entered into by a person indicated as heir, *fideicommissarius* or legatee in an inaccurate or revoked certificate of inheritance is valid. Articles 1918 and 2021 CC refer, respectively, to the possibility of the liquidator of a succession or of the executor of a will alienating immovables belonging to the succession. Article 147 BC lays down the conditions under which the trustee receiver in bankruptcy may alienate immovables belonging to a bankrupt individual. Finally, Article 13 paragraph 3 sub-paragraph b of L. 2664/1998 prescribes the conditions under which a third party may validly acquire a right from a person who appears in the land register as a beneficiary or from his or her heirs.[473]

B. *Agreement*

273. Although Article 1033 CC, in imitation of paragraph 925 BGB, uses the term 'agreement', there is no doubt that the relevant agreement forms the real contract which aims at the transfer of ownership.

C. *Just cause*

274. The real dispositive contract of Article 1033 CC is causal, in the sense that the production of its legal consequences presupposes the existence of a valid just cause without which ownership is not transferred.[474] The just cause lies in another

469. Derivative acquisition is that which is based on the preexisting right of another person. See also *supra* paras 100, 115.
470. Ownership (and also power of disposal) must exist not only on the date the relevant agreement is concluded but also on the date it is transcribed. This is because ownership is transmitted from the date of the transcription (see *infra* para. 277).
471. On the issue of whether the absence of ownership in the alienator results in the non-existence, nullification or non-effectiveness of the agreement, that is, of the real contract of Art. 1033 CC see D. Papasteriou, *The Real Contract of Art. 1033 Sub-para. a CC* (Thessaloniki: Sakkoulas, 1987), 13 et seq., 34 [in Greek] (who maintains that such absence implies incomplete conclusion of the relevant contract). See also Y. Karibali-Tsiptsiou, *The Approval of Juridical Acts* (Thessaloniki: Sakkoulas, 1990), 139 et seq., 141–143 [in Greek].
472. See *infra* paras 315 et seq.
473. See also *infra* para. 31 and n. 69.
474. This situation may not be changed by a different stipulation between the contracting parties because Art. 1033 CC is a mandatory rule.

juridical act and, as a rule, in a personal-promissory contract, such as contracts of sale, exchange and donation or the contract of a parental grant.[475] From this contract arises the obligation for the ownership to be transferred through the relevant real dispositive contract. This means that the just cause of the real dispositive contract of Article 1033 CC is the performance of the above personal-promissory contract, which is concluded before or at the same time as the real one.[476]

The causal character of the real contract of Article 1033 places the security of transactions at risk. This is because the invalidity of the juridical act which contains the just cause entails invalidity of the relevant real contract[477] and inhibits the transfer of ownership. On the other hand, the system of transcription registers adopted by the Civil Code – unlike the land registry system[478] – fails to provide general protection for the person who, aiming to acquire ownership of an immovable and trusting the transcription registers, deals with a non-owner while believing him or her to be owner.[479]

D. Notarial Deed

275. According to Article 1033 CC, an agreement between an owner and an acquirer, to the effect that ownership is transmitted for a just cause, must be incorporated in a notarial deed. This means that a notarial deed is required not only for the real contract of Article 1033 CC but also for the juridical act that contains it's just cause.[480] The notarial deed is constitutive in form. Consequently, its absence entails nullification of the relevant juridical acts (Article 159 paragraph 1 CC).

276. The following are also subject to incorporation in a notarial deed:

(a) a binder (Article 166 CC), that is, an agreement whereby the parties involved undertake to conclude in the future a contract, for example, of sale of an immovable;

475. On this subject see also *supra* para. 56.
476. However, in the case where the just cause of the real contract is a personal contract, the latter, as a rule, is concluded at the same time as the real one and is incorporated in the same notarial deed. Therefore, in the wording of the relevant notarial deeds, the phrase 'sells and transfers' or 'donates and transfers' is usually used in order to indicate the simultaneous conclusion of the above two juridical acts.
477. On the issue of whether the invalidity of the just cause entails the non-existence, nullification or non-effectiveness of the real contract of Art. 1033 CC see D. Papasteriou, *The Real Contract of Art. 1033 Sub-para. a CC*, 62 et seq. and chiefly, 117 et seq.; D. Papasteriou, *PrL I*, para. 8 II Nos 39 et seq., 141 et seq. (Papasteriou maintains that the invalidity of the just cause entails incomplete conclusion of the relevant real contract).
478. See *infra* para. 30, as well as *infra* paras 31 and 272.
479. See *infra* para. 30.
480. See also Art. 369 CC according to which 'contracts aiming at the constitution, transfer, alteration or extinction of real rights on immovables must be drawn up in the presence of a notary'.

(b) an optional agreement[481] and the declaration to the effect that an optional right is being exercised;
(c) a declaration to the effect that a power of attorney is given, in the case where the transfer of the immovable is to be made by a representative of the alienator or of the acquirer (Article 217 paragraph 2 CC);[482]
(d) the owner's consent or approval, in the case of alienation of an immovable by a non-owner (Article 239 CC);
(e) the approval of the person represented, in the case where the transfer of an immovable is made in the name of another without power of attorney (Article 229 CC).

E. Transcription

277. A condition of effect (*conditio juris*) for the real contract of Article 1033 CC is its transcription in the transcription registers of the district in which the immovable is located.[483] This means that ownership is transmitted from the time of transcription,[484] while, before this time, the relevant real contract, although constituted, does not produce its legal consequences (Article 1198 CC). Concomitantly, before transcription, the ownership of the immovable continues to belong to the alienator who has the legal power to transfer it to another person.

A transcription is an act of public authority that may be requested, at any time,[485] by any person who can show a lawful interest therein (Article 1194 paragraph 2 CC). On the other hand, transcription serves the principle of publicity in the area of immovables.[486]

II. Transfer by Death

278. Upon the death (or the declaration of disappearance) of a natural person (decedent), his or her property as a whole (estate) is transmitted, by virtue of the

481. Namely, an agreement by virtue of which one of the contracting parties is granted the right (optional right) to constitute a definite contract (e.g., purchase and acquisition of ownership of an immovable) by a unilateral declaration addressed to the other party.
482. Subsequent to the Plenary Session of AP 104/1975, 23 NoB, 1975, 653, it is generally accepted that a notarial deed is not required for the contract of mandate (Art. 713 CC) for the purchase of an immovable; see also AP 1925/2006, NOMOS; Court of Appeal of Athens 529/2009, EfAD 2009, 444 (446).
483. See also Art. 1192 point 1 CC, as well as Art. 12 para. 1 point a of L. 2664/1998 concerning, within the framework of the land registry system, the registration on the record sheet of the land register which is devoted to the relevant immovable.
484. Without delivery of possession being necessary. However, delivery also has legal consequences. Thus, in the case where possession is delivered before the transcription, the purchaser is entitled to repulse the revendicatory action of the owner-seller by invoking the plea deriving from Art. 1095 CC (see *infra* para. 373). Also, according to Art. 522 para. 1 CC, from the time of delivery of the sold immovable, the purchaser bears the risk of its destruction by a fortuitous event or its deterioration. Finally, the possibility of the possessor acquiring ownership by *usucaption* should also be borne in mind (see *infra* paras 280 et seq.).
485. Provided that, in the meantime, the immovable has not been transferred to a third party.
486. On this issue see, in details, *supra* para. 30.

law or a will (testament), to one or more natural persons or legal entities (heirs).[487] This hereditary succession, like transfer by contract, leads to a derivative acquisition of ownership. However, unlike the latter, this is a universal and not a particular succession. To be specific:

Provided the heirs, by virtue of a will (testament) or the law,[488] are alive or have at least been conceived at the time of devolution, namely at the time of the decedent's death,[489] the estate's assets and liabilities, as a whole, pass to them immediately at death. This process takes place automatically, by the operation of the law alone, before the heir has taken any step to put himself or herself in possession of the estate or has expressed any intention of accepting it. Nevertheless, insofar as the decedent's estate passes to the heir with all its advantages and its burdens and it is unified with the personal property of the heir, so that the latter is personally liable for the charges and debts of the succession, the law offers him or her the right to renounce the succession[490] within a certain period of time.[491] Owing to this right, at the time of devolution, the acquisition of the estate is temporary. The relevant acquisition becomes final as soon as the right of renunciation ceases to exist either because the period specified for the renunciation has lapsed or because the heir has accepted the estate. The acceptance takes the form of an informal, explicit or implicit,[492] declaration by the temporary heir that he or she wishes to become the definitive heir. However, if immovables are part of the estate, in order for the heir to acquire ownership or any other real right on them, the declaration of acceptance must be expressed in a public document and must be transcribed in the transcription registers of the district in which the immovable is located. By the transcription, the

487. The consequences of the death of a natural person with regard to the sum of the rights and obligations which he or she possessed as long as he or she was alive are regulated by the Law of Inheritance, which is covered mainly by Arts 1710–2035 CC.

488. According to Greek law, hereditary succession is determined either by will (testament) or by law, through its provisions concerning intestate succession and forced heirship. Greek law declares null and void contracts of inheritance (Art. 368 CC). With regard to testamentary devolution, it should be borne in mind that Greek law distinguishes between ordinary and extraordinary wills. The forms of ordinary will are: the holographic, the public and the mystic (secret), while extraordinary wills are: wills made at sea, military wills and wills made during a blockade (see Arts 1716 et seq. CC). On the other hand, with regard to intestate succession, it should be noted that Greek law recognizes six classes of intestate heir. The first five include persons related to the decedent by parental or marital ties, while in the sixth class the heir is the State (see Arts 1813 et seq. CC). An important provision is made by Art. 1819 CC, in accordance with which a relative may not be called upon to inherit so long as another relative takes precedence as heir. Finally, forced heirship (Arts 1825 et seq. CC) occurs in the case where the existing will makes no provision for a forced heir, that is, a descendant, a parent or the surviving spouse of the testator (on this issue see *supra* para. 40 [under g/iii]).

489. See Art. 1711 CC.

490. The law also offers an heir the right to accept the succession under the benefit of inventory. In this case, the heir is liable for the charges and debts of the succession only up to the net value of the estate, which constitutes a group of assets which is distinct from the personal property of the heir (see Arts 1902 et seq. CC).

491. The power of renunciation lapses four months after the heir learns of the devolution and its reason. In the case of devolution by will this period does not commence before the publication of the will. However, the aforementioned period is extended to one year if the decedent lived abroad or if the heir learned of the devolution while living abroad (Art. 1847 CC).

492. Thus, for example, the succession is deemed to be accepted after the expiration of the period of time set for the renunciation (Art. 1850 sub-para. b CC).

ownership or other real right is deemed to have been transmitted to the heir from the time of death of the decedent.[493]

279. The death of a person sometimes entails the transfer of benefits in favour of other successors than heirs. More specifically:

(a) We have already referred to the institution of *fideicommissum* (Articles 1923 et seq. CC) and we have pointed out that the *fideicommissarius* is a future heir and, concomitantly, a universal successor of the testator, who acquires the decedent's estate indirectly, that is, through the heir burdened with the *fideicommissum*.[494] In this place, we should only stress that, as the *fideicommissarius* is a heir, everything that has been stated about the acquisition of the decedent's estate by the heir also applies in the area of *fideicommissum*.[495]
(b) Moreover, the testator may confer a pecuniary advantage on a person without instituting him or her as his or her heir (legacy) (Articles 1714, 1967 et seq. CC). Consequently, the beneficiary (legatee) is not a universal successor, like the heir, but a particular one. Usually, the testator burdens the appointed heir (or the *fideicommissarius* or the legatee in the case of a sub-legacy) with the obligation to give the legacy to the legatee.[496] On the other hand, the legatee either has a personal right to claim the object bequeathed from the burdened person (Article 1995 CC) or acquires the said object immediately and *ipso jure* if the conditions of Article 1996 sub-paragraph a CC concur.[497] In any event, if the object of the legacy is the ownership of an immovable or any other real right thereon, the acquisition of the relevant right by the legatee presupposes an explicit acceptance of the legacy and fulfilment of the conditions that need to be met for the acquisition of a real right on an immovable by the heir.[498]
(c) Furthermore, the testator may obligate an heir or legatee to perform something (e.g., to distribute an amount of money for the publication of a book) without conferring on the beneficiary the right to demand the relevant performance (charge, modus; Articles 1715, 2011 et seq. CC). However, the enforcement of this testamentary burden may be demanded by the executor of the will, the heir, the coheir, the person immediately benefiting from the forfeiture of the person originally burdened with the charge or the State, if the performance of the charge concerns the public interest (Article 2014 CC).
(d) Finally, mention should be made of the *donatio mortis causa*. This is a donation which is concluded on the suspensive condition of the donor's predecease or of

493. On these points see in combination Arts 1846, 1193, 1195, 1198 and 1199 CC. See also Art. 12 para. 1 point vii and paras 3 and 4 of L. 2664/1998 within the framework of the land registry system.
494. See also *supra* para. 41.
495. See *supra* para. 278.
496. The legacy is nullified if the legatee dies before the testator (Art. 1978 CC).
497. That is, so long as the person burdened with the legacy is an heir, the object of the legacy is a specific thing or right belonging to the testator and the testator has not made different arrangements.
498. See *supra* para. 278 and Arts 1193, 1195, 1198, 1199 CC, as well as Art. 1996 CC. See also Art. 12 para. 1 point vii and paras 3 and 4 of L. 2664/1998 within the framework of the land registry system.

the simultaneous death of both parties contracting to the act of donation, without, in the meantime, the donee having the enjoyment of the objects donated (Articles 2032 et seq. CC). Although the legal consequences of the *donatio mortis causa* take effect after the donor's death, it seems correct to accept that it is a juridical act *inter vivos* and not *mortis causa*. This applies because as long as the donor is alive the donee has a right of expectation and also because the donee does not acquire anything from the decedent's estate. Insofar as the provisions governing donations apply in the area of *donatio mortis causa*, unless the law ordains otherwise (Article 2032 CC), the constitution of *donatio mortis causa* presupposes a notarial deed, regardless of whether it refers to movables or immovables (Article 498 CC). However, in the area of immovables, a transcription is also required in the transcription registers of the district in which the immovable is located (Article 1192 point 1 CC[499]).

III. Acquisition by *Usucaption* (Acquisitive Prescription)

A. *Concept, Justification and Types*

280. Usucaption entails, on certain conditions, original acquisition of ownership[500] on a movable or an immovable thing by its possessor. Hence, the institution of *usucaption* settles old outstanding uncertainties concerning ownership on certain things by recognizing real situations which have evolved in connection with these things over a relatively long period of time. In this way, on the one hand, diligent possessors are encouraged, while on the other, owners who have abandoned their property for many years to the prejudice of security in trade and the national economy in general are discouraged.

Usucaption leads to prescription, in the sense of extinction, of the previous owner's ownership, while, at the same time, it entails the constitution of a new ownership in favour of the possessor. Therefore, *usucaption* is usually described as 'acquisitive prescription'.

281. Usucaption is distinguished into two types: ordinary and extraordinary. According to Articles 1041 and 1043 CC, ordinary *usucaption* presupposes possession of the thing, good faith, a lawful or putative title and the lapse of a certain period of time. On the other hand, according to Article 1045 CC, extraordinary *usucaption* presupposes only possession of the thing during a certain period of time. However, both ordinary and extraordinary *usucaption* presuppose a thing susceptible of them.

The following sections examine the prerequisites and the results of ordinary and extraordinary *usucaption*.

---

499. See also Art. 12 para. 1 point a of L. 2664/1998 within the framework of the land registry system.

500. Original acquisition is that which is not based on the right of another person. Thus, in the area of original acquisition, neither predecessors in title nor successors exist. See also *supra* paras 100, 113.

B. Prerequisites of Ordinary Usucaption

1. Thing Susceptible of *Usucaption*

282. Not everything is susceptible of (ordinary or extraordinary) *usucaption*. Indeed, there are things which are not susceptible of and things which are exempted from *usucaption* and, in addition, things which on account of their nature may not become objects of *usucaption*. To be specific:

According to Article 1054 CC, things which are out of commerce[501] may not become objects either of ordinary or extraordinary *usucaption*.

Furthermore, there are things which, for certain reasons, are exempted by law from (ordinary or extraordinary) *usucaption*, although in principle they could be susceptible of the latter. This category includes things belonging to persons placed under parental care, tutelage or judicial assistance as long as these legal situations last (Article 1055 CC).[502] The category also includes immovables belonging to the State, municipalities or communal authorities and the Church.

Finally, insusceptible of *usucaption* on account of their nature are: (a) the essential component parts of a composite thing which may not become a distinct object of ownership or other real right[503] and (b) an aggregate of things or rights, as a whole, because it is not a thing in the legal sense.[504]

2. Possession

283. Ownership can be acquired by *usucaption* only by a person who enjoys possession over a thing. This possession must be exercised constantly during the period of time provided for by Article 1041 CC. However, as the exercise of constant possession over a thing is difficult to prove, Article 1046 CC provides a (rebuttable) presumption in accordance with which the person who possessed a thing at the commencement and at the termination of a certain period of time is presumed to have possessed the thing during the intervening period as well.

3. Good Faith

284. Good faith, in the sense of Article 1041 CC, exists in the case where the possessor is convinced,[505] without being guilty of gross negligence, that he or she has acquired ownership (Article 1042 CC). This good faith must exist at the time of acquisition of the possession. Subsequent bad faith is not prejudicial (Article 1044

501. On these see *infra* paras 70 et seq.
502. These things cannot be acquired either by the parent, tutor or judicial assistant (see also Art. 1047 CC in combination with Art. 256 points 2 and 3 CC) or by third persons.
503. See *supra* paras 81, 82.
504. See *supra* paras 59, 60.
505. Regardless of whether this conviction is due to an error concerning actual facts or law.

CC). In the case where possession has been acquired by a representative, the existence of good faith is considered by the representative (Article 214 CC), except if the latter has acted in accordance with certain instructions given by the represented person (Article 215 CC).

Good faith, which must be proved by the possessor,[506] cannot be justified without the existence of a lawful title. However, in view of the fact that each condition of ordinary *usucaption* is self-contained, the existence of a lawful title does not provide a presumption of good faith.

4. Lawful or Putative Title

285. A lawful title is any legal fact which results in the immediate (derivative or original) acquisition of ownership. Thus, for example, contracts of the type specified in Article 1033 CC and hereditary succession are lawful titles. However, a lawful title entails immediate acquisition of ownership only if it is valid, while ownership may not be acquired immediately in the case where the lawful title is defective. Nevertheless, this defective title forms a title-element of ordinary *usucaption* and in combination with the other condition-elements of ordinary *usucaption* may lead to acquisition of ownership. This means that a defective lawful title in combination with the aforementioned elements constitutes a new lawful title and, specifically, ordinary *usucaption*.

286. The Civil Code draws a distinction between lawful (Article 1041 CC) and putative (Article 1043 CC) titles, without defining the meaning of the first or the second. In any event, according to an initial opinion[507] (correct, in our view), a lawful title is an internally defective one, that is, an existing but null or voidable title, while a putative title is an externally defective one, namely a non-existent title.[508] On the other hand, according to a second opinion,[509] a lawful title is only one in which the defect lies in the absence of ownership in the alienator, while putative

---

506. This applies because Art. 1041 CC requires, positively, the existence of good faith. Compare Art. 1036 CC *infra* para. 317.

507. G. Balis, *PrL*, para. 66, 172 et seq.; K. Vavouskos, *PrL*, Nos 182, 183, 180–182; Ev. Alexandropoulou-Egiptiadou, *The Title in Ordinary Usucaption*, 2nd edn (Athens/Komotini: A. Sakkoulas, 1997), 147 et seq. [in Greek]; D. Papasteriou, *PrL II*, para. 48 Nos 60 et seq., 342 et seq., as well as AP 429/1984, 33 NoB, 1985, 406; AP 1577/1983, 51 EEN, 1984, 630; AP 1521/1980, 29 NoB, 1981, 867; AP 1247/1976, 25 NoB, 1977, 737; AP 192/1970, 18 NoB, 1970, 928; Court of Appeal of Athens 3965/1986, 27 HellD, 1986, 1323 (1324).

508. For example, a non-existent title exists in the case where a movable or an immovable thing belonging to the decedent's estate has passed to an intestate heir of the decedent, for example to his or her brother X, while, by virtue of the decedent's will, which prevails, the same thing ought to be transmitted to Z. In this case the lawful title of X, namely the hereditary succession, does not exist.

509. Vas. Ekonomidis, *Elements of Civil Law. Property Rights*, 2nd edn (Athens, 1912), para. 124 n. 25, 171 [in Greek]; Ap. Georgiades, *PrL*, para. 44 II 4 Nos 47 et seq., 530 et seq.; Ap. Georgiades, in *Civil Code*, Vol. V: *PrL*, ed. Ap. Georgiades & M. Sathopoulos, Art. 1041 No. 29, Art. 1043 No. 2; G. Koumantos, *Subjective Good Faith* (Athens: Pavlou, 1958), 160 et seq. [in Greek]; A. Tousis, *PrL*, para. 103 n. 24, 437, as well as AP 192/1960, 8 NoB, 1960, 918 (919); AP 107/1961, 28 EEN, 1961, 542; AP 122/1957, 5 NoB, 1957, 646 (947); Court of Appeal of Athens 2495/1960, 2 HellD, 1961, 608.

titles are non-existent titles, titles which are null and void due to any defect apart from the absence of ownership in the alienator, or voidable titles.

However, Article 1043 paragraph 1 CC, referring to putative titles, declares that the latter are sufficient for *usucaption* so long as the good faith of the possessor is justified. This means that the acquisition of ownership by a putative title presupposes not only the good faith of Article 1041 CC (as is defined in Article 1042 CC) but also additional good faith. In other words, the conviction (not due to gross negligence) of the possessor that he or she has acquired ownership (Article 1042 CC) must be accompanied by his or her conviction (not due to gross negligence) that a valid lawful title exists. However, the law, believing that this last conviction (good faith) is not always sufficient to cover the absence of the title, goes on to declare that, in the area of immovables, there cannot be a putative title without transcription in cases where a transcription is required (Article 1043 paragraph 2 CC).[510,511]

5. Lapse of a Certain Period of Time

287. Article 1041 CC declares that the period of time during which a person must have an immovable thing in his or her possession in order to acquire it by *usucaption* amounts to ten years. With regard to this period, it is useful to examine the issue of addition of time (Articles 1051–1052 CC) as well as the issues of suspension (Article 1047 CC) and interruption of *usucaption* (Articles 1048–1050 CC).

a. Addition of Time

288. According to Article 1051 CC, a person who has acquired possession of a thing as a universal or particular successor in title may add the length of time of his or her own *usucaption* to that of his or her predecessor.

According to the prevailing opinion, Article 1051 CC constitutes an addition of time (*accessio temporis*) and not *successio in usucapionem*.[512] Therefore, it is accepted that the application of Article 1051 CC presupposes that both predecessor

---

510. Concomitantly, in the example of *supra* n. 507, the acquisition of ownership on the relevant immovable by X presupposes, among other things, lawful acceptance of the estate/legacy by X and transcription at the registry of deeds of the district in which the immovable is located.

511. It is debatable whether the transcription specified in Art. 1043 para. 2 CC is required not only for the putative but also for the lawful title-element of *usucaption*. On this issue see, in particular, Ev. Alexandropoulou-Egiptiadou, *The Title in Ordinary Usucaption*, 187 et seq. (who, making a critical evaluation of the two diametrically opposed opinions that have been expressed on this subject, comes to the right, in our opinion, conclusion that transcription is necessary only for putative titles).

512. See G. Balis, *PrL*, para. 71, 181–182; K. Vavouskos, *PrL*, No. 186, 184; N. Papantoniou, *Law of Inheritance*, 5th edn (Athens: Sakkoulas, 1989), para. 9b, 47–48 [in Greek]; A. Tousis, *PrL*, para. 103, 449 and n. 57; D. Papasteriou, *PrL II*, para. 48 No. 76, 352; N. Psouni, *Law of Inheritance*, vol. I, 2nd edn (Athens-Thessaloniki, Sakkoulas, 2011), para. 2 VII 5, 98–99 [in Greek], as well as AP 1482/1983, 32 NoB, 1984, 1206 (1207); AP 567/1980, 28 NoB, 1980, 1957; AP 287/1967, 15 NoB, 1967, 1049 (1050); Court of Appeal of Athens 1579/1986, 27 HellD, 1986, 658 (659). Compare Em. Vousikas, *Law of Inheritance*, vol. I (Athens, 1972), para. 12 VB, 76 et seq. [in Greek] and Ap. Georgiades, *PrL*, para. 44 II 5 Nos 66, 67, 538–539 (who maintain that addition of time occurs only in the case of particular succession in title).

and successor satisfy the condition-elements of *usucaption* and, most importantly, the element of good faith.

289. Article 1052 CC, completing Article 1051 CC, declares that the time of *usucaption* which has elapsed in favour of the possessor of an estate[513] is calculated in favour of the true heir.

b. Suspension and Interruption of *Usucaption*

290. As has already been pointed out,[514] *usucaption* constitutes acquisitive prescription. Hence, as acquisitive prescription, it may be suspended or interrupted.

291. With regard to suspension, Article 1047 CC declares that *usucaption* does not commence and, if commenced, does not continue during the period in which the prescription of a revendicatory action is suspended or its completion is legally prevented. As can be clearly seen, Article 1047 CC refers to Articles 255, 256, 258 and 259 CC, dealing with the grounds of suspension, and also to Article 257 CC. The latter, referring to the consequences of suspension, stipulates that the period of time which has elapsed up until the suspension is not lost and continues after the cessation of the suspension.

292. Articles 1048, 1049 and 1050 CC refer to interruption of *usucaption*. The first two deal with the grounds of interruption, whereas the third specifies its consequences, declaring, on the one hand, that the time which has elapsed up until the interruption is not taken into consideration and, on the other, that a new acquisitive prescription commences after the termination of the interruption.

With regard to the grounds of interruption, Article 1048 CC stipulates that *usucaption* is interrupted by loss of possession and adds that this interruption is deemed not to have occurred in the case where the person who lost the possession resumes it within one year or even later but then by means of a legal action commenced within that year.[515] A second ground of interruption is introduced by Article 1049 CC. This is in respect of interruption caused by the commencement of a revendicatory action[516] against the possessor or the person who possesses the thing in his or her name. In this type of interruption, which occurs only in favour of the plaintiff,[517] the provisions governing the interruption of prescription by the commencement of a legal action, i.e., Articles 261–263 and 269 CC apply by analogy.

513. The possessor of an estate is a person who, in the capacity of heir, retains things belonging to the decedent's estate (Art. 1871 CC) or a person who has acquired by contract the estate from the above possessor (Art. 1882 CC).
514. See *supra* para. 280.
515. Compare Art. 992 CC *supra* para. 144.
516. Or any other legal action aiming to determine the right of ownership (on this point see K. Vavouskos, *PrL*, No. 190, 190; Ap. Georgiades, *PrL*, para. 44 II 5 No. 82, 544).
517. Or in favour of those who become successors of the plaintiff after the commencement of the relevant trial. In this sense, the above interruption is relative, contrary to the interruption of Art. 1048 CC which is absolute and may be invoked by anybody (see K. Vavouskos, *PrL*, No. 190, 189, 190; Ap. Georgiades, *PrL* , para. 44 II 5 No. 84, 544–545).

C. *Prerequisites of Extraordinary Usucaption*

293. Extraordinary *usucaption* is referred to in Article 1045 CC. From this article it may be concluded that the acquisition of ownership by extraordinary *usucaption* presupposes possession, even if defective, of a (susceptible of *usucaption*[518]) movable or immovable thing for a period of twenty years.[519]

D. *Results of Usucaption*

294. *Usucaption* entails, on the one hand, original acquisition of ownership on an immovable or movable thing[520] and, on the other, extinction of the limited real rights which probably encumber the thing (Article 1053 CC).[521] This extinction – which pertains only to rights which were constituted at the time of acquisition of possession by the acquirer through *usucaption* – presupposes that the acquirer through *usucaption* was of good faith in regard to the right of the third party at the time of acquisition of possession (Article 1053 CC).[522] The same extinction also presupposes that the time of *usucaption* must also have elapsed in regard to the above right (Article 1053 CC).

IV. Other Ways of Acquiring Ownership on Immovables

A. *Acquisition by Adjudication*

295. Ownership can be acquired by adjudication on the basis of a court decision only in the cases provided for by law (Article 1056 CC). Examples of such cases are: judicial distribution by physical division,[523] adjudication in the case where a building has been erected partially on a neighbouring immovable (Article 1010 CC),[524] determination of confused borders of bordering immovables by a court decision attributing the disputed area in equal parts to each of the immovables concerned (Article 1020 CC),[525] adjudication of a common enterprise which includes

518. On this point see *supra* paras 281, 282.
519. Articles 1046 CC (see *supra* para. 283), 1047–1050 CC (see *supra* paras 291–292) and 1051–1052 CC (see *supra* paras 288–289) govern extraordinary *usucaption* as well.
520. See also *supra* para. 280.
521. According to the prevailing opinion, a person who loses ownership or some other real right on account of *usucaption* does not have a claim against the acquirer in accordance with the provisions governing enrichment without just cause (compare Art. 1063 CC *infra* para. 334). This applies because Arts 1041–1055 CC offer the acquirer just cause for preserving the enrichment (see, among others, G. Balis, *PrL*, para. 72, 183; K. Vavouskos, *PrL*, No. 192, 191; Ap. Georgiades, *PrL*, para. 44 IV No. 100, 549–550).
522. This condition is required only in the case of acquisition by ordinary *usucaption*.
523. See *supra* para. 215.
524. See *supra* paras 185–186.
525. See *supra* paras 194–195.

immovables in favour of one of the coparceners (Article 483 CCProc), and confiscation.[526]

The court decision which adjudicates ownership entails original acquisition of ownership and, in this sense, is a constitutive decision. The same decision must be transcribed in the case where it refers to immovables (Article 1192 point 2 CC[527]).

B. Acquisition by Concession

296. By concession (Article 1056 CC) – which is an original means of acquisition of ownership – on the basis of a unilateral act by an administrative authority and in consequence of a certain procedure, a person may be deprived of his or her ownership on a thing (especially an immovable) against payment of compensation, while a new ownership is acquired on the same thing by a third party.[528]

The most characteristic cases of acquisition of ownership by concession are: compulsory expropriation, regularization (or making rectangular) of incomplete building plots and redistribution of land.

1. Compulsory Expropriation

297. The institution of compulsory expropriation,[529] which constitutes the most important restriction of ownership on the strength of rules of public law,[530] is justified by the principle whereby personal benefit must give way to the social purposes of the State.

Expropriation is the removal – on the basis of a unilateral act by an administrative authority and against payment of complete compensation determined by a court decision – of one's ownership[531] for a public benefit provided by law.[532] The ownership of the expropriated thing passes into the hands of the third party in favour of whom the expropriation has been performed. This party may be the State, a municipality, a communal authority or any other legal entity or even natural person.

526. Confiscation is imposed by a court decision as an additional penalty or provisional remedy in the case where a crime has been committed. It entails removal of one's ownership on a movable or an immovable thing and acquisition of a new ownership on the same thing by the State.
527. See also Art. 12 para. 1 point b of L. 2664/1998 within the framework of the land registry system.
528. Concessions which refer to immovables must be transcribed (Art. 1192 point 2 CC; see also Art. 12 para. 1 point b of L. 2664/1998 within the framework of the land registry system).
529. The institution of expropriation is regulated mainly by the Constitution (Art. 17 paras 2–7) and in detail by L. 2882/2001 and L. 2985/2002).
530. See also *supra* para. 168 n. 332.
531. In practice, expropriation is especially understood to be the removal of one's ownership on an immovable or the constitution of a limited real right thereon.
532. A distinction must be drawn between expropriation, confiscation (see *supra* para. 295 n. 526), redistribution of land (see *infra* para. 299) and requisition. The latter aims to resolve an urgent and direct public need and means the temporary removal of the use and collection of fruits of a movable or an immovable thing belonging to another and their transfer to the State or to a third party on the basis of an act by an administrative authority and against payment of reasonable compensation.

2. Regularization of Incomplete Building Plots

298. The regularization of incomplete building plots is accomplished by an act of an administrative authority for reasons relating to building alignment and the implementation of town-plans. This regularization is achieved, on the one hand, through concession of incomplete building plots to the owners of bordering building plots and, on the other hand, through concession of portions of the bordering building plots to the owners of incomplete building plots so that the latter may be made whole and fit for construction.

3.Redistribution of Land

299. The (rural or urban) redistribution of land is achieved on the basis of an act of the State and means the removal of the ownership of immovables which are located in an extensive rural or urban area and the redistribution of the land between the initial owners of the above immovables. It aims either to improve the agricultural exploitation of the land (in cases of rural immovables) or to satisfy housing needs (in cases of urban immovables).

C. Acquisition by Accession

300. Accession entails original acquisition of ownership so long as the conditions imposed by law are fulfilled, without an act of the State or payment of compensation being necessary. Acquisition by accession is achieved in cases of alluvion, avulsion, an islet which has risen in a river and an abandoned river bed.

301. Alluvion occurs when new land is added in small quantities and imperceptibly by a river to a property situated on the bank of a river. This land is acquired by the owner of the property situated on the bank of the river (Article 1069 CC).

302. Avulsion occurs when through the action of the current of a river a portion of land suddenly becomes detached from a property and attaches itself to another property situated on the same or the opposite bank. This portion of land is acquired by the owner of the property to which it has become attached provided that within one year its original owner has not resumed possession thereof or has not commenced a legal action to recover possession (Article 1070 CC).

303. According to Article 1071 CC, as has been implicitly amended by Law 116/1975, an islet which rises in a non-navigable river, on account of geological and not technical grounds,[533] belongs to the owners of the properties situated on the banks of the river. To each belongs the portion located between an ideal line drawn along and in the middle of the river and the perpendicular lines drawn thereon from the end of the side of each property. However, in the case where the islet has been created because of the encirclement of the property situated on the banks of a river or

533. In the latter case the islet belongs to the State (Art. 1 L. 116/1975).

of a portion of such property by a branch of the river, the ownership thereof is not lost (Article 1073 CC).

304. Finally, according to Article 1072 CC, as has been implicitly amended by Law 116/1975, the abandoned bed of a non-navigable river, on geological grounds and not because of the execution of public works,[534] belongs to the owners of the properties situated on the banks of the river. The distribution is made in the manner specified by Article 1071,[535] which applies by analogy. However, the relevant acquisition presupposes a final abandonment of the bed. This abandonment may not become final before the lapse of a period of one year from the time it first becomes abandoned. This applies because the owners of the land on which the new river bed is formed have the right to reinstate, within one year, the flow of the former river bed (Article 1072 paragraph 2 CC) without in the meantime losing their ownership on the land which was temporarily flooded by the water (Articles 1073–1074 CC).

V. Renunciation or Abandonment of Ownership on Immovables

305. The owner of an immovable has the possibility of renouncing his or her ownership[536] without determining the person who will benefit from the renunciation.[537] This occurs, for example, when the charges[538] which encumber an immovable exceed its value or when the incomes originating from the latter are insufficient for its maintenance.

The renunciation of ownership takes the form of a unilateral, non-addressed and non-causal juridical act of disposition which is formal. It is carried out by a unilateral declaration of the owner in front of a notary and submitted to transcription.[539]

306. By the transcription of a notarial deed concerning the renunciation of the ownership of an immovable, the latter becomes ownerless and passes into the ownership of the State (Article 972 CC)[540] automatically, by operation of the law alone. The State automatically acquires also the possession of the immovable without taking any steps to put itself in this possession.

---

534. In the latter case the abandoned bed belongs to the State (Art. 1 L. 116/1975).
535. See *supra* para. 303.
536. The renunciation may concern the ownership of the whole immovable or a part of it and also an ideal share of co-ownership, when the immovable belongs to several co-owners in undivided shares (see also *infra* para. 343), or to a horizontal or vertical ownership (see also *infra* para. 347).
537. Otherwise, the 'renunciation' constitutes transference.
538. In the sense of Art. 965 CC (see *supra* para. 90).
539. The necessity of drawing up a notarial deed is not explicitly stipulated by the law. Nevertheless, it may be concluded by drawing an analogy with Arts 1134, 1169 and 1319 CC concerning renunciation of other real rights on immovables or it may be based in Arts 369, 1033 CC on account of the identical nature of the legal ground. On the other hand, the need for transcription is based on Art. 1192 point 1 and Art. 1198 CC (or Art. 12 para. 1 point a and para. 3 of L. 2664/1998 within the framework of the land registry system) concerning the acts which must be transcribed (registered) and the results connected with the transcription (registration) (on all these points see, in particular, Ap. Georgiades, *PrL*, para. 47 II Nos 5, 6, 578–579).
540. Compare, however, Art. 34 E.L. 1539/1938 concerning protection of State lands.

The acquisition of ownership, in the present case, is original. However, the limited real rights which probably encumber the abandoned immovable continue to exist even after the abandonment.[541]

307. Finally, it should be noted that, according to Article 972, the estates of persons who die without leaving heirs also belong to the State.[542]

§2. Acquisition and Loss of Ownership on Movables

I. Acquisition by Contract

A. *The Rule: Acquisition from a Person Who is the Owner*

308. Article 1034 CC declares that the transfer of ownership of a movable requires delivery of its possession by the owner to the acquirer and an agreement by both to the effect that ownership is transmitted.[543] Concomitantly, the transfer of ownership of a movable presupposes: (a) ownership of the alienator; (b) agreement between the owner and the acquirer to the effect that ownership is transmitted, and (c) delivery of the possession of the movable by the owner to the acquirer. With regard to these prerequisites mention should be made of the following:

1. Ownership of the Alienator

309. The principle *nemo plus juris ad alium transferre potest, quam ipse habet* applies in the area of movables as well. It should, however, be borne in mind that Article 1036 CC introduces a serious exception to this principle.[544] However, in spite of this exception, the need for the alienator to be owner of the movable which is transferred continues to constitute the rule.

541. Ap. Georgiades, *PrL*, para. 47 III No. 14, 581.
542. See also Art. 1824 CC according to which the State is called to be intestate heir in the sixth class (see also *supra* para. 278 n. 488). However, special provisions of laws, such as the laws which refer to the hereditary succession of monks, introduce exceptions to the rules of Arts 972 and 1824 CC.
543. Money, title deeds in bearer form, things-objects of intellectual property (e.g., a work of art or a cinematographic film) and accessories (see *supra* paras 85–87) are transmitted in the way specified in Art. 1034 CC. The transfer of registered shares presupposes fulfilment of the conditions of Art. 1034 CC and also registration in the relevant register of the company in order for it to be recognized as valid by the latter. Cars and motor-cycles are transferred in the manner provided for by L. 722/1977. Ships and aeroplanes are transmitted like immovables (see Arts 6 CPrMarL and 41 CAL respectively). However, here, the relevant real contract may be incorporated in a private deed and is transcribed, respectively, in the registers of ships or aeroplanes.
544. See *infra* paras 315 et seq.

2. Agreement and Delivery of Possession (The Real Contract of Article 1034 CC)

310. The agreement between the owner and the acquirer to the effect that ownership is transmitted and the delivery of possession of the movable by the former to the latter form the real contract which leads to acquisition of ownership.[545] This contract is non-causal. The same contract may be concluded by a legal or voluntary, direct or indirect,[546] representative of the alienator or the acquirer.

311. Below the elements which form the real contract of Article 1034 CC and its non-causal character are examined.

a. Agreement

312. The type of agreement specified in Article 1034 CC is a non-formal contract. Consequently, it is governed by the general provisions relating to the capacity to carry out juridical acts, defects of will, representation, conditions and terms, consent and approval. It seems correct to accept that the aforementioned agreement constitutes a real contract.[547]

---

545. G. Balis, *PrL*, para. 53 No. 5, 143; K. Vavouskos, *PrL*, No. 213, 210; Ap. Georgiades, *PrL*, para. 48 I 1 Nos 2, 3, 584, para. 49 I 2 No. 4, 597; I. Spyridakis & M. Spyridakis, *PrL*, vol. B/1, No. 141.2.2., 571. See also J. Baur & R. *Stürner*, *SachR*, para. 5 I 2 b No. 3, 43, para. 51 A I 1 b No. 1, 636; F. Quach, in *MünchKomm*, vol. 6: *SachR*, para. 929 No. 113. However, the opinion has also been expressed that the agreement specified in Art. 1034 CC forms the relevant real contract, whereas the delivery is an additional material element (see H. Westermann et al., *SachR*, para. 37 No. 1, 274–275). According to a third opinion, the delivery of possession constitutes a condition of effect (*conditio juris*) of the relevant real contract (Chr. Kousoulas, *PrL*, para. 44 II 1, 311).

546. As is well-known, an indirect representative acts in his or her own name. Hence, in the case where the acquirer is indirectly represented, the ownership of the thing is acquired by the representative, who is bound to transfer it to the person he or she represents. The danger of the movable being seized by the creditors of the representative may be averted by an agreement between the representative and the represented person to the effect that the ownership of the thing which is going to be acquired is transferred beforehand to the represented person by *constitutum possessorium anticipatum* (see *supra* para. 120). Furthermore, it is accepted that, in sale contracts where the price is paid from hand to hand and in cash, ownership and possession are acquired immediately by the represented person on condition: (a) that the identity of the acquirer and possessor is of no importance to the seller, and (b) that the intention of the 'purchaser' to acquire for the benefit of the represented person (transfer 'to whom it may concern') may be deduced with certainty from the circumstances. Consequently, in this case – although it is not apparent that the representative acts in the name of the person represented – the results of direct representation are produced. (On all these points see Ap. Georgiades, *PrL*, para. 49 II 2, 3 Nos 14 et seq., 600–602.)

547. Thus, I. Spyridakis & M. Spyridakis, *PrL*, Vol. B/1, No. 141.2.1, 570; P. Filios & Chr. Filios, *PrL*, para. 90 A, 188, as well as J. Baur & R. Stürner, *SachR*, para. 51 B 1 No. 6, 638; W. Brehm & Chr. Berger, *Sachenrecht*, 2nd edn (Tübingen: Mohr Siebeck, 2006), para. 27 I No. 1, 403; M. Habersack, *Examens-Repetitorium Sachenrecht*, 4th edn (Heidelberg: Müller, 2005), para. 8 III No. 144, 65; H. Prütting, *SachR*, para. 32 II No. 372, 151; K. Schreiber, *Sachenrecht*, 5th edn (Stuttgart: Boorberg, 2008), No. 155, 92; K. Vieweg & A. Werner, *Sachenrecht*, 5th edn (München: Vahlen, 2011), para. 4 II 2a No. 6, 76; H.J. Wieling, *Sachenrecht*, 5th edn (Berlin/Heidelberg: Springer, 2007), para. 9 I 1, 95; M. Wolf & M. Wellenhofer, *Sachenrecht*, 26th edn (München: Beck, 2011), para. 7 II 1 No. 4, 77. See, however, K. Vavouskos, *PrL*, No. 215, 213, who maintains that the relevant agreement constitutes a personal contract.

b. Delivery of Possession

313. Delivery of possession serves the concept of (formal) publicity in the area of movables.[548] It is accomplished by any of the ways stipulated by Articles 976–978 CC[549] and also by assignment (to the acquirer) of a revendicatory action (Article 1035 CC). Indeed, if the alienator has neither possession nor detention of the movable because it is in the possession of a third party (e.g., a thief), the assignment to the acquirer of the revendicatory action against the third party is sufficient for the purpose of transfer of ownership. This assignment substitutes the delivery of possession and together with the agreement provided for by Article 1034 CC forms the real contract specified in the same article. Due to the fact that the relevant assignment pertains to a real and not to a personal claim, the notification of the third (probably unknown) party specified in Article 460 CC is not required.

c. Non-causal (Abstract) Character of the Real Contract of Article 1034 CC

314. From the text of Article 1034 CC, which – unlike the text of Article 1033 CC – does not refer to just cause, it may be concluded that the real contract of Article 1034 CC is non-causal (abstract). This means that, in the field of movables, acquisition of ownership by contract is achieved regardless of whether a valid just cause exists. However, in the case where a valid just cause does not exist, the alienator is entitled to demand from the acquirer retransfer of the ownership in accordance with the provisions concerning enrichment without just cause (Article 904 et seq. CC).

B. The Exception: Acquisition from a Person Who is Not the Owner

315. The protection and facilitation of transactions, as well as the principle of protection of confidence in the apparent rights, justify recognition of the institution of acquisition of ownership of a movable from a person who is not the owner (Articles 1036 et seq. CC).

As may be concluded from Article 1036 paragraph 1 CC, the acquisition of ownership of a movable which does not belong to the alienator depends: (a) on the condition that the elements of the real contract of Article 1034 CC (agreement and delivery of possession) exist, and (b) on the condition that the acquirer is of good faith. With regard to these conditions, as well as the results of acquisition from a person who is not the owner, mention should be made of the following.

1. Agreement and Delivery of Possession (The Real Contract of Articles 1036/1034 CC)

316. Everything that has been stated above[550] about the real contract of Article 1034 CC also applies in the case of Article 1036 CC. Therefore, there is no need to

548. On this issue see *supra* para. 29.
549. On this point see *supra* paras 117 et seq.
550. Paragraphs 310, 312–314.

repeat the points already made. Nevertheless, it should be stressed that, according to the most correct opinion,[551] within the framework of Article 1036 CC, the delivery of possession must be accomplished materially, that is, in the ways stipulated by Articles 976 and 978 CC[552] and not by Articles 977 and 1035 CC.[553] This is due to the nature of the institution introduced by Articles 1036 et seq. CC. In fact, only in the case where the alienator has the possession or detention of the thing and delivers it materially to the acquirer, may the good faith of the latter be justified in that it is founded on an objective basis.

2. Good Faith

a. Concept of Good Faith

317. Article 1036 paragraph 1 CC declares that the acquirer must not be of bad faith. This negative expression does not alter the essential point that the acquirer must be of good faith. The same expression has procedural importance connected with the allocation of burden of proof. To be specific, it means that the acquirer's good faith is presumed. Therefore, an owner who vindicates the thing or any third party who invokes the invalidity of the transmission carries the burden of proof of the acquirer's bad faith.

The sense of 'bad faith', as mentioned in Article 1036, is defined in Article 1037 CC. According to the latter, the acquirer is of bad faith when he or she knows or, owing to gross negligence, is ignorant of the fact that the alienator is not the owner of the alienated movable. In contradistinction to the previous article, it may be concluded that an acquirer of good faith is one who is convinced,[554] without being guilty of gross negligence, that the alienator is the owner of the alienated movable.

318. Gross negligence, which excludes good faith, applies in cases where the acquirer has not collected information concerning the ownership of the alienator, although he or she should have done so, thereby showing the required diligence in trade. Thus, for example, the acquirer is obliged to check up if ownership exists: when there are basic suspicions that the alienator is not the owner (e.g., the seller of an item of jewellery is suspect); when the movable alienated is of the type usually sold on retention of title (e.g., purchase of a machine from an insolvent person without checking if he or she had paid the price); or when the purchase concerns movables for which registers are kept (e.g., purchase of a boat from an unknown person without checking, in the relevant registers, if the seller is registered in them as the owner). However, the acquirer's good or bad faith is judged in the light of the circumstances of each particular case.

551. Thus, K. Vavouskos, *PrL*, No. 220, 218; Ap. Georgiades, *PrL*, para. 50 III 2 Nos 8–9, 613–616. On the opposing view see G. Balis, *PrL*, para. 56 b, 151.
552. See *supra* paras 117, 118, 122.
553. See *supra* paras 119, 121 and 313.
554. This conviction may be due to an error concerning real facts or law.

b. Persons to Whom Good Faith Must Apply

319. As may be concluded from Article 1036, the acquirer is the only one who must act in good faith. However, in the case of representation, the existence of good faith should be considered by the representative (Article 214 CC), except if the latter has acted in accordance with certain instructions given by the person represented (Article 215 CC).[555]

c. Time at Which Good Faith Must Exist

320. According to Article 1036 paragraph 1 CC, the acquirer must possess good faith at the time of the delivery of possession. Concomitantly, neither is subsequent bad faith prejudicial nor is previous or subsequent good faith useful. Good faith must exist at the time of delivery even when the relevant real contract is dependent on a suspensive condition or term. However, when agreement is preceded by delivery, it is correct to accept that good faith must exist at the time of the agreement.[556]

d. Object of Good Faith

321. According to Article 1037 CC, the object of the acquirer's good faith is the fact that the ownership of the thing acquired is held by the alienator. This means that the good faith of the acquirer covers only the absence of the above ownership. Consequently, absence of other conditions required for a valid conclusion of the relevant real contract, such as capacity to carry out legal transactions or power of disposal, is not covered by the good faith of the acquirer.

Nevertheless, it seems correct to adopt the opinion[557] that good faith also covers the absence of the power to dispose owing to a relevant prohibition of law for the benefit of certain persons (Article 175 sub-paragraph b CC).[558] Indeed, insofar as good faith covers the complete absence of ownership (major), it should also cover the absence of power to dispose (minor). On the other hand, the fact that the alienator possesses the alienated movable justifies not only the acquirer's conviction that

555. The correct opinion has been expressed that Art. 215 CC applies by analogy in the cases of indirect representation, too. Thus, for example, the good faith of the (indirect) representative B does not cover the bad faith of the person represented, A, and the acquisition of ownership by A is not achieved in the case where A, who knows that the movable concerned does not belong to the alienator, gives mandate to B to buy this movable in his or her name (i.e., in the name of B) and to transfer it afterwards to him or her (i.e., to A) (see Ap. Georgiades, *PrL*, para. 50 III 4 No. 25, 622).

556. See Ap. Georgiades, *PrL*, para. 50 III 4 No. 30, 623.

557. See K. Vavouskos, *Acquisition of Ownership of Movables from a Person Who is Not the Owner and Its Protection* (Thessaloniki, 1956), 87–88 [in Greek]; K. Vavouskos, *PrL*, No. 225, 223; Ap. Georgiades, *PrL*, para. 50 III 3 No. 14, 617–618; G. Koumantos, *Subjective Good Faith*, 230; M. Karasis, in *Civil Code*, Vol. I: *General Principles*, ed. Ap. Georgiades & M. Stathopoulos (Athens: Sakkoulas, 1978), Arts 175–177 No. 2 [in Greek]; I. Spyridakis & M. Spyridakis, *PrL*, vol. B/1, No. 142.3.3, 596–597. Contra: G. Balis, *PrL*, para. 56 a, 151; G. Balis, *GenPrinc*, paras 61, 68, 174, 195; A. Tousis, *PrL*, para. 100, 418; P. Filios, Chr. Filios, *PrL*, para. 95 D a, 194, as well as Court of Appeal of Thessaloniki 174/1983, 37 Arm, 1983, 580 (581).

558. See also (corresponding to Art. 175 sub-para. b CC) para. 135 BGB, which declares (Satz 2) that 'the provisions for the benefit of those who are acquiring rights from a person who is not the owner apply by analogy'.

the alienator is the owner but also his or her conviction that the alienator has the power of disposal.

Furthermore, another convincing opinion[559] is that which holds that the good faith also covers the nullity specified in Article 206 CC.[560] Consequently, insofar as the acquirer was justifiably ignorant of the fact that the ownership of the alienated movable was dependent on a resolutory condition, the alienation, which was accomplished while the relevant condition was pending, remains valid even after the fulfilment of this condition. In fact, considering that the condition is a restriction of ownership, it seems correct to accept that the good faith, which covers the complete absence of ownership, may also cover its partial absence.

3. Results of Acquisition from a Person Who is Not the Owner

322. Provided that the conditions specified in Article 1036 CC occur, the acquirer becomes the definite owner of the transferred movable[561] and the true owner loses his or her ownership definitively, retaining probably only personal claims against the alienator.

323. It is debatable whether the acquisition of ownership from a person who is not the owner is derivative or original. Thus, one opinion,[562] attaching importance to the fact that the relevant acquisition presupposes the conclusion of a real contract, considers it derivative. Nevertheless, it seems correct to adopt a second,

559. K. Vavouskos, *Acquisition of ownership etc.*, 88–89; K. Vavouskos, *PrL*, No. 225, 223–224; Ap. Georgiades, *PrL*, para. 50 III 3 Nos 15–16, 618–619; Ap. Georgiades, *GenPrinc*, para. 44 VI 5 No. 41, 578; G. Koumantos, *Subjective Good Faith*, 229; G. Rammos, in *ErmAK*, Art. 206 No. 36 [in Greek]; K. Simantiras, *GenPrinc*, para. 48 IV No. 904, 671; M. Karasis, *GenPrinc*, 147; P. Kornilakis, *Law of Obligations. Special Part I* (Athens-Thessaloniki: Sakkoulas, 2002), para. 56 III 1 a, 349–350 [in Greek]; I. Spyridakis & M. Spyridakis, *PrL*, Vol. B/1, No. 142.3.3, 597; Asprogerakas-Grivas, *General Principles of Civil Law* (Athens/Komotini: A. Sakkoulas, 1981 [in Greek], para. 89 V 2 A, 377–378, as well as Court of Appeal of Athens 2748/1982, 31 NoB, 1983, 511 (514). Contra: G. Balis, *PrL*, para. 56 a, 151; G. Balis, *GenPrinc*, paras 68, 100, 194, 272; A. Tousis, *PrL*, para. 100, 418; A. Tousis, *General Principles of Civil Law*, vol. II, 2nd edn (Athens: Sakkoulas, 1978), para. 137 n. 1, 644 [in Greek]; A. Kritikos, in *Civil Code*, Vol. I: *GenPrinc*, ed. Ap. Georgiades & M. Stathopoulos, Art. 206 No. 6.

560. See also (corresponding to Art. 206) para. 161 BGB, which declares (Satz 3) that 'the provisions for the benefit of those who are acquiring rights from a person who is not the owner apply'.

561. Consequently, he or she (e.g., A) may transfer the movable to anybody (e.g., B) who becomes the owner, regardless of whether he or she is acting in good or bad faith. However, in the case where B was not the owner and, despite his or her awareness of this fact, transferred the movable to A, the relevant transfer (from A to B) does not entail acquisition of ownership by B but reinstatement of the former situation, that is, return of the ownership to its initial owner (thus, K. Vavouskos, *Acquisition of Ownership etc.*, 123–124; Ap. Georgiades, *PrL*, para. 50 IV 3 Nos 41 et seq., 626–628; G. Koumantos, *Subjective Good Faith*, 276–277).

562. G. Balis, *PrL*, para. 57 No. 3, 154; G. Balis, *GenPrinc*, para. 30, 96; A. Tousis, *PrL*, para. 100 n. 1, 415; P. Filios & Chr. Filios, *PrL*, para. 97 A, 196. See also K. Larenz & M. Wolf, *AllgT*, para. 14 IV 1 b No. 28, 246; H. Prütting, *SachR*, para. 35 VIII No. 441, 190; H. Westermann et al., *SachR*, para. 45 IV 2, 372; J. Oechsler, in *MunchKomm*, Vol. 6: *SachR*, para. 932 No. 69; W. Wiegand, in *Staudinger Komm zum BGB, Buch 3: SachR* (2011), para. 932 No. 108.

opposing opinion.[563] This view, attaching importance not to the method of transfer but to its result – namely to the fact that, in this case, a new right is acquired which did not belong to the alienator – considers the same acquisition original.

C. *Lifting of the Exception and Return to the Rule*

324. The exception to the rule of Article 1034 CC (i.e., that the alienator must be owner of the movable which is transmitted) which is introduced by Article 1036 paragraph 1 CC, is restricted by Article 1036 paragraph 2 CC. Indeed, the latter declares that the provision of Article 1036 paragraph 1 CC applies particularly in those cases where an alienation without right has been made by a person enjoying a right of usufruct or pledge on the thing or by a lessee or a depositary or by a person who has a similar relationship with the owner. Considering that the persons enumerated indicatively in Article 1036 paragraph 2 CC have possession or detention over the thing with the consent of the owner, it becomes obvious that the acquisition of ownership of a movable from a person who is not the owner is achieved to the extent that the alienator possesses or detains the movable with the consent of the true owner.

325. In consequence to the regulation of Article 1036 paragraph 2, Article 1038 CC stipulates that transfer by a person who is not the owner to an acquirer of good faith is not valid if the transferred thing has been removed from the possession of the owner as a result of theft[564] (Article 372 PC)[565] or loss.[566] Concomitantly, in this case, the true owner is entitled to vindicate the thing from anybody who possesses it, that is, not only from the person (A) to whom it was transferred by the thief or the discoverer but also from the person (B) to whom it was transmitted by A.[567]

D. *Partial Restoration of the Exception*

326. According to Article 1039 CC, the transfer of money or title deeds in bearer form by a person who is not the owner to an acquirer of good faith is effective even if the owner was dispossessed of them by theft or loss. The same article adds that

563. K. Vavouskos, *Acquisition of Ownership etc.*, 127 et seq.; K. Vavouskos, *PrL*, No. 227, 225–226; Ap. Georgiades, *PrL*, para. 50 IV 2 Nos 37 et seq., 625–626. See also G. Koumantos, *Subjective Good Faith*, 266–267 (who, however, comes to the conclusion [p. 267] that the relevant acquisition is a mixed phenomenon which contains elements of derivative and original acquisition; for a similar opinion see also I. Spyridakis & M. Spyridakis, *PrL*, vol. B/1, No. 142.2, 592).
564. Regardless of whether: (a) the movable had been stolen from the owner or from the person through whom the owner's possession was exercised, and (b) a penal conviction had been imposed.
565. And not on account of misappropriation (Art. 375 PC).
566. 'Loss' in the sense of Art. 1038 CC occurs when the thing has escaped from the owner's possession without his consent and without the consent of the person (e.g., the usufructuary or the lessee) through whom the owner's possession is possibly exercised (on this point see Ap. Georgiades, *PrL*, para. 50 V 3 Nos 50 et seq., 630 et seq., as well as Ach. Koutsouradis, *The Discovery of Lost Property in the Field of Civil Law* (Thessaloniki: Sakkoulas, 1987), 113 et seq. [in Greek]). Compare, however, *infra* para. 339 n. 599 on the same issue in the area of Arts 1081 et seq. CC.
567. In the case of acceptance of the revendicatory action, A or B is bound to restore the thing to its true owner, while retaining only personal claims against the alienator.

this rule also applies in regard to other movable things which have been alienated by public auction or in a fair or a market.

The regulation of Article 1039 CC is justified partly by the fact that money and title deeds in bearer form constitute the basis in trade and partly by the fact that alienation by public auction or in a fair or market eliminates the possibility of theft being encouraged and stolen goods being received. However, it is rightly accepted that alienation in a fair or market entails acquisition of ownership provided: (a) that the alienation is accomplished by a seller who sells things of the same kind as the stolen or lost thing, and (b) that the sold thing belongs to the sort of things which are usually alienated in the fair or market. Thus, for example, the alienation of a lost jewel in a fair where only animals are sold does not entail acquisition of ownership.

E. The Rights of Third Parties on the Thing Transferred

327. The possibility of the ownership of the true owner becoming extinguished, in the case where the conditions of Article 1036 CC occur, would be strange if the law did not provide for a similar possibility in regard to the limited real rights (usufruct or pledge) which probably encumber the transmitted movable. Therefore, Article 1040 CC declares that the transfer of a movable to the ownership of the acquirer extinguishes any real rights which exist thereon in favour of third parties, except if the acquirer has acted in bad faith in regard to the right of the third party at the time of delivery of the possession.[568]

The application of Article 1040 CC presupposes good faith on the part of the acquirer, that is, a conviction not due to gross negligence that the movable is not encumbered with a limited real right.[569] Furthermore, in the belief that the regulation of Article 1040 CC is based on similar reasoning to that of Article 1036 CC, it has been claimed that the application of Article 1040 CC presupposes material delivery of the possession to the acquirer,[570] while the view has also been expressed that Articles 1038–1039 CC apply, in the area of Article 1040 CC, by analogy.[571]

II. Transfer by Death

328. Everything that was stated above with regard to the transfer by death to an heir, a *fideicommissarius* or a legatee in the context of immovables[572] also applies

568. The opinion has also been expressed that Art. 1040 CC applies not only in cases of acquisition from a person who is not the owner but also in cases of acquisition from a person who is the owner. This view is based partly on the wording of Art. 1040 CC ('by the transfer of the movable to the ownership of the acquirer … ') and partly on the thought that the interest of the acquirer in acquiring ownership free from encumbrances is the same in both of the above cases (see G. Balis, *PrL*, para. 60, 158; Ap. Georgiades, *PrL*, para. 50 VI 2 No. 68, 637. Contra: K. Vavouskos, *Acquisition of Ownership etc.*, 132; K. Vavouskos, *PrL*, No. 226, 224).

569. See also *supra* para. 317.

570. Ap. Georgiades, *PrL*, para. 50 VI 2 Nos 69–70, 637–639. See also *supra* para. 316.

571. See G. Balis, *PrL*, para. 60 No. 1, 158–159; K. Vavouskos, *Acquisition of Ownership etc.*, 133; K. Vavouskos, *PrL*, No. 226, 225; Ap. Georgiades, *PrL*, para. 50 VI 2 No. 73, 639.

572. See *supra* paras 278, 279 (under a, b).

in the field of movables. However, in cases where the object of the estate, the *fideicommisum* or the legatee is a movable, the ownership on it may be acquired without the need for an explicit declaration of acceptance or, naturally, a transcription in the transcription registers.

III. Acquisition by *Usucaption* (Acquisitive Prescription)

329. Movable things may be acquired by ordinary or extraordinary *usucaption* provided the already mentioned conditions of Articles 1041 et seq. CC occur.[573] Nevertheless, it ought to be borne in mind that, in the area of movables, the time period of ordinary *usucaption* amounts to three, instead of ten years.

IV. Acquisition by Adjudication

330. The ownership of a movable may be acquired by adjudication[574] in cases of judicial distribution by physical division and confiscation[575] as well as in the case provided for by Article 1062 CC.[576]

V. Acquisition by Union, Connection, Amalgamation or Merger

331. According to Article 1057 CC, if a movable thing has been attached to an immovable in such a manner as to become a component part of the latter, the ownership of such immovable extends to the movable as well (acquisition by union). This provision conforms with the mandatory rule of Article 953 CC.[577] Therefore, like the latter, it excludes, on the one hand, an alternative arrangement between the parties (e.g., an agreement about retention of title on the movable) and, on the other, a revival of the original ownership on the movable in the case where it subsequently becomes separated from the immovable.

332. The content of the rule in Article 953 CC is also reflected in Article 1058 CC. The latter, excluding an alternative arrangement between the parties, regulates, in a categorical way, the fate of the ownership of movables which belong to different owners and have been connected so as to become component parts of a unitary thing. To be precise, according to Article 1058 CC, the erstwhile owners of these movables become co-owners of the unitary thing, while their shares therein are determined by reference to the value of the things at the time they were united, except if one of the things must be considered the principal thing, in which case the owner thereon acquires ownership of the whole.

573. See *supra* paras 282 et seq.
574. See *supra* para. 295.
575. See *supra* para. 295 n. 526.
576. On this point see *infra* para. 335.
577. See *supra* para. 82.

333. Finally, according to Article 1059 CC, the provision of Article 1058 applies by analogy where solid or liquid things, belonging to different owners, have been amalgamated or merged in such a way that their separation becomes impossible or would entail disproportionate disbursements.

334. Acts of union, connection, amalgamation or merger, which are material acts, entail original acquisition of ownership and insofar as the ownership of a thing is extinguished as a result of their actions, so too are extinguished the real rights thereon belonging to others (Article 1060 CC).[578]

However, as the law does not wish to permit a person to become richer to the detriment of another on account of the loss of ownership or other real right, Article 1063 CC provides that the person who has lost ownership[579] or some other real right has a claim against the person who has benefited thereby,[580] in accordance with the provisions governing enrichment without just cause.[581] Furthermore, according to the same article, the above person also has a right to compensation, provided that the conditions of an unlawful act occur, or a right to reimbursement of disbursements incurred, or to removal of a construction. However, a claim for reinstatement of the former situation is excluded.

VI. Things Specified

335. According to Article 1061 CC, a person who through an elaboration or transformation of material[582] owned by another has produced a new movable thing acquires ownership thereof only if the value of the work performed is obviously higher than the value of the material.[583] Nevertheless, as this solution may lead to abuses and injustices, Article 1062 CC adds that the court may on reasonable grounds adjudicate ownership of the new thing to the owner of the material if the person who produced the thing was acting in bad faith, that is, he or she knew or was ignorant through his or her own fault of the fact that the material belonged to another.

---

578. Consequently, Art. 1060 CC does not apply in cases of establishment of co-ownership.
579. And, concomitantly, not the one who has become co-owner.
580. And also against his or her universal successors or his or her particular successors in title on the condition that they have benefited gratuitously (see Art. 913 CC).
581. Consequently, the relevant claim may not be commenced in the case where the loss of one's right and the enrichment of the other person has resulted from an agreement.
582. Examples of elaboration are: writing, painting, design, photography, printing, engraving as well as any other similar means of fashioning surfaces (Art. 1061 para. 1 sub-para. b CC), such as sculpture or drawing cartoons. However, the law requires a creative form of elaboration or transformation and not a simple repair, restoration or act of maintenance, such as, for example, the repair of a car, the polishing of a piece of furniture or cleaning of a cloth.
583. Ownership is acquired by the producer in the case where the elaboration or transformation of the material has been achieved by himself or herself or by workmen or artisans employed by him or her, though not by a representative (in the sense of Arts 211 et seq. CC) of the producer. This applies because elaboration or transformation are material acts and, therefore, insusceptible of representation.

The application of Article 1061 CC leads to original acquisition of ownership by the producer. The same application entails extinction of the ownership of the material as well as extinction of any real rights thereon belonging to third parties (Article 1061 paragraph 2 CC). However, as the law does not wish to permit the enrichment of a person to the detriment of the owner of the material or of the holder of the limited real right thereon, it offers the latter the claims provided by Article 1063 CC.[584]

VII. Acquisition of Fruits of a Thing

336. The fruits of a thing, on account of the fact that they are (essential) component parts,[585] cannot become a distinct object of ownership before their separation from the fruit-producing thing. However, the acquisition of ownership on fruits sometimes presupposes only separation (Articles 1064–1066 CC)[586] and at other times, besides separation, acquisition of possession as well, that is, gathering (Articles 1067–1068 CC).[587]

As may be concluded from Articles 1064–1068 CC, the fruits of a thing,[588] after their separation, belong in order of priority to the following persons:

(a) The person who is entitled to receive them by virtue of a personal relation, e.g., the lessee of a piece of agricultural land (Article 1067 CC), even when the person who granted him or her the relevant right was not entitled to do so, e.g., the lessor was not the owner of the agricultural land (Article 1068 CC). However, in the latter case, the fruits are acquired provided that, at the time of acquisition of their possession, the acquirer was acting in good faith[589] and the grantor of the relevant right enjoyed possession[590] of the fruit-producing thing.

584. See *supra* para. 334.
585. See *supra* para. 81 and n. 159.
586. In this case, it is almost unanimously accepted that the acquisition is original (see E. Kounougeri-Manoledaki, in *Civil Code*, Vol. V: *PrL*, ed. Ap. Georgiades & M. Stathopoulos Art. 1064 No. 13, 1065 No. 4, 1066 No. 8).
587. In this case, it is debatable whether the acquisition is original or derivative. For the first opinion see E. Kounougeri-Manoledaki, *Law of Fruits*, 113; E. Kounougeri-Manoledaki, in *Civil Code*, Vol. V: *PrL*, ed. Ap. Georgiades & M. Stathopoulos, Arts 1067 No. 9, 1068 No. 5. For the second opinion see G. Balis, *GenPrinc*, para. 29, 91 (only for the case provided for in Art. 1067); K. Vavouskos, *PrL*, No. 206, 203.
588. Articles 1064–1068 CC regulate, as a rule, the acquisition of natural fruits (on which see *supra* para. 88 and nn. 176, 177, 179) as well as the acquisition of other components of a thing which are not fruits. Examples of such components are building materials after the demolition of a building. Exceptionally, Art. 1066 CC regulates only the acquisition of fruits and of other products considered to be fruits, while the same is accepted with regard to Art. 1065 CC, too (E. Kounougeri-Manoledaki, in *Civil Code*, Vol. V: *PrL*, ed. Ap. Georgiades & M. Stathopoulos, Art. 1064 No. 5).
589. In the sense of being convinced, without being guilty of gross negligence, that the grantor was entitled to grant the relevant right (G. Balis, *PrL*, para. 83 No. 1, 205; E. Kounougeri-Manoledaki, in *Civil Code*, Vol. V: *PrL*, ed. Ap. Georgiades & M. Stathopoulos, Art. 1068 No. 2; Ap. Georgiades, *PrL*, para. 53 III 2 No. 20, 671–672).
590. Of bad faith, as, otherwise, he or she should be entitled to grant the relevant right (see Art. 1066 CC).

(b) In the case where a beneficiary with the aforementioned characteristics does not exist, the fruits belong to the person who, acting in good faith, enjoys, over the fruit-producing thing, possession or quasi possession with the intention of acting as owner or usufructuary, provided that this person is of good faith[591] at the time of separation of the fruits as well[592] (Article 1066 CC).
(c) In the case where not even a beneficiary in the latter category exists, the fruits belong to the person who is entitled to acquire them on the strength of a limited real right, e.g., usufruct, on the fruit-producing thing (Article 1065 CC).
(d) Finally, in the case where a holder of such a right does not exist, the fruits belong to the owner of the thing (Article 1064 CC).

VIII. Acquisition by Occupancy of Movables without an Owner

337. Things without an owner, that is, things which do not belong to anybody, consist first and foremost of wild animals, as long as they remain in a state of natural freedom, and, second, the products of the sea (Article 1077 CC).[593] On the other hand, movables which become ownerless are those which are derelict. Indeed, according to Article 1076 CC, a movable thing becomes ownerless if its owner has abandoned the possession thereof with the intention of renunciating the ownership.[594]

Dereliction, in the sense of Article 1076 CC, is a juridical act which includes, on the one hand, a unilateral and non-addressed declaration of renunciation of the ownership and, on the other hand, the physical abandonment of the thing, through which the intention of renunciation is usually expressed.[595]

Derelict movables are acquired originally by the person who has taken them in his or her possession (Article 1075 CC), that is, by the person who has occupied[596]

591. In the sense of being convinced, without being guilty of gross negligence, that he or she is owner or usufructuary of the thing and that a third party does not have a real right on the fruits (G. Balis, *PrL*, para. 83 No. 3, 207; E. Kounougeri-Manoledaki, in *Civil Code*, Vol. V: *PrL*, ed. Ap. Georgiades & M. Stathopoulos, Art. 1066 Nos 2, 3, 9; Ap. Georgiades, *PrL*, para. 53 II 3 No. 14, 669).
592. G. Balis, *PrL*, para. 83 No. 3, 206–207; K. Vavouskos, *PrL*, No. 208, 206; Ap. Georgiades, *PrL*, para. 53 II 3 No. 14, 669. Compare E. Kounougeri-Manoledaki, *Law of Fruits*, 95–96; E. Kounougeri-Manoledaki, in *Civil Code*, Vol. V: *PrL*, ed. Ap. Georgiades & M. Stathopoulos, Art. 1066 No. 5.
593. To be precise, according to Art. 1077 CC: 'Wild animals are without a master as long as they remain in a state of natural freedom. Wild animals within an enclosed space and fish in a fishery or other closed private waters are not without a master. A wild animal which has been captured is deemed to be without a master when it recovers its freedom and its owner has not taken without delay on his part steps for its pursuit. A tamed animal is deemed to be without a master if it loses the habit of returning'. Further on, Art. 1078 CC likens a swarm of bees to untamed wild animals (Art. 1077 sub-para. c CC), Art. 1079 CC refers to the right of the owner of a swarm of bees to pursue and capture it within the immovable of another and Art. 1080 CC regulates the issue of ownership in the case of the amalgamation of swarms of bees belonging to several owners.
594. The dereliction entails extinction of ownership, though not also extinction of the limited real rights which probably encumber the movable (see, in particular, Ap. Georgiades, *PrL*, para. 54 II No. 6, 675).
595. See, in particular, Ap. Georgiades, *PrL*, para. 54 II No. 3, 674.
596. It is debatable whether occupancy is a real fact (for this opinion see K. Vavouskos, *PrL*, No. 160, 159; A. Tousis, *PrL*, para. 118 n. 2, 525; P. Filios & Chr. Filios, *PrL*, para. 119 A, 230, as well as J. Baur & R. Stürner, *SachR*, para. 53 F III 2 No. 72, 734, as well as H. Prütting, *SachR*, para. 42

them. However, occupancy does not entail acquisition of ownership in those cases where it is prohibited by law, for example, by the law which prohibits hunting or fishing either generally or in a certain season or region.

IX. Acquisition by Discovery of Lost Property

338. The discovery of lost property (Articles 1081–1092 CC) entails the establishment of an *ex lege* personal relationship between the discoverer and the person who has lost the thing or anyone else who has a right thereon. From this relationship derive rights and obligations for the benefit or to the detriment of the discoverer. Therefore, the institution of the discovery of lost property ought to be regarded as part of the law of obligations. However, owing to the fact that the discovery of lost property may lead to original acquisition of ownership on the lost thing by the discoverer, the above institution has been included in property law.[597]

339. A lost thing, in the sense of Articles 1081 et seq. CC,[598] is a movable thing the ownership of which belongs to somebody, while its possession has been lost[599] without the consent[600] of the possessor.

Lost things are acquired by discovery[601] so long as the thing is subsequently retained by the discoverer. However, lost things which exceed one hundred drachmas in value (Article 1081 sub-paragraph c CC) are not acquired immediately by the discoverer.[602] On the contrary, the discoverer is bound: (a) to notify without delay on his or her part the person who has lost the thing or its owner or anyone else who has a right thereon and, in the case where such notification is difficult, to notify the police authority (Article 1081 sub-paragraphs a, b CC); (b) to keep and maintain the thing, unless he or she prefers to hand it over to the police authority (Article 1082 CC) and (c) to hand the thing over to the police authority when this is demanded by the latter (Article 1084 paragraph 1 CC). After a lapse of one year from the date of notifying the police authority, provided that in the meantime the

---

I No. 486, 208) or a juridical act (for this view see G. Balis, *PrL*, para. 85, 211; Ap. Georgiades, *PrL*, para. 54 III No. 7, 675–676). See also *supra* para. 114 nn. 220, 221.

597. On this point see Ap. Georgiades, *PrL*, para. 55 I No. 1, 679 and for a more detailed treatment Ach. Koutsouradis, *Discovery etc.*, 37 et seq.
598. For a detailed discussion of this point see Ach. Koutsouradis, *Discovery etc.*, 69 et seq.
599. In the case where the movable has been thrown away with the intention of abandonment by the lessee-detentor, it is lost in respect to the owner (K. Vavouskos, *PrL*, No. 164, 162; Ap. Georgiades, *PrL*, para. 55 I 1 No. 2 n. 1, 680). Compare, however, *supra* para. 325 n. 566 on the same issue in the area of Art. 1038 CC. See also Ach. Koutsouradis, *Discovery etc.*, 113 et seq.
600. Compare K. Fourkiotis, 'On Art. 1081 et seq. of the Greek Civil Code', AID 9 (1942): 139 [in Greek]; Ap. Georgiades, *PrL*, para. 55 I 1 No. 2, 679–680; N. Livanis, in *Civil Code*, Vol. V: *PrL*, ed. Ap. Georgiades & M. Stathopoulos, Art. 1081 No. 5.
601. Which is a material act (see G. Balis, *PrL*, para. 87, 212; Ap. Georgiades, *PrL*, para. 55 I 2 No. 4, 681; N. Livanis, in *Civil Code*, Vol. V: *PrL*, ed. Ap. Georgiades & M. Stathopoulos, Art. 1081 No. 13).
602. In the case where the thing has been found in an inhabited building or a place destined for the use of the public, the discoverer is bound to hand it over to the owner of the building or the lessee or the person in charge of the supervision of the place. In such a case the discoverer will be deemed to be the person to whom the thing was handed over (Art. 1092 CC).

person entitled to the thing has not been made known to the police authority or to the discoverer, the latter acquires the ownership of the lost thing, free from any real right which may have encumbered it, from the time of the discovery (*ex tunc*) (Article 1088 CC).[603] If the discoverer does not take delivery of the thing acquired within the time period set by the police authority, the ownership is transferred to the municipality or the communal authority of the locality where the discovery was made (Article 1091 CC). Finally, it should be borne in mind that the lost thing may be acquired by the discoverer even if the person entitled to the thing has been made known before the aforementioned one year period lapses. This applies provided that the discoverer demanded his or her disbursements[604] and reward,[605] while setting a time-limit for this purpose, and the person entitled let this time-limit expire without effect (Article 1089 CC).

X. Acquisition of a Hoard

340. A hoard is a movable thing of value which has been hidden in another movable or immovable thing for so long that the owner thereof cannot be ascertained (Article 1093 CC). According to Article 1093 CC, the person who finds and takes the hoard into his or her possession becomes owner of one half of it, while the other half belongs to the owner of the thing in which the hoard was hidden.[606]

The acquisition of a hoard by the above persons is original and presupposes, on the one hand, a discovery, which is a material act, and, on the other hand, a taking of possession of the hoard, that is, occupancy. From the moment occupancy by the discoverer commences, the latter and the owner of the thing in which the hoard was hidden become, by virtue of the law, co-owners of the hoard in equal shares.

603. During the aforementioned one year period the discoverer has an expectation that he or she will acquire ownership. This expectation, which is extinguished as soon as the person entitled to the thing has been made known, is transferable and inheritable (see, in particular, Ap. Georgiades, *PrL*, para. 55 III No. 19, 685).

604. See Arts 1085, 1087 CC.

605. See Art. 1086 CC.

606. Things of archaeological, historical or artistic value which are useful for the study of the history of the Greek nation do not fall within the scope of application of Art. 1093 CC. The ownership of such things is determined by L. 3028/2002 concerning protection of archaeological things and the cultural heritage in general.

Chapter 2. Acquisition and Loss of Specific Types of Ownership

§1. Constitution and Loss of Co-ownership

341. Co-ownership is constituted by a juridical act, by virtue of the law or by *usucaption*. Constitution by juridical act occurs, for example, when A transfers to B the undivided half of his or her building plot, when A transfers his or her car in undivided shares to B and C or when B, C and D inherit by virtue of a will (testament) an apartment belonging to the testator A. Co-ownership by virtue of the law is achieved, for example, in the case where B, C and D inherit by intestate succession an immovable belonging to the estate of the decedent A or in the cases of Articles 1058, 1059 or 1093 CC.[607] Finally, for example, A, B and C, who possess in common a movable or an immovable thing belonging to another, acquire co-ownership thereon by ordinary or extraordinary *usucaption* in the case where the conditions specified in Article 1041 or 1045 CC[608] concur in respect to them all.

342. An ideal share of co-ownership may be acquired by contract just like ownership, that is, by application of Article 1033, in the area of immovables, and in accordance with Articles 1034 et seq. CC, in the area of movables.[609] However, an ideal share may also be acquired by ordinary[610] or extraordinary[611] *usucaption*.

343. Finally, it should be borne in mind that, like an owner, so too a co-owner may renounce his or her ideal share of the co-ownership at any time.[612] In such a case, the relevant ideal share does not accrue to the ideal shares of the other co-owners. It becomes ownerless and, consequently, it comes into the ownership of

607. See *supra* paras 332, 333, 340.
608. See *supra* paras 282 et seq., 293, 329.
609. The acquisition of an ideal share from a person who is not the owner (Arts 1036 et seq. CC) is achieved, for example, in the case where A, the depositary of a car, appears as the owner of the car, sells the undivided half of it to B, who acts in good faith, and delivers to the latter the possession of the car.
610. For example, in the case where the undivided half of an immovable is 'transferred' to A on the basis of a defective lawful title.
611. Thus, for example, in the case where A and B are co-owners of a field, A may acquire the ideal share of B by extraordinary acquisition by possession after twenty years' exercise of possession over the whole immovable with the mind of an exclusive owner. However, in such a case, the time period of *usucaption* begins from the time the decision of A to enjoy possession of the common thing exclusively for himself or herself is brought to the knowledge of B (K. Vavouskos, *PrL*, No. 177, 177; Ap. Georgiades, *PrL*, para. 44 II 2 No. 32, 525, para. 45 II 2 No. 11, 556–557, para. 65 III 3 No. 23, 811; AP 1431/2010, NOMOS; AP 1429/2010, NOMOS; AP 815/2010, NOMOS; AP 810/2010, NOMOS; AP 718/2010, NOMOS; AP 1744/2009, NOMOS; Plenary Session of AP 485/1982, 31 NoB, 1983, 55; AP 645/2001, 50 NoB, 2002, 697; AP 1117/1998, 66 EEN, 1999, 906; AP 309/1997, 38 HellD, 1997, 1850; AP 689/1996, 65 EEN, 1998, 46; AP 1109/1984, 33 NoB, 1985, 773; AP 919/1981, 49 EEN, 1982, 586; AP 237/1981, 29 NoB, 1981, 1475; AP 641/1980, 28 NoB, 1980, 1992; AP 1535/1979, 28 NoB, 1980, 1086; AP 1075/1979, 28 NoB, 1980, 494; Court of Appeal of Thessaloniki 1691/1987, 42 Arm, 1988, 425).
612. See also *supra* para. 305 and n. 536.

the State, in the area of immovables (Article 972 CC),[613] or into the ownership of the person who occupied it, in the field of movables (Article 1075 CC).[614]

§2. Constitution and Loss of Horizontal and Vertical Ownership

344. Horizontal and vertical ownership may be constituted by a contract between the co-owners of the whole immovable, by a contract between the owner (or co-owners) of the whole immovable and a future co-owner, by a unilateral juridical act *inter vivos* of the owner of the whole immovable or by a will (testament) of the latter (Article 1002 sub-paragraph a CC, 14 L. 3741/1929 and 2 L.D. 1024/1971).

In addition, horizontal and vertical ownership may be constituted, on the one hand, by virtue of a court decision published in the context of a trial for the distribution of a common building plot with a building or separate buildings thereon (Article 480 A CCProc) and, on the other, by virtue of a court decision and an agreement by a 65% majority of the co-owners of a building plot (Articles 1–8 Law 1562/1985).

Finally, considering that the grounds which justify the institution of *usucaption* also apply in the area of horizontal and vertical ownership, it seems correct to interpret positively[615] (and not negatively[616]) the silence of Article 1002 CC, 14 Law 3741/1929 and 2 L.D. 1024/1971 and to accept that horizontal and vertical ownership may be constituted by *usucaption* as well. Indeed, the above articles regulate the constitution of horizontal and vertical ownership on the basis of the private will and do not seem to exclude their constitution by virtue of the law and, specifically, by *usucaption*.

---

613. See *supra* para. 306.
614. See *supra* para. 337.
615. Thus, Ap. Bournias, *Horizontal Ownership As it Functions in Greece Today* (Athens, 1969), 21 et seq. [in Greek]; Ap. Bournias, 'Constitution of Horizontal Ownership by Usucaption', *NoB* 20 (1972): 1232 et seq. [in Greek]; Ap. Georgiades, *PrL*, para. 66 II 2 Nos 32–33, 835–836; D. Christophilopoulos, *Vertical Co-ownership* (Athens: Simopoulos, 1976), 119 [in Greek]; M. Karasis, in *Civil Code*, Vol. V: *PrL*, ed. Ap. Georgiades & M. Stathopoulos, Art. 1117 No. 14.
616. As the prevailing opinion does. See G. Balis, *PrL*, para. 121, 283; K. Vavouskos, *PrL*, No. 283 and n. 3, 279–280; M. Kallimopoulos, in *ErmAK*, Art. 1002 No. 157 [in Greek]; A. Tousis, *PrL*, para. 144, 667–668; I. Spyridakis, *Law of Horizontal and Vertical Ownership* (Athens/Komotini: A. Sakkoulas, 1996), 157–158 [in Greek]; P. Filios & Chr. Filios, *PrL*, para. 163 A II, 297 [in Greek]; Ph. Tsetsekos, *Horizontal and Vertical Ownership (Divided Ownership)*, 3rd edn (Athens: Sakkoulas, 2002), 110–112 [in Greek]; A. Patsourakos, *Horizontal Ownership* (Athens: Sakkoulas, 1973), n. 11, 27 [in Greek]; P. Konstantopoulos, *Horizontal Ownership in Greece* (Athens, 1974), 138–139 [in Greek], as well as AP 79/2008, 49 HellD, 2008, 1520; AP 630/2006, 47 HellD, 2006, 1068; AP 761/2002, 43 HellD, 2002, 1702; AP 602/2001, 43 HellD, 2002, 153 (154); AP 502/2001, 42 HellD, 2001, 1632; AP 722/1993, 36 HellD, 1995, 99; AP 885/1985, 34 NoB, 1986, 839; AP 1642/1983, 32 NoB, 1984, 1375; AP 579/1982, 31 NoB, 1983, 366; AP 195/1982, 31 NoB, 1983, 386; AP 1705/1981, 30 NoB, 1982, 1060; Court of Appeal of Athens 3289/2009, 50 HellD, 2009, 1511; Court of Appeal of Patras 1155/2007, NOMOS = AchN, 2008, 756; Court of Appeal of Athens 6920/1991, 34 HellD, 1993, 650 (651); One-member District Court of Thessaloniki 20915/2006, 62 Arm, 2008, 396 (397); One-member District Court of Rhodos 185/2006, NOMOS; One-member District Court of Mytilini 219/1999, 52 ArchN, 2001, 64.

345. The contract by which horizontal or vertical ownership is constituted must be incorporated in a notarial deed and transcribed. Furthermore, in the case where horizontal or vertical ownership is constituted by a will (testament) or in accordance with Article 480 A CCProc, the acceptance of the estate (or legacy) or the relevant final court decision must be transcribed, respectively (Article 1193 CC, 489 paragraph 2 CCProc). Finally, in the case provided for by Law 1562/1985, transcriptions must be made of: (a) notarial deeds which incorporate an act of constitution of horizontal ownership which has been formed by the majority of the co-owners, and (b) the court decision which permits the relevant constitution.

346. The issue of constitution of horizontal or vertical ownership must be distinguished from the issue of acquisition of ownership on a storey or an apartment on which horizontal or vertical ownership has already been constituted. In fact, in the latter case, the general provisions governing acquisition of ownership on immovables apply. Consequently, in this case, possible means of acquisition of ownership are transfer by contract or death and *usucaption*.

347. Finally, it should be borne in mind that, like owners of immovables in general, so too the owner of a storey or an apartment may renounce or abandon his or her ownership.[617] In such a case, the abandoned ownership becomes ownerless and, concomitantly, comes into the ownership of the State (Article 972 CC).[618]

617. See also *supra* para. 305 and n. 536.
618. See *supra* para. 306.

Chapter 3. Constitution and Extinction of Servitudes

§1. Constitution of Servitudes

I. Constitution of Real Servitudes

348. Real servitudes may be constituted by means of a juridical act, either *inter vivos* (a contract) or *mortis causa* (a testament),[619] by *usucaption* (Article 1121 CC) or on the strength of a court decision[620] or a compulsory expropriation based on the constitution of a real servitude.[621]

349. According to Article 1121 CC, the provisions governing *usucaption* of immovables and the transfer thereof by agreement apply by analogy to the constitution of real servitudes. Consequently, for the constitution of a real servitude by contract an agreement (real contract) incorporated in a notarial deed and submitted to transcription is required between the owners of the dominant and the servient tenements to the effect that a real servitude is constituted for a just cause (Article 1033 CC).[622] On the other hand, the constitution of a real servitude by *usucaption* presupposes an immovable susceptible of *usucaption* and, in the case of ordinary *usucaption*, the exercise of quasi possession with the intention of acting as holder of a certain real servitude for a period of ten years, good faith and a lawful or putative title (Articles 1041–1043 CC). However, in the case of extraordinary *usucaption*, a necessary precondition is the exercise of quasi possession with the intention of acting as holder of a certain real servitude for a period of twenty years (Article 1045 CC).

Finally, consideration ought to be given to Articles 1122 and 1123 CC. The former, holding that a real servitude is an undivided right,[623] stipulates that, in the case where the dominant or the servient tenement belongs to several persons, the constitution of a servitude by means of a juridical act requires the consent of all (Article 1122 CC). On the other hand, according to Article 1123 CC, where the servitude consists in an obligation to abstain from doing something,[624] possession commences, insofar as extraordinary *usucaption* is concerned, from the time the owner of the dominant tenement prohibits the owner of the servient tenement from performing an act abstention from which forms the substance of the servitude.

619. See also *supra* para. 278 and n. 493, as well as para. 279 (under (a), (b)).
620. According to Art. 481 point 2 CCProc, in the context of a trial for the distribution of a common immovable and in order to render unequal parts equal, the court may decide to allow the constitution of servitudes on certain parts in favour of other co-owners.
621. See Art. 1 para. 1 L. 2882/2001.
622. In this case the acquisition of the relevant right is derivative and 'creative'.
623. See *supra* para. 231.
624. See *supra* para. 234 (under (a)).

II. Constitution of Personal Servitudes

A. *Constitution of Usufruct*

350. The constitution of usufruct[625] is referred to in Articles 1143 and 1144 CC.[626] From these articles it can be concluded that usufruct may be constituted, even on an undivided ideal share of a thing, by means of a juridical act, either *inter vivos* (a contract) or *mortis causa* (a testament),[627] or by *usucaption*. Furthermore, according to Article 1143 CC, the provisions governing *usucaption* of movables or immovables and transfer of the ownership thereof by agreement apply by analogy to the constitution of usufruct on such movables or immovables. Consequently, in the case of constitution of usufruct by contract,[628] depending on whether the usufruct is constituted on an immovable or a movable thing, the conditions laid down by Article 1033 CC[629] or by Articles 1034 et seq. CC,[630] respectively, need to be met. Likewise, the constitution of usufruct by ordinary or extraordinary *usucaption*, presupposes fulfilment of the conditions laid down by Articles 1041–1043 or 1045 CC, respectively, and, naturally, that the thing in question is susceptible of *usucaption*.[631]

B. *Constitution of Habitation*

351. Insofar as in the area of habitation the general provisions governing usufruct of immovables apply by analogy (Article 1187 CC), habitation is constituted just like the usufruct on immovables.[632]

---

625. Here, we will speak of the constitution of usufruct on immovable and on non-consumable movable things. On the issue of constitution of usufruct on consumable things (quasi usufruct) and on incorporeal objects see, respectively, *supra* para. 259 and paras 261, 263 and n. 450, 264 and n. 454, 265, 267, 268 n. 463, 269, 270.
626. In the area of usufruct also apply Art. 481 point 2 CCProc (thus, Ap. Georgiades, *PrL*, para. 75 II 1 No. 18 p. 923; M. Karasis, in *Civil Code*, Vol. VI: *PrL*, ed. Ap. Georgiades & M. Stathopoulos, Art. 1143 No. 31) and Art. 1 para. 1 L. 2882/2001 (on which see *supra* para. 348 and nn. 619, 620).
627. See also *supra* para. 278 and n. 493 and para. 279.
628. By the relevant contract the owner either constitutes usufruct and preserves naked ownership or transfers naked ownership and withholds usufruct in favour of himself or herself or a third party (on this issue, which appears in the area of habitation as well, see, in particular, Y. Karibali-Tsiptsiou, *Habitation*, 118–119).
629. See *supra* para. 349 and n. 622.
630. Namely, agreement between the owner (except if the conditions in Arts 1036 et seq. CC arise) and the usufructuary to the effect that usufruct is constituted and delivery of quasi possession of the thing from the former to the latter occurs.
631. See *supra* para. 349, though bearing in mind that in the area of movables the period of *usucaption* extends to three years.
632. See *supra* para. 350 and, for a detailed treatment of this point, Y. Karibali-Tsiptsiou, *Habitation*, 117 et seq.

C. Constitution of Limited Personal Servitudes

352. Limited personal servitudes are constituted like real servitudes.[633] This is because, according to Article 1191 CC, in the field of limited personal servitudes the provisions governing real servitudes apply, insofar as these are compatible with the nature of the personal servitudes.

§2. Extinction of Servitudes

I. Extinction of Real Servitudes

A. General Grounds of Extinction

353. The grounds on the basis of which a real servitude may be extinguished are distinguished into general (which also pertain to other real rights) and special.

Examples of general grounds are:

(a) fulfilment of the resolutory condition or expiration of the resolutory term upon which the real servitude was constituted (Articles 202, 210 CC);
(b) acquisition of the servient tenement by *usucaption* (Article 1053 CC);[634]
(c) compulsory expropriation of the servient tenement;[635] and
(d) compulsory auction of the servient tenement provided that such auction was precipitated by a mortgagee whose mortgage was inscribed before the constitution of the relevant real servitude.

B. Special Grounds of Extinction

1. Renunciation by the Beneficiary (Article 1134 CC)

354. The renunciation by the beneficiary entails extinction not only of a real servitude but of other real rights on immovables as well.[636]

In the area of real servitudes, the renunciation is effected either by a unilateral, non-addressed and non-causal juridical act created *inter vivos*, which must be incorporated in a notarial deed and transcribed, or by a will (testament). In the latter case, the renunciation takes the form of a *legatum liberationis* with the owner of the servient tenement as legatee. In the same case, the real servitude is extinguished from the moment the acceptance of the legacy by the legatee is transcribed.[637]

633. See *supra* paras 348–349. However, the opinion has been expressed that Art. 481 point 2 CCProc (see *supra* para. 348 n. 620) does not apply in the area of limited personal servitudes (I. Sontis, *Limited Personal Servitudes*, 247 n. 11; K. Vavouskos, *PrL*, No. 360, 360–361).

634. See *supra* para. 294.

635. In this case the real servitude is converted into a personal claim on the compensation that was paid to the owner of the servient tenement (Art. 9 para. 4 L. 2882/2001).

636. See, for example, Arts 1169 (*infra* para. 362), 1187 (*infra* para. 364), 1318 point 2 CC (*infra* para. 441).

637. See *supra* para. 279 and n. 498.

If a third party has a real right on the dominant tenement, his or her consent is also essential if his or her right is affected by the renunciation (Article 1134 sub-paragraph b CC).

Due to the undivided character of real servitudes, the renunciation of an ideal share of such a servitude is impossible. For the same reason, in the case where there are several beneficiaries, the renunciation must be made by all of them in order for the renunciation to be legally effective.

2. Destruction of the Dominant or Servient Tenement (Article 1135 CC)

355. The destruction of the dominant or servient tenement entails extinction of a real servitude if it is total. This occurs, for example, in the case where the dominant or servient tenement has been irreversibly flooded by the waters of a river.

3. Inability of Exercise (Article 1136 CC)

356. A real servitude is extinguished in the case where it cannot be exercised on account of actual or legal events. This impossibility must be constant and not transient and also absolute and not partial. In fact, in the latter case, the servitude is not extinguished on account of its undivided character.

4. Confusion (Article 1137 CC)

357. The passing of the ownership of the dominant and the servient tenements to the same person (confusion) entails extinction of the relevant real servitude.[638,639] In such a case, the extinction occurs automatically without a declaration of will or a transcription being necessary. The same extinction is final, in the sense that the servitude does not revive if the dominant or the servient tenement is later transferred to a third party.

5. Disuse (Articles 1138 et seq. CC)

358. The continuous disuse of a real servitude during a period of twenty years[640] leads to its extinction (Article 1138 sub-paragraph a CC), regardless of the

638. See also *supra* paras 162, 230 (under (c)).
639. However, if the owner of the dominant tenement becomes the owner not of the whole but of a part of the servient tenement, the servitude is maintained on the remaining part insofar as it may be exercised on this part (Art. 1131 sub-para. (b) CC). Along the same lines, if the owner of the servient tenement becomes the owner of a part of the dominant tenement, the servitude is maintained on behalf of the remaining part provided that it continues to be useful for this part (Art. 1131 sub-para. (b) CC).
640. In respect to this twenty-year period of disuse the following ought to be noted: (a) it commences, in the area of intermittent servitudes, from the time of the last use and, in the field of continuous servitudes (on the distinction between continuous and intermittent servitudes see *supra* para. 234 (under (b)), from the time a construction has been erected on the servient tenement that impedes

ground for the disuse. The disuse must be complete, in the sense that it must refer to all the utilities contained in the relevant servitude and not to a part of them. Owing to the undivided character of a real servitude, its partial exercise does not entail partial extinction on account of disuse.

If several beneficiaries exist, the exercise of the servitude by one of them is sufficient to prevent extinction (Article 1138 sub-paragraph b CC). This is also due to the undivided character of the real servitude.

The extinction of a servitude through disuse is not prevented when the servitude is exercised in a manner or at a time differing from those that are appropriate to the servitude (Article 1140 CC).

II. Extinction of Personal Servitudes

A. *Extinction of Usufruct*

1. General Grounds of Extinction

359. Like real servitudes, usufruct[641] may also be extinguished on general or special grounds. Thus, examples of general grounds are: fulfilment of the resolutory condition or expiration of the resolutory term upon which the usufruct was constituted (Articles 202, 210 CC); acquisition of the encumbered thing by *usucaption* (Article 1053 CC), and transfer of the encumbered movable from a person who is not the owner to an acquirer of good faith (Article 1040 CC).[642]

2. Special Grounds of Extinction

a. Demise of the Usufructuary (Article 1167 CC)

360. As may be concluded from Article 1167 CC, unless otherwise stipulated, the demise (or the declaration of disappearance) of the usufructuary[643] entails extinction of usufruct. On the other hand, a usufruct constituted for the benefit of a legal entity is extinguished with the dissolution of the said entity.[644] However, if the

---

the exercise of the servitude (Art. 1139 para. 1 CC); (b) it is interrupted by the commencement of a legal action (i.e., of a confessory action [on which see *infra* para. 405] or of the corresponding declaratory action), by the beneficiary (Art. 1139 para. 2 CC; see also Arts 261–263, 269 CC); (c) it is suspended during the period in which the prescription of the legal action for the protection of the servitude (i.e., of the confessory action) is suspended or its completion is legally prevented (Art. 1141 CC; see also Arts 255–259 CC).

641. Here we shall speak of the extinction of usufruct on immovable and non-consumable movable things. On the issue of extinction of usufruct on consumable things (quasi usufruct) and incorporeal objects see, respectively, *supra* para. 259 and n. 445 and *supra* paras 262, 263, 268 n. 463.

642. See *supra* para. 327.

643. Even in the case where the usufruct is uninherited, by the demise of the usufructuary, his or her quasi possession is transmitted to his or her heirs (Art. 983 CC) who must, however, restore the thing to the owner (see *supra* para. 124 and n. 236).

644. The usufruct is not maintained at the stage of liquidation of the legal entity in that it does not serve the purpose of the liquidation (see Art. 72 CC).

usufruct had been constituted on behalf of several beneficiaries in undivided ideal shares, the demise of one of them leads to the extinction of the relevant ideal share of usufruct.

Article 1167 CC, declaring the extinction of usufruct by the demise of the usufructuary, unless otherwise stipulated, introduces a non-mandatory rule. However, the possibility of the parties constituting an inherited usufruct is rightly censured by certain authors who perceive in this possibility the danger of usufruct perpetuated and the function and content of ownership becoming degraded. Therefore, it has been argued that, in cases where the usufruct is stipulated as being inherited, its duration must be determined in advance.[645]

b. Confusion (Article 1168 CC)

361. Like all limited real rights, usufruct is also extinguished by merger (confusion) of usufruct and ownership in the same person. This occurs, for example, when the usufructuary inherits the naked ownership. The extinction of usufruct in this case is final, in the sense that the latter does not revive if the thing is transferred to a third party by the present owner and former usufructuary.

c. Renunciation by the Usufructuary (Article 1169 CC)

362. The renunciation, which is a special ground of extinction of usufruct, takes the form of a juridical act which contains a unilateral and non-causal declaration of will addressed to the naked owner. The relevant juridical act, in the area of immovables, must be incorporated in a notarial deed, of which the naked owner must be notified, and transcribed.

d. Other Grounds of Extinction

363. Article 1170 CC provides for, as grounds for the extinction of usufruct, the destruction of the encumbered thing, the inability of exercising the usufruct and the disuse of the usufruct by drawing an analogy with Articles 1135, 1136 and 1138–1141 CC[646] concerning extinction of real servitudes on the above grounds. The same article also states that the twenty-year period of disuse begins from the time the right of usufruct was last exercised.

An exception to the rule that the usufruct is extinguished by the destruction of the encumbered thing (Article 1170 CC) is introduced by Article 1171 CC. According to the latter, the usufruct of a thing also extends to whatever is due in exchange thereof or to the amount of compensation payable in respect thereof, particularly as a result of its destruction or an insurance policy or its compulsory expropriation. This means that, when the conditions of Article 1171 CC concur, the usufruct is *ex lege* converted into a personal claim or into usufruct on consumable things (i.e., on

645. On all these points see Ap. Georgiades, *PrL*, para. 76 IV 2 No. 15, 951–952; K. Roussos, in *Civil Code*, Vol. VI: *PrL*, ed. Ap. Georgiades & M. Stathopoulos, Art. 1167 No. 7 et seq.

646. See *supra* paras 355, 356, 358.

money). However, if the given exchange is another thing, it is obvious that the usufruct continues to pertain to a thing.

Article 1171 CC is completed by Article 1172 CC which states that, in the case contemplated in Article 1171 CC, the owner or the usufructuary is entitled to demand that the amount collected be spent on the restoration or replacement of the thing so long as such an action conforms to the rules of an orderly exploitation. As is obvious, in this case, the usufruct encumbers the restored or the new thing.

B. Extinction of Habitation

364. Insofar as in the area of habitation the general provisions governing usufruct of immovables apply by analogy (Article 1187 CC), habitation is extinguished just like the usufruct on immovables.[647]

C. Extinction of Limited Personal Servitudes

365. Owing to the fact that, in the field of limited personal servitudes, the provisions governing real servitudes apply, insofar as these are compatible with the nature of the personal servitudes, limited real servitudes are extinguished like real servitudes.[648] Furthermore, Article 1190 CC should also be borne in mind in that, according to the latter, unless otherwise stipulated, a limited real servitude is extinguished by the demise of the beneficiary or from the time of dissolution of the legal entity that was the beneficiary.[649] However, the demise of one of several beneficiaries does not entail extinction of the relevant servitude if the said servitude has been constituted as an undivided right.[650]

647. See *supra* paras 360 et seq. See, however, in particular, Y. Karibali-Tsiptsiou, *Habitation*, 219 et seq.
648. See *supra* paras 353 et seq.
649. See also *supra* para. 253.
650. On this point see *supra* para. 254.

Part VI. Protection of Property Rights

Chapter 1. Protection of Ownership

§1. General Classification

366. An owner's direct and absolute power over the thing he or she owns may be violated in two ways: (a) wholly, that is, by deprivation or retention of the thing or (b) partly, namely by disturbance which falls short of dispossession. In these cases the owner needs protection. In this respect, the law offers him or her real claims which aim to restore his or her direct and absolute power over the thing.[651] To be precise, by these claims the owner may demand from the offender either (in the first case) acknowledgment of his or her right of ownership and the restitution of the thing (Article 1094 CC: revendicatory action) or (in the second case) the cessation of such disturbance and its non-recurrence in the future (Article 1108 CC: negative action). Revendicatory and negative actions are considered to be general actions in the sense that they are available for both immovables and movables.

367. In addition to the above general actions, the law also recognizes specific actions. Thus, the publician action is applicable to immovable property (Article 1112 CC), whereas, in regard to movable property, an action to conduct a search for a movable is provided for. The latter is regulated by Article 1109 CC,[652] according to which the owner of a movable which has been brought into the immovable of another has the right to demand from the possessor of this immovable permission to search for and recover the movable against payment of compensation for any damages caused by the search.[653]

368. The following sections deal in detail with revendicatory, negative and publician actions.

---

651. See also *supra* para. 48 n. 124.

652. Compare Art. 995 CC (on which see *supra* para. 135 and n. 253). However, in the case where the owner is possessor as well, he or she may exercise the claim derived from Art. 995 CC in addition to the claim generated by Art. 1109 CC.

653. This action is dependent on the condition that the owner of the immovable has not already acquired possession or detention over the movable, as, in the former case, a violation of the ownership has taken place, thus permitting the true owner to commence a revendicatory action.

§2. Revendicatory Action

I. Procedure

A. *Content and Procedural Issues*

369. As emerges from Article 1094 CC (in combination with Article 1108 paragraph 1 sub-paragraph a CC), a revendicatory action protects the ownership of an immovable or movable thing which is violated wholly, that is, by deprivation or retention of the thing. This action is brought by a dispossessed owner[654] against a non-owner who possesses or detains the thing at the time the action is brought and has as requested relief acknowledgement of the right of ownership and restitution of the thing.[655] This means that a revendicatory action operates at the same time as a declaratory action and an action for performance. Thus, in the case where only acknowledgement of the right of ownership is requested, the relevant action is not revendicatory but declaratory (Article 70 CCProc).[656] However, on the other hand, when only restitution of the thing is requested, the action is revendicatory. This is because the judge may not order the restitution of the thing to the plaintiff before being persuaded that the latter is its owner.

370. The legal document of a revendicatory action, besides the requested relief and the other elements required in any legal document (Article 118 CCProc), must contain the legal and actual facts which support it and justify its commencement[657] (historical basis of the action), as well as an exact description of the thing under litigation (Article 216 CCProc).

The competent courts in terms of subject-matter for the hearing of revendicatory actions are either the Magistrates' Courts or One or Three-member District Courts, depending on the value of the object of the dispute (Articles 14 paragraphs 1a and 2, 18 CCProc). As regards territorial competency, it should be noted that, in the area

---

654. The plaintiff may also be the co-owner (see also *infra* paras 400, 401, 402), the owner of a storey or an apartment on which horizontal ownership has been constituted (see also *infra* para. 403), a person in favour of whom compulsory expropriation has been carried out, a naked owner (who, however, may not bring the relevant action against a usufructuary), creditors of the owner, when the conditions of Art. 72 CCProc concur (see *infra* para. 414 under (a)), a trustee in bankruptcy and a testamentary executor. Furthermore, on the issue of whether the revendicatory action may be assigned to a person who is not the owner of the thing under litigation see Ap. Georgiades, *PrL*, para. 58 I 2 No. 3, 703 and, especially, the same author in Ap. Georgiades & M. Stathopoulos (eds), *Civil Code*, Vol. V: *PrL*, Introd. 1094–1112 No. 16 where further references may be found.

655. The restitution of the thing may also be requested by an eviction action (see also *supra* para. 139) or by a personal (obligational) action, for example, against the lessee who refuses to make the relevant restitution on the expiration of the lease.

656. In such a case the plaintiff must invoke and prove his or her legal interest in the relevant acknowledgment. In current practice, declaratory actions are preferred because the hearing of such actions does not presuppose the payment of a judicial stamp-tax. In contrast, in revendicatory actions, the plaintiff who does not pay judicial stamp-tax proportionate to the value of the object of the dispute is deemed to be judged by default.

657. Namely, the legal and actual facts from which it may be concluded, on the one hand, that the plaintiff is the owner of the thing under litigation and, on the other, that the defendant possesses or detains the thing without right.

of immovables, the competent court is that of the district in which the immovable is situated (Article 29 CCProc), while, in the field of movables, the competent court is that of the district in which the defendant has his or her domicile or residence (Articles 22, 23 CCProc).

Revendicatory actions that concern immovables must be registered, within thirty days of the date of their deposition, in the vindication register of the registry of the district in which the immovable is situated. Otherwise they are dismissed as inadmissible (Article 220 CCProc[658]).

Finally, it should be borne in mind that a revendicatory action against the State, which arbitrarily occupies an immovable, may not be commenced without a preceding application to the State aiming to solve the dispute out of court and a lapse of six months from the date of service of the above application, provided that in the meantime the applicant has not received a notification that his or her claims have been accepted (Article 24 L. 2732/1999).

B. Defence of the Defendant

371. The defendant may deny the basis of the revendicatory action, alleging that the plaintiff is not the owner and (or) that he or she himself or herself has not deprived or retained the possession or detention of the thing.[659] In the case of denial, the onus is on the plaintiff to prove the facts which support his or her action (Article 338 paragraph 1 CCProc).

372. The defendant is also entitled to advance the allegation that, already, he or she and not the plaintiff is the owner of the thing under litigation. In this case, the defendant is bound to prove his or her ownership.

A claim asserting one's own right of ownership may be filed either by a cross action or by a plea.[660] By a cross action, the defendant seeks not only dismissal of the action by the plaintiff but also acknowledgement of his or her own ownership on the thing under litigation by a court decision which will have a res judicata effect on the plaintiff. On the other hand, acceptance of the relevant plea entails only dismissal of the revendicatory action.

373. Furthermore, the defendant, who in relation to the owner has a right to possess or detain the thing under litigation, may refuse to restore the thing (Article 1095 CC). In this case, the defendant, without denying the historical basis of the revendicatory action, namely the ownership of the plaintiff, maintains – by means of a

---

658. See also Art. 12 para. 1 point xii of L. 2664/1998 within the framework of the land registry system.
659. The denial may be simple (e.g., 'the plaintiff is not the owner' or 'I do not have possession or detention over the thing') or justified (e.g., 'the plaintiff is not the owner as the ownership belongs to X').
660. A claim asserting one's own right of ownership takes the form either of a justified denial of a revendicatory action or a plea, depending on whether it is based on facts which are anterior to or simultaneous with (justified denial of the action) or posterior to (plea) those facts contained in the historical basis of the action (see Ap. Georgiades, *PrL*, para. 58 II 1, 3 No. 27, 710–711, No. 35, 713–714).

genuine dilatory plea[661] – that he or she has a right to possess or detain the thing and, therefore, refuses its restitution.[662]

Possession is invoked by a defendant who has a limited real right – such as usufruct, habitation or a pledge – on the thing under litigation. It may also be invoked by a defendant to whom the plaintiff has alienated and delivered the immovable claimed, so long as the revendicatory action is commenced before the transcription provided for in Article 1033 CC ('plea of the thing sold and delivered': *exceptio rei venditae et traditae*).[663] On the other hand, the detention of the thing by the defendant may be based on a personal (obligational) right originating, for example, from a contract of hire, loan for use or deposit of the thing under litigation. However, the possession or detention of the thing by the defendant must be based on a valid legal relation, while the manner of its acquisition is of no consequence.

A plea concerning possession or detention may be raised not only by the direct possessor or detentor of a thing but also by a person who derives the relevant power from the latter, for example, by a sub-lessee. Acceptance of this plea, which presupposes that the real facts which support it have been proved by the defendant, entails dismissal of the revendicatory action.

374. In addition, the defendant may refuse to restore the thing under litigation by advancing the plea of prescription of the revendicatory action.[664] Indeed, the relevant action is prescribed after a period of twenty years (Article 249 CC) from the time a third party occupies the thing (Article 251 CC), provided that, during this period of time, the owner does not exercise his or her right.[665]

375. Finally, it should be borne in mind that, in cases where the conditions of Article 281 CC[666] occur, the defendant may request dismissal of the revendicatory action by raising the plea of abuse of right.

661. According to the prevailing opinion (on this point see Ap. Georgiades, *PrL*, para. 58 II 3 No. 38 and n. 59, 714; D. Papasteriou, *GenPrinc*, para. 19 III B No. 19, 254).
662. Consequently, the relevant plea may not be raised against an action which contains only a declaratory claim (see *supra* para. 369).
663. See Ap. Georgiades, *PrL*, para. 58 II 3 No. 42, 717 (who characterizes the relevant plea as subversive). See also *supra* para. 277 n. 484.
664. The prescription of a revendicatory action must be distinguished from the term of extinction of Art. 1020 CCProc, concerning actions for the vindication of a thing not belonging to a debtor and sold by auction. This action is commenced by the owner against the highest bidder within a term of extinction which differs according to the kind of property sold. It is one year for movables, running from the time they are delivered to the highest bidder, and five years for immovables, running from the transcription of the summary of the act of adjudgment.
665. Articles 255–270 CC, concerning suspension and interruption of prescription, apply in the area of prescription of revendicatory actions as well.
666. According to Art. 281 CC, the exercise of a right is prohibited if such exercise obviously exceeds the limits imposed by good faith or morality or by the social or economic purpose of the right.

C. Proof of Ownership

376. The plaintiff (or the defendant who has advanced the plea that he or she is the owner of the thing under litigation) is bound to prove the facts which, according to the law, led to the acquisition of the ownership. More precisely:

377. If the thing under litigation is an immovable and the manner of acquisition of ownership which is invoked is original (e.g., *usucaption*, adjudication, concession or accession) the facts that justify the relevant acquisition must be proved. On the other hand, in the case where the method of acquisition invoked is derivative (e.g., transfer by contract or death), the ownership of the predecessor in title must also be proved. This is because any derivative acquisition presupposes the status of owner in the person of the predecessor in title. Furthermore, in cases of successive transfers, the ownership of the most distant predecessors in title must also be proved until there is a case of original acquisition and, as a rule, extraordinary *usucaption* (*probatio diabolica*).[667]

378. In the area of movables proof of ownership is easier. This is because, first of all, movables may be acquired from a person who is not the owner (Article 1036 CC) and, second, because of the presumptions of ownership which are recognized by Articles 1110–1111 CC.[668]

In fact, the above articles constitute two legal rebuttable[669] presumptions. The first works on behalf[670] of the current possessor[671] of a movable property, who is presumed to be the owner (Article 1110 CC),[672] while the second works in favour of the previous possessor of a movable, who is presumed to have been owner during the period of his or her possession (Article 1111 CC). In the light of these presumptions, the (current or previous) possessor of a movable whose ownership is disputed only needs to prove his or her possession. On the other hand, the opposite party who seeks to rebut the relevant legal presumption must prove that the possessor is not or was not the owner.

As is obvious, on account of the presumptions of Articles 1110–1111 CC, when a movable is claimed, the defendant possessor is presumed to be the owner. Therefore, acceptance of the revendicatory action presupposes an attempt on the part of the plaintiff to refute the relevant presumption and prove his or her own ownership. Along the same lines, the plaintiff may invoke and prove the allegation, for

667. This method of proving ownership – which is necessary in the system of transcription registers adopted by the Civil Code – will not be necessary under the land registry system. This is because the latter is based on the presumption that the person who appears in the land register as owner really is the owner (for further details on this point see *supra* para. 31 and n. 69).

668. The presumptions set out in Arts 1398 CC and 115 IntrLCC apply to spouses.

669. Ap. Georgiades, *PrL*, para. 58 III 2 No. 61, 724. Compare K. Vavouskos, *PrL*, No. 316, 323.

670. And not against the current possessor. Thus, for example, in the case of disbursements which may be claimed from the owner of a movable, the plaintiff may not invoke the presumption of Art. 1110 CC in order to prove the ownership of the defendant possessor.

671. And not on behalf of the quasi possessor or the detentor.

672. However, the current possessor may not use the relevant presumption against a previous possessor who was deprived of the thing by theft or loss, unless money or title deeds in bearer form are involved (Art. 1110 sub-paras (b), (c) CC).

example, that the defendant is not possessor but quasi possessor or detentor[673] who recognizes him or her (the plaintiff) as possessor,[674] or that he or she (the plaintiff) was the previous possessor who was deprived of the thing by theft or loss.[675]

II. Consequences of Acceptance of Revendicatory Action

379. If a revendicatory action is accepted, the defendant is bound to restore the thing under litigation to the plaintiff. However, in this case, the defeated defendant or the winning plaintiff may bear a liability. This means that the acceptance of the revendicatory action sparks off reciprocal personal claims between the owner (plaintiff) and the possessor or detentor (defendant).

A. *Liability of the Defendant*

1. Content of the Defendant's Liability

380. The liability of the defeated defendant (possessor or detentor) towards the winning plaintiff relates, on the one hand, to the benefits derived from the thing under litigation and, on the other, to the deterioration, destruction and impossibility of restitution of the above thing for some other reason. The relevant liability is determined by the Civil Code on the basis of four criteria, which are as follows:

(a) the service or not of the revendicatory action;
(b) the good or bad faith of the defendant possessor or detentor;
(c) the entry of the possessor or detentor of bad faith into a state of default; and
(d) the acquisition of possession or detention by the defendant through an illegal act.

381. Thus, after the service of the revendicatory action, the defendant possessor or detentor (of good or bad faith) is liable: (a) to restore not only the benefits derived from the thing but also those which through his or her own fault he or she has not collected although he or she could have done so according to the rules of orderly management (Article 1096 CC); and b) to compensate the owner if through his or her own fault the thing has deteriorated or been destroyed or cannot be restored for some other reason (Article 1097 CC).

673. See *supra* n. 671.
674. One consequence of proving this fact is that the plaintiff-possessor is presumed to be the owner (Art. 1110 CC) and, concomitantly, he or she is absolved from the burden of proving his or her ownership.
675. If such a thing is proved, on the one hand, the presumption set out in Art. 1110 CC does not work in favour of the defendant (see *supra* n. 672) and, on the other, the presumption set out in Art. 1111 CC works in favour of the plaintiff.

382. On the other hand, before the service of the revendicatory action, the liability of the defendant possessor or detentor varies depending on whether he or she is of good or bad faith. Indeed, Article 1100 CC, referring to the period before the service of the revendicatory action, declares that a person who has taken possession of a thing in good faith and continued such possession in good faith is not liable either for restitution of benefits derived from the thing or for damages on account of deterioration or destruction or impossibility of restitution of the thing.[676] In contrast, according to Article 1098 sub-paragraph a CC, the possessor who was of bad faith at the time he or she took hold of the thing or later became aware that he or she was not entitled to possess it bears from such time and in regard to both the thing and the benefits derived therefrom the same responsibility as would arise in the period following the service of the revendicatory action.[677]

383. The liability of a possessor of bad faith increases in the case where he or she has entered into a state of default with regard to the restitution of the thing (Article 1098 sub-paragraph b CC). In fact, in this case, for as long as he or she delays restitution, the possessor is liable for any negligence and also for fortuitous events (e.g., fortuitous deterioration, destruction or impossibility of restitution of the thing), unless he or she can prove that the prejudice would have resulted even if the thing had been restored in time (Article 344 CC).

384. Finally, it should be borne in mind that a possessor (of good[678] or bad faith) who has acquired possession of a thing by an illegal act is also liable to compensate the owner in accordance with the provisions governing unlawful acts[679] (Article 1099 CC).

2. Exercise of the Rights Derived from Articles 1096–1100 CC

385. Claims derived from Articles 1096–1100 CC are effected by a legal action, which may be commenced either by a self-contained legal document or by the legal document of a revendicatory (or declaratory of ownership) action. The same claims may also be effected by a cross action or a plea or a counter-plea to set off the claims of the possessor or detentor for disbursements.

---

676. On the possibility that, in this case, the provisions governing enrichment without just cause might be applied (Arts 904 et seq. CC) see, in particular, Ap. Georgiades, *PrL*, para. 59 III 1 No. 16, 743–744 and para. 60 III 1 No. 8, 753).

677. See *supra* para. 381.

678. An example of a possessor of good faith who has acquired possession of a thing by an illegal act is a purchaser, X, who has violently taken possession of an immovable sold to him or her by a seller, A, believing that he or she (X) is the owner and ignoring, without being guilty of gross negligence, that the contracts of sale and transfer of ownership to him or her were null and void (see E. Kounougeri-Manoledaki, *Law of fruits*, 157; Ap. Georgiades, *PrL*, para. 59 II 4 No. 14, 742).

679. Providing that the conditions of tort occur as well (see Art. 914 CC).

With regard to the time-limit for their prescription, it seems correct to accept the opinion which holds that the relevant claims are subject to the twenty-year prescription of Article 249 CC, except for the claim arising from Article 1099 CC, which is subject to the five-year prescription of Article 937 CC.[680]

B. *Liability of the Plaintiff*

1. Content of the Plaintiff's Liability

386. The liability of the winning plaintiff towards the defeated possessor or detentor relates to disbursements incurred on the thing under litigation and to the settlement of charges encumbering the same thing. This liability, just like the liability of the defendant, is determined by the Civil Code on the basis of certain criteria, which are as follows:

(a) the service or not of the revendicatory action;
(b) the good or bad faith of the defendant possessor or detentor; and
(c) the division of the disbursements into the two categories of 'necessary'[681] and 'useful'.[682]

387. Thus, after the service of the revendicatory action, the possessor (of good or bad faith) is entitled to compensation for necessary disbursements or for the settlement of charges encumbering the thing solely in accordance with the provisions governing the management of another's affairs (Article 1102 CC).[683]

680. See Ap. Georgiades, *PrL*, para. 60 IV 4 Nos 34, 35, 761 and nn. 32, 33 (where other different opinions may be found).
681. 'Necessary' disbursements are those incurred in respect of the thing with a view to preserving it in a condition proper for an orderly exploitation (Art. 1101 sub-para. (a) CC). Necessary disbursements are treated by the Civil Code in the same manner as disbursements for the settlement of charges (Art. 1101 sub-para. (a) CC).
682. 'Useful' disbursements are those which entail an increase in the value of the thing (Art. 1103 CC). It is accepted that useful disbursements are treated like disbursements for luxuries, namely those aiming to satisfy particular aesthetic needs or caprices.
683. According to a first opinion (G. Balis, *PrL*, para. 99, 238; Ap. Georgiades, *PrL*, para. 61 II 2 Nos 29–30, 771–772; A. Tousis, *Prl*, para. 134, 597; P. Filios, Chr. Filios, *PrL*, para. 144 C I, 269; AP 837/1973, 22 NoB, 1974, 337; AP 1059/1972, 21 NoB, 1973, 623 [625], as well as J. Baur & R. Stürner, *SachR*, para. 11 A II 5 c No. 19, 115; H. Prütting, *SachR*, para. 48 VI 2 b No. 553, 235), Art. 1102 CC refers to the 'genuine management of another's affairs'. Thus, depending on whether the relevant disbursements have been made or not in the interest of and in conformity with the actual or presumed will of the owner, the latter is bound, respectively, either to reimburse the possessor completely (Art. 736 in combination with Art. 722 CC) or to reimburse him or her only in accordance with the provisions governing enrichment without just cause (Art. 737 CC). According to a second opinion (K. Vavouskos, *PrL*, No. 300, 310–311; G. Rammos, in *ErmAK*, Arts 1101–1107 No. 36; G. Kallimopoulos, *The Non-genuine Management of Another's Affairs* (Athens: A. Sakkoulas, 1978), 133 [in Greek]), which it seems correct to accept, Art. 1102 CC refers to the 'non-genuine management of another's affairs' and, therefore, the owner is bound to reimburse the possessor in accordance with the provisions governing enrichment without just cause (Art. 739 CC).

388. On the other hand, before the service of the revendicatory action, whereas a possessor of bad faith has the aforementioned claims provided for by Article 1102 CC, a possessor of good faith has the right to demand compensation: (a) for necessary disbursements and for the settlement of charges encumbering the thing (Article 1101 sub-paragraph a CC) and (b) for useful disbursements (and disbursements for luxuries[684]) only insofar as at the time of the restitution of the thing the increase in value has been preserved (Article 1103 CC). However, the above possessor of good faith is not entitled to compensation in respect of usual disbursements for the maintenance of the thing if the benefits derived therefrom have been retained by him or her (Article 1101 sub-paragraph b CC).

389. Finally, the following should be borne in mind: (a) in the case where the disbursements made by a possessor (of good or bad faith) relate to a (movable) thing that was adjoined to the thing under litigation as a component of the latter,[685] the possessor has, as a rule,[686] a right of removal[687] (Article 1104 CC), regardless of whether the union was necessary or useful and, concomitantly, regardless of whether the relevant disbursements were necessary or useful; (b) the claim for compensation and the right of removal exist even when the disbursements were made by the possessor's predecessor in title (Article 1105 paragraph 1 CC); (c) the obligation of the owner also extends to disbursements incurred before he or she acquired ownership (Article 1105 paragraph 2 CC).

2. Exercise of the Rights derived from Articles 1101–1104 CC

390. The right of a possessor or detentor to demand compensation for disbursements may be exercised by an action, a cross action or a plea to set off the claim of the owner for restitution of benefits or for compensation. The same right may also be exercised by a plea of retention against the revendicatory action.

Indeed, according to Article 1106 CC, a possessor who has not acquired the thing through an illegal act performed intentionally has the right to retain the thing until he or she has been satisfied in respect of disbursements repayable to him or her. The right of retention of Article 1106 CC constitutes a specific expression of the right provided for by Article 325 CC and, especially, by Article 326 CC. Therefore, Articles 325–329 CC also apply in the present case. Thus, the exercise of the above right entails the obligation of the defendant possessor or detentor to restitute the

684. See *supra* para. 386 n. 682.

685. In the sense of Art. 953 CC (see *supra* paras 81–82).

686. The right of removal is excluded: (a) in the case of usual disbursements for the purpose of maintenance in respect of which the possessor, having enjoyed the benefits, is not entitled to compensation; (b) if the possessor does not derive any advantage from the removal; (c) if the possessor receives the value that would have been attributable to the component after the separation (Art. 1104 para. 2 CC).

687. The possessor, exercising this right, is bound, at his or her own expense, to restore the thing to its former condition (Art. 302 sub-para. (a) CC). However, if the thing under litigation has reverted to the owner, the latter has the right to prevent the removal as long as no security has been provided to protect him or her from any prejudice that might be caused by the removal (Art. 302 sub-para. b CC).

thing on condition that at the same time the plaintiff owner repays the disbursements made on the thing (Article 329 CC). Also, the plaintiff owner is entitled to rebut the plea of retention by advancing the counter-plea of providing security, which, however, cannot be provided through a surety (Article 328 CC).

391. The right of removal of Article 1104 CC is exercised by a plea[688] and also without preceding judicial acknowledgment, in the case where the thing under litigation is still occupied by the possessor.[689]

392. With regard to the time-limit for extinction[690] of a claim for compensation or removal on account of disbursements, Article 1107 CC stipulates that the relevant claim is extinguished, in the case of movables, on the expiration of one month and, in the case of immovables, on the expiration of six months following the restitution of the thing.

§3. Negative Action

393. A negative action, unlike a revendicatory action, protects ownership in the case where it is violated partly and not wholly; in other words, in the case where ownership is violated other than by deprivation or retention of the thing (Article 1108 paragraph 1 sub-paragraph a CC).[691] This means that a negative action is available to an owner[692] whose right of ownership is disturbed[693] (or simply debated[694]). The relief requested by such an action is, as a rule, a cessation of the relevant disturbance and its non-recurrence in the future, while a further claim for compensation in accordance with the provisions governing unlawful acts is not excluded (Article 1108 paragraph 1 CC).

---

688. K. Vavouskos, *PrL*, No. 303, 314.
689. Ap. Georgiades, *PrL*, para. 61 III No. 36, 773. See also G. Rammos, in *ErmAK*, Arts 1101–1107 No. 75.
690. Thus, G. Balis, *PrL*, para. 103, 244; K. Vavouskos, *PrL*, No. 307, 316; A. Tousis, *PrL*, para. 134, 605; Court of Appeal of Athens 6473/1986, 41 Arm, 1987, 495 (496). Compare Ap. Georgiades, *PrL*, para. 61 IV 3 No. 63, 779 and K. Papadopoulos, *Actions of Property Law* (Athens, 1989), 282 [in Greek] (who hold the opinion that Art. 1107 CC constitutes prescription and not a term of extinction in the sense of Arts 279–280 CC).
691. In the case where a partial violation of ownership also constitutes a disturbance of the possession, the owner and possessor may choose between the negative action and the disturbance action of Art. 989 CC (see also *supra* para. 140).
692. And also to a co-owner (see also *infra* paras 400, 401, 402) or to the owner of a storey or an apartment on which horizontal ownership has been constituted (see also *infra* para. 403).
693. The disturbance must be illegal (Ap. Georgiades, *PrL*, para. 62 II 3 Nos 16–18, 789). However, it is accepted that the fault or imputability of the offender is immaterial (K. Vavouskos, *PrL*, No. 308, 317; K. Papadopoulos, *The Negative Action* (Athens/Komotini: A. Sakkoulas, 1984), 78 [in Greek]).
694. See K. Vavouskos, *PrL*, No. 308, 317; Ap. Georgiades, *PrL*, para. 62 II 2 No. 13, 786; G. Rammos, in *ErmAK*, Art. 1108 No. 3; K. Papadopoulos, *The Negative Action*, 66. See also G. Mitsopoulos, *The Declaratory Action according to the Greek Civil Procedural Law* (Athens: Rodakis-Pavlou, 1947), 105 [in Greek].

394. The legal document of a negative action, besides the requested relief and the other elements required in any legal document (Article 118 CCProc), must contain the legal and actual facts which support it and justify its commencement[695] (historical basis of the action) as well as an exact description of the thing under litigation (Article 216 CCProc).

The competent court in terms of subject-matter for the hearing of negative actions is, according to the most correct opinion,[696] the Three-member District Court (Article 18 CCProc). This is because the object of the relevant action may not be evaluated in monetary terms.[697] On the other hand, the territorial competency is determined in the way provided for revendicatory actions.[698]

Any negative action which concerns an immovable must be registered, within thirty days of the date of its deposition, in the vindication register of the registry of the district in which the immovable is situated (Article 220 CCProc[699]).

395. With regard to the defence of the defendant, in the context of negative actions, the points set out above concerning revendicatory actions apply *mutatis mutandis*.[700] However, to the plea derived from Article 1095 CC,[701] corresponds, in the field of negative actions, the plea deriving from Article 1108 paragraph 2 CC. According to the latter, a negative action may not be granted in the case where the offender has acted in accordance with a (real or personal[702]) right.

---

695. Namely, the legal and actual facts which provide evidence of the ownership of the plaintiff and the disturbance of this ownership by the defendant.
696. Thus, Ap. Georgiades, *PrL*, para. 62 V 2 No. 26, 792 and note 56 (where there are also references to the opinion that the competency is determined on the basis of the value of the object of the dispute (Art. 14 paras 1a and 2 and Art. 18 CCProc)); K. Papadopoulos, *The Negative Action*, 153, as well as Court of Appeal of Patras 256/2006, NOMOS = AchN, 2007, 149; Court of Appeal of Athens 5518/2003, 45 HellD, 2004, 181 (182); Court of Appeal of Larissa 69/2001, NOMOS = Dikografia, 2001, 84; Court of Appeal of Athens 1115/2000, 41 HellD, 2000, 797; Court of Appeal of Athens 1115/2000, 41 HellD, 2000, 797; Court of Appeal of Athens 3690/1985, 26 HellD, 1985, 1173 (1174); Three-member District Court of Rhodos 22/2006, NOMOS; Three-member District Court of Preveza 113/1997, 51 ArchN, 1999, 123 (indirectly); Three-member District Court of Samos 8/1990, 21 D, 1990, 549; One-member District Court of Syros 46/2010, NOMOS; One-member District Court of Rhodos 80/2009, NOMOS; Magistrates' Court of Paramythias 17/1999, 51 ArchN, 1999, 844.
697. Court of Appeal of Patras 256/2006, NOMOS = AchN, 2007, 149; Court of Appeal of Athens 5518/2003, 45 HellD, 2004, 181 (182); Court of Appeal of Larissa 69/2001, NOMOS = Dikografia, 2001, 84; Court of Appeal of Athens 1115/2000, 41 HellD, 2000, 797; One-member District Court of Rhodos 80/2009, NOMOS; see also Court of Appeal of Athens 486/2010, 16 DEE, 2010, 579 (581). Therefore, the hearing of a negative action (unlike the hearing of a revendicatory action; see *supra* para. 369 n. 656) does not presuppose payment of a judicial stamp-tax (see Ap. Georgiades, *PrL*, para. 62 V 3 No. 27, 792, as well as Court of Appeal of Athens 3690/1985, 26 HellD, 1985, 1173 [1174]).
698. See *supra* para. 370.
699. See also Art. 12 para. 1 point xii of L. 2664/1998 within the framework of the land registry system.
700. See *supra* paras 371 et seq.
701. See *supra* para. 373.
702. A personal right is one, for example, which springs from a provision concerning legal restriction of ownership (on this point see *supra* paras 166 et seq.).

396. The legal and actual facts which support the negative action and justify its commencement[703] must be proved by the plaintiff.[704] In addition, the plaintiff who demands compensation in accordance with the provisions governing unlawful acts must also prove that the conditions of an unlawful act occur. On the other hand, the defendant who advances the plea deriving from Article 1108 paragraph 2[705] is bound to prove his or her allegation.

§4. Publician Action

I. General Remarks

397. Publician actions, unlike revendicatory and negatory actions, are considered to be a specific type of action, as they are available only for the protection of immovable property.[706] Strictly speaking, a publician action is a fictitious action of ownership. This is because it aims to protect the person who has acquired the possession of an immovable in the conditions allowing an ordinary *usucaption* and whose right was violated, wholly or partly, before the period of *usucaption* expired, i.e., before he or she became owner of the immovable. However, it is self-evident that a publician action may also be commenced by an owner who exercises possession on an immovable under the conditions allowing an ordinary *usucaption.* The choice of a publician action by this owner is justified on account of the fact that, in this case, the plaintiff owner is not bound to prove his or her ownership. It suffices that he or she should prove that he or she acquired the possession of the immovable in the conditions allowing an ordinary *usucaption* and that his or her right was violated, wholly or partly, before the ten-year period of *usucaption* expired.

Publician actions are provided for by Article 1112 CC. From this article it emerges that the relevant action works either as a revendicatory or a negatory action. On this, the following points should be noted:

II. The Publician Action as a Revendicatory Action

398. Article 1112 paragraph 1 CC, referring to the publician action as a revendicatory action, declares that a person who acquired possession of an immovable in the conditions allowing an ordinary *usucaption* and who was deprived of possession before the term of *usucaption* expired[707] is entitled to demand from the possessor lacking a lawful or putative title the restitution of the thing in accordance with the provisions governing revendicatory actions, which apply by analogy.

703. See *supra* para. 394 and n. 695.
704. With regard to the proof of ownership the points set out above concerning revendicatory actions apply *mutatis mutandis* (see *supra* paras 376 et seq.).
705. See *supra* para. 395.
706. See also *supra* para. 367.
707. In the event of the death of the above person, a publician action may be raised by his or her heir provided that the latter has transcribed his or her declaration of acceptance of the estate (AP 492/1956, 5 NoB, 1957, 122). However, in the case where the above person had sold (after his or her

The text of the above article makes it obvious that the publician action is brought against an offender who possesses an immovable without the conditions allowing an ordinary *usucaption* having arisen. Concomitantly, the relevant action may not be raised against the real owner or the person who has taken possession of the immovable under conditions allowing an ordinary *usucaption*. The latter is preferred because he or she is the one who detains the immovable.[708]

In view of the fact that Article 1112 paragraph 1 CC provides application by analogy of the provisions governing revendicatory actions, the following may be accepted:

(a) that a publician action which is raised as a revendicatory action has as requested relief the acknowledgement that the plaintiff is a possessor who is acting in good faith and bears a lawful or putative title and the restitution of the thing under litigation to the plaintiff (Article 1112 paragraph 1 in combination with Article 1094 CC);
(b) that the defence of the defendant by a publician action is analogous to the defence of the defendant by a revendicatory action;[709]
(c) that the consequences of the acceptance of a publician action are the same as those of a revendicatory action;[710]
(d) that with regard to the subject-matter and territorial competence of the court, the need to register the relevant action in the vindication register and the need to pay the judicial stamp-tax, the points set out above concerning revendicatory actions[711] also apply to publician actions as revendicatory actions.

III. The Publician Action as a Negatory Action

399. Article 1112 paragraph 2 CC, referring to the publician action as a negatory action, stipulates that a person who acquired possession of an immovable under the conditions allowing an ordinary *usucaption* and whose right was violated other than by deprivation or retention of the thing (namely by disturbance) before the period of *usucaption* expired is entitled to the same protection as the owner. Consequently, the above person has the right to commence a publician action as a negatory action and request from the offender cessation of the disturbance and its nonrecurrence in the future. Furthermore, the points set out above regarding negatory actions also apply by analogy to publician actions as negatory actions.[712]

---

deprivation) the immovable to a third party, the purchaser is entitled to commence the publician action only on the condition that it has been assigned to him or her (AP 677/1978, 27 NoB, 1979, 520).

708. This justification is based on the Roman rule *beati possedentes*.

709. Consequently, the defendant may deny the basis of the relevant action, alleging that the plaintiff did not acquire the immovable under the conditions allowing an ordinary *usucaption*; he or she may advance the allegation that he or she is owner or possessor under conditions allowing ordinary *usucaption*; he or she may also advance the plea that he or she has a right to possess or detain the immovable under litigation (see also *supra* paras 371 et seq.).

710. See *supra* paras 379 et seq.

711. See *supra* paras 370, 369 n. 655.

712. See *supra* paras 393 et seq.

Chapter 2. Protection of Specific Types of Ownership

§1. Protection of Co-ownership

400. In the context of co-ownership, in the case where the common thing is violated, wholly or partly, by a third party, any of the co-owners is entitled to bring against the offender the claims arising from ownership relating to the whole of the thing (Article 1116 sub-paragraph a CC). Thus, depending on the nature of the case, any co-owner may commence a revendicatory, negatory or publician action, as well as an action to conduct a search for a movable. However, a co-owner who vindicates the whole thing is bound to request its restitution to all the co-owners (Article 1116 sub-paragraph b CC). Therefore, the legal document of a revendicatory action must determine the ideal share of each co-owner, while the plaintiff is bound to prove not only his or her co-ownership but the co-ownership of the other co-owners as well.

401. Any co-owner whose ideal share has been violated, wholly or partly, by a third party also enjoys the above protection. However, in this case, the requested relief of the revendicatory action is acknowledgement of the ideal share and restitution of the co-possession of the thing.

402. Finally, similar protection is enjoyed by any co-owner whose ideal share has been violated by another co-owner. Thus, in the case where one of the co-owners possesses the whole thing exclusively, any of the other co-owners may bring a revendicatory action against him or her and request the acknowledgement of his or her ideal share and the restitution or delivery of the co-possession (Article 1094 CC). Also, in the case where one of the co-owners exercising his or her right to use the common thing excludes simultaneous use of the thing by the other co-owners, any of the latter is protected by the negatory action (Article 1108 CC).[713]

§2. Protection of Horizontal and Vertical Ownership

403. Considering the fact that horizontal and vertical ownership constitute a combination of exclusive ownership and compulsory co-ownership, it is obvious that they are protected in the same way as ownership or co-ownership, depending on whether the relevant violation refers to the object of the exclusive ownership or the objects of compulsory co-ownership. In addition, the provisions governing protection of possession or co-possession apply by analogy, whereas quarrels between co-owners are also regulated in accordance with the provisions of Law 3741/1929.

713. Thus, Ap. Georgiades, *PrL*, para. 65 III 4 No. 25, 812. Compare K. Vavouskos, *PrL*, No. 322, 327 (who expresses the opinion that, in such a case, the provisions governing undivided joint rights apply).

Chapter 3. Protection of Servitudes

§1. Protection of Real Servitudes

I. General Classification

404. The protection of real servitudes is achieved by two actions:[714] the confessory action (1132 CC) and the publician action concerning servitudes (Article 1133 CC).[715]

II. Confessory Action

405. The holder of a real servitude (i.e., each individual owner of a dominant tenement) and, in the case where several beneficiaries exist, each one of them,[716] in the event of a (whole or partial) violation of his or her right, is entitled to commence a confessory action against the offender (the owner of the servient tenement or a third party), whereas a further claim for compensation in accordance with the provisions governing unlawful acts is not excluded (Article 1132 paragraph 1 CC). The relief requested by the confessory action is an acknowledgement of the right of servitude[717] and a cessation of the violation as well as its non-recurrence in the future.

The defendant in a confessory action may repulse it through claiming – by means of a subversive plea[718] – that he or she had acted by virtue of a (real[719] or personal[720]) right (Article 1132 paragraph 2 CC).

III. Publician Action Concerning Servitudes

406. As in the area of ownership,[721] so too in the context of real servitudes, the law protects any person who has acquired quasi possession of a certain real servitude under the conditions of ordinary *usucaption* and whose exercise of the servitude has been violated, before the term of the *usucaption* has expired, by a possessor

714. The holder of a real servitude is protected as quasi possessor as well.
715. The competent court in terms of subject-matter for hearing the above actions is determined on the basis of the value of the object of the dispute (see Arts 7, 10, 11 point 3 CCProc), while the court with territorial competency is that in the district where the servient tenement is situated (Art. 29 CCProc). The relevant actions must be registered in the vindication register (Art. 220 CCProc and, within the framework of the land registry system, Art. 12 para. 1 point xii of L. 2664/1998).
716. The plaintiff may also be the usufructuary of the dominant tenement and the holder of habitation on it, though not the person who detains the tenement on the basis of a personal right (e.g., its lessee).
717. The burden is on the plaintiff to prove the conditions allowing the constitution of the relevant servitude.
718. Thus, Ap. Georgiades, *PrL*, para. 73 II No. 8, 903–904.
719. For example, a preceding servitude of the same content.
720. For example, relevant permission from the owner of the dominant tenement.
721. See *supra* paras 397 et seq.

of the servient tenement without lawful or putative title. Indeed, according to Article 1133 CC, such a person, who does not have the status of the holder of a real servitude, is entitled to bring against the offender the confessory action specified in Article 1132 CC.

§2. Protection of Personal Servitudes

I. Protection of Usufruct

407. A usufructuary is protected as holder of the relevant real right and quasi possessor. As holder of the relevant real right, he or she enjoys protection similar to that of the owner.[722] In fact, according to Article 1173 CC, where the right of a usufructuary is violated (by the naked owner[723] or a third party), the provisions governing the protection of ownership apply by analogy.

II. Protection of Habitation

408. In view of the fact that, in the area of habitation, the general provisions governing usufruct of immovables apply by analogy (in all other respects) insofar as they are compatible with the nature of habitation (Article 1187 CC), the holder of habitation is protected in the same way as the usufructuary of an immovable.

III. Protection of Limited Personal Servitudes

409. The holder of a limited personal servitude is protected in the same way as the holder of a real servitude.[724] This is because, according to Article 1191 CC, as far as limited personal servitudes are concerned, the provisions governing real servitudes apply (in all other respects) insofar as they are compatible with the nature of the personal servitudes.

722. See *supra* paras 366 et seq.
723. The usufructuary may also file against the naked owner the claims deriving from the personal relationship which binds him or her with the naked owner (on this relationship see *supra* para. 239 (under h)).
724. See *supra* paras 404 et seq.

Part VII. Real Security

Chapter 1. General Issues

§1. General Classification

410. The Greek Civil Code recognizes two types of securities which may be granted to creditors for the satisfaction of their claims: personal and real.[725] Personal security is acquired if the creditor is able to find a second debtor who, as co-debtor (Article 477 CC) or guarantor (Article 847 CC), is responsible towards the creditor for the payment of the debt. On the other hand, in the area of real security, the creditor acquires a real right on an object belonging to the debtor (or to a third person) and, in the case where the debtor does not pay the debt, he or she (the creditor) has the power to sell the thing by auction and gain satisfaction by way of privilege from the proceeds of the auction.

In the area of personal security, the situation improves for the creditor only in quantitative and not always qualitative terms. This is because the satisfaction of the creditor's claim depends on the creditworthiness and financial standing of individuals. Real security, on the other hand, is stronger and ensures greater stability as it relates to a certain thing which is placed under the authority of the creditor.

411. The Greek Civil Code accepts and regulates two rights of real security: the pledge, which is constituted on movables and incorporeal objects, and the mortgage, which may be obtained on immovables[726] or on the usufruct thereof. However, the prenotice of mortgage is also of great importance.[727]

412. In addition to the above rights of real security, special laws and everyday practice have created other types of real security as well. In this respect, the following should be noted:

725. On this distinction see, in particular, Ach. Koutsouradis, 'Present and future of real and personal security' (Hellenic National Reports XVIth Int'l Congress of Comparative Law 2002), 55/1 R. Hell. D.I., 2002, 49 et seq.; see also D. Papasteriou, *PrL III*, para. 82 IV Nos 7–9, 247.

726. However, certain movables, such as ships and aeroplanes (see, respectively, Arts 195 et seq. CPrMarL and Arts 50 et seq. CAL), may also be the objects of mortgages.

727. See Th. Papazissi, 'Les problèmes actuels de sûretés réelles', in *Les garanties de financement, Travaux de l'Association Henri Capitant des Amis de la Culture Juridique Française*, Vol. XLVII (Paris, L.G.D.J., 1996), 186 et seq.

(a) The increase in sales on credit, especially in the area of movables, and the concomitant need for the vendor to be secured have led to the recognition of the pact of retention of title (Article 532 CC) as an important type of real security, mainly in the field of movables.
(b) In the light of the finding that, in the case of the constitution of a pledge, the required delivery of the quasi possession of the thing from the owner to the creditor (or to a third party) is desired neither by the owner, who needs the thing in order to continue his or her financial activities, nor by the creditor (especially credit institutions with numerous debtors), who faces problems of storage, the institution of securing transfer of ownership of a movable (*Sicherungsübereignung*) has been created. Likewise, the disadvantages of the legal treatment of pledges on claims have led to the development of the institution of securing assignment of claims (*Sicherungsabtretung*).[728]
(c) Along the same lines, special laws – aiming at the support of certain productive classes (who, in each case, need the thing in order to continue their productive activities) and through them of the national economy – have recognized the possibility of pledges being constituted without delivery of the thing pledged (special fictitious pledges) with a view to securing claims derived from contracts of loan. However, the provisions concerning special fictitious pledges have been abolished by Law 2844/2000 (Article 20). This law recognizes the possibility of pledges being constituted on movables without delivery of the detention of the thing pledged. It refers to pledges on claims and other rights originating from business activities. It introduces into the Greek legal system the institution of the so-called floating charge and it also contains provisions concerning other security contracts, such as sale contracts with the pact of retention of title and fiduciary contracts.

413. The present section of the monograph will be devoted to real security, as personal security is not a component of property law. To be precise, after a reference (in the following paragraph 2) to the general principles governing real security, the following topics will be examined: first of all (Chapter 2), real security on immovables and on the usufruct thereof, that is, mortgages on the ownership or usufruct of an immovable and the prenotice of mortgage; second (Chapter 3), real security on movables, that is, the various types of pledges on movables and pacts of retention of title in contracts for the sale of movables; third (Chapter 4), real security on incorporeal objects, namely pledges on rights, claims and negotiable instruments; finally (Chapter 5), the institution of the 'floating charge'. The institutions of securing transfer of ownership of a movable and of securing assignment of claims will be dealt with in the following and last section (Part VIII) of the book.

414. However, before the aforementioned issues are discussed, the following points ought to be made clear:

728. See also *supra* paras 44, 45.

(a) The constitution of a pledge or mortgage offers the creditor a privilege (priority) in the form of a right to be paid from the proceeds of the auction of the encumbered thing before any creditors whose claims are not secured with a real right (unsecured or general creditors). However, this privilege must not be confused with the general and special priorities of Articles 975–978 and 1007 CCProc, the importance of which becomes evident at the stage of compulsory execution, and more particularly, at the stage in which the table of classification, namely the list setting forth the order of priority of the creditors, is compiled.[729] In any case, these priorities fall within the sphere of civil procedural law and will not therefore be examined in the present monograph.[730]

On the other hand, the creditor's right to demand judicial protection, by exercising his or her debtor's rights, if the latter himself or herself does not exercise them (Article 72 CCProc),[731] also falls within the sphere of civil procedural law and therefore beyond the scope of this book.

(b) In Greece, the term 'charge', with the exception of 'floating charge', does not signify a type of real security. It is used either as a general term which includes the various limited rights that may encumber the ownership of a thing or to denote the various liabilities (e.g., public taxes) that are connected with the thing and follow it.[732]

(c) The right or plea of retention (lien) which is specified in Articles 325 et seq. CC,[733] while a specific expression of it is provided for by Article 1106 CC,[734] is not regarded as a type of real security in Greece.[735]

(d) The rights of retention and compensation or setting off of claims (Articles 440 et seq. CC)[736] as well as the institution of delegation (Articles 876 et seq.

---

729. See also *infra* para. 438 n. 786.
730. On these priorities see P. Yesiou-Faltsi, *Civil Procedure in Hellas*, No. 554, 421–423.
731. On this issue see, in particular, N. Nikas, in *Interpretation of the CCProc*, Vol. I, ed. K. Kerameus, D. Kondilis & N. Nikas, Art. 72 with a further wealth of references [in Greek].
732. See also *supra* para. 90.
733. On this right see, in particular, Ast. Georgiades, *Law of Obligations. General Part*, Vol. II, 5th edn (Athens-Thessaloniki: Sakkoulas, 2007), 41 et seq. [in Greek]; M. Stathopoulos, *Contract Law in Hellas*, Nos 225, 242.
734. See *supra* para. 390.
735. Possessory and vendor's or purchaser's liens are considered to be types of real security according to English law. A possessory lien is the right to retain possession of the property of another person until a debt owed by that person is paid; for example, the right of a watchmaker to retain the watch repaired by him or her until he or she is paid for his or her work on it. A vendor's lien arises where a vendor of land conveys the land to a purchaser, but allows the purchaser to delay part or the whole of the price. It constitutes a kind of equitable interest in the land which exists in favour of the vendor until he or she is paid in full. On the other hand, once an agreement to purchase land has been made, the purchaser is entitled, should the vendor fail to convey it to him or her, to a decree ordering the vendor to convey the land to him or her. In such a case, although the purchaser is not yet the owner of the land at law, he or she is already regarded as owner for the purposes of equity or he or she has an equitable interest (the so-called purchaser's lien) in the land. (On all these points see F.H. Lawson & B. Rudden, *PrL*, 189, 199–200; Roger Sexton, *Land Law*, 86; E.H. Burn, *Real Property*, 66.)
736. On which see, in particular, Ast. Georgiades, *Law of Obligations. General Part*, Vol. II, 281 et seq.; M. Stathopoulos, *Contract Law in Hellas*, Nos 239–240.

CC),[737] fall within the sphere of the law of obligations and therefore beyond the scope of this book.

§2. General Principles Governing Real Security

415. Rights of real security, as real rights, are governed by the principles of *numerus clausus* of real rights, of (formal and substantive) publicity and of specificity.

The principle of *numerus clausus*[738] means that individuals of their own volition can neither constitute other rights of real security apart from those provided for by law nor change the content of such rights from that specified by the law.

The principle of publicity[739] is realized, in the area of real security on immovables, through due registration in the mortgage registers and, within the framework of the land registry system, on the record sheet of the land register which is devoted to the relevant immovable.[740] In the context of pledges, on the other hand, formal publicity is achieved through delivery of the quasi possession of the movable from its owner to the creditor (or to a third person) and, in the case of a pledge which is constituted without delivery, through registration in a public register. In the same context, substantive publicity is achieved insofar as the law (Article 1215 in combination with Articles 1036 et seq. CC) recognizes the possibility of a right of pledge being acquired on a thing not belonging to the pledger by a person acting in good faith.

Finally, the principle of specificity means that the rights of real security secure a clearly defined claim and are constituted on an individually determined thing.[741]

416. Rights of real security may be constituted only on a thing belonging to another person (*nemini res sua pignori esse potest*). This is because of the universal character of ownership, which renders the constitution of mortgages or pledges on something belonging to oneself meaningless and which also implies the extinction of the above rights because of confusion in the case where their holders acquire the ownership of the thing encumbered.[742]

417. Rights of real security, which are constituted with a view to securing the satisfaction of a certain claim, are accessory rights (Articles 1210, 1258 CC), in the sense, primarily, that their constitution presupposes the existence of such a claim and, secondarily, that they follow the legal fate of the latter.[743] On the other hand, the securing of the relevant claim constitutes the just cause of the real juridical act which aims at the constitution of a mortgage or pledge. Concomitantly, in the case

737. On which see *infra* para. 505 n. 945.
738. On this see also *supra* paras 26, 27.
739. On which see *supra* paras 28 et seq.
740. See also *infra* paras 428, 429.
741. See also *supra* para. 32 and *infra* Nos 428, 430.
742. See also *supra* paras 162 and 230 (under (c)).
743. See, for example, Art. 458 CC, according to which, in the assignment of a claim the mortgages or pledges securing the claim are also transferred.

where such a claim does not exist or is null and void, the relevant causal[744] juridical act does not generate its legal consequences.

The claim secured by a right of real security must be a personal money claim or a claim susceptible of evaluation in monetary terms. It may arise from a valid juridical act, an unlawful act or directly from the law. It can exist either prior to or at the same time as the constitution of a mortgage or pledge and it may be realized in the future or be dependent on a (suspensive) condition (Articles 1210, 1258 CC) or term. It is debatable whether a claim originating from a natural obligation,[745] for example, a prescribed claim or a claim arising from a game or a wager, may be secured by a mortgage or pledge. In this respect, it seems correct to accept that the principle of freedom of contracts justifies an affirmative answer only in the case where the debtor – and not a third party – is the one who grants the mortgage or the pledge.[746] In any event, it should be borne in mind that, according to Article 272 paragraph 2 sub-paragraph b CC, the security granted[747] with a view to satisfying a prescribed claim, in ignorance of the prescription, is valid.

418. According to Articles 1231 and 1281 CC, pledges and mortgages are undivided rights. However, this rule does not mean that these rights may not be constituted on an ideal share.[748] The rule means that, in the case where a part of the claim secured is paid, the pledge or the mortgage is not limited to a part of the encumbered thing or to a part of its value but continues to encumber the whole thing, which secures each remaining part of the debt. The rule also means that, in the case where the encumbered thing is divided into more than one self-contained part, each of them continues to secure the whole claim.

419. Finally, mention should be made of Article 1239 CC, which, although it concerns pledges, applies in the area of mortgages as well. This article declares the nullity of any agreement, made before (and not after) the secured debt falls due,

744. Thus, G. Balis, *PrL*, para. 242 No. 6, 518; para. 205 No. 5, 444; K. Vavouskos, *PrL*, No. 383, 378–379; Ap. Georgiades, *PrL*, para. 6 III 4 No. 36, 76; para. 86 II 1 No. 25, 1029; para. 89 III 2 No. 51, 1119; Ath. Kritikos, in *Civil Code*, Vol. VI: *PrL*, ed. Ap. Georgiades & M. Stathopoulos; Art. 1266 No. 6. For the opposite view see P. Filios & Chr. Filios, *PrL*, para. 199 A I, 365; para. 235, 424 and, from the scope of German law, J. Damrau, in *MünchKomm*, Vol. 6: *SachR*, para. 1205 No. 2; H. Westermann et al., *SachR*, para. 128 I 3, 894; W. Wiegand, in *Staudinger Komm zum BGB, Buch 3: SachR* (2009), Vorbem zu paras 1204 et seq. Nos 21–22, para. 1205 No. 33.

745. This concerns obligations in which the creditor cannot compel the debtor to settle his or her debt, but, if the latter has settled it of his or her own free will, he or she is not deemed to have settled it without 'just cause' (see, among others, M. Stathopoulos, *Contract Law in Hellas*, para. 15, 31).

746. Thus, Ap. Georgiades, *PrL*, para. 85 I 3 No. 19, 1026–1027. See also K. Vavouskos, *PrL*, No. 379, 375–376; Al. Ligeropoulos, 'Natural Obligations and Related Legal Structures', *Miscellany in Honour of Gh. Fragistas*, Vol. IB-issue 6 (Thessaloniki, 1970–1971), 258 et seq. [in Greek]; Contra: A. Tousis, *PrL*, para. 252 note 3, 949; Ath. Kritikos, in *Civil Code*, Vol. VI: *PrL*, ed. Ap. Georgiades & M. Stathopoulos, Art. 1258 No. 7; P. Filios & Chr. Filios, *PrL*, para. 199 A 1, 365.

747. By the debtor or a third party with the consent of the debtor (see Al. Ligeropoulos, 'Natural Obligations and Related Legal Structures', 259; Ap. Georgiades, *PrL*, para. 85 I 3 No. 19, 1026–1027; Ph. Doris, *Real Security* (Athens/Komotini: A. Sakkoulas, 1986), para. 7 IV, 63 [in Greek]).

748. See Art. 1216 CC, according to which a pledge may be constituted on an ideal share of a movable thing.

which specifies that if the creditor is not satisfied in due time, either the ownership of the pledged thing is passed or must be transferred to him or her or he or she is to be released wholly or in part from the obligation to carry out the formalities required for the alienation of the thing.

Chapter 2. Real Security on Immovables and on the Usufruct Thereof

§1. Mortgage on the Ownership of an Immovable

I. Concept of Mortgage

420. From Article 1257 CC it emerges that a mortgage is a real right which secures the satisfaction of a creditor's claim from the value of an immovable belonging to another by way of privilege. However, it seems correct to accept that like any other real right so too mortgages establish real relations from which derive not only the relevant real right (as is defined above), but also other rights, as well as obligations, charges or commitments.[749] The elements of the concept of a mortgage are as follows: an immovable belonging to another, the claim secured and the satisfaction of the creditor by way of privilege.

421. As the elements 'claim secured' and 'satisfaction of the creditor by way of privilege' have already been discussed,[750] here it remains for the element 'an immovable belonging to another' to be examined.

Strictly speaking, the object of a mortgage is the full, naked[751] or revocable ownership[752] of an immovable[753] which belongs to another and which is susceptible of alienation (Article 1259 CC). A mortgage may be acquired on the whole immovable, on a divisible part of it or on an ideal share of the ownership on it. The object of the mortgage may also be a horizontal or vertical ownership even before the erection of the relevant building.[754] Finally, with a view to securing the satisfaction of the relevant claim, it is possible for several immovables belonging to the same or to different owners to be encumbered with mortgages (multiple or unique mortgage).[755]

---

749. See also D. Papasteriou, *PrL III*, para. 88 No. 10, 339.
750. See, respectively, *supra* paras 417 and 410, 414 (under (a)).
751. Namely, ownership encumbered with usufruct (see also *supra* paras 15, 238). In this case the extinction of usufruct entails the extension of the mortgage onto the complete ownership (K. Vavouskos, *PrL*, No. 417, 407).
752. Namely, ownership dependent on a suspensive or resolutory condition or term (see also *supra* para. 15). In the case where the ownership of the immovable is dependent on a resolutory condition, the relevant mortgage is recallable until fulfilment or frustration of the condition. On the other hand, in the case where the ownership is dependent on a suspensive condition, before the fulfilment of the latter, the object of the mortgage refers to the right of expectation of the owner, while, after the relevant fulfilment, the object of the mortgage becomes *ipso jure* the ownership of the immovable. However, frustration of the condition entails an extinction of the mortgage.
753. I. Spyridakis & M. Spyridakis, *Property Law*, Vol. C (Athens/Komotini: Sakkoulas, 2001), No. 257a, 98 [in Greek]; I. Spyridakis & M. Spyridakis, *Property Law* (Athens/Komotini: Sakkoulas, 2004), No. 257.1., 328 [in Greek].
754. See Art. 10 para. 2 L. 3741/1929 and 1 para. 1 L.D. 1024/1971.
755. In this case, the extinction of the claim entails the extinction of the mortgages on each of the encumbered immovables. Furthermore, if, in the case where the encumbered immovables belong to different owners, the mortgagee is satisfied by the proceeds of the auction of one of them, the owner of the relevant immovable is subrogated to the rights of the creditor against the other owners (see, in particular, Ap. Georgiades, *PrL*, para. 85 I 2 No. 14, 1025).

II. Acquisition of Mortgage

422. According to Article 1260 CC, a title conferring a right of mortgage and a registration in the mortgage register are required for the acquisition of a mortgage.

A. *Title*

423. The title[756] is the legal ground which confers on the creditor the right to acquire (register) a mortgage. Titles conferring the right to acquire a mortgage are gained by means of the law, court decisions or the private will of an individual (Article 1261 CC). The latter is specific in the sense that it confers the right to register a mortgage on a certain immovable or immovables. The titles provided by the law and court decisions are of general nature. Consequently, unless otherwise stipulated by the law,[757] they confer on the creditor the right to register a mortgage on any immovable belonging to the debtor. However, the registration is valid only for a given amount and certain immovables (Article 1264 CC).

424. Art. 1262 CC specifies those individuals who have the right to acquire a mortgage by virtue of the law.[758] These are as follows:

(1) the State on the immovables of its debtors for claims relating to unpaid (direct or indirect) taxes;
(2) the State, municipalities, communal authorities, religious institutions or public utilities and legal entities belonging to the public sector on the immovables of their managers or guarantors with regard to claims arising from the management;
(3) those placed under parental care or tutelage, on the immovables of the parents or the tutor in respect of the assets managed by the latter and for any claim arising from such management;
(4) any spouse for his or her claim concerning increases in the assets of the other spouse according to Article 1400 CC;
(5) legatees, on the immovables of the deceased's estate, in respect of their claims;
(6) heirs, on the immovables of the deceased's estate, for their claims concerning equalization of their portions of the estate or by reason of legal defects of the assets attributed to them;
(7) mortgagees, on the mortgaged immovable, in respect of interest overdue on the claim and of disbursements relating to the registration of the mortgage or in respect of court fees, as long as the mortgaged immovable has not been transferred to another.

---

756. On which see I. Spyridakis, *Title Conferring a Right to Register a Mortgage* (Athens/Komotini: A. Sakkoulas, 2001), 9 et seq. [in Greek].
757. See, for example, Art. 1262 point 7.
758. However, titles of this type are provided by other legislative provisions as well. One example is Art. 66 para. 2 BC, according to which a trustee in bankruptcy, after the declaration of bankruptcy, is bound to register a mortgage on the immovables of the bankrupt person in favour of the group of creditors in the bankruptcy case.

425. With regard to the titles conferred by court decisions, Article 1263 CC declares that the final decisions of civil, criminal, administrative or other special courts, as well as enforceable decisions made by arbitrators or foreign courts may confer titles for the acquisition of a mortgage so long as they order payment of a sum of money or adjudicate a claim that can be valued in monetary terms. Likewise, according to Article 29 paragraph 1 IntrLCCProc, an order to pay a money claim also confers a title for the acquisition of a mortgage so long as no objection has been raised to it within due time or any objection that was raised has been rejected by a final court decision.[759]

426. Finally, a private title exists in the case where the right to register a mortgage is conferred by the owner[760] of the immovable, regardless of whether he or she is the debtor or a third party who is acting on behalf of the debtor (Article 1265 CC).[761] The relevant right is conferred by a unilateral declaration made before a notary (Article 1266 CC). This declaration, which may not be withdrawn, is a unilateral and causal[762] real juridical act *inter vivos* or a juridical act *mortis causa*, that is, a public testament which is drawn up before a notary (Article 1724 CC). However, the granting of a mortgage by a contract made before a notary is possible and indeed usual in practice.

The juridical act by which the mortgage is conferred must identify the person who is conferring the mortgage, the creditor, the encumbered immovable and the claim secured[763] (i.e., its creditor and debtor, its proximate cause and its amount). The same juridical act may be dependent on a particular condition or term. However, in the case where the relevant condition or term is suspensive, the mortgage takes effect after the fulfilment of the condition or term and not from the moment of its due registration, as Article 1268 CC ordains. Nevertheless, on account of the

759. See also *infra* para. 452.
760. According to Art. 1271 CC, in the case where, at the moment of registration, the immovable does not belong to the person who is conferring the mortgage, the registration of a mortgage decided by private will is null and void and cannot be validated by a subsequent approval or acquisition of ownership (according to Art. 238 or 239 para. 2 CC). Although Art. 1271 CC speaks of mortgages decided by private will, it is self-evident that it also covers mortgages registered by virtue of a title by law or a court decision. However, it is accepted that the section of the same article which prohibits the subsequent validity of the registration refers only to mortgages decided by private will. Furthermore, it should be noted that the above prohibition relates only to the registration and not to the juridical act by which the mortgage is conferred. Thus, the latter may be validated by a subsequent approval or acquisition of ownership, whereas the final acquisition of a mortgage requires a new registration. Along the same lines as Arts 1271 CC, 1267 CC declares that anyone who has knowingly conferred a mortgage on the immovable of another or concealed from the creditor the restrictions and encumbrances burdening the ownership of the immovable is under an obligation to pay forthwith the debt if he or she is not in the position to confer another similar mortgage. The incurment of further liability by such a person (according to the provisions governing unlawful acts) is not excluded.
761. The above persons can act through a representative invested with a general power of attorney for the alienation of immovables.
762. See also *supra* para. 417 and n. 744.
763. See also *infra* para. 430.

regulation laid down by Article 206 sub-paragraph a CC,[764] by the fulfilment of the condition or term, the mortgage is to be considered as coming into effect at the moment of its registration.

B. Registration

427. The second prerequisite for the acquisition of a mortgage is registration in the mortgage register (Article 1260 CC).[765] With regard to the real juridical act by which the mortgage is conferred, the above registration is considered to be a condition of its effect (*conditio juris*).

According to Article 1268 CC, a mortgage takes effect from the moment of its due registration[766] in the mortgage register of the district in which the immovable is situated.[767] On the other hand, the registration interrupts the prescription of the claim for the benefit of the person whose rights are secured by the mortgage, while the prescription is deemed as never having been interrupted in the case where the mortgage is subsequently deleted (Article 1273 CC).

428. The registration of a mortgage realizes the principles of publicity (formal and substantial) and specificity,[768] as well as the principle of temporal priority.

429. Formal publicity, that is the ability of any person to be informed about the legal situation of any immovable from the point of view of real security, is achieved insofar as the mortgage registers are public and accessible to all who wish to consult them (Article 1339 CC), while the registrar of mortgages is bound to issue to applicants certified copies or summaries from the mortgage register (Article 1340 CC).

Substantial publicity, that is the ability of persons of good faith who trust the mortgage registers to receive protective cover, is not achieved effectively.[769] This is because Article 1335 CC – according to which acts made by a mortgage registry, within the limits set by the law, as well as copies of the contents of a mortgage register carry the authority of public documents – presupposes not a valid registered act but a valid registration which does not cover the probable defects of the registered act.

---

764. According to Art. 206 sub-para. a CC, 'after the fulfilment of the condition any disposal of the object of the juridical act attempted while the condition was pending shall become *ipso jure* null and void, if such disposal has frustrated or impaired the effect that was dependent on the condition'.
765. And, within the framework of the land registry system, on the record sheet of the land register which is devoted to the relevant immovable (Art. 12 para. 1 point viii of L. 2664/1998).
766. Articles 1302 and 1303 CC define the persons who may apply for the registration of a mortgage, while Arts 1305–1307 CC specify the documents required to support an application for a registration.
767. Consequently, in the case where, before the registration, a juridical act for the transfer of the ownership of the immovable or for the constitution of another real right (e.g., of usufruct) thereon has been transcribed, the mortgage is not acquired or is acquired on an encumbered immovable, respectively.
768. On these principles see also *supra* para. 415.
769. The principle of substantial and formal publicity will be satisfied effectively within the framework of the land registry system. On this subject see *supra* para. 31.

430. The principle of specificity is expressed in particular by Articles 1266 and 1306 point 5 CC, which state the necessity of identifying the immovable encumbered with a mortgage, and Articles 1269 sub-paragraphs a, b and 1329 point 1 CC, which refer to the claim secured. From these articles it emerges that the amount of the claim secured must result from the registration and that the latter is invalid if it gives rise to any uncertainty with regard to the above amount.

431. The principle of temporal priority, which is expressed by the well-known rule *prior tempore potior jure*, means that in the case where several mortgages encumber the same immovable,[770] the first one to have been contracted is satisfied before the others. In fact, Article 1300 CC ordains that the priority among mortgagees is determined by reference to the chronological order of the registrations of their mortgages, whereas Article 1272 CC clarifies that the date of registration determines the priority ranking of each mortgage and adds that all the mortgages which were registered on the same day have the same ranking. Therefore, they are satisfied pro rata (Article 1301 CC).

The principle of temporal priority has been partially amended by E.L. 612/1968. According to the latter, the ranking of mortgages or of prenotices of mortgage which have been successively registered may be interchanged.[771] The relevant interchange presupposes a contract, incorporated in a notarial deed, between the mortgagees involved and takes effect as soon as a relevant note is entered in the mortgage register next to the corresponding registrations.

III. Relationship between the Parties Involved in a Mortgage

432. The constitution of a mortgage entails the production of personal rights and obligations for the owner of the mortgaged immovable, debtor or third party, and also for the mortgagee.

433. With regard to the debtor in a mortgage, mention should be made of his or her right to demand a proper reduction of the amount of the claim secured in the case where the registered amount of money is exaggerated (Article 1269 sub-paragraph c CC). In addition, it should be borne in mind that, where a mortgage has been registered by virtue of the law or a court decision on several immovables

770. According to Art. 1290 CC, the registration of a mortgage does not deprive the owner of the right to confer on another person a mortgage on the same immovable, while an agreement to the contrary is valid only in regard to those who acquire a mortgage by declaration of private will and only if such agreement (has been incorporated in a notarial deed and) has been registered in the mortgage register. The above agreement actually means that the conferment and registration of another mortgage on the same immovable, in spite of this agreement, is null and void (compare Art. 177 CC). However, this nullity is relative and may be invoked by those who are prejudiced by a breach of the agreement (see Ap. Georgiades, *PrL*, para. 86 I 4 No. 16, 1058–1059).

771. It seems correct to adopt the opinion which holds that an interchange is permitted even between mortgages or prenotices of mortgage which are not registered successively (i.e., between mortgages of first and third rank), so long as this interchange does not harm the intermediate mortgagees (on this point see I. Spyridakis, *Interchange in the ranking of mortgages* (Athens: Zacharopulos, 1969), 218–219 [in Greek]; Ap. Georgiades, *PrL*, para. 86 I 2 No. 8, 1056).

belonging to the debtor, the latter is entitled to request that the mortgage be limited to only those immovables whose value provides sufficient security for the claim (Article 1270 CC).

434. With regard to the mortgagee, the following should be noted:

(a) If the mortgaged property runs the risk of deteriorating or losing value on account of wrongful behaviour on the part of the debtor, the creditor is entitled to demand the cessation of the harmful acts or removal of their causes or an immediate settlement of the debt or the granting of another similar mortgage, while a claim for damages according to the provisions governing unlawful acts is not excluded (Article 1284 CC). The above rights, except for the right to demand the grant of another similar mortgage, also belong to the creditor in the case where the mortgaged property runs the risk of deteriorating or losing value as a result of the actions of a third party owner of the mortgaged property (Article 1299 CC).
(b) If the mortgaged property is a building, the creditor has the right to insure it against fire or other risk at the expense of the debtor and, if the latter fails to pay the relevant premiums, the creditor is entitled to demand immediate payment of the debt (Article 1285 CC). The above provision also applies with regard to the insurance of any mortgaged immovable, if the insurance against the risk is required according to the rules of an orderly management of the immovable (Article 1286 CC).
(c) If the mortgaged immovable is insured, the occurrence of the insured risk entails the substitution of the immovable by the insurance indemnity. Consequently, the mortgagee becomes the beneficiary of the part of the latter which covers the secured claim (Article 1287 sub-paragraph a CC).[772,773] Likewise, in the case of a compulsory expropriation[774] of the mortgaged immovable, the latter is substituted by the relevant indemnity and consequently the mortgagee is entitled to be satisfied by way of privilege by the (received) indemnity (Article 1288 CC). In this case, as well as the one mentioned above, we speak of 'conversion of the mortgage into a personal claim'.

772. However, in the case where, in spite of the occurrence of the insured risk (e.g., fire), part of the mortgaged immovable (e.g., a building plot) is preserved, this part continues to secure the relevant claim if the latter is not completely satisfied by the insurance indemnity.
773. However, if the mortgaged immovable is a building, its owner is entitled, within six months from the occurrence of the insured risk, to demand that the insurance indemnity be applied to the restoration of the building (Art. 1287 sub-para. c CC).
774. Compulsory expropriation in the sense of Art. 1288 CC also occurs in the case of a concession of the mortgaged immovable due to reasons relating to the city plan (see *supra* para. 296), as well as in the cases of Art. 1010 or 1012 CC (see *supra* paras 184–185 and 187 et seq.).

IV. Extent of Mortgage

A. Extent of Responsibility with Regard to the Object

435. A mortgage extends to the whole of the mortgaged immovable (Article 1282 CC) and, more specifically, to the ownership thereof in the legal status it holds on the date of the registration. Consequently, if, on this date, the ownership was encumbered by a real right – for example, usufruct or habitation – the mortgage extends to the ownership limited with the relevant right (principle of temporal priority) and, in the event of an auction, the purchaser (highest bidder) acquires the immovable with the burden of the above right.[775] On the other hand, real rights constituted on the mortgaged immovable after the registration of the mortgage do not affect the mortgage (principle of temporal priority) and, in the event of an auction, the highest bidder acquires the immovable free of encumbrances. However, the mortgagee and, in the case of an auction, the highest bidder enjoy the real servitudes which serve the mortgaged dominant tenement, regardless of whether they were constituted before or after the acquisition of the mortgage.[776] This is due to the fact that the real servitudes are rights which follow (accompany) the ownership of the dominant tenement.[777] Finally, it ought to be borne in mind that the erection of a building or buildings on a mortgaged plot or the establishment of horizontal or vertical ownership do not prejudice the rights of the mortgagee. Indeed, unless otherwise stipulated between the owner or co-owners of the immovable and the mortgagee, the mortgage will extend to the erected building or buildings.

436. According to Article 1282 CC, a mortgage extends to the whole of the mortgaged immovable as well as its component parts and accessories. However, in the light of the legal treatment of accessories,[778] it should be stressed that the mortgage extends to them insofar as they belong to the owner of the mortgaged immovable. Furthermore, it should be borne in mind that in the case where a movable which constitutes a component part or accessory of the mortgaged immovable has been separated from the immovable and transferred to a third party, the mortgagee does not have the right to claim it back from the third party (Article 1283 CC).

B. Extent of Responsibility with Regard to the Claim Secured

437. As has already been mentioned, the amount of the claim secured must result from the registration, which is invalid if it gives rise to any uncertainty with regard to the above amount.[779] However, the registered amount of money does not

---

775. Provided that it has not been extinguished in the meantime.
776. This applies provided the relevant servitude has not been extinguished. However, a real servitude constituted before the registration of the mortgage is preserved in favour of the mortgagee when the owner of the mortgaged dominant tenement renounces the servitude without the consent of the mortgagee (Art. 1134 sub-para. b CC). (See Ap. Georgiades, *PrL*, para. 85 IV 1 No. 79, 1044).
777. See *supra* para. 231 (under (c)) and n. 394.
778. See *supra* para. 87.
779. See *supra* para. 430.

always correspond with the real amount of the claim secured and may be bigger or smaller than the latter. In such a case, it seems correct to accept that the mortgage secures the registered amount of money even if it is smaller than the one actually due, and the amount actually due even if it is smaller than the registered one.[780]

Another issue concerns the interest on the claim secured which is covered by the mortgage. On this point it should be noted that, if the mortgage has been registered for a certain amount of money, this amount also includes the interest on the claim secured and constitutes the maximum amount the creditor may receive by way of privilege from the mortgaged immovable.[781] On the other hand, if the mortgage has been registered for a certain amount of principal and the latter has been registered as interest-bearing, the mortgage, regardless of who has the ownership of the immovable, will also secure, on the same priority ranking, the interest due for a period of one year before the attachment as well as the interest that becomes due after the attachment until payment of the debt or until the table of classification is finalized (Article 1289 CC). Consequently, the amount which is to be paid by way of privilege to the mortgagee out of the proceeds of the auction will be the total of the above interest and of the registered as interest-bearing principal.[782]

V. Liquidation of Mortgage

438. As soon as the debt has become due, if the debtor does not pay it voluntarily, the mortgagee is entitled to claim its payment by commencing, as he or she sees fit, either a personal or a real legal action (Article 1291 sub-paragraph a CC). In the first case, he or she proceeds, as any (unsecured or general) creditor would,

780. Thus, K. Vavouskos, *PrL*, No. 428, 414. See also Ph. Doris, *Real Security*, para. 7 III, 62; I. Spyridakis, *The Law of Real Security*, Vol. I (Athens: A. Sakkoulas, 1974), 94–95 [in Greek]; Ath. Kritikos, in *Civil Code*, Vol. VI: *PrL*, ed. Ap. Georgiades & M. Stathopoulos; Art. 1269 No. 3; P. Filios & Chr. Filios, *PrL*, para. 236 A, 425, as well as AP 711/1992, 35 HellD, 1994, 102; AP 562/1968, 17 NoB, 1969, 168 (169). Compare, however, Ap. Georgiades, *PrL*, para. 85 IV 2 No. 91 et seq., 1047–1049, as well as AP 5543/1999, 40 HellD, 1999, 1624; AP 872/1996, 39 HellD, 1998, 1621.

781. Ap. Georgiades, *PrL*, para. 85 IV 2 No. 95 p. 1049, as well as AP 454/2000, 41 HellD, 2000, 1668; AP 813/1998, 39 HellD, 1998, 1620; AP 613/1998, 40 HellD, 1999, 152; AP 300/1976, 24 NoB, 1976, 850; Court of Appeal of Larissa 785/2002, 52 NoB, 2004, 261 (262); Court of Appeal of Thessaloniki 2022/1998, 39 HellD, 1998, 1416; Court of Appeal of Athens 7481/1989, 34 HellD, 1933, 643; Court of Appeal of Athens 7126/1979, 20 HellD, 1979, 681; Court of Appeal of Thessaloniki 1013/1977, 29 ArchN, 1978, 503 (504).

782. Thus, I. Spyridakis, *The Law of Real Security*, Vol. I, 97–98; Ap. Georgiades, *PrL*, para. 85 IV 2 No. 96, 1050. However, especially, in the area of jurisprudence it is argued that the total of the principal of the claim secured and of the above interest may not exceed the registered amount secured by the mortgage and that the surplus interest is not covered by the mortgage (see AP 400/2003, 51 NoB, 2003, 1861; AP 304/2003, NOMOS; AP 303/2003, NOMOS; AP 340/2001, 42 HellD, 2001, 1353; AP 813/1998, 39 HellD, 1998, 1621; AP 1424/1997, 40 HellD, 1999, 151; AP 1126/1997, 40 HellD, 1999, 348; AP 613/1998, 40 HellD, 1999, 152; AP 307/1996, 38 HellD, 1997, 137; AP 941/1995, 45 NoB, 1997, 1110; AP 1247/1985, 34 NoB, 1986, 857; AP 136/1977, 25 NoB, 1977, 1145; AP 1058/1974, 42 EEN, 1975, 573; AP 562/1968, 17 NoB, 1969, 168; Court of Appeal of Patras 511/2004, NOMOS = AchNom 2005, 155; Court of Appeal of Patras 992/2002, NOMOS = AchNom 2003, 181; Court of Appeal of Thessaloniki, 1020/1997, 41 Arm, 1997, 1021; One-member District Court of Thessaloniki 12869/2004, 59 Arm, 2005, 1093 (1097), as well as Ph. Doris, *Real Security*, para. 7 V, 64–66; P. Filios & Chr. Filios, *PrL*, para. 236 B II, 426).

with a compulsory execution in respect of the assets of the debtor and, if other creditors are involved, he or she is satisfied with them on a pro rata basis, if they are general creditors, and after them, if they are creditors in a mortgage or other privilege. In the latter case, so long as the mortgagee is in possession of an executory title (final court decision, order of payment, etc.[783]), he or she may proceed with a compulsory execution[784] in respect of the mortgaged immovable[785] (Article 1292 CC) – regardless of whether it belongs to his or her personal debtor or to a third party – aiming at the satisfaction of his or her claim from the proceeds of the relevant auction by way of privilege.[786]

The above personal and real legal actions are not subject to any order of priority. The creditor may commence, as he or she himself or herself sees fit, either the first or the second, while the commencement of a personal action does not preclude the initiation of a real one (Article 1291 CC) and *vice versa*. Indeed, according to Article 1293 CC, a creditor whose claim has not been wholly or partially satisfied by the mortgaged immovable has the right to commence a personal legal action against any person who is bound to pay. The creditor is also entitled to commence both of the above actions at the same time and in parallel.[787] However, the complete satisfaction of the claim secured as a result of the commencement of one of them precludes the possibility of initiating the other.

439. Mention has already been made of the right of a mortgagee to commence a relevant real legal action not only against his or her personal debtor but also against any third party who has conferred a mortgage on his or her own immovable with a view to securing the debt of another. The term 'third party' also includes[788] any individual possessing the mortgaged immovable by virtue of a lawful title (Article 1294 CC), that is, the universal or particular successor in title of the third party who has conferred a mortgage on his or her own immovable, the particular successor in title of the debtor-owner of the mortgaged immovable or any person who has acquired the ownership of the mortgaged immovable by *usucaption* after

783. See Art. 904 para. 2 CCProc.
784. This execution is carried out according to Arts 904 et seq., 951, 992 et seq. CCProc.
785. In the case where, after the registration of the mortgage, the mortgaged immovable is divided into two or more self-contained parts, on account of the undivided character of mortgage (on which see *supra* para. 418), the compulsory execution may be pursued in respect of any of these immovables. Likewise, if, after the relevant registration, the mortgaged immovable is joined with another contiguous immovable, the compulsory execution may be pursued in respect of the whole new immovable (see Ap. Georgiades, *PrL*, para. 86 II 2 No. 29, 1063–1064).
786. From Art. 1007 CCProc, in combination with Arts 975–978 CCProc, the following points emerge: the claim secured by a mortgage is provided with a special priority and, therefore, it is satisfied after claims which are provided with a general priority. The latter, however, are satisfied by way of privilege only up to a share of one-third of the proceeds of the auction, while the remaining share of two-third is offered, in order of priority, for the satisfaction of claims arising from disbursements on the mortgaged immovable and for the satisfaction of the claim secured by the mortgage. Exceptionally, of the claims provided with a general priority, claims concerning performance of paid services which have arisen within the two years before the day of the first auction are satisfied out of the total of the proceeds of the auction (Art. 31 L. 1545/1985).
787. See Ap. Georgiades, *PrL*, para. 86 II 1 No. 19, 1059.
788. See Ap. Georgiades, *PrL*, para. 86 II 4 No. 37, 1067–1068.

the registration of the mortgage, providing that the mortgage has not been extinguished according to Article 1053 CC.[789]

The commencement of a real legal action against the third party above displays certain peculiarities, some of which are regulated by Articles 1294–1298 CC as follows:

(a) the third party is sued by the real legal action, except if he or she prefers to pay all the claims to the extent that they are secured by the mortgage (Article 1294 CC);
(b) the commencement of the compulsory execution against the third party presupposes his or her being served with an order for payment as well (Articles 1295 CC, 993 paragraph 1 CCProc);
(c) the extent of obligation of the third party may not exceed the value of the mortgaged immovable, provided that the said third party is not personally liable, e.g., as guarantor (Article 1296 CC);
(d) in the case where the mortgage secures not the main claim but a personal guarantee, the third party is entitled to advance a plea of distraint (Article 855 CC), that is, to demand that the principal debtor be sued first of all (Article 1297 CC);
(e) third party who has paid the debt secured by the mortgage or has been deprived of the mortgaged immovable as a result of its sale by auction is subrogated to the rights of the mortgagee (Article 1298 CC).

VI. Abolishment of Mortgage

440. Just as the acquisition of a mortgage presupposes a title and a registration in the mortgage register, the abolishment of a mortgage presupposes an extinction, with regard to the title, and also a deletion (cancellation), with regard to the registration.

A. *Extinction of Mortgage*

441. The grounds leading to the extinction of a mortgage relate to the claim secured, the object of the mortgage, the title and the right of the mortgage itself.

More precisely, a mortgage may be extinguished by the following:

(a) the complete[790] extinction, in any fashion,[791] of the claim secured or the prescription of the latter (Articles 1317, 1320 CC);

789. See *supra* para. 294 and *infra* para. 441.
790. Owing to the undivided character of a mortgage, the partial extinction of the claim secured does not entail extinction of the mortgage (see also *supra* para. 418).
791. Compare, though, Arts 439 CC and 475 para. 1 CC.

(b) the total (material or legal[792]) disappearance of the mortgaged immovable (Article 1318 point 1 CC),[793] its sale in a public auction and the payment of the proceeds of the auction (Articles 1318 point 3 CC and 1005 paragraph 3 CCProc)[794] and also the acquisition of the same immovable by *usucaption*, provided that the conditions of Article 1053 CC are fulfilled;[795]
(c) the expiration of the time period for which the mortgage was granted (Article 1318 point 4 CC); and finally
(d) the renunciation of the creditor (Article 1318 point 2 CC)[796] and the merger in the same person of the right of ownership and the right of mortgage (confusion) (Article 1321 CC).[797]

B. Deletion (Cancellation) of Mortgage

442. The extinction itself does not entail abolishment of the mortgage without deletion of the registered mortgage from the mortgage register. The relevant deletion is effected either with the consent of the creditor or by a final court decision (Article 1324 CC) or as a result of an application by the highest bidder who has paid the proceeds of the auction (Article 1005 paragraph 3 sub-paragraph b CCProc).

The creditor's consent for deletion is given by a unilateral declaration before a notary (Article 1325 CC) which may not be revoked. However, in the case where the creditor does not consent to the deletion, this is ordered by the court following a (personal[798]) legal action by whoever has an interest in the matter (Articles 1327–1328 CC).

§2. Mortgage on the Usufruct of an Immovable

443. According to Article 1259 CC, a mortgage may also be obtained on the usufruct of an immovable which is susceptible of alienation for as long as such usufruct lasts. On the other hand, as is generally accepted,[799] Article 1259 CC serves as an exception to the rule that usufruct is non-transferable[800] and permits the relevant

792. An example of legal disappearance is the fulfilment of the resolutory condition or term upon which the ownership of the mortgaged immovable depended.
793. Not, however, its alteration or change in form or kind (Art. 1322 CC).
794. However, according to Art. 1008 CCProc, the mortgage is preserved if the highest bidder assumes the debt with the consent of the mortgagee.
795. See *supra* para. 294.
796. The renunciation is effected by a unilateral declaration made before a notary and does not abolish a right of action that exists against any person who holds a relevant personal obligation (Art. 1319 CC).
797. For example, in the case where the secured claim has been assigned by the mortgagee to the third party owner of the mortgaged immovable.
798. Thus, Ap. Georgiades, *PrL*, para. 86 III 4 No. 68, 1077 (which includes the debate on the issue of whether the relevant action is personal or constitutive). See also Court of Appeal of Athens 13609/1988, 41 ArchN, 1990, 106; One-member District Court of Chalkida 16/2008, 39 D, 2008, 388 (390).
799. K. Vavouskos, *PrL*, No. 348, 349–350; Ap. Georgiades, *PrL*, para. 87 I 1 No. 3, 1079; D. Papasteriou, *PrL III*, para. 92 No.7, 416; Ph. Doris, *Real Security*, 54; K. Roussos, in *Civil Code*, Vol. VI: *PrL*, ed. Ap. Georgiades & M. Stathopoulos, Art. 1166 No. 17.
800. See *supra* paras 247–248.

encumbrance even in the case where the usufruct has not been stipulated as being transferable.

The constitution of a mortgage on the usufruct of an immovable does not prevent the naked owner from conferring a mortgage on his or her naked ownership.[801] Thus, it is possible for two mortgages to exist on the same immovable: one on the usufruct and one on the naked ownership.

444. To mortgages on the usufruct of immovables also applies everything that was stated above regarding mortgages on the ownership of immovables. However, the following should be borne in mind:

(a) a mortgage on the usufruct of an immovable extends to the components and accessories of that immovable which are covered by the usufruct (Article 1282 CC);
(b) the mortgagee may commence a real legal action provided by Article 1291 CC even against the naked owner, who is considered to be a third-party possessor in the sense of Article 1294 CC;[802]
(c) the relevant action leads to seizure,[803] an auction and, finally, to the transfer of the right of usufruct to the highest bidder[804] who will retain it for as long as such usufruct lasts;[805]
(d) mortgages on usufructs are extinguished in the same way as mortgages on ownership and also on account of the extinction of the encumbered usufruct (Article 1259 CC). However, grounds relating to the protection of the mortgagee justify the view that the extinction of usufruct due to a merger of usufruct and ownership in the same person (Article 1168 CC) and to the renunciation of the usufructuary (Article 1169 CC) should not entail extinction of the mortgage.[806]

§3. Prenotice of Mortgage

I. Concept of Prenotice of Mortgage

445. A prenotice of mortgage[807] aims to secure the claim of a creditor who does not possess any title deed conferring on him or her a right to acquire a mortgage

801. See also *supra* para. 421 and n. 751.
802. Thus, Ap. Georgiades, *PrL*, para. 87 IV No. 10, 1081. On Art. 1294 CC see *supra* para. 439.
803. Even if the encumbered usufruct has not been specified as being transferable (see also *supra* para. 248).
804. The highest bidder acquires the relevant real right and not only the personal right to exercise the usufruct, even in the case where the encumbered usufruct has not been specified as being transferable (Ap. Georgiades, *PrL*, para. 87 V No. 12, 1082).
805. This is because the highest bidder must not have more rights than the debtor in the mortgage.
806. See G. Balis, *PrL*, para. 174 No. 2, 3, 379–380; K. Vavouskos, *PrL*, No. 417, 407 (in respect of the extinction of usufruct due to the renunciation of the usufructuary); Ap. Georgiades, *PrL*, para. 76 IV 3, 4 Nos 18–19, 21, 953–954; para. 87 VI Nos 14 et seq., 1082–1083; D. Papasteriou, *PrL III*, para. 92 No. 12, 417; I. Spyridakis, *The Law of Real Security*, Vol. II (Athens: A. Sakkoulas, 1975), 100; Ath. Kritikos, in *Civil Code*, Vol. VI: *PrL*, ed. Ap. Georgiades & M. Stathopoulos, Art. 1259 Nos 22, 23; P. Filios & Chr. Filios, *PrL*, para. 233 B III, 421.
807. For a detailed discussion of prenotice of mortgage, especially within the scope of civil procedural law, see Ch. Apalagaki, *Prenotice of Mortgage. A Procedural Approach* (Athens–Thessaloniki: Sakoulas, 2005), passim [in Greek].

and who runs the risk of the immovable or immovables of his or her debtor being alienated or encumbered with a mortgage, on behalf of a third party, until he or she himself or herself acquires a title and, more specifically, a final court decision adjudicating the relevant claim in his or her favour.

A prenotice of mortgage, which currently serves as a provisional remedy (Article 706 CCProc), confers solely a priority right for the acquisition of a mortgage, in the sense that, as soon as a final court decision adjudicating the claim has been issued, the prenotice is converted into a mortgage which is considered to be registered as from the date of the prenotice (Article 1277 CC). Consequently, the prenotice may be defined as a mortgage which is dependent on two suspensive conditions: the condition of the final adjudication of the claim secured and the condition of the conversion of the prenotice into a mortgage.

II. Acquisition of Prenotice of Mortgage

446. Like the acquisition of a mortgage, the acquisition of a prenotice of mortgage presupposes a title conferring a right of prenotice and a registration in the mortgage register.[808]

A. *Title*

447. The principal title for a prenotice of mortgage is a court decision (Article 1274 CC) which is issued through the procedure of provisional remedies (Article 706 CCProc). However, orders for payment, which are not judgments, also confer an entitlement to register a prenotice (Article 724 paragraph 1 CCProc). Finally, while the private will may not officially confer a title for a prenotice of mortgage, procedural practice in Greece tends to allow such an additional method, most often in order to avoid the increased expense of a conventional mortgage. This is very frequently attempted through the participation and prompt consent of the opposing party before the competent judge (Article 687 paragraph 2 CCProc). Thus, an essentially unopposed order for issuing this provisional remedy is immediately obtained.[809]

448. The aforementioned court decision is issued in consequence of an application by the creditor to the competent (according to Articles 683 et seq., 22 and 23 CCProc) court. The requested relief of this application is the registration of a prenotice of mortgage, as a provisional remedy, on an immovable or on immovables of

808. And, within the framework of the land registry system, on the record sheet of the land register which is devoted to the relevant immovable (Art. 12 para. 1 point viii of L. 2664/1998).

809. This is in respect of the so-called consensual prenotice of mortgage, on the legality of which some reservations have been expressed in theory. On this point see Ph. Doris, *Real Security*, 82–83; Ap. Georgiades, *PrL*, para. 88 I No. 2, 1087; N. Livanis, in *Civil Code*, Vol. VI: *PrL*, ed. Ap. Georgiades & M. Stathopoulos, Art. 1274, Nos 8–9.

the debtor.[810] The acceptance of the application depends on the applicant making convincing claims regarding the existence of an imminent danger or an urgent circumstance (Article 682 paragraph 1 CCProc) and also on whether the existence of the claim secured has been shown to be probable. A negative condition for acceptance of the application is the creditor's lack of a title conferring on him or her a right of mortgage. If such a title exists, the application is rejected on account of absence of a legal interest.[811]

The court decision allowing the registration of a prenotice of mortgage[812] must specify the exact amount of the claim secured (Article 706 paragraph 2 CCProc). The same decision probably bases the registration of the prenotice on various conditions, such as the granting of surety by the applicant (Article 694 CCProc) or the commencement of a regular legal action concerning the claim secured within a certain term which cannot be less than thirty days (Article 693 CCProc).

449. Until the court decision ordering the registration of the prenotice of mortgage has been issued, the risk of the immovable of the debtor being alienated or encumbered with a mortgage, in favour of a third party, persists. Therefore, the application for the registration of prenotice may also request the prompt rendering of a provisional order in favour of the applicant (691 paragraph 2, 700 paragraph 3 CCProc). This order provisionally prohibits further transfer of ownership or establishment of a mortgage with regard to an immovable, under the penalty of invalidity (Article 176 CC), until the judgment on the requested prenotice has been rendered. The same provisional order is also registered in the mortgage register.[813]

B. Registration

450. A prenotice of mortgage is registered in the same manner as a mortgage but with the mention that it is in respect of a prenotice (Article 1276 CC). This registration, just like the registration of a mortgage, is null and void in the case where the immovable does not already belong at the time of registration to the person conferring the prenotice. However, the relevant null registration may be validated by a subsequent approval or acquisition of ownership (Article 239 CC).[814] Finally, it should be borne in mind that a prenotice of mortgage, just like the mortgage itself, takes effect from the time of its due registration in the mortgage register (Article

810. The above application, as well as the relevant court decision, may refer either to a certain immovable (specific title) or to any immovable or immovables of the debtor (general title). Thus, K. Beis, *Proceedings II*, 303; Ap. Georgiades, *PrL*, para. 88 II 2 No. 8, 1089; N. Livanis, in *Civil Code*, Vol. VI: *PrL*, ed. Ap. Georgiades & M. Stathopoulos, Art. 1274 No. 22. For the opposite view see I. Spyridakis, *The Law of Real Security*, Vol. II, 129–130, who recognizes specific titles only.
811. See Ap. Georgiades, *PrL*, para. 88 II 2 No. 7, 1089; One-member District Court of Piraeus 917/1974, 22 NoB, 1974, 1442.
812. The relevant decision is revocable (Arts 696 et seq. CCProc).
813. However, the prenotice of a mortgage takes effect from the time of its registration in the mortgage register (see *infra* para. 450) and not from the time of the registration of the above provisional order.
814. In this case, Art. 1271 sub-para. b CC does not apply in that it relates to the registration of a mortgage by private will (see *supra* para. 426 n. 760).

1268 CC), while its registration, like the registration of a mortgage (Article 1273 CC), interrupts the prescription of the claim for the benefit of the person whose rights are secured by the prenotice (Article 1280 CC).

III. Conversion of Prenotice of Mortgage into a Mortgage

451. According to Article 1277 CC, a prenotice of mortgage which is registered on the strength of a court decision issued through the procedure of provisional remedies may be converted into a mortgage (which will be considered to be registered as from the date of the prenotice) providing a final court decision adjudicating the claim secured has been issued. The necessity of this judgment becomes obvious in the light of the fact that the relevant conversion presupposes certainty in regard to the existence of the claim secured and also of the fact that the existence of the latter has solely been regarded as probable by the court of provisional remedies. From Article 1277 CC it may also be concluded that the relevant conversion requires a note in the mortgage register that the prenotice has been converted into a mortgage. This note must be effected within ninety days of the date the court decision adjudicating the claim secured by the prenotice has become final (Article 1323 point 2 CC).[815] This time-limit is exclusive and, consequently, it may be suspended if the creditor has been impeded by force majeure from effecting the relevant note (Article 279 in combination with Article 255 CC).[816]

The conversion of a prenotice into a mortgage is not prevented in the case where the ownership of the immovable is transferred to another (Article 1278 CC). In such a case, the latter will acquire the immovable encumbered by the mortgage from the date of the registration of the prenotice. On the other hand, where before the conversion of a prenotice into a mortgage a compulsory execution has been pursued against the immovable, the claim for the benefit of which the prenotice was registered receives no priority ranking (is classified at random)[817] and the immovable is transferred to the highest bidder free from encumbrance (Article 1279 CC).

452. According to Article 29 IntrLCCProc, in the case where a prenotice has been registered on the basis of an order for payment, it may be converted into a mortgage upon expiration of the two successive time limits for raising an objection

815. The expiration of the relevant time limit entails the extinction of the prenotice (Art. 1323 point 2 CC). Therefore, a note which is effected after the above expiration leads to the establishment of a mortgage on the basis of a final judgment. The chronological ranking of this mortgage will be determined, though, by reference to the date of its registration and not by reference to the date of the registration of the prenotice (K. Vavouskos, 'The Prenotice of a Mortgage in Greek Law under the New Code of Civil Procedure', *Volume in Honour of K. Karavas*, Vol. I–B (Thessaloniki, 1978), 832; K. Vavouskos, *PrL*, No. 455 n. 1, 439; K. Beis, *Proceedings II*, 308; Ap. Georgiades, *PrL*, para. 88 II 1 No. 29, 1096–1097; I. Spyridakis, *The Law of Real Security*, Vol. II, 135–136).

816. K. Vavouskos, *PrL*, No. 455, 440; Ap. Georgiades, *PrL*, para. 88 II 1 No. 29, 1097. See also AP 1858/1986, 36 NoB, 1988, 345 (346).

817. This is due to the fact that the above claim depends on the suspensive condition of its final adjudication. On this issue see Art. 978 CCProc and for further details P. Yessiou-Faltsi, *Civil Procedure in Hellas*, No. 555, 422–423.

to the order for payment (Articles 632, 633 paragraph 2 CCProc) or upon final rejection of such an objection.[818] In addition, a relevant note in the mortgage register is required within ninety days of the date of expiration of the time limits for raising the above objection or of the final rejection of the same objection (Article 1323 case 2 CC).

IV. Abolishment of Prenotice of Mortgage

453. Just like the abolishment of a mortgage, the abolishment of a prenotice presupposes its extinction and its deletion (cancellation).

454. A prenotice of mortgage may be extinguished on the same grounds as a mortgage[819] and also: (a) by a revocation of the court decision which ordered the prenotice, and (b) if the prenotice has not been converted into a mortgage within ninety days of the date of the final judgment that adjudicated the claim (Article 1323 CC).

455. According to Article 1330 CC, a prenotice may be deleted as follows:

(a) with the consent of the creditor, which must be given as in the case of the deletion of a mortgage, that is, by a unilateral declaration before a notary (Article 1325 CC);[820]
(b) if a court decision revoking the judgment that ordered the registration or ordering the deletion of the prenotice is adduced;
(c) if ninety days have elapsed since the date of the final judgment that adjudicated the claim secured without the prenotice having been converted into a mortgage.

In addition, pursuant to Article 1005 paragraph 3 sub-paragraph b CCProc, a prenotice may be deleted in consequence of an application by the highest bidder who has paid the proceeds of the auction.

818. It is further accepted that, under the above two conditions, even prenotices which have been registered on the basis of a specific judgment (Arts 706, 682 CCProc) may now be converted into a mortgage based on the order of payment (see Ap. Georgiades, *PrL*, para. 88 III 2 No. 36, 1099–1100; P. Yessiou-Faltsi, *Civil Procedure in Hellas*, No. 470, 380; N. Livanis, in *Civil Code*, Vol. VI: *PrL*, ed. Ap. Georgiades & M. Stathopoulos, Arts 1277–1278 No. 14).

819. See *supra* para. 441.

820. If the creditor refuses his or her consent, it is replaced by a judgment of the One-member District Court, which is issued through the procedure of provisional remedies in consequence of an application by the debtor (see Ap. Georgiades, *PrL*, para. 88 IV 2 No. 39, 1100–1101, as well as Three-member District Court of Athens 2468/1987, 31 HellD, 1990, 1630.

Chapter 3. Real Security on Movables

§1. Pledges on Movables

I. Concept of a Pledge

456. From Article 1209 CC it emerges that a pledge is the real right which secures the satisfaction of a creditor's claim from the value of a movable thing belonging to another by way of privilege. However, it seems correct to accept that like any other real right so too pledges establish real relations from which derive not only the relevant real right (as is defined above), but also other rights, as well as obligations, charges or commitments.[821] The elements of the concept of a pledge are as follows: a movable belonging to another, the claim secured and the satisfaction of the creditor by way of privilege.

457. The elements 'claim secured' and 'satisfaction of the creditor by way of privilege' have already been discussed.[822] However, with regard to the claim secured, it is important to add that it must be determined or susceptible of determination[823] (principle of specificity) and that the privilege issuing from a pledge takes effect from the moment of its constitution, even if it has been constituted to secure a future or a conditional claim (Article 1217 CC).

With respect to the element 'a movable thing belonging to another', the following should be noted:

(a) strictly speaking, the object of a pledge is the full, naked or revocable ownership[824] of the movable of another;[825]
(b) any defined movable (principle of specificity) which is in commerce and which may be alienated can be the object of a pledge;[826]
(c) a pledge may also be constituted on an ideal share of the ownership of a movable (Article 1216 CC);
(d) items of movable property that are exempt from attachment (in the sense of Article 953 CCProc) may be pledged only when the debtor-pledger, in whose favour the relevant prohibition works, has renounced this prohibition;

821. See also D. Papasteriou, *PrL III*, para. 83 No. 7, 262.
822. See, respectively, *supra* paras 417 and 410, 414 (under (a)).
823. Compare Art. 1269 CC concerning mortgages.
824. On the same issue in the area of mortgage see *supra* para. 421 and nn. 751, 752.
825. Insofar as the constitution of a pledge presupposes delivery of the thing to the creditor (see Art. 1211 CC), future things (e.g., things under construction), may not be pledged. However, the pledging of a future thing means that the pledge will be constituted as soon as the thing is acquired by the debtor and delivered to the creditor (K. Vavouskos, *PrL*, No. 388, 382; Ap. Georgiades, *PrL*, para. 89 I 2 No. 9, 1107; D. Papasteriou, *PrL III*, para. 83 II No. 12, 264; as well as AP 408/1966, 15 NoB, 1967, 206 (207)).
826. This is because pledges, as rights of value, offer the pledgee the power to alienate the thing, under certain conditions, in order to gain satisfaction from its value (see also *supra* para. 50 (under b)).

(e) consumable things, especially money, are possible objects of pledges as well.[827] However, in this case, after the payment of the debt, depending on whether the pledgee had the power to consume the thing[828] or not, he or she is bound to restitute either other things of the same quantity and quality (irregular pledge) or the same thing[829] in kind (regular pledge).

II. Types of Pledges

A. *Common Pledges*

1. Concept of a Common Pledge

458. A common pledge is that which, like pledges on movables without delivery,[830] is constituted by a contract between the pledger (debtor or third party) and the creditor. However, the constitution of a common pledge, unlike the constitution of a pledge on a movable without delivery, also presuposes the delivery of the thing by the pledger to the pledgee or – by their common consent – to a third party.

2. Constitution of a Common Pledge

459. According to Article 1211 CC, the constitution of a pledge requires the delivery of the thing by the owner to the creditor and an agreement by both, which must be incorporated in a notarial deed or in a private deed bearing an officially certified date, to the effect that the creditor has acquired a right of pledge on the thing.

From the above article it emerges that the pledger, debtor or third party who acts on behalf of the debtor, must be the owner of the thing pledged. However, Article 1215 CC, permitting the application by analogy of Articles 1036 et seq. CC[831] within the framework of pledges, offers the possibility of a pledge being acquired even if the thing does not belong to the pledger.

From Article 1211 CC it emerges, furthermore, that the constitution of a pledge presupposes the conclusion of a real contract which includes, on the one hand, an agreement (i.e., a real contract which constitutes a constituent part of the aforementioned real contract[832]) between the owner of the thing, debtor or third party, and the creditor to the effect that the latter acquires a right of pledge on the thing and, on the other hand, the delivery of the quasi possession[833] of the thing by the pledger to the creditor.

827. On this point see G. Balis, *PrL*, para. 201 No. 10, 436–437; K. Vavouskos, *PrL*, No. 388, 382; Ap. Georgiades, *PrL*, para. 89 I 2 No. 6, 1106–1107.
828. In this case the constitution of a pledge is identical to a transfer of the ownership of the thing.
829. For example, the money which was delivered to him or her in a sealed envelope.
830. On which see *supra* para. 412 (under (c)) and *infra* paras 468 et seq.
831. On which see *supra* paras 315 et seq. However, the part of Art. 1039 sub-para. b CC which refers to things alienated by public auction does not apply in the field of pledges.
832. See D. Papasteriou, *PrL III*, para. 84 No. 23, 282.
833. See *supra* para. 107.

The above agreement, for reasons of protection of third parties,[834] is formal and must be incorporated in a notarial deed or in a private deed bearing an officially certified date. The same agreement must define the claim secured and describe the thing pledged. However, instead of a description incorporated in the document itself, it is sufficient to attach thereto a special list describing the thing or things.

On the other hand, the delivery of the quasi possession of the thing may be carried out in one of the ways provided by Articles 976–978 CC,[835] except for delivery through *constitutum possessorium* (Article 1213 CC).[836] In any event, according to Article 1212 CC, the relevant delivery may also be made to a third party (usually, a depositary)[837] by the common consent of the creditor and the pledger.

3. Relationship between the Parties Involved in a Pledge

460. The constitution of a pledge entails not only the establishment of the relevant real right but also the creation – on the strength of the law – of a personal relationship between the pledgee and the pledger. This relationship includes a set of reciprocal rights and obligations on the part of the above persons and is regulated by Articles 1219–1240 CC, unless otherwise stipulated by the parties.

461. The most important rights of the pledgee until the claim secured becomes due are as follows:

(a) He or she has the quasi possession of the thing pledged (Article 975 CC) and, as quasi possessor, he or she is protected as the possessor (Article 996 CC).[838] In addition, as holder of the relevant real right, he or she is protected as the owner of a movable (Article 1236 CC).[839]
(b) He or she is entitled to receive the benefits of the thing pledged in accordance with the provisions of Articles 1221–1222 CC.
(c) He or she has, on the one hand, the right to claim, according to the provisions governing the management of another's affairs, the disbursements incurred by him or her in respect of the thing and, on the other hand, the right to remove a piece of work added by him or her to the thing (Article 1225 CC).
(d) In the case where his or her security is threatened by an impending act of destruction or a substantial reduction in the value of the thing pledged, he or she has the right to obtain court permission for the sale of the thing by auction, except if the pledger has completed the security within a reasonable period set

834. See Ap. Georgiades, *PrL*, para. 89 III 4 No. 53, 1120.
835. On this point see *supra* paras 117 et seq.
836. Article 1213 CC, prohibiting an agreement between the creditor and the pledger that the latter will remain in detention of the thing, protects third parties from the risk of believing that the thing is free from pledges.
837. The debtor is also considered to be a third party in the case where the pledger is not the debtor but a third party (Ap. Georgiades, *PrL*, para. 89 III 5 No. 58, 1121).
838. See *supra* para. 152.
839. See *supra* paras 366, 367.

for him or her (Article 1228 CC). However, in the case of an auction, the proceeds of the auction substitute the thing (Article 1228 paragraph 1 sub-paragraph c CC) and, consequently, the pledge on the thing is converted into a pledge upon a claim.

462. With regard to the obligations of the pledgee until the claim secured becomes due, it should be mentioned that this creditor is bound:

(a) to preserve the thing (Article 1224 sub-paragraph a CC), provided that he or she detains it;
(b) not to use or pledge the thing without the consent of the pledger (Article 1224 sub-paragraph b CC);
(c) to restitute the thing to the pledger as soon as the right of pledge is extinguished (Article 1232 CC).[840]

463. Finally, with regard to the rights of the pledger, it ought to be noted that he or she has all the powers deriving from his or her right of ownership and may exercise them to the extent that such exercise does not infringe the right of pledge. Hence, the pledger may transfer or encumber with a limited real right the ownership of the thing pledged and he or she may protect himself or herself as owner. However, he or she cannot use the thing as he or she does not detain it. Moreover, it ought to be borne in mind that the pledger is the possessor of the thing pledged who exercises possession through another[841] and consequently is protected as possessor.

Furthermore, the pledger has the following rights:

(a) In the case where the creditor infringes his or her rights, he or she may demand the delivery of the thing to a receiver or its public deposition or its restitution against repayment of the debt even if it has not matured (Articles 1226–1227 CC).
(b) If destruction or substantial reduction in the value of the thing pledged is threatened, he or she is entitled either to obtain court permission for the sale of the thing by auction or to demand the restitution of the thing against the provision of another security, except for a security through a guarantor (Article 1229 CC).
(c) If an opportunity for a favourable sale of the thing arises, he or she may demand, even before the debt matures, court permission for the sale of the thing (Article 1230 CC). In this case the price will substitute the thing and, consequently, the pledge on the thing will be converted into a pledge on a claim.
(d) The third party pledger has the right, upon the debt becoming due, to settle such debt and take back the thing. By such a settlement, the third party pledger is subrogated to the rights of the creditor (Article 1234 CC).
(e) Unless the law ordains otherwise, the third party pledger is entitled to advance against the creditor the pleas that the debtor has in regard to the claim (e.g., the

840. See, however, *infra* para. 467.
841. On this possibility see *supra* paras 128, 130.

plea of prescription) even if the debtor has renounced such pleas (Article 1219 CC).

4. Liquidation of a Common Pledge

464. In the case where the debtor does not voluntarily pay the claim secured, although the latter has become due and payable, the pledgee has the right to commence a personal legal action against him or her (e.g., the action arising from the contract of loan) aiming at a compulsory execution on the assets of the debtor. In this case, depending on whether in addition to the pledgee there are other general (ordinary) creditors or creditors in a pledge or mortgage, he or she runs the risk of being satisfied on a pro rata basis with or following them, respectively.

The pledgee is also entitled to follow the procedure provided by Article 1237 CC. To be precise, provided that he or she possesses an executory title (final court decision, order for payment, notarial deed, etc.[842]), he or she may bring against the debtor a so-called real legal action, that is, he or she may pursue a compulsory execution in respect of the thing pledged and a sale of the latter by public auction in order to gain satisfaction from the proceeds of the auction by way of privilege over the general creditors and the pledgees following him or her. On the other hand, a pledgee who does not possess an executory title may obtain a court decision ordering the sale of the thing by public auction.[843] In any case, by the auction and the adjudication of the thing to the purchaser (highest bidder), the latter will acquire the ownership of the thing free of any encumbrances,[844] except for the encumbrance of usufruct that existed before the constitution of the pledge (Article 1240 CC).

5. Extinction of a Common Pledge

465. Common pledges are extinguished primarily on general grounds. Examples of such grounds are the destruction of the thing pledged, the fulfilment of the resolutory condition upon which the ownership of the thing pledged was dependent, the fulfilment of the resolutory condition or the expiration of the resolutory term upon which the pledge was constituted (Articles 202, 210 CC) and the acquisition of the thing pledged by *usucaption* (Article 1053 CC)[845] or by contract with a person who was not the owner (Article 1040 CC).[846]

842. See Art. 904 para. 2 CCProc.

843. This decision is indispensable in the case where the pledger is not the personal debtor but a third party who has acted on behalf of the debtor. Indeed, even when an executory title against the debtor exists, it is impossible to pursue, on the basis of the latter, a compulsory execution against the third party owner of the thing pledged.

844. Consequently, even when the claim secured has not been satisfied, in whole or in part, from the proceeds of the auction (e.g., because the pledge which secured it had a lower ranking in relation to other pledges which encumbered the same movable), the relevant pledge will be extinguished. In this case, the creditor will be entitled as a general creditor to pursue the satisfaction of his or her claim by commencing against the debtor the above-mentioned personal legal action.

845. See *supra* para. 294.

846. See *supra* para. 327.

466. Furthermore, common pledges may be extinguished by the auction of the thing pledged[847] and on other special grounds which are specified in Article 1243 CC. These grounds are:

(a) the extinction of the claim secured by any method;[848]
(b) the voluntary restitution of the thing by the creditor to the pledger or the owner;
(c) a unilateral declaration[849] by the creditor to the pledger or the owner to the effect that he or she is renouncing the pledge;
(d) the merger in the same person of the right of ownership and the right of pledge (confusion). This occurs, for example, in the case where the ownership of the thing pledged is inherited by the pledgee.

467. As has already been mentioned,[850] upon the right of pledge being extinguished, the creditor is bound to restitute the thing to its owner (Article 1232 CC). An exception to this rule is introduced by Article 1233 CC. Indeed, according to the latter, with the permission of the court, the creditor, even after the extinction of his or her claim, is entitled to refuse the restitution of the thing to the debtor if he or she has against him or her another claim that has arisen from a contract concluded subsequently to the constitution of the pledge and has become due and payable before the maturity of the claim secured by the pledge. The creditor has the same right in regard to the third party pledger, if he or she also has against such a party a claim under the same conditions. As is obvious, Article 1233 CC offers the pledgee a right of retention, that is, a right to refuse the restitution of the thing until repayment of the aforementioned claim.[851]

B. Fictitious Pledges (Pledges on Movables without Delivery)

1. Fictitious Pledges before Law 2844/2000

468. Pledges which are constituted solely by agreement, that is, without material delivery of the thing pledged to the creditor – or to a third party by the common consent of the creditor and the pledger – are usually characterized as 'fictitious pledges'.[852] Here, the relevant real alteration is publicized either by the registration

847. See *supra* para. 464 and n. 844.
848. It is accepted that the prescription of the claim secured entails extinction of the pledge as well (Ap. Georgiades, *PrL*, para. 89 VI 2 No. 94, 1131).
849. This declaration is a unilateral, addressed to a specific individual, non-causal (abstract), non-formal and irrevocable real juridical act.
850. See also *supra* para. 462 (under c).
851. See Arts 325 et seq CC.
852. This type of pledge is also characterized as 'chattel-mortgage' (Ath. Yiannopoulos, 'Property', in *Introduction to Greek Law*, ed. K. Kerameus & Ph. Kozyris, 164) or as 'quasi (or "putative") pledge' (Ach. Koutsouradis, 'Present and Future of Real and Personal Securities', 61). For detailed discussion on the institution of fictitious pledges see P. Mazis, *The Fictitious Pledge* (Athens, 1977), passim [in Greek] as well as K. Simitis, *The Reformation of the Fictitious Pledge* (Athens, 1968), passim [in Greek]. On the issue of justification of the institution of fictitious pledges see *supra* para. 412 (under (c)).

of the above agreement in special registers created by the law or through other ways provided by special laws.

Fictitious pledges are distinguished into general and special ones. A general one is that which is constituted on any movable with a view to securing any claim, whereas a special one is that which is constituted on certain kinds of movables with a view to securing claims of a certain kind.

469. General fictitious pledges are referred to in Article 1214 CC, according to which 'a pledge may be constituted solely by agreement without delivery if the relevant agreement has been registered in a public register created by the law for this purpose'. However, since the above register has not yet been published, Article 1214 CC remains inactive. Hence, general fictitious pledges have not worked in practice so far. On the other hand, special laws which recognize and regulate various types of special fictitious pledges have been passed.[853]

The most important types of special fictitious pledges are as follows:

(a) pledges on the machines of an enterprise and pledges on mining equipment, which secure claims of banks derived from contracts of loan. Their constitution presupposes an agreement incorporated in a private deed bearing an officially certified date and registration in a public register which is kept in the District Court of the region in which the registered office of the enterprise is situated;
(b) cinematographic pledges which secure claims originating from contracts of loan between banks and film producers. These have as their object machines, films or claims relating to the exploitation of films and they are constituted by a written contract subject to registration in a special register which is kept in the District Court of Athens;
(c) pledges on tourist buses which secure the claims of any creditor against any debtor and are constituted by a contract incorporated in a notarial deed and registered in a special register which is kept in the registry office;
(d) agricultural pledges which secure claims derived from contracts of loan between agricultural associations and farmers or stock-farmers or between any creditor (e.g., a bank) and agricultural associations. They encumber the technical equipment, products or animals of the debtor and are constituted by the issue of an agricultural warrant;
(e) tobacco pledges which secure claims originating from contracts of loan between banks and tobacco producers and have as their object the production of tobacco which is written on the relevant license for detention or cultivation of tobacco. Their constitution presupposes the delivery of one of the two copies of the above license, by the producer (debtor) to the bank (creditor), and a note on both copies that a loan has been granted.

470. Special fictitious pledges, the most important of which have been mentioned above, have been abolished by the Law 2844/2000, concerning contracts on movables or claims subject to publicity and other security contracts. Indeed,

853. These pledges do not come within the scope of application of Art. 1214 CC.

according to Article 20 of this law, 'the provisions concerning pledges on movables without delivery, on behalf of certain creditors and claims, shall be abolished as soon as the present law shall come into force'[854] whereas 'pledges which had already been constituted by the above date, on the basis of the abolished provisions, shall be preserved and shall continue to be governed by the abolished provisions'.

2. Fictitious Pledges after Law 2844/2000

a. Concept and Legislative Status of a Fictitious Pledge

471. Law 2844/2000 'generalizes' the fictitious pledges which could be constituted on the basis of special provisions in special cases up until that time.[855] Thus, Article 1 paragraph 1[856] states that a pledge on a movable is also[857] constituted without delivery of its detention, in the case where, on the one hand, the creditor and the debtor are enterprises or businessmen and, on the other, security is provided for the needs of the enterprise or of the business of the debtor.

The above article, which recognizes the possibility of a pledge being constituted without delivery of the detention of the movable pledged, means that only the detention of the thing is not delivered to the pledgee, and not its quasi possession, which is acquired by *constitutum possessorium.*[858] This means of acquisition is permitted here, in spite of the regulation of Article 1213 CC,[859] because in the area of fictitious pledges publicity is achieved by the registration of pledges in public registers.

Article 1 paragraph 1 makes the constitution of a fictitious pledge dependent on two restrictions. The first refers to the contracting parties, who must be enterprises[860] or businessmen,[861] while the second relates to the claim secured, which must derive from a professional activity. In addition, Article 2 paragraph 1 sub-paragraph a, which excludes the constitution of fictitious pledges on money, negotiable instruments, household objects and movables susceptible of mortgage themselves,[862] adds a third restriction to the constitution of fictitious pledges relating to their object. However, also susceptible of fictitious pledges are all movable things,[863] an ideal share of a movable (Article 2 paragraph 2 sub-paragraph c), things which are due to be acquired in the future, so long as they are defined or are

854. The relevant law entered into force on 13 Oct. 2001 according to the P.D. 253/2001.
855. See the preamble to L. 2844/2000 under A2, where the term 'pledge on movables without delivery' is used instead of the synonymous term 'fictitious pledge' (see also under A3). However, in the present book, the above terms will be used interchangeably.
856. From this point on only the number of the relevant article without reference to the above law will be mentioned.
857. Consequently, the relevant constitution is potential.
858. Concomitantly, the pledgee is protected as quasi possessor. (On all these points see the preamble to L. 2844/2000 under B1.)
859. See *supra* para. 459 and n. 836.
860. The enterprise may belong to a natural person or to a legal entity (P. Filios & Chr. Filios, *PrL*, para. 220 C I, 395).
861. Namely persons who systematically practice a liberal or non-liberal profession by which they earn their livelihood, e.g., lawyers, doctors, architects or artisans.
862. On these see *supra* para. 411 n. 726.
863. And, as a rule, types of movable professional equipment and merchandise which is ready for sale, half-fashioned or in a raw material (see the preamble to L. 2844/2000 under B1).

capable of being defined (Article 2 paragraph 1 sub-paragraph b) and also an aggregate of things, especially merchandise, or a percentage of the relevant aggregate (Article 2 paragraph 3).

472. Pledges on movables without delivery are mainly governed by the provisions of Law 2844/2000. In addition, they are governed by the provisions concerning common pledges and already by Article 42 point d BC, insofar as the relevant provisions are reconcilable with the nature of the type of pledge in question (Article 8 paragraph 1). Finally, certain provisions relating to mortgages[864] also apply here by analogy (Article 8 paragraph 2).

b. Constitution of a Fictitious Pledge

473. For the constitution of a pledge on a movable thing without delivery of its detention, Article 1 paragraph 1 requires a written agreement between the owner (pledger) and the creditor and publication of the agreement in public registers in the manner specified in Article 3.[865] Consequently, the constitution of a fictitious pledge presupposes: (a) ownership of the pledger, (b) written agreement between the pledger and the creditor to the effect that a pledge is being constituted and (c) publication in the public registers in the manner described in Article 3. In regard to these points, the following should be stressed:

474. The constitution of a fictitious pledge presupposes that the pledger is the owner of the thing pledged. However, from Articles 6 paragraph 3 and 8 paragraph 1 emerges the possibility of a pledge being acquired even in the case where the pledger is not owner, so long as the conditions of Article 1215 CC concerning common pledges are fulfilled.[866] This applies in spite of the fact that, in the area of fictitious pledges, the quasi possession of the thing pledged is acquired by the pledgee through *constitutum possessorium*, while Article 1036 CC, which applies by analogy in the field of pledges (Article 1215 CC), presupposes, according to the most correct opinion, material delivery of the possession.[867] However, the relevant choice of Law 2844/2000 is, in our view, correct. This is because the reasons justifying the above opinion within the context of Article 1036 CC do not exist in the area of fictitious pledges. Indeed, here, the publication specified in Article 3 constitutes, instead of material delivery of the quasi possession, the objective basis which may justify the good faith of the pledgee.

---

864. Articles 1284, 1290, 1294–1299, 1314–1316 sub-para. a, 1324, 1327–1329, 1331, 1332, 1334, 1335 and 1339–1341 CC.

865. Agreement and publication are also necessary for any amendments to the above agreement (Art. 5 para. 1).

866. See *supra* para. 459. However, here, the good faith of the acquirer must exist at the time of the conclusion of the agreement to the effect that a pledge is being constituted (Art. 8 para. 1 sub-para. b).

867. See *supra* para. 316. Therefore, before L. 2844/2000, those who supported the above opinion refused to accept the possibility that fictitious pledges could be constituted by a non-owner, contrary to those who hold that the delivery of possession in the area of Art. 1036 CC may be accomplished not only materially (on the relevant debate see Ap. Georgiades, *The Securing of Credits*, 2nd edn (Athens: Sakkoulas, 2008), 512–514 [in Greek]).

475. As has already been mentioned, the constitution of a fictitious pledge presupposes an agreement, namely a contract, between the owner of the thing, debtor or third party,[868] and the creditor to the effect that the latter acquires a right of pledge and the quasi possession of the thing pledged. This agreement must be incorporated in a deed that may be public or private and which may or may not bear an officially certified date. The same agreement must specify the claim secured and the amount of money up to which the relevant claim will be secured (Article 1 paragraph 2 sub-paragraph a). It must also describe the thing pledged and state, on the one hand, the place in which it will be found or its type of use (if the relevant thing according to its very purpose does not remain constantly in the same place) and, on the other, the address of the residence or the registered office of the pledger (Article 1 paragraph 2 sub-paragraphs a, b). Furthermore, the pledging of an ideal share of the thing which (share) does not represent the majority of the shares is null and void without the (written and published, according to Article 3) consent of the majority of the co-owners concerning the place where the thing pledged will be located or its type of use (if the thing according to its very purpose does not remain constantly in the same place) (Article 1 paragraph 2 sub-paragraph c).

476. Finally, the constitution of a fictitious pledge presupposes publication in public registers in the manner described in Article 3.[869]

The date of publication determines the order of priority in cases where several pledges have been constituted on the same thing, while pledges published on the same day have the same ranking and the creditors are satisfied pro rata (Article 6 paragraph 1 sub-paragraphs a, b).[870] However, provision is made for the above priority to be changed following a written and published (according to Article 3) agreement between two or more pledgee (Article 6 paragraph 2). On the other hand, it is stipulated that a (written and published according to Article 3) agreement, between pledger and pledgee, to the effect that, for a certain amount of money, another pledge not yet constituted will have priority, should be valid (Article 6 paragraph 2).[871]

c. Special Rights and Obligations of the Pledger

477. With regard to the rights of the pledger, it is worth noting that, according to Article 2 paragraph 4, if several things are encumbered by a pledge, the pledger is entitled to request from the creditor and, if he or she refuses, from the court, that the pledge be limited only to those movables whose value provides sufficient security for the claim.[872] This right of the pledger arises when there is partial

868. This third party is not necessarily a businessman (P. Filios & Chr. Filios, *PrL*, para. 220 C II, 395).
869. To be precise, as a rule (compare Art. 3 para. 3), pledges should be published in public registers which should be kept in the registry of pledges of the region in which the residence or registered office of the pledger is situated and, if the latter does not have a residence or registered office in Greece, in the pledges registry in Athens. However, until registries of pledges are established, pledges should be published in the mortgage registries or land registries (Art. 19 para. 1 sub-para. b).
870. However, pledges constituted by law (on which see *infra* para. 482) will follow (Art. 6 para. 1 sub-para. d).
871. This possibility corresponds with the institution of the so-called negative mortgage which is known in other legal systems (see preamble to Law 2844/2000 under B3).
872. Compare Art. 1270 CC *supra* para. 433.

extinction of the claim secured or a disproportion, due to another reason, between the value of the claim secured and the value of the things pledged.

478. On the pledger, who reserves the detention and the use of the thing pledged, the law (Article 7) also imposes obligations.[873] Thus, every six months or when a serious ground arises, he or she is bound to tolerate the checking of the existence and state of the thing, by the creditor. Also, unless otherwise stipulated, he or she is obliged not to transfer the ownership of the thing,[874] nor to deliver its detention to a third person, nor to move it to another place or, if the thing according to its very purpose does not remain constantly in the same place, to change its type of use without the consent of the creditor.

d. Liquidation of a Fictitious Pledge

479. Everything stated above regarding the liquidation of common pledges[875] also applies to fictitious pledges. However, Article 8 paragraphs 4 and 5 elucidate issues relating to the procedure of the auction.

e. Abolishment of a Fictitious Pledge

480. The abolishment of a fictitious pledge presupposes an extinction of the right of pledge and deletion (cancellation) from the pledge register. The latter is carried out in the manner prescribed by Articles 1324 and 1327–1328 CC concerning mortgages,[876] which apply here by analogy.[877]

With regard to the extinction of the right of pledge, it should be noted that a fictitious pledge may be extinguished on the same grounds as those leading to the extinction of a common pledge[878] and also after ten years from the date of its registration, with the possibility of an extension (Article 4). Furthermore, if, on account of union, connection, amalgamation, merger, elaboration or transformation, the ownership of the thing pledged and the limited real rights which probably encumber it are extinguished, according to Articles 1057–1061 CC,[879] the fictitious pledge is also extinguished, except if the relevant material acts were carried out by the pledger and there was no stipulation to the contrary (Article 2 paragraph 2 subparagraphs a and b).

---

873. Any essential infringement of these obligations gives the creditor the right to render the debt due and payable through a declaration to the pledger, while any fraudulent infringement of the same obligations is punished according to the provisions of Art. 399 PC (Art. 7 paras 3, 4).
874. The disposal of the thing subsequent to the relevant publication does not have any effect on the existence of a pledge, except if the things pledged were merchandises destined to be transferred or if, at the time of the delivery of the possession of the thing, the acquirer, without being at fault, was ignorant of the fact that a pledge existed (Art. 6 para. 4).
875. See *supra* para. 464.
876. On this point see *supra* para. 442.
877. However, the consent of Art. 1324 CC may be given by a private deed (Art. 8 para. 2 sub-para. b).
878. On this point see *supra* paras 465–467.
879. On which see *supra* paras 331 et seq.

C. Pledges under Common Detention

481. According to Article 9 of Law 2844/2000, a pledge may also be constituted in the case where the thing is not delivered to the creditor but is placed under the common detention of the creditor and the pledger in such a way that neither of them can undertake the thing without the cooperation of the other. This type of pledge is governed by the provisions of Articles 1209–1243 CC concerning common pledges, insofar as they are reconcilable with the nature of the type of pledge in question. On the other hand, the provisions of Articles 35, 36 paragraph 2, 38, 40–47 L.D. 17.7/13.8.1923 also apply, provided that the conditions of their application occur.

D. Pledges Constituted by Law

482. A pledge constituted by law is that which is not constituted on the basis of an agreement but by the operation of the law alone.

Thus, the Civil Code recognizes the following types of legally constituted pledges:

(a) the pledge of the lessor of an immovable, which secures payment of arrears of rent and has as its object the movables brought into the leased thing by the lessee or his or her spouse and children, if they live with him or her, so long as such movables do not fall into the category of objects that may not be seized (Article 604 CC);
(b) the pledge of the lessor of agricultural land, which secures rent due to him or her and concerns the fruits of the land, so long as they do not fall into the category of objects that cannot be seized (Article 626 CC);
(c) the pledge of the contractor, which secures claims arising from a contract for work and extends to the movables (belonging to the employer) which have been constructed or repaired by the contractor and which are detained by the latter (Article 695 CC);
(d) the pledge of the hotel owner, which secures claims arising from a client's residence in the hotel and related services and concerns things brought into the hotel by the client (Article 838 CC).[880]

483. In the area of legally constituted pledges the provisions governing common pledges apply by analogy (Article 1246 CC), insofar as they are reconcilable with the nature and the function of the legally constituted pledge in question. Thus, for example, Article 1215 CC (concerning the possibility of a pledge being constituted on a thing not belonging to the pledger) does not apply by analogy to those legally constituted pledges whose constitution does not presuppose acquisition of the quasi possession of the thing by the creditor. An example of such a pledge is

880. The relevant provision applies by analogy to persons who keep stables, warehouses, garages or airports, concerning animals, coaches, automobiles, aircraft and things related thereto which have been brought in by clients (Art. 839 CC).

that of the lessor (Articles 604, 605 CC), though not that of the contractor (Article 695 CC).[881]

E. Commercial Pledges

484. L.D. 17.7/13.8.1923, concerning special provisions governing companies limited by shares (A.E.), in its Articles 35–47, provides for a special commercial pledge which secures claims belonging especially to banks. This pledge, which is not fictitious but common in character, has not been abolished by Law 2844/2000.[882] This type of pledge is governed by the provisions of the above legislative decree which introduces deviations from the Civil Code mainly on the issues relating to the constitution and liquidation of pledges. However, issues not regulated specifically by the relevant legislative decree are governed by Articles 1211 et seq. CC.

§2. Pact of Retention of Title in Sales of Movables

485. As has already been mentioned,[883] the increase of sales on credit, especially in the area of movables, and the concomitant need to achieve security for the vendor – who delivers the thing to the purchaser without being sure if the latter will pay the purchase price – led to the evolution of the pact of retention of title specified in Article 532 CC[884] into a special type of real security on behalf of the vendor mainly of a movable thing. On the other hand, contracts of sale and transfer of ownership of movables on the suspensive condition of full payment of the purchase price are also dealt with by Law 2844/2000.

I. The Provisions of the Civil Code

486. Article 532 CC, pertaining to contracts of sale (of a movable or an immovable thing) which include the clause that the vendor retains the ownership of the

881. On all these points see Ap. Georgiades, *PrL*, para. 89 II 3 No. 38, 1115–1116.
882. See Arts 8 paras 4, 9 para. 2 and also the preamble to L. 2844/2000 under B4.
883. See also *supra* para. 412 (under (a)).
884. On which see, in particular, A. Gazis, in *ErmAK*, Art. 532 [in Greek]; I. Deliyiannis & P. Kornilakis, *Law of Obligations. Special Part*, Vol. I (Thessaloniki: Sakkoulas, 1992), paras 71 et seq., 273 et seq. [in Greek]; P. Kornilakis, *Law of Obligations. Special Part I*, para. 56, 341 et seq.; Ap. Georgiades, *The Securing of Credits*, 521 et seq.; P. Filios, *Law of Ogligations. Special Part*, Vol. I/1, 7th edn (Athens/Komotini: A. Sakkoulas, 2007), paras 14–14 c, 84 et seq. [in Greek]; I. Schinas, in *Civil Code*, Vol. III: *Law of Obligations. Special Part*, Ap. Georgiades & M. Stathopoulos (Athens: Sakkoulas, 1980), Art. 532 [in Greek]; A. Karabatzos, in *SEAK*, Vol. I, ed. Ap. Georgiades, Arts 1–946 (Athens: Sakkoulas, 2010), Art. 532 [in Greek]; N. Triantos, in *Civil Code*, Vol. 4: *Law of Obligations. Special Part*, ed. I. Karakostas (Athens: Nomiki Bibliothiki, 2008), Art. 532 [in Greek]. On the same issue from the scope of German law see B. Grunewald, in *Erman Bürgerliches Gesetzbuch*, Vol. I, 12th edn (Köln: Dr. Otto Schmidt, 2008), para. 449; R.-M. Beckmann. Mader, in *Staudinger Komm zum BGB, Buch 2: Recht der Schuldverhaltnisse* (Berlin, Sellier-de Gruyter, 2004), para. 449; W. Weidenkaff, in *Palandt Bürgerliches Gesetzbuch*, 70th edn (München: Beck, 2011), para. 449; H.P. Westermann, in *MünchKomm*, Vol. 3: *Schuldrecht. Besonderer Teil I*, 5th edn (München: Beck, 2008), para. 449.

thing sold until full payment of the credited purchase price,[885] contains two interpretative rules.[886] The first, which determines the 'real effect' of the above clause, states that, in case of doubt, this clause does not refer to the sale contract but to the real dispositive contract concerning the transfer of ownership, which is regarded as being agreed on the suspensive condition[887] of payment of the purchase price.[888] On the other hand, the second interpretative rule, which determines the 'personal (obligational) effect' of the relevant clause, stipulates that, in case of doubt, the vendor, in the event of default by the purchaser, is entitled either to demand the purchase price or to rescind the contract of sale,[889] exercising his or her rights deriving from ownership.

487. With regard to the real effect of a pact of retention of title, the following ought to be borne in mind:

While the suspensive condition of full payment of the purchase price is pending, the vendor remains the owner and possessor of the thing. Consequently, he or she is protected as owner and possessor against all parties, except for the purchaser who is the rightful detentor of the thing. He or she may also raise the 'third party opposition' specified in Article 936 CCProc, if the thing has been seized by a creditor of the purchaser. In the case where the purchaser has been declared bankrupt the vendor's rights are not affected (Article 35 paragraph 2 BC).[890] Finally, as the ownership of the vendor is revocable, any disposal of the thing made by him or her while the relevant condition was pending becomes *ipso jure* null and void upon the fulfilment of the condition (Article 206 CC).[891]

On the other hand, during the aforementioned period of time, the purchaser is the detentor of the thing. Hence, he or she is protected by Article 997 CC[892] against third parties, he or she may repulse the revendicatory action of the vendor by raising the plea which derives from Article 1095 CC[893] and he or she is also entitled to

885. This clause must be inserted not only in the personal promissory contract of sale (Art. 513) but also in the real dispositive contract concerning the transfer of ownership (Arts 1033, 1034 CC) (P. Kornilakis, *Law of Obligations. Special Part I*, para. 56 II 1, 343).
886. However, insofar as Art. 532 CC is a non-mandatory rule, the parties are basically free to make a different agreement about the consequences (see, among others, M. Stathopoulos, *Contract Law in Hellas*, para. 351. See also P. Kornilakis, *Law of Obligations. Special Part I*, para. 56 II 2, 344–345).
887. The relevant condition may also be stipulated as resolutory and only in case of doubt it is considered to be suspensive.
888. The fulfilment of the relevant condition entails an extinction of the pact of retention of title. However, the same pact may also be extinguished, for example: (a) by a unilateral declaration of renunciation by the vendor-owner; (b) in the case where the thing is alienated with the consent of the vendor-owner (Art. 239 para. 1) or is acquired by a third person of good faith (Art. 1036 CC); or (c) in the event that a ground leading to extinction of ownership, according to Arts 1057–1061 CC, occurs (see P. Kornilakis, *Law of Obligations. Special Part I*, para. 56 VI, 355–356).
889. This contract, which is not dependent on a condition, may not be rescinded automatically (P. Kornilakis, *Law of Obligations. Special Part I*, para. 56 II 3, 346).
890. For detailed discussion see L. Kotsiris, *Law of Bankruptcy*, 8th edn (Athens-Thessaloniki: Sakkoulas, 2011), paras 241 et seq., 390 et seq. [in Greek].
891. See, however, *supra* para. 321 and n. 559.
892. On which see *supra* para. 155.
893. On which see *supra* para. 373.

repulse actions protecting the possession of the vendor by claiming that he or she had not illegally violated the possession of the plaintiff. In addition, the purchaser, as the beneficiary under a suspensive condition, has a right to expect acquisition of the ownership. This is a property right which is transferable, inheritable, susceptible of pledge and seizure (Articles 1022 et seq. CCProc) and also protected (Articles 206, 914, 997 or 1095 CC).[894]

Furthermore, as soon as the suspensive condition of full payment of the purchase price has been fulfilled, the purchaser's right to expect acquisition of the ownership and his or her detention are converted *ipso jure* into ownership and possession, respectively. On the other hand, frustration of the relevant condition[895] makes the vendor the definitive owner and possessor, validates the disposals of the thing possibly made by him or her and entails extinction of the purchaser's right to expect acquisition of the ownership and the possibility of the vendor vindicating the thing from the latter.

488. With regard to the personal (obligational) effect of a pact of retention of title, it should be noted that, in the event of default by the purchaser, the vendor is entitled either to demand the purchase price and also compensation (according to Articles 343 paragraph 1 and 345 CC) or to rescind the contract of sale or to demand compensation on the ground of impossibility of performance (according to Article 383 CC).[896]

II. The Provisions of Law 2844/2000

489. Law 2844/2000 completes the provisions made by the Civil Code regarding pacts of retention of title as follows. It stipulates that 'contracts of sale and transfer of ownership of movables on the suspensive condition that the ownership is preserved until full payment of the purchase price' may be subject to the publication specified in Article 3[897] and adds that, in this case, those provisions concerning fictitious pledges[898] which are reconcilable with the nature and purpose of the above contracts apply to them by analogy (Article 10 paragraphs 1 and 2).[899] On the other hand, the combination of Article 13 paragraph 3 sub-paragraph a and Article 12 paragraph 1 gives rise to the possibility that the so-called extended or prolonged retention might be stipulated.[900] Consequently, in cases where the purchaser is a middleman whose task is to alienate the merchandise bought by him or her with

894. On these points see Ap. Georgiades, *Die Eigentumsanwartschaft beim Vorbehaltskauf* (Tübingen: J.C.B. Mohr [Paul Siebeck], 1963), 4 et seq.
895. This occurs in the case of default by the purchaser on the condition that the vendor has rescinded the contract of sale (P. Kornilakis, *Law of Obligations. Special Part I*, para. 56 III 3, 351).
896. See P. Kornilakis, *Law of Obligations. Special Part I*, para. 56 IV, 351 et seq.
897. See *supra* para. 476.
898. See *supra* paras 471 et seq.
899. For the relevant application, the vendor and the purchaser are considered, respectively, as pledger and pledgee (Art. 10 para. 2 sub-para. b).
900. On the various forms of the pact of retention of title, including the so-called extended or 'prolonged' retention, see, among others, P. Kornilakis, *Law of Obligations. Special Part I*, para. 56 VII, 356–358.

retention of title, the pact of retention of title may be combined with a stipulation that the purchaser is entitled to alienate the thing, while the security of the vendor's claim, relating to the payment of the credited purchase price, will be achieved through a prior assignment of the future claims of the purchaser on the proceeds of the relevant alienation or through the constitution of a pledge on the same claims.

Chapter 4. Real Security on Incorporeal Objects

§1. Pledges on Rights

I. Pledges on Rights in General

490. The possibility of pledges being constituted on (real or personal, absolute or relative) rights belonging to another[901] is provided by Article 1247 CC, while Article 1256 CC stipulates that, in the context of pledges on rights, so long as Articles 1247–1255 do not stipulate otherwise, the provisions governing pledges on things apply by analogy.[902]

The constitution of a pledge on a right is effected in the same manner as a transfer of the right (Article 1247 sub-paragraph b CC) – that is, by assignment, unless the law ordains otherwise (Articles 470, 455 CC) – whereas the contract constituting the pledge must be incorporated in a notarial deed or in a private deed bearing an officially certified date (Article 1247 sub-paragraph c CC). However, a right which is encumbered by a pledge must be transferable (Article 1247 sub-paragraph a CC) and also a right of financial value.[903] This last necessity, although not mentioned in the law, is based on the fact that pledges, and therefore pledges on rights, are real rights of value.[904] Indeed, a pledge on a right confers on its holder the ability to gain satisfaction from the value of the encumbered right upon its alienation (Articles 1237, 1256 CC) or collection (Articles 1253, 1254 CC, in the area of claims). In the light of the above remarks, pledges may be constituted on, for example, the purchaser's right of expectation in the case of purchase of a movable with retention of title (Article 532 CC) and the right of intellectual property.

II. Pledges on Business Rights

491. According to Article 15 of L. 2844/2000, in the area of pledges on business rights, that is, on rights deriving from business activities, the provisions concerning pledges on business claims apply by analogy,[905] unless otherwise provided for by law.

901. On the nature of a real right which is constituted on a right belonging to another see *supra* para. 260.
902. Such provisions are contained, for example, in Arts 1216 para. 1, 1217, 1219, 1231, 1239, 1243 CC, in Art. 1237 CC (which applies in combination with Arts 1022 et seq. CCProc) and also in Arts 1221 para. 1, 1222–1224, 1227, 1232, 1234, 1235 CC. On the other hand, Art. 1215 CC (concerning the constitution of a pledge on a thing not belonging to the pledger) for example, and Art. 1236 CC (referring to protection of the right of pledge) presuppose the existence of a corporeal object and, therefore, are not reconcilable with the nature of pledges on rights.
903. On this point see Ap. Georgiades, *PrL*, para. 90 I 2 Nos 5 et seq., 1150–1151.
904. See *supra* para. 50 (under b).
905. See *infra* paras 495–497.

§2. Pledges on Claims

I. Pledges on Claims in General

492. This section is devoted to the pledges regulated by the Civil Code on any kind of pecuniary claim or claim which can be valued in monetary terms, regardless of whether they arise from a contract or directly from the law or whether they are business claims, liquidated, mature, dependent on a condition or term, already in existence or might exist in the future.

In the light of the fact that claims are personal rights, pledges on claims are similar to pledges on rights. Therefore, Articles 1247 and 1256 CC, concerning pledges on rights, also apply in the area of pledges on claims. Nevertheless, the Civil Code also devotes special provisions to pledges on claims: to be precise, Articles 1248–1250 CC. Thus, the constitution of a pledge on a claim presupposes a concurrence of the conditions mentioned in Article 1247 sub-paragraphs b and c[906] and also notification of the debtor by the pledger regarding the pledge (Article 1248 CC). This notification is informal and corresponds with the delivery of the thing in the field of pledges on movables.[907] On the other hand, according to the prevailing opinion,[908] the constitution of a pledge is not complete without the above notification, in the sense that, before the notification, the creditor does not acquire a right of pledge either with regard to the debtor of the claim pledged and the third parties or with regard to the pledger.[909]

493. Even after the constitution of a pledge, the pledger remains the holder of the claim pledged. Concomitantly, he or she is entitled to alienate it, so long as the relevant alienation does not prejudice the rights of the pledgee. Thus, for example, he or she may assign or re-pledge the claim pledged,[910] though not abolish it through release from debt, setting off the claim or compromising it.[911]

494. With regard to the collection of the claim pledged, the following should be borne in mind:

As long as the debt secured has not matured, and provided that the claim pledged is not monetary, the pledgee is entitled to collect it alone, whenever he or she acquires a pledge on the 'collected' thing (Article 1252 CC). However, in the case where the claim pledged is monetary, the pledgee and the pledger have the right and

906. On which see *supra* para. 490.
907. See *supra* para. 459.
908. E. Vouzikas, *Acquisition of a Pledge from a Person Who Is Not the Owner* (Athens: Zacharopoulos, 1950), 23, n. 6, 23 [in Greek]; Ap. Georgiades, *PrL*, para. 90 II 2 No. 17, 1154; Ph. Doris, *Real Security*, para. 15 III, 121; I. Spyridakis, *The Law of Real Security*, Vol. III (Athens: Sakkoulas, 1974/1976), para. 190 No. 2, 136; Ph. Dimakou, in *Civil Code*, Vol. VI: *PrL*, ed. Ap. Georgiades & M. Stathopoulos, Arts 1247–1248 Nos 63, 64. Compare A. Cazis, *Conflict of Rights* (Athens, 1959), n. 3, 186 [in Greek].
909. For example, in the case where the pledger gave power of attorney to the pledgee to notify the debtor of the constitution of the pledge and the pledgee neglected to do so.
910. See also Art. 1250 CC.
911. See Ap. Georgiades, *PrL*, para. 90 II 3 No. 21, 1156.

the obligation to proceed jointly with the collection. Instead of or after this collection, each of them is entitled to demand the safe deposit of the money in an interest-bearing account, reserving the right of pledge. The kind of deposit is determined by the pledger (Article 1253 CC).

Upon maturity of the debt secured, provided the claim pledged is not monetary, the pledgee is entitled to collect it alone and the consequences of a pledge on a thing belonging to the pledger take effect. However, in the case where the claim pledged is monetary, the creditor has the right either to collect it to the extent necessary for the satisfaction of his or her claim or to demand its assignment to him or her in lieu of payment (Article 1254 CC).

II. Pledges on Business Claims

495. Pledges on claims arising from business activities (business claims) are specifically regulated by Articles 11–14 of Law 2844/2000.[912] However, according to Article 14, in the context of this type of pledge, certain articles of Law 2844/2000 referring to fictitious pledges[913] and certain articles of the Civil Code concerning mortgages apply by analogy,[914] while the provisions of the Civil Code concerning pledges on claims also apply.

496. According to the provisions of Law 2844/2000, the types of business claims upon which pledges may be constituted are the claims of providers against issuers of credit cards, claims that may be realized in the future or are dependent on a condition,[915] aggregates of claims, though not claims against consumers (Article 11 paragraph 1 and Article 12). In accordance with the law (Article 12), future claims may be pledged even when the grounds for their creation do not exist at the date the pledge is made, provided that they are defined or may be defined. However, in this case, the pledge takes effect from the date on which the claim pledged is created. Therefore, the pledger is bound to inform the pledgee of the relevant creation.

497. The aforementioned claims are pledged in the way provided for by the Civil Code.[916] However, the contract constituting the pledge, insofar as it has been constituted in written form, as well as the notification of the debtor regarding the pledge[917] may be subject to publication through registration in the public register

912. However, the same claims may also be pledged according to the provisions of the Civil Code (see the preamble to L. 2844/2000 under D2).
913. And, to be precise, Art. 2 para. 4 (see *supra* para. 477), Art. 4 (see *supra* para. 480), Art. 5 (see *supra* para. 473 n. 865), Art. 8 para. 2 sub-paras b, c (see *supra* para. 480 n. 877).
914. Articles 1314–1316 sub-para. a, 1324, 1327–1329, 1331, 1332, 1334, 1335 and 1339–1341 CC.
915. See the preamble to L. 2844/2000 under D2.
916. See *supra* para. 492 in combination with para. 490.
917. In the case where a future claim is pledged, the pledger may notify the future debtor of the constitution of the pledge if he or she is well-known to him or her(Art. 12 para. 1 sub-para. d).

specified in Article 3[918] (Article 11 paragraphs 1, 2 and Article 14 paragraph 1 sub-paragraph b). Furthermore, the pledgee is entitled, although not obliged, to inform the debtor of the relevant publication (Article 11 paragraph 3).

Until publication, the relevant pledge is governed by the provisions of Articles 1248–1250 CC (Article 13 paragraph 1), while, from the time of the first publication the order of priority among several pledgees is determined on the basis of the date of publication (Article 13 paragraph 2 sub-paragraph a). However, this order may be changed in the way provided for by Article 6 paragraph 2[919] (Article 13 paragraph 2 sub-paragraph b). In addition, in the case of retention of title in the sale of a movable (merchandise), a privilege is recognized in favour of the vendor: (a) in regard to his or her right of pledge on the future claims of the purchaser on the proceeds of a further alienation of the thing sold[920] and (b) in regard to his or her claims arising from Article 1063 CC,[921] in the case where he or she has lost the ownership of the thing sold on account of union, amalgamation, elaboration or transformation (Article 13 paragraph 3).

§3. Pledges on Negotiable Instruments

498. In the light of the general classification of negotiable instruments into title deeds in bearer form, title deeds made payable to order and registered title deeds, pledges on negotiable instruments are classified into pledges on title deeds in bearer form, pledges on title deeds made payable to order and pledges on registered title deeds.

The Civil Code refers explicitly to pledges on title deeds in bearer form (Articles 1244, 1245 CC), regarding them as pledges on movables (Article 1244 sub-paragraph a),[922] and also to pledges on title deeds made payable to order (Articles 1251, 1255 CC), treating them as pledges on rights and, more specifically, pledges on claims.

The Civil Code makes no reference at all to pledges on registered title deeds. However, this omission does not mean that registered title deeds may not constitute the object of a pledge. Indeed, so long as there is no reason for the relevant titles to be treated differently from other negotiable instruments, with regard to the possibility of being pledged, it seems correct to accept that they may be pledged and also that the pledge on them should be treated as a pledge on a right. This is because

918. See *supra* para. 476. In the relevant register is also published the full payment of the claim pledged (Art. 14 para. 1 sub-para. b).
919. See *supra* para. 476.
920. The relevant provision of the law is taking into account here the case of the so-called extended or prolonged retention, on which see *supra* para. 489.
921. See *supra* para. 334.
922. However, it must be borne in mind that, pursuant to Art. 49 of L. 2396/1996, as superseded by Art. 107 of L. 2533/1997, the constitution of a pledge or other encumbrance on dematerialized shares requires submission of the relevant document by bailiff to the Central Securities Depository S.A. (CSD), which is based at the Athens Stock Exchange. Pledges or other forms of encumbrance on dematerialized shares are binding on all parties from the date of their registration in the archives of the CSD. The CSD will promptly send the issuing company all agreements relating to the constitution of pledges or other encumbrances on its shares.

registered title deeds are characterized by absence of the element of complete incorporation, in the sense that the right which derives from the title deed surpasses the right which exists on the title deed.[923] Consequently, in the area of pledges on registered title deeds the provisions governing pledges on rights apply, as well as the provisions governing pledges on a thing, properly adopted (Article 1256 CC).

499. With regard to pledges on title deeds made payable to order, it should be mentioned that they are governed by Articles 1251 and 1255 CC, as well as the provisions concerning pledges on rights/claims and certain articles (e.g., 19 and 77 of Law 5325/1932) concerning negotiable instruments.

From Article 1251 CC it may be concluded that the constitution of this type of pledge is effected either in the manner provided for by Articles 1247–1248 CC regarding the constitution of pledges on claims[924] or through endorsement to the order of the creditor, without another written agreement being required.[925] On the other hand, Article 1255 CC permits the conclusion that the pledgee is entitled to proceed alone with the collection of the claim incorporated in the title even if the debt secured has not matured. However, in the latter case, the pledgee is bound to proceed with the safe deposit of the amount collected in an interest-bearing account, the right of pledge being reserved.

923. See *supra* para. 269.

924. Consequently, by a contract, which must be incorporated in a notarial deed or in a private deed bearing an officially certified date, and by delivery of the quasi possession of the title to the pledgee, without the notification of Art. 1248 CC being required according to the most correct opinion (on this point see Y. Karibali-Tsiptsiou, 'Pledging of Bills of Exchange', 5 EpiskEmbD, No. C (July–August), 1999, 656–658 [in Greek]).

925. In this case are required a (informal) contract to the effect that a pledge is constituted, delivery of the quasi possession of the title to the pledgee and endorsement of the title (on this point see Y. Karibali-Tsiptsiou, 'Pledging of Bills of Exchange', 658–660).

Chapter 5. Floating Charges

§1. Concept and Legislative Status

500. A floating charge is a type of real security on an aggregate of things or rights[926] which offers the person who grants it two important advantages: primarily, the advantage of retaining the detention of the things which form the aggregate; and, secondarily, the advantage of retaining the power to dispose (free from encumbrances) of the objects which form the aggregate, while being bound, as a rule, to replace the objects disposed of, within a reasonable period of time, with other objects of similar value.[927]

The institution of the floating charge has been introduced into the Greek legal system by Law 2844/2000 and is governed by Articles 16–18 of the latter.

§2. The Provisions of the Law

501. Article 16, in defining the concept of a floating charge, states that the parties may stipulate the granting of security on an aggregate of things or rights of changing composition, in accordance with the provisions of Law 2844/2000. From the same article emerge two interpretative rules. According to the first, in the case where merchandise destined for disposal or consumption is included in the aggregate, the parties are deemed to have agreed the constitution of a floating – and not a stable – charge, unless otherwise stipulated. According to the second, in the context of floating charges, the person who grants the security and who is entitled to dispose of the objects belonging to the relevant aggregate free from encumbrances is bound, unless otherwise stipulated, to replace, without delay for which he or she is accountable, the disposed (consumed, lost or disappeared for other reasons) objects with others of similar value.

502. The power of disposal of the person who grants the floating charge is offset by the following obligations which are imposed on him or her by Article 17:[928]

(a) the obligation to send to the creditor, every three months, a brief list of the objects which make up the aggregate and of the changes that have occurred during these three months;
(b) the obligation to tolerate the check provided for by Article 7 paragraph 1[929] so long as this check is reconcilable with the nature of the objects belonging to the aggregate;

926. In the sense of Arts 2 para. 3 and 12 para. 2 of L. 2844/2000 (see the preamble to L. 2844/2000 under E).
927. See Art. 16 of L. 2844/2000 and the preamble to L. 2844/2000 under E.
928. Any infringement of these obligations offers the creditor the rights mentioned in *supra* para. 478 n. 873 (Art. 17 para. 3, Art. 7 paras 3, 4).
929. On which see *supra* para. 478.

(c) in the case where it has been stipulated that the security will extend to the claim relating to the proceeds of the alienation of the objects of the security, the obligation to bring immediately to the knowledge of the creditor the debtors of the above proceeds.

503. Finally, Article 18 should be borne in mind, which refers to the grounds for 'crystallization' of the floating charge, that is, to the grounds on which the power of disposal of the person who granted the security ceases. Thus, the entry into a state of default by the above person offers the receiver of the security (creditor) the power to 'crystallize' the security through seizure or any provisional remedy or other measure which entails loss of the power to dispose. However, the parties may provide other ways of 'crystallization', and may also stipulate that, after the 'crystallization', the person who granted the security will be released from all or some of the obligations which are imposed on him or her by Article 17.[930]

930. See *supra* para. 502.

Part VIII. Fiduciary Mechanisms

Chapter 1. General Remarks and Classification

504. Under the term 'fiduciary mechanisms' could be included the institutions of trust, *fideicommissum* and fiduciary juridical acts (*Treuhandgeschäfte*). However, as has already been mentioned, trusts do not exist in Greece.[931] On the other hand, the institution of *fideicommissum*, which is regulated by the Greek Civil Code, comes under the law of inheritance and does not fall within the sphere of property law. Therefore, it was discussed in general terms in the 'General Introduction' to the present book.[932] Finally, with regard to the fiduciary juridical acts, it has already been noted[933] that Greek doctrine and judicial rulings recognize them, though not without reservations. Also, whereas the Greek Civil Code does not include any provision relating to them, Articles 190–194 CPrMarL regulate the fiduciary transfer of ownership of ships and Article 10 paragraph 1b as well as Articles 11–15 of Law 2844/2000 recognize, respectively, the fiduciary transfer of ownership of movables and the fiduciary assignment of business claims or other rights with a view to securing a claim. Furthermore, reference has also been made to the concept, general attributes and possible forms of fiduciary juridical acts.[934]

In this chapter, first of all, we will determine the practical usefulness of each form of fiduciary juridical act and then we will state which forms of fiduciary juridical acts will be examined in the following chapters.

505. The practical usefulness of fiduciary juridical acts varies in accordance with their exact nature. More specifically:

(a) One type of fiduciary juridical act which is useful in practice is the fiduciary transfer of ownership of a movable with a view to securing a claim on the part of the acquirer against the alienator (securing transfer of ownership of a movable [*Sicherungsübereignung*]). This is considered to be a more advantageous form of real security as compared with that of a common pledge.[935] This is due to the fact that the constitution of common pledges presupposes, among other

931. See *supra* paras 36, 39–40.
932. See *supra* paras 41–43, 279 (under (a)).
933. See *supra* para. 44.
934. See *supra* para. 45.
935. See Ap. Georgiades, *The Securing of Credits*, 546, 560; Ap. Georgiades, in *Civil Code*, Vol. V: *PrL*, ed. Ap. Georgiades & M. Stathopoulos, Art. 1034 Nos 80–81; M. Karasis, *GenPrinc*, 54.

conditions, delivery of the quasi possession of the thing by the pledger to the creditor, which delivery may not be carried out through *constitutum possessorium*.[936] The said delivery, though, is desired neither by the pledger, who needs the thing in order to continue his or her financial activities, nor by the creditor (especially credit institutions with many debtors), who faces problems of storage.[937] This particular disadvantage is overcome by securing transfer of ownership of a movable from the debtor to the creditor by stipulating that the alienator will remain in detention of the thing on the strength of a certain legal relation (e.g., lease or loan for use) thus retaining the ability to use the thing.

However, after the entry into force of Law 2844/2000, which recognizes the institution of pledges on movables without delivery (fictitious pledges), in cases where a fictitious pledge may be constituted,[938] the securing transfer of ownership of movables loses its practical usefulness with regard to debtors. Indeed, the constitution of a fictitious pledge is preferable for a debtor, compared with a securing transfer, not only because, he or she preserves the ownership of the thing but also because he or she has the ability to encumber the thing pledged with a second or third fictitious pledge. On the other hand, securing transfers continue to be profitable for creditors and useful for both creditors and debtors in cases where a fictitious pledge may not be constituted. It should be borne in mind, though, that the possibility of a creditor choosing the securing transfer of a movable instead of the constitution of a fictitious pledge is contrary to the interests of the debtors.

In any event, Law 2844/2000, in addition to the institution of the fictitious pledge also recognizes the securing transfer of ownership of movables (Article 10 paragraph 1b),[939] mainly with the justification[940] that the possibility of a fictitious pledge being constituted does not preclude recourse to *fiducia*. The various needs of transactions are usually combined with various means of satisfying them insofar as an important ground justifying the restriction of the freedom of contracts does not exist.

(b) The fiduciary transfer of ownership of an immovable with a view to securing a claim on the part of the acquirer against the alienator (securing transfer of ownership of an immovable) is extremely rare. This is due not only to reservations regarding whether the securing of a claim may constitute a valid just cause for the transfer of ownership of an immovable,[941] but mainly to the fact that, in the area of immovables, the needs of real security are completely satisfied by the institution of mortgages.[942]

(c) The fiduciary transfer of a thing so that the latter might be managed by the acquirer (*Verwaltungstreuhand*) is relatively rare. This is due to the existence of

936. See *supra* para. 459.
937. See also *supra* para. 412 (under b).
938. On the conditions upon which the constitution of a fictitious pledge is dependent see *supra* para. 471.
939. To be precise, from Art. 10 para. 1b it emerges that the securing transfer of ownership of a movable may be subject to the publication specified in Art. 3 (on which see *supra* No. 476).
940. See the preamble to L. 2844/2000 under Γ.
941. See *infra* para. 508.
942. See M. Karasis, *GenPric*, 54.

institutions (such as, for example, the power of attorney,[943] consent[944] and delegation[945]) which satisfy the needs which are served by the above transfer.[946]

(d) Another type of fiduciary juridical act which is of practical usefulness is the fiduciary assignment of claims with a view to securing a claim on the part of the assignee against the assignor (securing assignment of claims [*Sicherungsabtretung*]). It constitutes, in comparison with pledges on claims, a simple and more effective form of security for creditors.[947] In fact, while for the constitution of pledges on claims several formalities are required, particularly notification of the debtor by the pledger about the pledge,[948] the securing assignment of claims is carried out by a non-formal contract, which need not include the notification of the assignment to the debtor. On the other hand, whereas the Civil Code prescribes a complex system with regard to the collection of the claim pledged,[949] in the area of the securing assignments, the assignee becomes creditor of the assigned claim himself or herself and is entitled to collect the claim himself or herself, thus becoming owner of the collected money or 'collected' thing, depending on whether the assigned claim is of a monetary form or not.

(e) Finally, the fiduciary assignment of a claim so that this claim can be managed and, more specifically, collected by the assignee in his or her own name but in the interest of the assignor (*Inkassozession*)[950] is used in cases where the holder of the claim does not want either to appear as litigant in a trial aimed at securing the collection of the relevant claim or his or her debtor to find out that he or she is the person who is pursuing a compulsory execution on his or her (the debtor's) assets. In the context of fiduciary assignment, the assignee acquires the assigned claim and becomes its sole holder with regard to the debtor and third parties. However, in relation to the assignor, the assignee is a mere mandatory who is bound, on the strength of a particular agreement between him or her and the assignor, to collect the claim in his or her own name and in the interest of the assignor and to restore the proceeds of the collection to the latter.

Results similar to those connected with the fiduciary assignment of claims for the purpose of their collection by the assignee are also achieved through the related institution of indirect representation.[951] On the other hand, if secrecy is not desired,

943. See *supra* para. 40 (under c).
944. See *supra* para. 40 (under d).
945. 'In a delegation an instrument is handed to the authorized payee whereby the latter is authorized to collect in his own name from an authorized payer a payment in money or other fungible things and the authorized payer is authorized to effect payment to the payee on the account of the delegating party' (Art. 876 CC). On delegation see, in particular, M. Stathopoulos, *Contract Law in Hellas*, No. 387.
946. See M. Karasis, *GenPric*, 54.
947. See relevantly P. Kornilakis, *The Fiduciary Assignment of Claims*, 33, 43–45; Ap. Georgiades, *The Securing of Credits*, 589–590; M. Karasis, *GenPrinc*, 54–55.
948. See *supra* para. 492.
949. See *supra* para. 494.
950. For a detailed discussion see P. Kornilakis, *The Fiduciary Assignment of Claims*, 134 et seq. See also M. Karasis, *GenPrinc*, 55.
951. On the relationship between these two institutions see P. Kornilakis, *The Fiduciary Assignment of Claims*, 139–141.

the holder of a claim can pursue its collection through a direct representative supplied with a power of attorney. In this case, though, the collection is carried out by the representative (attorney) in the name and interest of the represented holder of the claim.

506. Of the aforementioned forms of fiduciary juridical acts, the practical usefulness of which has already been outlined, the following chapters will examine the securing transfer of ownership of movables (Chapter 2) and the securing assignment of claims (Chapter 3). This choice is due to their practical usefulness together with the fact that they have a bearing on property law, insofar as they both constitute types of real security.[952]

952. See *supra* para. 412 (under b).

Chapter 2. Securing Transfer of Ownership of Movables

§1. STRUCTURE

507. As has already been mentioned,[953] in the case of a securing transfer of ownership of a movable, the debtor, with a view to securing a claim on the part of his or her creditor, instead of constituting a pledge in favour of the latter, transfers to him or her the ownership of a movable by stipulating that he or she (the transferor) remains in detention of the thing on the strength of a certain legal relations (e.g., lease or loan for use). This means that, in the case in question, the real dispositive contract of Article 1034 CC[954] is performed through the realization of its 'delivery of possession' element by means of *constitutum possessorium.*[955]

Within the framework of the securing transfer of ownership, in addition to the aforementioned real dispositive contract, a personal (obligational) promissory contract, the so-called securing agreement (*Sicherungsabrede*[956]), is also carried out. This second contract contains the clause for the transfer of ownership and specifies the rights and obligations of the contracting parties.[957] More specifically, on the basis of the securing agreement, the debtor is obliged to transfer the ownership of the movable to the creditor, to treat with care the thing which remains in his or her detention and probably to insure the thing at his or her own cost.[958] On the other hand, again on the basis of the above agreement, the creditor undertakes to use the legal powers arising from his or her ownership within the scope of the intended purpose. Thus, he or she must avoid any disposal of the thing which does not serve the said purpose and to transfer it back to the debtor after the debt is settled by the latter. In the case where the relevant retransfer is impossible because the creditor, in his or her capacity as owner, has in the meantime validly[959] transferred it to a third party, delivering the possession of the thing to the latter through delegation,[960] the creditor is bound to compensate the prejudice resulting therefrom to the debtor (Article 335 CC).

953. See *supra* paras 45 and 505 (under a).
954. On which see *supra* paras 310 et seq.
955. On which see *supra* para. 119. Theoretically, the delivery of the possession may also be effected through one of the other ways prescribed in Arts 976–977 CC (see Ap. Georgiades, *The Securing of Credits*, 550; Ap. Georgiades, in *Civil Code*, Vol. V: *PrL*, ed. Ap. Georgiades & M. Stathopoulos, Art. 1034 No. 86; P. Filios & Chr. Filios, *PrL*, para. 256 B, 455).
956. M. Henssler, in *Soergel Komm zum BGB*, Vol. 14: *Sachenrecht*, 13th edn (Stuttgart: Kohlhammer, 2002), para. Anh 930 Nos 52 et seq.
957. If a securing agreement has not been explicitly concluded, it seems correct to accept that the issues which arise in each case will be solved in the light of the purpose of the securing transfer of ownership and its special nature as a means of real security; that is, by application of the provisions relating either to ownership or to pledges, depending on the particular case (on this point see Ap. Georgiades, *The Securing of Credits*, 553–554). On the other hand, if the securing agreement does not regulate certain issues, as is rightly accepted, the gaps can be filled in by the so-called complementary interpretation of contracts (see P. Kornilakis, *The Fiduciary Assignment of Claims*, 55; Ap. Georgiades, *The Securing of Credits*, 554).
958. Ap. Georgiades, *The Securing of Credits*, 553.
959. See also Art. 177 CC.
960. On which see *supra* para. 121.

§2. THE PROBLEM OF WHAT IS PERMISSIBLE

508. The validity of the securing transfer of ownership of movables is strongly disputed.[961] Indeed, the view has been expressed that such a transfer is null and void because, through the latter, the regulation of Article 1213 CC, which prohibits the constitution of pledges through *constitutum possessorium*, is violated.[962] On the other hand, according to prevailing opinion, the securing of a claim may not constitute a valid just cause for the transfer of ownership.[963] Therefore, the said opinion – in the light of the fact that real dispositive contracts aiming at the transfer of ownership of immovables and movables are, respectively, causal[964] and non-causal[965] – holds that the securing transfer of ownership is null and void in the area of immovables[966] and valid in the field of movables.[967] Finally, the view has also been put forward[968] which, criticizing negatively the prevailing one, maintains that the securing transfer of ownership must, in any event, be null and void. This view puts forward the argument that the securing transfer of ownership seriously disturbs the reconciliation of the conflicting interests of debtors and creditors, a reconciliation which is achieved only through the institutions of pledges and mortgages. The same opinion holds that the relevant transfer must be null and void in the area of immovables due to the lack of a valid just cause and null and void in the field of movables due to its opposition to the purpose of the law, which renders null and void not only the securing agreement but also the transfer itself.

---

961. On this point see K. Simitis, *The Reformation of the Fictitious Pledge*, 44.
962. See P. Mazis, *The Fiduciary Transfer of Ownership of a Thing with a View to Securing a Claim according to Greek Law and Practice*, 27 NoB, 1979, 311, 318–319 [in Greek]; see also the reservations of Ph. Doris, *Real Security*, 114–116.
963. G. Balis, *GenPrinc*, para. 41, 131–132; G. Balis, *PrL*, para. 200 No. 6, 433; A. Tousis, *PrL*, para. 251 n. 1, 945; Mazis, *Fiduciary Transfer etc.*, 313 et seq., as well as AP 999/1996, 39 HellD, 1998, 847; AP 1307/1994, 44 NoB, 1996, 419 (420); AP 1315/1989, 41 NoB, 1993, 87; AP 91/1984, 33 NoB, 1985, 241; AP 1662/1980, 29 NoB, 1981, 1076; AP 1154/1980, 29 NoB, 1981, 529; AP 369/1978, 27 NoB, 1979, 173; AP 733/1975, 24 NoB, 1976, 138; Court of Appeal of Thessaloniki 308/1994, 48 Arm, 1994, 790; Court of Appeal of Athens 6125/2002, 44 HellD, 2003, 269; Court of Appeal of Athens 7199/2000, 53 ArchN, 2002, 644; Court of Appeal of Athens 7212/1991, 32 HellD, 1991, 1644; Three-member District Court of Thessaloniki 26994/2007, NOMOS; Three-member District Court of Veria 166/1996, 45 NoB, 1997, 76.
964. See *supra* para. 274.
965. See *supra* para. 314.
966. See K. Vavouskos, *PrL*, No. 236, 234 and the writers in *supra* n. 962. See also AP 999/1996, 39 HellD, 1998, 847; AP 1315/1989, 41 NoB, 1993, 87; AP 91/1984, 33 NoB, 1985, 241; AP 1154/1980, 29 NoB, 1981, 529; AP 733/1975, 24 NoB, 1976, 138; Court of Appeal of Athens 6125/2002, 44 HellD, 2003, 269; Court of Appeal of Athens 7199/2000, 53 ArchN, 2002, 644; Court of Appeal of Thessaloniki 308/1994, 48 Arm, 1994, 790; Court of Appeal of Athens 7212/1991, 32 HellD, 1991, 1644; Three-member District Court of Veria 166/1996, 45 NoB, 1997, 76.
967. G. Balis, *GenPrinc*, para. 41, 132; G. Balis, *PrL*, para. 200 No. 6, 433; A. Tousis, *PrL*, para. 251, 944–945, para. 97 C, 406, as well as AP 1307/1994, 44 NoB, 1996, 419 (420); Three-member District Court of Veria 166/1996, 45 NoB, 1997, 76. However, it is obvious that due to the absence of a valid just cause, the relevant valid transfer may be subverted in accordance with the provisions concerning enrichment without just cause (Art. 904 CC) (see also *supra* para. 314).
968. P. Filios & Chr. Filios, *PrL*, para. 257a, 459–461.

509. However, also convincing are the opinions which, refuting the arguments of the aforementioned views, hold that the securing transfer of ownership of movables is valid. Thus, the view[969] has been expressed that the above transfer is not contrary to Article 1213 CC insofar as the prohibition arising from the latter refers exclusively to the constitution of pledges. The same view is corroborated by also invoking the principle of contractual freedom together with the fact that there is no legal rule prohibiting the securing transfer of ownership of a movable. Furthermore, the view has also been expressed[970] that the securing transfer of ownership is valid regardless of whether it is a non-causal or a causal juridical act. This opinion, by invoking, on the one hand, the principle of contractual freedom and, on the other, the fact that the law does not expressly specify the causes justifying the transfer of ownership, in its final version,[971] rightly holds that the securing of a claim constitutes the just cause for the securing agreement, while the latter (from which arises the obligation for the ownership to be transferred) constitutes the just cause for the fiduciary transfer of ownership.

§3. Forms of Appearance

510. The securing transfer of ownership of a movable is considered to be obvious (clear or simple) in the case where the parties stipulate explicitly that the transfer of ownership aims at the securing of a claim. However, it is possible for the securing agreement to be concealed under another apparent contract and, as a rule, a contract of sale dependent on a resolutory condition or accompanied by an agreement providing for repurchase (Articles 565 et seq. CC). In such a case, the contract of sale is simulated and, therefore, null and void (Article 138 paragraph 1 CC), while the concealed securing agreement is valid (Article 138 paragraph 2 CC).[972]

969. See Em. Vouzikas, 'The Transfer of Ownership with a View to Securing a Claim according to the Civil Code', 18 EEN, 1951, 658 et seq., 662 [in Greek]; Ap. Georgiades, *The Securing of Credits*, 548; N. Papantoniou, *GenPrinc*, para. 54 d, 278; M. Karasis, *GenPrinc*, 56, as well as Court of Appeal of Thessaloniki 2642/1992, 35 HellD, 1994, 629 (631); Court of Appeal of Athens 1142/1957, 6 NoB, 1958, 557.

970. Em. Vouzikas, 'The Transfer of Ownership with a View to Securing a Claim Etc.', 663; A. Gazis, in *ErmAK*, Introd. to Arts 513–573 Nos 62–63 [in Greek]; Pan. Kanellopoulos, 'Das Gültigkeitsproblem von Sicherungsübertragungen in griechishen Zivilrecht', 21 Rev. Hell. D.I., 1968, 115 et seq.; K. Simantiras, *GenPrinc*, para. 33 X No. 599, 438; Kornilakis, *The Fiduciary Assignment of Claims*, 58 et seq.; Ap. Georgiades, *The Securing of Credits*, 549; N. Papantoniou, *GenPrinc*, para. 54 d, 278; M. Stathopoulos, 'Claims as a Means of Funding', 3 EpiskEmbD, No. A (January–March), 1997, 7–8 [in Greek]; M. Karasis, *GenPrinc*, 56; G. Archaniotakis, *Transfer of Property or Enterprise. Incorporation of Art. 479 CC into the System of Protecting Creditors from the Insolvency of the Debtor* (Thessaloniki: Sakkoulas, 1997), 217–218 [in Greek], as well as Court of Appeal of Athens 1142/1957, 6 NoB, 1958, 557 (558).

971. See, amongst the writers in the previous note, P. Kornilakis, Ap. Georgiades, N. Papantoniou, M. Stathopoulos, G. Archaniotakis.

972. On this point see Ap. Georgiades, *The Securing of Credits*, 550; Ap. Georgiades, in *Civil Code*, Vol. V: *PrL*, ed. Ap. Georgiades & M. Stathopoulos, Art. 1034 No. 87; P. Kornilakis, *The Fiduciary Assignment of Claims*, 11–12, 73–74; P. Kornilakis, *Law of Obligations. Special Part*, para. 57, 359–360.

Furthermore, the securing transfer may be concluded either on the resolutory condition of full payment of the debt or not. Thus, after the debt has been paid, in the first case, the ownership of the thing is restored *ipso jure* to the debtor (Article 202 CC), whereas, in the second case, the creditor is obliged, on the basis of the securing agreement, to restore the ownership of the thing.[973]

Finally, the securing transfer of ownership of a movable may be concluded as an 'extended' or 'prolonged' type, in the sense that the ownership of the creditor will extend to the new thing which is likely to be produced by the debtor through an elaboration or transformation of the movable which is fiduciary transferred.[974]

§4. Function

I. The Satisfaction of the Creditor-Owner by the Thing

511. In the event of the creditor-owner not being satisfied in due time, he or she may bring against the debtor, who detains the thing and unjustly refuses to restore it, either a revendicatory or an eviction action.[975] On the other hand, after the creditor has acquired detention of the thing, it seems correct to accept that the provisions concerning pledges apply by analogy. This means that the creditor can neither hold for good the thing 'in lieu of payment' nor sell the thing freely,[976] but he or she must sell it by public auction, observing the formalities of Article 1237, in order to gain satisfaction from the proceeds of the auction.[977] The situation is different in the case where, the contracting parties, after the secured claim has become due, stipulate that the creditor may alienate the thing freely, that is, without observing the formalities of Article 1237 CC. If such a stipulation does not exist, while the free alienation of the thing by the creditor, in his or her capacity as owner, is valid, the creditor is bound to compensate the debtor who can prove that, through a public auction, a higher purchase price could be obtained.[978]

---

973. It is argued that the fiduciary transfer must be regarded as being concluded on the resolutory condition of full payment of the debt in the case where the contracting parties have not provided for the fate of the thing after the relevant payment (see, in particular, P. Kornilakis, *The Fiduciary Assignment of Claims*, 124 with further numerous references to those who support this and the opposite opinion; see also Ap. Georgiades, *The Securing of Credits*, 550–551).
974. Ap. Georgiades, *The Securing of Credits*, 551.
975. Ap. Georgiades, *The Securing of Credits*, 555.
976. Any different agreement made before the secured claim has become due opposes Art. 1239 CC which applies here by analogy (see G. Balis, *GenPrinc*, para. 59, 169–171; Em. Vouzikas, 'The Transfer of Ownership with a View to Securing a Claim Etc.', 662; A. Gazis, *GenPrinc*, Vol. III: *The Juridical Acts* (Athens, 1973), 49–50 [in Greek]; Ap. Georgiades, *The Securing of Credits*, 555; K. Simitis, *The Reformation of the Fictitious Pledge*, 34; A. Tousis, *PrL*, para. 251 n. 1, 945; I. Spyridakis, *The Law of Real Security*, Vol. III, para. 169 n. 2, 109, as well as AP 1307/1994, 44 NoB, 1996, 419).
977. Thus, Ap. Georgiades, *The Securing of Credits*, 556; K. Simitis, *The Reformation of the Fictitious Pledge*, 34. However, the possibility of a free alienation is also accepted (see Court of Appeal of Thessaloniki 2642/1992, 35 HellD, 1994, 629 (631)).
978. Thus, Ap. Georgiades, *The Securing of Credits*, 556.

II. Securing Transfer and Compulsory Execution or Bankruptcy

512. The movable object of a securing transfer may be attached either by the creditors of the debtor who detains it or by the creditors of the creditor who owns it. In the former case, the creditor-owner may raise the 'third party opposition' specified in Article 936 CCProc demanding recognition of his or her ownership on the thing and recognition of the invalidity of the seizure.[979] In the latter case, if the securing transfer has been concluded on the resolutory condition of full payment of the debt, once the relevant condition is fulfilled, the debtor is entitled to raise the 'third party opposition' specified in Article 936 CCProc.[980] On the other hand, if the securing transfer has not been concluded on the aforementioned condition, it seems correct to accept that the debtor may not raise the said opposition.[981]

513. In the case where the debtor has been declared bankrupt, the creditor, in his or her capacity as an owner of the thing, may separate it from the property in bankruptcy and request the delivery of the thing to him or her (Article 37 paragraph 4 BC).[982] On the other hand, if the creditor-owner is the one who has been declared bankrupt, the debtor may pay the debt to the trustee receiver in bankruptcy. In such a case, depending on whether the securing transfer was concluded on the resolutory condition of full payment of the debt or not, either the debtor becomes *ipso jure* owner again or he or she has a personal claim aiming at the retransfer of ownership to himself or herself.[983]

979. See, in particular, P. Kornilakis, *The Fiduciary Assignment of Claims*, 124–126 (on the same issue in the area of securing assignment of claims); Ap. Georgiades, *The Securing of Credits*, 557.

980. See, in particular, P. Kornilakis, *The Fiduciary Assignment of Claims*, 127 (on the same issue in the area of securing assignment of claims); Ap. Georgiades, *The Securing of Credits*, 558 (who, by invoking Art. 69 para. 1e CCProc, accepts that the 'third-party opposition' may also be raised even before the relevant condition is fulfilled).

981. See, in particular, Ap. Georgiades, *The Securing of Credits*, 558. Compare P. Kornilakis, *The Fiduciary Assignment of Claims*, 128–129 (on the same issue in the area of securing assignment of claims).

982. See Ap. Georgiades, *The Securing of Credits*, 558.

983. See, in particular, Ap. Georgiades, *The Securing of Credits*, 558–559.

Chapter 3. Securing Assignment of Claims

§1. Structure

514. As has already been mentioned,[984] in the case of a securing assignment of a claim, the debtor, with a view to securing a claim on the part of his or her creditor, assigns to him or her a claim that he or she has against a third-party debtor. Such an assignment is carried out in the manner specified by Articles 455 et seq. CC;[985] that is, through a non-causal and non-formal personal dispositive contract between the debtor-assignor and the creditor-assignee to which (contract) the third-party debtor does not need to consent. According to the most correct opinion,[986] the relevant claim is detached from the assignor's property and transferred to the assignee following an agreement by the parties to the effect that the claim is assigned, regardless of whether the notification of the assignment to the third-party debtor prescribed in Article 460 CC has taken place or not. As emerges from Articles 455, 460 and 461 CC, as well as from a comparison of Article 455 CC with Article 1248 CC,[987] the above notification does not constitute a component of the securing assignment; it merely aims at the protection of the third-party debtor (or third parties, e.g., a probable second assignee). Consequently, before notification occurs, the debtor may and is obliged to make payment to the assignor and such payment releases him or her (Article 461 CC), while, after notification, he or she is relieved only if he or she makes payment to the assignee.

As in the area of the securing transfer of ownership of movables,[988] so too in securing assignments of claims, in addition to the aforementioned personal dispositive contract, a personal-promissory contract, the 'securing agreement' (*Sicherungsabrede*), is also carried out.[989] By this agreement, the debtor, with a view to securing a claim on the part of his or her creditor, undertakes to assign to the latter the claim that he or she has against his or her own debtor. On the basis of the same agreement,[990] the creditor commits himself or herself to use the claim within the scope of the intended purpose. To be precise: he or she undertakes to avoid any use or disposal of the claim which does not serve the above purpose; to

984. See *supra* paras 45, 505 (under d).
985. On the assignment of claims (Arts 455 et seq. CC) see, in particular, M. Stathopoulos, *Contract Law in Hellas*, Nos 203 et seq.
986. See, in particular, P. Kornilakis, *The Fiduciary Assignment of Claims*, 64 et seq., where references are also made: (a) to the opinion which holds that, before notification occurs, the assignment is effective only between the assignor and the assignee; and (b) to the view which maintains that, before notification, the contract of assignment is not completed.
987. On the pledger's notification of the pledge to the debtor as a precondition, provided for by Art. 1248 CC, for the constitution of pledges on claims see *supra* para. 492.
988. See *supra* para. 507.
989. On securing agreements see, in particular, P. Kornilakis, *The Fiduciary Assignment of Claims*, 49 et seq.
990. The probable gaps in this agreement are filled in through the 'complementary interpretation of contracts' (P. Kornilakis, *The Fiduciary Assignment of Claims*, 55, 85; Ap. Georgiades, *The Securing of Credits*, 599). See also *supra* para. 507 n. 957.

reassign it to the assignor once the debt is settled;[991] and, finally, in the case where full payment of the debt has not been made in due time, to collect the claim himself or herself from the third-party debtor and, after withholding the amount necessary for the satisfaction of his or her claim, to return the remainder to the assignor. The assignee who fails to fulfil the aforementioned obligations, is in breach of his or her contractual obligations and is bound to compensate the prejudice resulting therefrom to the assignor.[992]

§2. The Problem of What is Permissible

515. Following the prevailing view which holds that the securing of a claim may not constitute a valid just cause for the transfer of ownership or other right,[993] it ought to be accepted that a causal securing agreement, from which the obligation of assigning the claim arises, is null and void on account of the illegality of its just cause (Article 174 CC), while the non-causal assignment of a claim is valid, susceptible though to subversion, according to the provisions concerning enrichment without just cause (Article 904 CC), on account of the invalidity of the securing agreement which constitutes its just cause.[994]

However, it seems correct to adopt the view which, invoking the principle of contractual freedom and the fact that the law does not explicitly state the causes justifying the transfer of ownership or the assignment of claims, holds that:[995] (a) the securing of a claim constitutes a valid just cause for the securing agreement, which therefore is valid, and (b) the securing assignment of the claim, regardless of its causal or non-causal character, is valid insofar as it aims at the performance of an obligation which arises from a valid securing agreement.

In any event, it should be noted that, since the entry into force of Law 2844/2000, which recognizes that the securing assignment of claims (or other rights) which arise from business activities is possible (Articles 11–15), the problem of what is permissible no longer exists.[996]

991. In the case where the relevant assignment has been concluded on the resolutory condition of full payment of the debt, the claim is restored *ipso jure* to the assignor (Art. 202 CC).
992. In particular, on the problem of the protection of the assignor in the event of an uncontractual disposal of the assigned claim by the assignee see P. Kornilakis, *The Fiduciary Assignment of Claims*, 107 et seq.
993. On which see *supra* para. 508.
994. For a detailed discussion see P. Kornilakis, *The Fiduciary Assignment of Claims*, 58 et seq.
995. P. Kornilakis, *The Fiduciary Assignment of Claims*, 63; Ap. Georgiades, *The Securing of Credits*, 591.
996. In view of the fact that L. 2844/2000 regulates both pledges and the securing assignments of business claims (or other rights), whatever was stated (in *supra* paras 495–497) in regard to pledges on business claims also applies *mutatis mutandis* in the area of securing assignments of business claims.

§3. Forms of Appearance

516. Securing assignments of claims appear in current praxis, mainly, in one of the following forms:[997]

(a) As a simple or composite assignment, depending on whether it is used as the only method for securing credit or not. In the latter case, it may be combined, for example, with an extended or prolonged retention of title.[998]
(b) As a global assignment, in the sense that all the existing or future business claims of the debtor against an indefinite number of his or her clients are assigned. In such a case, the clients must be defined by certain criteria (e.g., the clients whose names begin from A–K) and the assigned claims must be at least capable of definition.
(c) As a mantle-assignment, that is, an assignment combined, on the one hand, with the delegation to the assignor of the right to collect the assigned claims and, on the other, with a commitment on the part of the latter to assign continuously new business claims so that the total amount of the assigned claims constantly exceeds, by a certain percentage (e.g., 30%), the amount of the credit secured.
(d) As an implicit assignment, which exists in the case where, according to the term agreed by the contracting parties, the assignor (e.g., a worker) is entitled to collect, for a period of time, the assigned claim (e.g., the claim for future salaries).
(e) Finally, a securing assignment may have as its object a future claim which must be defined or at least be capable of definition.[999]

§4. Function

I. Collection of the Claim

517. Once the assigned claim matures, provided that the relevant assignment has been notified to the third party-debtor, the assignee is entitled to collect the claim regardless of whether it is monetary or not.[1000] The proceeds of such a collection, as long as the debt secured has not matured, substitute the assigned claim. However, once the debt secured matures, so long as the latter has been fully paid, the said proceeds are returned to the debtor-assignor. On the other hand, in the case where the full payment of the debt secured has not been made in due time, the assignee gains satisfaction from the proceeds of the above collection and returns the surplus to the debtor-assignor. However, if the proceeds of the collection take the form of a thing, the assignee may sell it freely and gain satisfaction from the purchase price.[1001]

997. See, in particular, Ap. Georgiades, *The Securing of Credits*, 592 et seq.
998. See *supra* para. 489.
999. See Art. 12 para. 1 L. 2844/2000.
1000. On the relation between the assignee and third party-debtor see, in particular, M. Stathopoulos, *Contract Law in Hellas*, para. 208 and, in greater detail, P. Kornilakis, *The fiduciary assignment of claims*, 103 et seq.
1001. For a detailed discussion of the issues set out in this paragraph see P. Kornilakis, *The Fiduciary Assignment of Claims*, 86 et seq.; see also 98 et seq., on which the view that Art. 1239 CC applies by analogy in the area of securing assignments of claims is founded. This view regards as null

II. Securing Assignments and Compulsory Execution or Bankruptcy

518. The assigned claim may be attached by the creditors of the assignor or the assignee-creditor.[1002] In the former case, the assignee, after having notified of the relevant assignment, may raise the 'third party opposition' specified in Article 936 CCProc, demanding recognition of his or her right on the seized claim and recognition of the invalidity of the seizure. In the latter case, if the securing assignment has been concluded on the resolutory condition of full payment of the debt secured, once the relevant condition is fulfilled, the assignor is entitled to raise the 'third party opposition' specified in Article 936 CCProc. On the other hand, if the securing assignment has not been concluded on the aforementioned condition, it seems correct to accept that the assignor may not raise the said opposition.[1003]

519. In the case where the assignor-debtor has been declared bankrupt, the assigned claim does not belong to the property in bankruptcy. Consequently, in the case where full payment of the debt secured has not been made in due time, the assignee (after having notified the assignation to the third-party debtor) is entitled to collect the claim and gain satisfaction from the proceeds of such a collection, while returning the probable surplus to the group of creditors in bankruptcy. However, if the debt secured has been fully paid by the trustee receiver in bankruptcy, depending on whether the securing assignment was concluded on the resolutory condition of full payment of the debt or not, either the assigned claim returns *ipso jure* to the property in bankruptcy or the assignee is bound to reassign it to the assignor (who is represented by the trustee receiver in bankruptcy).

On the other hand, if the assignee-creditor is the one who has been declared bankrupt, the assignor-debtor may pay the debt secured to the trustee receiver in bankruptcy. In such a case, depending on whether the securing assignment was concluded on the resolutory condition of full payment of the debt or not, either the assigned claim returns *ipso jure* to the property of the assignor or the assignor is entitled, as a member of the group of creditors in bankruptcy, to demand its reassignment to him or her. However, if the debt secured has not been fully paid in due time, the trustee receiver in bankruptcy is entitled to collect the assigned claim and hold, on behalf of the group of creditors, the amount necessary for the satisfaction of the debt secured, while returning the probable surplus to the assignor.[1004]

---

and void an agreement which is made before the secured claim has become due according to which, in the event of the assignee-creditor not being satisfied in due time, the assigned claim is acquired definitely by the latter who is relieved of any fiduciary commitment.

1002. For a detailed discussion of the relevant issue see P. Kornilakis, *The Fiduciary Assignment of Claims*, 124 et seq.

1003. See Ap. Georgiades, *The Securing of Credits*, 603. Compare P. Kornilakis, *The Fiduciary Assignment of Claims*, 128–129.

1004. For a detailed discussion of the issues set out in this paragraph see P. Kornilakis, *The Fiduciary Assignment of Claims*, 129 et seq.

Selected Bibliography

Alexandropoulou-Egyptiadou, Ev. *The Title in Ordinary Usucaption.* 2nd edn. Athens/Komotini: A. Sakkoulas, 1997 (in Greek).

Apalagaki, Ch. *Prenotice of Mortgage. A Procedural Approach.* Athens-Thessaloniki: Sakkoulas, 2005 (in Greek).

Archaniotakis, G. *Transfer of Property or Enterprise.* Thessaloniki: Sakkoulas, 1997 (in Greek).

Asprogerakas-Grivas, K. *General Principles of Civil Law.* Athens/Komotini: A. Sakkoulas, 1981 (in Greek).

Balis, G. *General Principles of Civil Law.* 8th edn. Athens-Thessaloniki: Sakkoulas, 1961 (in Greek).

Balis, G. *Property Law.* 4th edn. Athens: Sakkoulas, 1961 (in Greek).

Balis, G. *Law of Inheritance.* 5th edn. Athens: Sakkoulas, 1965 (in Greek).

Banakas, S. In *Civil Code*, Vol. VI: *Property Law*, edited by Ap. Georgiades & M. Stathopoulos. Athens: Sakkoulas, 1985 (Articles 1119–1120) (in Greek).

Baur, J.& R. Stürner. *Sachenrecht*, 18th edn. München: Beck, 2009.

Beckmann, R.-M. *Staudinger Komm zum BGB, Buch 2: Recht der Schuldverhältnisse.* Berlin: Sellier-de Gruyter, 2004 (paragraph 449 BGB).

Beys, K. *The Proceedings before the One-member District Court.* Vol. II. Athens: Klisiounis, 1969 (in Greek).

Bourandas, K. *Fideicommissum.* Vols. I, II. Thessaloniki: Sakkoulas, 1993 (in Greek).

Bournias, Ap. *Horizontal Ownership As It Functions in Greece Today.* Athens, 1969 (in Greek).

Bournias, Ap. 'Constitution of Horizontal Ownership by Usucaption'. NoB 20(1972), 1232–1238 (in Greek).

Brehm, W. & Berger, Chr. *Sachenrecht.* 2nd edn. Tübingen: Mohr Siebeck, 2006.

Burn, E.H. *Modern Law of Real Property.* 15th edn. London/Dublin/Edinburgh: Butterworths, 1994.

Chrysogonos, K. *Individual and Social Rights.* 3rd edn. Athens: A. Sakkoulas, 2006 (in Greek).

Christakakou-Fotiadi, K. *Usufruct on Enterprise.* Athens: Sakkoulas, 1994 (in Greek).

Christophilopoulos, D. *Vertical Co-ownership.* Athens: Simopoulos, 1976 (in Greek).

Selected Bibliography

Dagtoglou, P. 'Constitutional and Administrative Law'. In *Introduction to Greek Law*, edited by K. Kerameus & Ph. Kozyris. 3rd edn. AH Alphen aan den Rijn/Athens: Kluwer/Sakkoulas, 2008.

Damrau, J. In *MünchKomm*, Vol. 6: *Sachenrecht.* 5th edn. München: Beck, 2009 (paragraph 1205 BGB).

Daskarolis, G. 'Interruption of Prescription by Petition of Provisional Remedies in Disputes Concerning Possession'. EEN 36 (1969): 603–617 (in Greek).

Deliyianni-Dimitrakou, Chr. *Trust and Fiducia.* Thessaloniki: Sakkoulas, 1998 (in Greek).

Deliyiannis, I & P. Kornilakis, *Law of Obligations. Special Part.* Vol. I. Thessaloniki: Sakkoulas, 1992 (in Greek).

Deloukas, N. & E. Perakis. 'Commercial Law'. In *Introduction to Greek Law*, edited by K. Kerameus & Ph. Kozyris. 3rd edn. AH Alphen aan den Rijn/Athens: Kluwer/Sakkoulas, 2008.

Diamandopoulos, G. *The Contradictory Behaviour of Litigants in Civil Trials.* Athens/Komotini: A. Sakkoulas, 1996 (in Greek).

Dimakou, Ph. In *Civil Code*, Vols. V, VI: *Property Law*, edited by Ap. Georgiades & M. Stathopoulos. Athens: Sakkoulas, 1985 (Articles 958, 1247–1248) (in Greek).

Doris, Ph. *Introduction to the Civil Law.* Vol. I. Athens/Komotini: A. Sakkoulas, 1991 (in Greek).

Doris, Ph. *Real Security.* Athens/Komotini: A. Sakkoulas, 1986 (in Greek).

Ekonomides, Vas. *Elements of Civil Law. Property Rights.* 2nd edn. Athens, 1912 (in Greek).

Filios, P. *General Principles of Civil Law.* 3rd edn. Athens/Komotini: A. Sakkoulas, 2009 (in Greek).

Filios, P. *Law of Obligations. Special Part.* Vol. I/1. 7th edn. Athens/Komotini: A. Sakkoulas, 2007 (in Greek).

Filios, P. *ErmAK.* Vol. III/B, issue 6/4. Athens: Sakkoulas, 1974 (Article 788) (in Greek).

Filios, P. & Chr. Filios. *Property Law.* 3rd edn. Athens/Komotini: A. Sakkoulas, 2009 (in Greek).

Fourkiotis, K. 'On Art. 1081 et seq. of the Greek Civil Code'. AID 9 (1942): 125–139 (in Greek).

Franceskakis, Ph., D. Evrigenis & S. Symeonides. *Comparative Law.* Thessaloniki: Sakkoulas, 1978 (in Greek).

Gazis, An. *General Principles of Civil Law.* Vols. I (*Introduction*), II, III (*The Juridical Acts*). Athens, 1970, 1973 (in Greek).

Gazis, An. *ErmAK* (Introd. to Articles 513–573, Article 532) (in Greek).

Gazis, An. *Conflict of Rights.* Athens, 1959 (in Greek).

Georgiades, Ap. *General Principles of Civil Law.* 3rd edn. Athens/Komotini: A. Sakkoulas, 2002 (in Greek).

Georgiades, Ap. *Property Law.* 2nd edn. Athens-Thessaloniki: Sakkoulas, 2010 (in Greek).

Georgiades, Ap. *The Securing of Credits.* 2nd edn. Athens: Sakkoulas, 2008 (in Greek).

Georgiades, Ap. In *Civil Code*, Vol. V: *Property Law*, edited by Ap. Georgiades & M. Stathopoulos. Athens: Sakkoulas, 1985 (Articles 1034, 1041, 1043, Introd. 1094–1112) (in Greek).

Georgiades, Ap. 'Eigentumsbegriff und Eigentumsverhältnis'. *Volume in Honour of I. Sontis* München: Beck, 1977, 149–166.

Georgiades, Ap. *Die Eigentumsanwartshaft beim Vorbehaltskauf.* Tübingen: J.C.B. Mohr (Paul Siebeck), 1963.

Georgiades, Ast. *Law of Obligations. General Part.* Vol. II. 5th edn. Athens-Thessaloniki: Sakkoulas, 2007 (in Greek).

Grammatikaki-Alexiou, A. 'Sources and Materials'. In *Introduction to Greek Law*, edited by K. Kerameus & Ph. Kozyris. 3rd edn. AH Alphen aan den Rijn/Athens: Kluwer/Sakkoulas, 2008.

Gray, K. *Elements of Land Law.* 2nd edn. London/Dublin/Edinburgh: Butterworths, 1993.

Grunewald, B. *Erman Bürgerliches Gesetzbuch.* Vol. I. 12th edn. Köln: Dr. Otto Schmidt, 2008. (paragraph 449 BGB).

Habersack, M. *Examens-Repetitorium Sachenrecht.* 4th edn. Heidelberg: Müller, 2005.

Hech, Ph. *Grundriß des Sachenrechts.* Tübingen: Scientic Malen, 1960.

Herbots, J.H. 'Belgium/Contracts'. In *International Encyclopaedia of Laws.* The Hague: Kluwer, 1998.

Henssler, M. *Soergel Komm zum BGB*, Vol. 14: *Sachenrecht 1: §§ 854-984.* 13th edn. Stuttgart: Kohlhammer, 2002 (paragraph Anh 930).

Kallimopoulos, M. *The Non-genuine Management of Another's Affairs.* Athens: A. Sakkoulas, 1978 (in Greek).

Kallimopoulos, M. *ErmAK* (Article 1002) (in Greek).

Kanellopoulos, P. 'Das Gültigkeitsproblem von Sicherungsübertragung im griechischen Zivilrecht'. R. Hell. D.I. 21 (1968): 108–121.

Karabatzos, A. In *SEAK*, Vol. I: *Arts. 1–946*, edited by Ap. Georgiades. Athens: Sakkoulas, 2010 (Article 532) (in Greek).

Karakostas, I. *Environment and Law.* 2nd edn. Athens/Komotini: A. Sakkoulas, 2006 (in Greek).

Karasis, M. *Textbook of General Principles of Civil Law. The Law of the Juridical Act.* Thessaloniki: A. Sakkoulas, 1996 (in Greek).

Karasis, M. In *Civil Code*, Vol. I: *General Principles*, edited by Ap. Georgiades & M. Stathopoulos. Athens: Sakkoulas, 1978 (Articles 175–177). Vols V, VI: *Property Law.* Athens: Sakkoulas, 1985 (Articles 1113, 1117, 1143) (in Greek).

Karibali-Tsiptsiou, Y. *The Approval of Juridical Acts.* Thessaloniki: Sakkoulas, 1990 (in Greek).

Karibali-Tsiptsiou, Y. *The Complete Personal Servitude of Habitation.* Thessaloniki: Sakkoulas, 1986 (in Greek).

Karibali-Tsiptsiou, Y. 'Pledging of Bills of Exchange'. EpiskEmbD 5, No. C (July–August 1999), 646–671 (in Greek).

Karibali-Tsiptsiou, Y. 'Presumption of Precision of the Registrations in the Land Registers and Public Faith'. HellD 40 (1999): 1480–1487 (in Greek).

Karibali-Tsiptsiou, Y. 'Fundamental Principles governing Greek Property Law'. *Cyprus Law Review* 11, no. 43–44 (July-December 1993), 6409–6421 (in Greek).

Selected Bibliography

Karibali-Tsiptsiou, Y. 'Sources of Positive Law'. *Harmenopoulos/Scientific Year-Book* 1 (1980): 227–238 (in Greek).

Kerameus, K. *Civil Procedural Law. General Part.* Athens-Thessaloniki: Sakkoulas, 1986 (in Greek).

Kiandou-Pampouki, A. *Law of Negotiable Instruments.* 5th edn. Thessaloniki: Sakkoulas, 1997 (in Greek).

Kitsaras, L. *The Initial Entries in the Land Register.* Athens: P.N. Sakkoulas, 2001 (in Greek).

Klavanidou, D. 'Preventative Mechanisms of Environmental Protection in the System of Civil Law'. EpiskEmbD 5, no. B (April-June 1999), 370–396 (in Greek).

Klavanidou, D. & D. Papasteriou. *Law of Juridical Acts.* Athens-Thessaloniki: Sakkoulas, 2008 (in Greek).

Kornilakis, P. *Law of Obligations. Special Part I.* Athens-Thessaloniki: Sakkoulas, 2002 (in Greek).

Kornilakis, P. *Concise Law of Obligations. Special Part.* Athens-Thessaloniki: Sakkoulas, 2000 (in Greek).

Kornilakis, P. *The Fiduciary Assignment of Claims.* Thessaloniki: Sakkoulas, 1978 (in Greek).

Kornilakis, P. 'The Birth and Evolution of the Institution of Trusts in Anglo-Saxon Law'. Arm 31 (1977): 243–246 (in Greek).

Kornilakis, P. & I. Deliyiannis. *Law of Obligations. Special Part.* Vol. I. Thessaloniki: Sakkoulas, 1992 (in Greek).

Kotsiris, L. *Law of Bankruptcy.* 8th edn. Athens-Thessaloniki: Sakkoulas, 2011 (in Greek).

Koumantos, G. *Subjective Good Faith.* Athens: Pavlou, 1958 (in Greek).

Kounougeri-Manoledaki, E. *The Law of Fruits.* Thessaloniki: Sakkoulas, 1979 (in Greek).

Kounougeri-Manoledaki, E. In *Civil Code*, Vol. V: *Property Law*, edited by Ap. Georgiades & M. Stathopoulos. Athens: Sakkoulas, 1985 (Articles 1064–1068, 1069–1074) (in Greek).

Kousoulas, Chr. *Property Law.* Athens-Thessaloniki: Sakkoulas, 2003 (in Greek) Athens-Thessaloniki.

Kousoulas, Chr. *The Law Relating to the Land Register.* Athens-Thessaloniki: Sakkoulas, 2001 (in Greek).

Kousoulas, Chr. *Possession and Hereditary Succession.* Thessaloniki: Philotas, 1996 (in Greek).

Koutourisis, K. *The Compulsory Granting of Passage.* Athens: Sakkoulas, 1986 (in Greek).

Koutsoubinas, St. *Les peuple dans la constitution hellénique de 1975.* Nancy: Presses Universitaires, 1989.

Koutsouradis, Ach. *The Discovery of Lost Property in the Field of Civil Code.* Thessaloniki: Sakkoulas, 1987 (in Greek).

Koutsouradis, Ach. 'Present and Future of Real and Personal Security' (Hellenic National Reports XVIth Int'l Congress of Comparative Law 2002). R. Hell. D.I. 55, no. 1 (2002): 49–67.

Konstantopoulos, P. *Horizontal Ownership in Greece.* Athens, 1974 (in Greek).

Kritikos, Ath. In *Civil Code*, Vol. I: *General Principles*, edited by Ap. Georgiades & M. Stathopoulos. Athens: Sakkoulas, 1978 (Article 206), Vol. VI: *Property Law.* Athens: Sakkoulas, 1985 (Articles 1258, 1259, 1266, 1269) (in Greek).

Ladas, P. *General Principles of Civil Law.* Vols I, II. Athens-Thessaloniki: Sakkoulas, 2007, 2009 (in Greek).

Ladas, P. *From the Civil Code to the European Law. National Consciousness and European Spirit.* Thessaloniki: Sakkoulas, 1993 (in Greek).

Larenz, K. & M. Wolf. *Allgemeiner Teil des Bürgerlichen Rechts.* 9th edn. München: Beck, 2004.

Lawson, F.H. & B. Rudden. *The Law of Property.* 2nd edn. Oxford: Clarendon Press, 1982/reprinted 1991.

Livanis, N. In *Civil Code*, Vols. V, VI: *Property Law*, edited by Ap. Georgiades & M. Stathopoulos. Athens: Sakkoulas, 1985 (Artilces 1081, 1274, 1277–1278) (in Greek).

Ligeropoulos, Al. 'Natural Obligations and Related Legal Structures'. *Miscellany in Honour of Ch. Fragistas.* Vol. IB/6. Thessaloniki: 1970–1971, 227–330 (in Greek).

Ligeropoulos, Al. *Case-law As a Factor in the Formation of Private Law.* Thessaloniki: 1932/Athens/Komotini: A. Sakkoulas, 2000 (reprint) (in Greek).

Manitakis, An. *Greek Constitutional Law.* Vol. I. Athens-Thessaloniki: Sakkoulas, 2004 (in Greek).

Matthaiou, P. *National Land Register.* Athens: A. Sakkoulas, 2000 (in Greek).

Mazis, P. 'The Fiduciary Transfer of Ownership of a Thing with a View to Securing a Claim According to Greek Law and Practice'. NoB 27 (1979): 311–322 (in Greek).

Mazis, P. *The Fictitious Pledge.* Athens, 1977 (in Greek).

Michaelides-Nouaros, G. 'Les systèmes juridiques des peuples Européens'. R. Hell. D.I. 10 (1957): 40–131.

Michaelides-Nouaros, G. 'L'oeuvre créatrice de la jurisprudence grecque en cas de silence de la loi'. R. Hell. D.I. 4 (1951): 163–180.

Mitsopoulos, G. *The Declaratory Action According to the Greek Civil Procedural Law.* Athens: Rodakis-Pavlou, 1947/Athens/Komotini: A. Sakkoulas, 1989 (reprint) (in Greek).

Moffat, Gr. (G. Bean & J. Dewar). *Trust Law. Text and Materials.* 2nd edn. London/Dublin/Edinburgh: Butterworths, 1994.

Nakos, G. *History of Greek and Roman Law.* Thessaloniki: University Studio Press, 1991 (in Greek).

Nikas, N. In *Interpretation of the CCProc*, edited by K. Kerameus, D. Kondilis & N. Nikas. Vol. I. Athens-Thessaloniki-Komotini: Sakkoulas, 2000 (Articles 11, 14, 16, 72) (in Greek).

Oechsler, J. *MünchKomm*, Vol. 6: *Sachenrecht.* 5th edn. München: Beck, 2009 (paragraph 932 BGB).

Pantazopoulos, N. *Roman Law in a Dialectic Coherence to Greek Law.* Vol. I. Thessaloniki: Sakkoulas, 1974 (in Greek).

Papadopoulos, K. *Actions of Property Law.* Athens, 1989 (in Greek).

Papadopoulos, K. *The Negative Action.* Athens/Komotini: A. Sakkoulas, 1984 (in Greek).

Papantoniou, N. *General Principles of Civil Law.* 3rd edn. Athens: Sakkoulas, 1983 (in Greek).
Papantoniou, N. *Law of Inheritance.* 5th edn. Athens: Sakkoulas, 1989 (in Greek).
Papasteriou, D. *General Principles of Civil Law.* 2nd edn. Athens-Thessaloniki: Sakkoulas, 2009 (in Greek).
Papasteriou, D. *Property Law.* Vols I, II, III. Athens-Thessaloniki: Sakkoulas, 2008 (in Greek).
Papasteriou, D. 'The Principle of Legality within the Scope of the National Land Registry'. HellD 40 (1999): 1469–1479 (in Greek).
Papasteriou, D. *The Real Contract of Art. 1033 Sub-para. a CC.* Thessaloniki: Sakkoulas, 1987 (in Greek).
Papasteriou, D. & D. Klavanidou. *Law of Juridical Acts.* Athens-Thessaloniki: Sakkoulas, 2008 (in Greek).
Papazissi, Th. 'Les problèmes actuels des sûretés réelles'. In *Les garanties de financement (Journées portugaise), Travaux de l'Association Henri Capitant des Amis de la Culture Juridique Française.* Vol. XLVII. Paris: L.G.D.J., 1996, 183–198.
Patsourakos, A. *Horizontal Ownership.* Athens: Sakkoulas, 1973 (in Greek).
Petropoulos, G. *History and Institutions of Roman Law.* 2nd edn. Athens, 1963 (in Greek).
Pipsou, L. *Judicial Distribution.* Athens-Thessaloniki: Sakkoulas, 2006 (in Greek).
Pipsou, L. *Procedural Issues of Real Actions.* Thessaloniki: Sakkoulas, 2000 (in Greek).
Pipsou, L. 'Issues Arising from Interruption of Prescription by the Commencement of Legal Action or the Undertaking of other, Introductory to a Trial, Procedural Acts'. Arm 46 (1992), 323–328 (in Greek).
Prütting, H. *Sachenrecht.* 34th edn. München: Beck, 2010.
Psouni, N. *Law of Inheritance.* Vol. I. 2nd edn. Athens-Thessaloniki: Sakkoulas, 2011 (in Greek).
Rammos, G. *ErmAK* (Articles 206, 1101–1107, 1108) (in Greek).
Riddall, J.G. *Land Law.* 6th edn. London/Edinburgh/Dublin: Butterworths, 1997.
Roth, H. *Staudinger Komm zum BGB, Buch 3: Sachenrecht.* Berlin: Sellier-de Gruyter, 2009 (paragraphs 912, 920 BGB).
Roussos, K. In *Civil Code*, Vol. VI: *Property Law*, edited by Ap. Georgiades & M. Stathopoulos. Athens: Sakkoulas, 1985 (Articles. 1166, 1167) (in Greek).
Säcker, F.J. *MünchKomm*, Vol. 6: *Sachenrecht.* 5th edn. München: Beck, 2009 (paragraphs 912, 920 BGB).
Schinas, I. In *Civil Code*, Vol. III: *Law of Obligations. Special Part*, edited by Ap. Georgiades & M. Stathopoulos. Athens: Sakkoulas, 1980 (Article 532) (in Greek).
Schreiber, K. *Sachenrecht.* 5th edn. Stuttgart: Boorberg, 2008.
Sexton, R. *Land Law.* 2nd edn. Great Britain: Blackstone Press Limited, 1997.
Simantiras, K. *General Principles of Civil Law.* 4th edn. Athens/Komotini: Sakkoulas, 1988 (in Greek).
Simitis, K. *The Reformation of the Fictitious Pledge.* Athens, 1968 (in Greek).
Skouras, Th. In *Civil Code*, Vol. IV: *Law of Obligations, Special Part*, Athens: Sakkoulas, 1982 (Article 788) (in Greek).

Sontis, I. *Compulsory Servitudes.* Athens/Komotini: A. Sakkoulas, 1981 (in Greek).
Sontis, I. *Limited Personal Servitudes.* Athens: Sakkoulas, 1957 (in Greek).
Sontis, I. 'Strukturelle Betrachtungen zum Eigentumsbegriff'. *Volume in Honour of K. Larenz* München: Beck, 1973, 981–1002.
Sontis, I. 'Contribution to the Interpretation of Article 1010 CC'. NoB 2 (1954): 1024–1031 (in Greek).
Spyridakis, I. *Title Conferring a Right to Register a Mortgage.* Athens/Komotini: A. Sakkoulas, 2001 (in Greek).
Spyridakis, I. *Action on an Eviction from Possession.* Athens/Komotini: A. Sakkoulas, 1997 (in Greek).
Spyridakis, I. *Action on a Disturbance of Possession.* Athens/Komotini: A. Sakkoulas, 1997 (in Greek).
Spyridakis, I. *Law of Horizontal and Vertical Ownership.* Athens/Komotini: A. Sakkoulas, 1996 (in Greek).
Spyridakis, I. *The Law of Real Security.* Vols I, II, III. Athens: A. Sakkoulas, 1974, 1975, 1974/1976 (in Greek).
Spyridakis, I. *Interchange in the Ranking of Mortgages.* Athens: Zacharopoulos, 1969 (in Greek).
Spyridakis, I. & M. Spyridakis. *Property Law.* Athens/Komotini: A. Sakkoulas, 2004 (in Greek).
Spyridakis, I. & M. Spyridakis. *Property Law.* Vols A, B/1, C. Athens/Komotini: A. Sakkoulas, 2001 (in Greek).
Spyropoulos, Ph. *Constitutional Law in Hellas.* The Hague/Athens: Kluwer/Sakkoulas, 1995.
Stathopoulos, M. *Contract Law in Hellas.* The Hague/Athens: Kluwer/Sakkoulas, 1995.
Stathopoulos, M. 'Claims As a Means of Funding'. EpiskEmbD 3, no. A (January–March 1997), 3–30 (in Greek).
Stevens, J. & R.A. Pearce. *Land Law.* 3rd edn. London: Sweet&Maxwell, 2005.
Symeonides, S. 'The General Principles of Civil Law'. In *Introduction to Greek Law*, edited by K. Kerameus & Ph. Kozyris. 3rd edn. AH Alphen aan den Rijn/Athens: Kluwer/Sakkoulas, 2008.
Themeli, Chr. *The Contract of Time-sharing Hire.* Thessaloniki, 2003 (in Greek).
Thibaios, Chr. *Law of Possession.* Vols II, III. Athens: 1953, 1957 (in Greek).
Tousis, A. *General Principles of Civil Law.* Vol. II. 2nd edn. Athens: Sakkoulas, 1978 (in Greek).
Tousis, A. *Property Law.* 4th edn. Athens: Sakkoulas, 1988 (in Greek).
Triantos, N. In *Civil Code*, Vol. 4: *Law of Obligations. Special Part (Arts. 496–640)*, edited by I. Karakostas. Athens: Nomiki Bibliothiki, 2008, Article 532 (in Greek).
Tsatsos, D. *Constitutional Law.* Vol. I. 4th edn. Athens/Komotini: Sakkoulas, 1994 (in Greek).
Tsetsekos, Ph. *Horizontal and Vertical Ownership (Divided Ownership).* 3rd edn. Athens: Sakkoulas, 2002 (in Greek).
Tsetsekos, Ph. *Neighbour Law.* Athens: Sakkoulas, 2000 (in Greek).
Vavouskos, K. *Property Law.* 6th edn. Thessaloniki: Sakkoulas, 1986 (in Greek).

Vavouskos, K. 'The Prenotice of a Mortgage in Greek Law under the New Code of Civil Procedure'. *Volume in Honour of K. Karavas.* Vol. I–B. Thessaloniki, 1978, 751–836 (in Greek).
Vavouskos, K. *Acquisition of Ownership of Movables from a Person Who Is Not the Owner and Its Protection.* Thessaloniki, 1956 (in Greek).
Vieweg, K. & A. Werner. *Sachenrecht.* 5th edn. München: Vahlen, 2011.
Voulgaris, I. 'Issues in the Fiduciary Transfer of Ownership under the Anglo-Saxon Laws (Trust) According to Private International Law'. EEN 36 (1969): 797–803 (in Greek).
Vousikas, Em. *Law of Inheritance.* Vol. I. Athens, 1972 (in Greek).
Vousikas, Em. *Acquisition of a Pledge from a Person Who Is Not the Owner.* Athens: Zacharopoulos, 1950 (in Greek).
Vousikas, Em. 'The Transfer of Ownership with a View to Securing a Claim According to the Civil Code'. EEN 18 (1951): 657–666 (in Greek).
Waters, D. 'The Institution of the Trust in Civil and Common Law'. RCADI 252 (1995): 117–451.
Weidenkaff, W. *Palandt Bürgerliches Gezetsbuch.* 70th edn. München: Beck, 2011 (paragraph 449 BGB).
Westermann, H.P. *MünchKomm*, Vol. 3: *Schuldrecht. Besonderer Teil I.* 5th edn. München: Beck, 2008 (paragraph 449 BGB).
Westermann, H., et al. *Sachenrecht.* 7th edn. Heidelberg: Müller, 1998.
Westermann, H.P. *BGB-Sachenrecht.* 11th edn. Heidelberg: Müller, 2005.
Wiegand, W. *Staudinger Komm zum BGB, Buch 3: Sachenrecht.* Berlin: Sellierde Gruyter, paragraph 932 BGB (2011), Vorbem. zu paragraphs 1204 ff BGB, paragraph 1205 BGB (2009).
Wieling, H.J. *Sachenrecht.* 5th edn. Berlin/Heidelberg: Springer, 2007.
Wolf, M. & M. Wellenhofer. *Sachenrecht.* 26th edn. München: Beck, 2011.
Wolf, M. & L. Raiser. *Sachenrecht.* 10th edn. Tübingen, 1957.
Yessiou-Faltsi, P. *Civil Procedure in Hellas.* Athens/The Hague: Sakkoulas/Kluwer, 1995.
Yiannopoulos, Ath. *Louisiana Civil Law Treatise*, Vol. 2: *Property Law.* 3rd edn. St. Paul, Minn.: West Publishing Co., 1991.
Yiannopoulos, Ath. 'Historical Development'. In *Introduction to Greek Law*, edited by K. Kerameus & Ph. Kozyris. 3rd edn. AH Alphen aan den Rijn/Athens: Kluwer/Sakkoulas, 2008.
Yiannopoulos, Ath. 'Property'. In *Introduction to Greek Law*, edited by K. Kerameus & Ph. Kozyris. 3rd edn. AH Alphen aan den Rijn/Athens: Kluwer/Sakkoulas, 2008.
Zepos, P. 'The Greek Legal System'. R. Hell. D.I. 14 (1961): 1–13.
Zepos, P. & M. Tourtoglou. 'Griechenland'. In *Handbuch der Quellen und Literatur der neuren europäischen Privatrechtsgeschichte*, edited by H. Coing (Hrsg). Vol. III/5. Max Planck Institut, München: Beck, 1988, 473–535.

Index

The large numbers refer to the paragraph numbers in the text and the numbers within the parenthesis to the notes.

Index

Index

www.ingramcontent.com/pod-product-compliance
Lightning Source LLC
Chambersburg PA
CBHW071430230926
51846CB00001B/177
* 9 7 8 9 0 4 1 1 4 7 0 8 0 *